D0843252

MIES VAN DER ROHE

Ludwig Mies van der Rohe, 1962
© Karsh, Ottawa

MIES VAN DER ROHE

A Critical Biography

FRANZ SCHULZE

in association with the Mies van der Rohe Archive
of the Museum of Modern Art

The University of Chicago Press   Chicago and London

FRANZ SCHULZE is the Betty Jane Hollender
Professor of Art at Lake Forest College. He is a
contributing editor to *Artnews* and *Inland Architect*
and a corresponding editor to *Art in America*. In
addition to many articles and book reviews, he is
the author of *Fantastic Images: Chicago Art since
1945* and *One Hundred Years of Chicago
Architecture: Continuity of Structure and Form.*

The University of Chicago Press, Chicago 60637
The University of Chicago Press, Ltd., London
© 1985 by Franz Schulze
All rights reserved. Published 1985
Printed in the United States of America

94 93 92 91 90 89 88 87 86 85   54321

Library of Congress Cataloging in Publication Data

Schulze, Franz, 1927–
    Mies van der Rohe.

    Bibliography: p.
    Includes index.
    1. Mies van der Rohe, Ludwig, 1886–1969.
2. Architects—Germany—Biography. 3. Architects—
United States—Biography.   I. Mies van der Rohe
Archive.   II. Title.
NA1088.M65S38   1985   720'.92'4   [B]   85-8488
ISBN 0-226-74059-5

Contents

Illustrations

Acknowledgments

The greatest boon to Miesian scholarship in the past forty years has been the establishment in 1968 of the Mies van der Rohe Archive at the Museum of Modern Art. With the acquisition and assembly of most of the architect's professional files and many of his personal papers, as well as a treasury of his drawings numbering in the thousands, it became possible to begin filling in a multitude of gaps in Mies's history which had frustrated students even while Mies was still alive. An additional quantity of archival material, obtained in 1965 by the Library of Congress, proved to be a windfall of nearly comparable magnitude.

I clearly could not have undertaken a study as detailed as this one without access to these two major sources, and especially without the personal assistance and counsel of the staff of the Museum of Modern Art's Department of Architecture and Design. I am grateful to Arthur Drexler, director of the department, whose encouragement has been as constant as it has been generous. My thanks go also to the keepers of the archive: to Ludwig Glaeser, curator from 1968 to 1980, and to Pierre Adler, archivist since 1980. Other departmental members at MoMA have been similarly helpful: Robert Coates, Marie-Anne Evans, Sue Evens, Mary Jane Lightbown, and Cara McCarty.

The family of Mies van der Rohe has also made invaluable contributions to this recording of his life and career. His two surviving daughters, Georgia van der Rohe and Marianne Lohan, have been unfailingly forthcoming, while no individual has offered more of his personal knowledge and professional wisdom than Dirk Lohan, Mies's grandson and an architect in his own right, who with Joseph Fujikawa and Bruno Conterato continued the Mies atelier in Chicago. The files in Lohan's office, now called FCL and Associates, have yielded more than a little important visual and literary data. Lohan's late father, Wolfgang Lohan, graciously submitted to several interviews, as did Ulrike Schreiber, Mies's granddaughter, and her husband, the architect Detlef Schreiber, and their son Markus Schreiber. At no time did any members of the family seek to fetter my efforts to assess Mies's career as objectively as possible.

The list of Mies's students and colleagues who made themselves available for advice in general or interviews in particular is long indeed. None of them has earned more of my gratitude than George Danforth, the Chicago architect who, having studied with Mies following World War II, succeeded him as director of the School of Architecture at Illinois Institute of Technology in 1959.

I have likewise gained greatly from conversations with Jacques Brownson, Gordon Bunshaft, Alfred Caldwell, Alfred Clauss, Pafford

Keatinge Clay, Edward Duckett, Joseph Fujikawa, Bertrand Goldberg, Bruce Graham, John Holabird, Jr., Philip Johnson, Gyorgy Kepes, Phyllis Lambert, William Wesley Peters, Bruce Pfeiffer, James Prestini, William Priestley, Louis Rocah, Kevin Roche, John Barney Rodgers, Paul Schweikher, Robert A. M. Stern, Gene Summers, Stanley Tigerman, John Turley, and Robert Venturi in the United States, and with Dietrich von Beulwitz, Hermann Blomeier, Herbert Hirche, Manfred Lehmbruck, Fritz Neumeyer, Sergius Ruegenberg, Peter C. von Seidlein, and Selman Selmanagic in Europe. These men and women are professional architects or designers and as such possess knowledge unique to their calling. Insights of a different kind but no less instructive have come from friends and acquaintances of Mies, or from friends of friends: Ross J. Beatty, Jr., Barbara and Fairbank Carpenter, Marian Carpenter, Elaine Eliat van der Velde, Ise Gropius, Mrs. John Holabird, Lora Marx, Mathilde Meng, Peter Palumbo, the late Lilly von Schnitzler, Mia Seeger, Katherine Logan de Tugendhat, Renate Werner, and Ruth Winter; as well as from scholars and critics: Manfred Bock, Nina Bremer, Tilmann Buddensieg, the late Harold Joachim, Katharine Kuh, Christian Norberg-Schulz, Julius Posener, Pieter Singelenberg, James Johnson Sweeney, and Allan Temko. I appreciate the information provided by a number of people in a variety of institutional roles: Dr. Herbert Lepper of the Aachen Stadtarchiv, the late Dr. Hans Wingler of the Bauhaus Archiv, West Berlin, Carter Manny of the Graham Foundation for Advanced Studies in the Fine Arts, and John Zukowsky, curator of architecture at the Art Institute of Chicago. Without the material assistance of FCL and Associates, the Graham Foundation for Advanced Studies in the Fine Arts, the Mies van der Rohe Archive of the Museum of Modern Art, the National Endowment for the Humanities, and the Skidmore, Owings and Merrill Foundation, this book could not have been completed.

Finally, while the end product is a vita, it would have little meaning if it were not more than that: if it did not deal centrally with Mies's work and thought. In this connection, communication with a number of art and architectural historians—Mies scholars in particular—has provided me with the most important intellectual raw material for the text, not to mention the most valued critical refinements. I am indebted to Professors Kevin Harrington of Illinois Institute of Technology, Christian Otto of Cornell University, Richard Pommer of Vassar College, David van Zanten of Northwestern University, Wolf Tegethoff of the University of Kiel, and Amelia Carr of Lake Forest College, as well as Arthur Drexler of the Museum of Modern Art for their scrupulous reading of the manuscript and their elegant commentary. Further personal encouragement came from other colleagues at Lake Forest College: from President Eugene Hotchkiss and my departmental chairman, Alex F. Mitchell. My two sons, Matthew and Lukas, meanwhile, have shown me a forebearance over the years required to finish my researches that is hardly compensated by my dedication of the completed book to them.

Preface

It is not uncommon for great artists to die twice. Personal extinction is followed by public questioning of the real magnitude of the man, leading his survivors as they bury his body to tear his icon from the altar they themselves raised during his lifetime. Thus death comes as a release not only to him but to those who have gradually found his presence as oppressive as it is inescapable. Often as not the image is later restored, by a generation no longer forced to share the world with him, though the effigy they fashion is likely to reflect as much of themselves as of him. Similar modifications continue through time.

Seventeen years—nearly one full generation—separate the death of Ludwig Mies van der Rohe from the observance of his centenary in 1986. During his later maturity he was widely regarded as one of the twentieth century's several most important architects, whose only peers were Frank Lloyd Wright and Le Corbusier. Critics frequently contended that, the excellence of his work aside, he influenced building more than any other designer of his day. He was the most rigorous of rationalists in a time little blessed with rationality, a stern disciplinarian who insisted that those styles which had grown out of other epochs had no place in this one. Instead, Mies argued, modern building must be the concrete realization of the modern spirit, which in architecture is most evident in the technology of steel and glass. The lucidly rectilinear forms he created seemed to his contemporaries so ineluctable in their logic that the building art itself must be, as he said it was, a reasonable process leading to an unassailable truth. Nostalgia for the ideals of the past was a false end, mere self-expression an equally inadmissible means.

The time to take issue with such an understanding of things coincided more or less with Mies's death; thus in the late 1960s and early 1970s his philosophy was repeatedly attacked as simplistic and even inhumane, just as modernism in the arts fell under the suspicion that it had failed to remake the world while neglecting to appreciate the richness of history and its residual meaning to contemporary minds. While Mies was not the only modernist architect accused of such error, because of his stature he became a lightning rod that attracted most of the thunderbolts of the so-called postmodernist revolution.

Yet he rose well above most of the storm-tossed modernist landscape, and when the elements subsided at the turn of the 1980s, he was still there, occupying as high an elevation as any structure in sight. Rationalists and romantics alike, structuralists and pictorialists, took his work as the prime standard by which they measured their own endeavors either in emulation or rejection of him. Such a position must be sufficient reason for a book like this.

Indeed with Mies the span of one generation may not be enough to enable us to form an appropriately lasting judgment of his contribution to twentieth-century culture. But it is time we began. If he was overpraised during his lifetime or celebrated for the wrong reasons, it follows that the rebellion against him has often prompted proportionately dubious interpretations of the lessons he taught. Even now, as the work of architects who took him as master seems to us often more simply vapid than rational, the counterefforts of many of his detractors already appear mannered and more than a little grotesque. Allowing that his devotion to logic was all too easily reduced to the chilliest sort of dogma, postmodernist fascination with caprice, charm, and the willful gesture has provided us with an architecture all in all changed rather than improved, the product more of insurgency than of liberation.

During the very time that Mies's reputation was thrown open to question—the 1960s and 1970s—archival material was being assembled that students could not have known in the days when his position seemed firmer to us and our concept of him clearer. The most instructive papers have been collected by the Mies van der Rohe Archive of the Museum of Modern Art and the Library of Congress. It seems only fitting that these augmented sources reveal to us an image of Mies more complex than any we earlier formed, whether we revered him or turned away from him. Admittedly, no fundamentally new assessment emerges from them: as we have long supposed, Mies the architect was given to the most deliberate formulation of his goals, which he pursued and refined with remarkable consistency, as if he had surveyed the long road before he ever set foot on it. Creativity for him was a process of distillation rather than of inspiration. Mies the thinker and Mies the man bear out this view. His building was rooted in ideas, even in a metaphysic, to which he so ardently dedicated himself that social existence—his relation to communities as large as a nation or as small as a family—were relegated to a secondary, if not a distantly secondary, place in his life.

For all of these basic traits, however, he was capable also of self-doubt, confusion, and deviation from principle, of friendship and loyalty as well as their opposites, of actions, in short, that are perplexing and inconstant only if we presume he was as simple and fixed a character as his legend suggests. He did not always know the road after all, or follow it unswervingly. Indeed he was more convoluted in his introversion, more ambiguous in his thinking and the architecture it yielded, than most writers have been willing to acknowledge. These qualifications make him a more, not less, enthralling human being, a brilliant and vexing artist no less worthy than ever of a major place in history and, on that account, of the most serious critical and biographical examination.

Buildings and Projects by
Mies van der Rohe

This list is confined to works that Mies designed exclusively or that, especially in his later American career, were carried out in substantial design detail by his office under his supervision. It does not include projects that did not reach the working or presentation drawing stage.

1907	Riehl House, Berlin-Neubabelsberg
1910	Project: Bismarck monument, Bingerbrück-Bingen
1910–11	Perls House (later Fuchs House), Berlin-Zehlendorf
1912	Project: Kröller-Müller House, Wassenaar, The Netherlands
1912–13	Werner House, Berlin-Zehlendorf
1913	House on the Heerstrasse, Berlin
1914	Project: House for the Architect, Berlin-Werder
1914/15– 17	Urbig House, Berlin-Neubabelsberg
1919	Monument for Laura Perls, Berlin(?)
1919(?)	Haus K. (Kempner or Kiepenheuer House project?)
1921	Project: Friedrichstrasse Office Building 1, Berlin
1921	Project: Petermann House, Berlin-Neubabelsberg
1921–22	Kempner House, Berlin-Charlottenburg (demolished)
1921–22	Feldmann House, Berlin-Grünewald
1922	Project: Glass Skyscraper
1922	Eichstaedt House, Berlin-Wannsee
1922/23	Project: Concrete Office Building
1923	Project: Concrete Country House
1923	Project: Lessing House, Berlin-Neubabelsberg
1923	Project: Ryder House, Wiesbaden
1923	Project: Kiepenheuer House(?)
1923/24	Project: Brick Country House
1924–26	Mosler House, Berlin-Neubabelsberg
1925	Project: Dexel House, Jena
1925	Project: Eliat House, Nedlitz (near Potsdam)
1925	Project: Traffic Tower

1950	Preliminary Study, Apartment interior for Byron Harvey, 860 Lake Shore Drive
1950	Project: Dormitory and Fraternity Houses, IIT
1950	General Housing and Landscaping Plan, IIT
1950–51	Project: Steel Frame Prefabricated Row House
1950–51	Project: 50 by 50 House
1950–51	Project: Apartment for the Architect, 860 Lake Shore Drive
1950–52	Mechanical Engineering Research Building 1, IIT Research Institute
1950–52	Test Cell, Armour Research Foundation of IIT
1950–52	Project: Berke Office Building, Indianapolis
1950–56	Architecture, City Planning, and Design Building (Crown Hall), IIT
1951	Project: Television Station, IIT
1951–52	McCormick House, Elmhurst, Illinois
1951–52	Project: Pi Lambda Phi Fraternity House, Bloomington, Indiana
1951–53	Carman Hall, faculty housing, IIT
1951–53	Project: 9000 Jefferson Avenue Apartments, Detroit
1951–53	Morris Greenwald House, Westport, Connecticut
1951–53	Herbert Greenwald Apartment, 860 Lake Shore Drive
1951–53	Project: Riverside Apartments, Trenton, New Jersey
1952	Project: Association of American Railroads Mechanical Engineering Building, IIT
1952–53	Commons Building, IIT
1952–53	Project: National Theater, Mannheim
1952–53	Project: Berke Apartment Building, Indianapolis
1952–55	Cunningham Hall and Bailey Hall, faculty housing, IIT
1953	Project: 1300 Lake Shore Drive Apartments, Chicago
1953–54	Project: Convention Hall, Chicago
1953–56	900–910 Lake Shore Drive Apartments (known also as 900 Esplanade), Chicago
1953–56	Commonwealth Promenade Apartments, Chicago
1953–56	Institute of Gas Technology Storage Building, IIT
1954	Master Plan for the Museum of Fine Arts, Houston
1954	Cullinan Hall, Museum of Fine Arts, Houston (Brown Wing extension completed in 1974)
1954	Project: Association of American Railroads Car Press Building, IIT

1954–57	Electrical Engineering and Physics Building (Siegel Hall), IIT
1954–58	Seagram Building, New York
1955	Remodeling of west entrance, Gunsaulus Hall, IIT
1955	Project: Lubin Apartment Hotel, New York
1955–56	Master Plan for Lafayette Housing Development, Detroit
1955–57	Association of American Railroads Laboratory Building, IIT
1955–57	Project: National Arts Club, New York
1956	Project: Hyde Park Redevelopment, Chicago
1956	Project: Blue Cross–Blue Shield Building, Chicago
1956–58	Metals Research Building Addition, IIT
1956–58	Commonwealth Promenade Apartments, second addition, Chicago
1956–58	Maquettes for sculpture, Seagram Building Plaza, New York
1957	Project: Bacardi Office Building, Santiago, Cuba
1957	Project: United States Consulate, São Paulo, Brazil
1957	Project: Quadrangles Apartments, Brooklyn
1957	Project: Kaiser Office Building, Chicago
1957	Project: Commercial Housing Building, Pratt Institute, Brooklyn
1957	Project: Willoughby Walk Apartments, Pratt Institute
1957	Project: Michigan Avenue Office Buildings, Chicago
1957–58	Project: Chemical Research Building, IIT
1957–58	Project: Battery Park Apartment Development, New York
1957–59	Project: Seagram Office Building, Chicago
1957–61	Bacardi Office Building, Mexico City
1958	Project: Marina Site Apartments, San Francisco
1958	Project: Rimpau Site, Los Angeles
1958	Pavilion Apartments and Town Houses, Lafayette Park, Detroit
1958	Project: Skid Row, Detroit
1958–60	Pavilion Apartments and Colonnade Apartments, Colonnade Park, Newark
1959	Project: Brookfarm Apartments, Brookline, Massachusetts
1959	Project: Exhibition of Mies van der Rohe, V Bienal, São Paulo
1959	Project: Rockhill Center Development, Kansas City, Missouri

1959–64	Federal Center, Chicago
1960–61	Project: Schaefer Museum, Schweinfurt
1960–63	Project: Friedrich Krupp Administration Building, Essen
1960–63	One Charles Center, Baltimore
1960–63	2400 Lakeview Apartments, Chicago
1960–63	Lafayette Towers Apartment Building, Detroit
1960–63	Home Federal Savings and Loan Association of Des Moines, Des Moines, Iowa
1960–63	Project: Millbrook Commercial Center, Newark
1961	Project: Mountain Place, Montreal
1962	Project: Pavilion Recreation Area, Detroit
1962–65	Meredith Memorial Hall, Drake University, Des Moines
1962–65	Science Center, Duquesne University, Pittsburgh
1962–65	Social Service Administration Building, the University of Chicago
1962–65	Highfield House Apartment Building, Baltimore
1962–67	New National Gallery, Berlin
1963	Lafayette Towers, Lafayette Park, Detroit
1963–69	Dominion Centre, Toronto
1964–66	Project: Foster City Apartment Development, San Mateo, California
1964–68	Westmount Square, Montreal
1965–68	Martin Luther King Memorial Library, Washington, D.C.
1965–74	Brown Wing, Museum of Fine Arts, Houston
1966	Master Plan, Church Street South Redevelopment, New Haven, Connecticut
1966	Project: K–4 School, New Haven
1966–69	Highrise Apartment Building No. 1, Nuns' Island, Montreal
1966–69	IBM Regional Office Building, Chicago
1967	Project: Mansion House Square and Office Tower, London
1967–69	Project: King Broadcasting Studios, Seattle
1967–69	111 East Wacker Drive, Illinois Central Air Rights Development, Chicago

MIES VAN DER ROHE

1   Aachen: Youth in Imperial Germany, 1886–1905

In 1905 Mies van der Rohe, then Ludwig Mies, boarded a train in Aachen, the city of his birth, and headed for Berlin for good. He was nineteen years old, little accustomed to long-distance travel by rail, still less to a destination as formidable as the capital of the German Empire. Thirty miles underway he developed acute nausea, which subsided only slightly at the first stop, Cologne. "Around 8:15," he recalled later, "the train started up again, and at 8:16, I opened the window, stuck my head out, and threw up."[1] His distress persisted until he felt the firm ground of Berlin beneath his feet hours hence, though as soon as he mounted a taxi headed for the suburb of Rixdorf,[2] he lost his stomach again.

He deserted the cab, sat down on a curbstone, and waited for the return of equilibrium. Then he hoisted himself on a trolley and endured long enough to reach the municipal architectural office in Rixdorf, where he had been promised a job as a studio assistant.

Thus, Mies's unspectacular entry into the great metropolis of Berlin, the profession, the world. Between that day of his tender years and the time when international homage was a fact of his daily life, decades would pass. He would live to see the ascendancy and eventual collapse of the empire, the establishment and failure of the republic that succeeded it, the rise and still more shattering fall of the Reich that Adolf Hitler promised would last a thousand years. He would finally be forced to abandon his homeland and emigrate to the country that laid it waste, yet in both places—Germany and the United States—he would so transform the art of architecture that by the time of his death in 1969 every major city in the Western world bore his imprint.

For now, however, 1905, eager to breathe the air of a new century in one of its most stimulating climates, he had ample reason to put up with his physical discomfort, short-lived as it was. All he knew of life he had learned in Aachen, a provincial city certain to remain one. His family, modest, middle class, piously Catholic in the Rhineland tradition and limited in outlook, was likewise liable to stay that way. He might have spent his own life accordingly, save for a talent that asserted itself during his early adolescence and grew increasingly urgent as he approached manhood, finally firing an ambition to reach horizons far beyond the family hearth.

How he spent his youth is known to us only from the scantest records. No personal letters of any account survive, no diaries, few recorded recollections of acquaintances. Mies, young and old, never took eagerly to writing. There are several interviews, the best of them conducted by his grandson Dirk Lohan as late as 1968, a year before the old man died.[3] Even in that conversation he was inclined at first to

resist autobiographical accounting ("That's schoolboy stuff, isn't it?"),
though once Lohan got him moving, he talked volubly enough. He
just did not talk very long: much of what we can make out of his early
personal life remains inferential.

Still, we can begin to learn something from Aachen itself. If it was
a parochial city in Mies's day, it looked back on a glorious history,
long past but proudly remembered by any local youth of his generation. Late in the eighth century Charlemagne made it the capital of
his empire, the first great unified state in Northern Europe, a domain
that extended from the Pyrenees east to Saxony, from the North Sea
south to Rome. The intellectual energies of the scholars appointed to
the Carolingian court generated the first major revival in the West of
the classical spirit that apparently had died with the collapse of the
Roman Empire. Charlemagne's close personal identification with the
emperors of Rome together with his passionate admiration of Rome's
cultural legacy—and the fateful alliance he forged with the pope—
contributed seminally to the shape of the Middle Ages and, eventually,
to the emergence of the Renaissance.

Aachen was the site of his palace, now long vanished. Originally it
stood across a court from the splendid domed chapel that survives
today, testament to another architect, Odo of Metz, who built it after
the example of the Byzantine church of San Vitale in Ravenna. The
most sophisticated northern European structure of its day, it served
as the coronation hall for German kings from the tenth to the sixteenth
century.

Mies knew the chapel as a boy and recollected it as a man, keenly
enough that the impression he claimed it made on him, as he later
spoke of it, must have awakened associations with the concept of "universal space" which he explored in his own mature designs. He remembered standing next to and occasionally behind the powerful piers
that separate the octagonal area beneath the dome of the chapel from
the aisles and perceiving that "one could apprehend everything that
went on. The whole space was a unity, everywhere alive with the
sights and sounds of the ceremony, even the smells of it."[4] So saying,
Mies may have seen the chapel less with the unaided eye, as it were,
than through the glass of his own architecture, since the interior is
not so undifferentiated as he implied. Still, the specificity of his memory of it may be taken as a sign of the impact the venerable pile made
upon him. The image of its construction was no less vivid in his recall.
He was forever telling interviewers late in his life of the boyhood occasions when he accompanied his mother to morning mass in the chapel.
There, he reported, he would sit in rapt silence, transfixed by the
scale and strength of the "great stones" that comprise the columns
and arches of the building. Today enough of the Aachen Cathedral,
of which Charlemagne's chapel is a part, looks as it did when Mies
was a youth that one can readily imagine how intently the son of a
stonemason, whose children were accustomed to work in the family
yard, might have studied the lively assortment of materials that make
up the whole ecclesiastical complex. Where the original atrium of
Charlemagne's chapel once stood, for instance, a cobblestoned courtyard is now surrounded, as it was in Mies's day, by unpretentious but

charming three-story houses that hint at the nearness of France. Within
them are the cathedral treasury, administrative offices, and clerical
residences. The houses are built mostly of limestone on the first story,
brick in English bond on the second, and Mansard slate roofs on the
third. The court is accessible either from the west, past a Romanesque
gatehouse topped by a baroque roof, or from the south, where, across
the Münsterplatz, a wall of slender town houses rears up, as disparate
in their materials, manners, and ornament as the cathedral itself is a
catchall of period styles. The chapel leads eastward to a fifteenth-
century Gothic choir surrounded by a veritable wall of glass and surmounted by spidery vaulting. It prompts associations with the openness and transparency of Mies's later works.

Beyond the Münsterplatz, in the oldest part of town, Mies's Aachen
was a maze of tight streets hemmed in by flat-faced medieval houses
mostly in brick, intimately related to the tradition of Holland and Belgium, whose borders lie within walking distance of Aachen's city limits. Mies described these anonymous vernacular structures with en-
compassing affection: "mostly very simple, but very clear . . . did not
belong to any epoch . . . had been there for a thousand years and
were still impressive . . . All the great styles passed, but [they re-
mained] . . . they were *really* built."[5]

This is typical Miesian sentiment, as we have learned to know it
from those published pronouncements he did leave us: the explicit
affirmation of clarity and generality in the design and construction of
buildings, especially over the long reach of time, plus the implicit
negation of personality, of self-conscious "style," or of anything
ephemeral.

Yet just as we have noted more variety than unity in the architecture of the cathedral and the Münsterplatz, there was far more of
"style" and less of clarity, more of clamorous change than of perma-
nence, in the rest of the Aachen of Mies's youth, especially in the

Aachen: Youth in Imperial Germany

part of the city he would probably have seen more frequently and steadily than he saw the chapel and its environs.[6] This part of his experience and what he learned from it are no less important to the present account than are the lessons of the timeless dome.

He must have learned something from the new Aachen, even if, as one is tempted to suspect, it took the form of a glandular antipathy toward the superabundance of historicist ornamentation that was one of the salient characteristics of German architecture during the last several decades of the nineteenth century. Mies was born on 27 March 1886, in a house at Steinkaulstrasse 29. Though his family moved several times during his early childhood, they remained in the same neighborhood until he was fifteen; thus it is reasonable to assume he watched the rebuilding in the 1890s of the extraordinary facades along the Oppenhoffallee, a kilometer to the south. Earlier the Kaiserallee, the Oppenhoffallee was and still is the most elegant residential boulevard in Aachen, and there is no more complete an example anywhere in Germany of Wilhelmine architectural decoration at its most ostentatious. The street consists of row houses, each boasting a *piano nobile* that surveys the world through a generous bay window. Aside from that common feature and a typical Aachen three-window width, the houses are a riot of surface decor, with multiple cornices, columns, pilasters, and pediments, swags, brackets, scrolls, and oeils-de-boeuf, lions', warriors', and giants' heads, lifesize nudes and knights—all in polychrome—bristling from the house fronts, most of which are neobaroque, not a few Gothic, and others wildly mixed in origins.

Late nineteenth-century building throughout the Western world was marked by a comparable imperialist braggadocio of ornamental form, though in Germany it seems to have come closer than in other places to confusion and bumptious excess. Several factors may account for this. At the time of Mies's birth the country was newly seized with a sense of national identity and military power following political unification and victory over the French in the early 1870s. National pride and confidence swelled during the eighties and nineties, and along with it, ambition, abetted by the explosively swift pace of German industrialization. The floridity of early Wilhelmine architecture was thus a symptom of national self-esteem and bourgeois high hopes that grew violently, in an aesthetic and symbolic sense almost unmanageably, in the hothouse atmosphere of the last quarter of the century.

Aachen was fertile ground for such a fanfaronade. It was a wealthy city, even by nineteenth-century German standards, with notably more millionaires than its population would have indicated. (One of them went so far as to outfit the entire municipal firefighting arm out of his own pocket.) Meanwhile, the city was growing at an unprecedented rate. In 1825, Aachen had a population of 35,428. By 1905 that number was 151,971, a rise of more than 400 percent, with the greatest increase occurring in the two decades of Mies's residence and coinciding with the historic crest of the city's economic prosperity. While Aachen continued to enjoy the tourist trade that had been attracted to the hot sulphur springs of its Elisenbrunnen since the days of the Romans, it now witnessed the flash growth of its modern industry as well. Traditionally noted as a textile center, it drew upon the extensive coalfields in its neighboring districts following the Franco-Prussian War. By the 1890s, the largest and best-equipped steelworks in Germany, the Rothe Erde, employed between 4000 and 5000 Aacheners.

This furious activity was reflected in institutional proliferation as well. The Technical Institute (*Technische Hochschule*) was founded in 1870, rapidly gaining a reputation as the most distinguished, and conservative, architectural school in northwestern Germany. Mies would have studied there had his family been able or inclined to send him. Public schools popped up like spring shoots: eighteen *Volksschulen* built between 1880 and 1900, eleven more before the outbreak of World War I. Added to these were an assemblage of other and specialized educational facilities: the Trade School (*Gewerbeschule*), the Secondary Science School (*Oberrealschule*), plus academies (*Gymnasien*) devoted alternatively to the science and humanities curricula. A main post office was completed in 1898, in neo-Romanesque, its portal flanked by a pair of grandiose, larger-than-life statues of Kaiser Wilhelm I and Charlemagne. Seven years later the new train station opened, its Jugendstil reflecting the dernier cri of turn-of-the-century styles. Meanwhile, the municipal trolley system had been electrified in 1892 and motion pictures were shown at the Kurhaus in 1896. The fourteenth-century Town Hall, a huge edifice built on the foundations of Charlemagne's palace and badly damaged by fire in 1883, was redesigned three years later and rebuilt by 1902, its two proud towers restored— or rather inflated—to the belligerently majestic scale beloved of the Wilhelmine era.

3. Kapuzinergraben with main Post Office at right, Aachen, about 1910
Stadtarchiv Aachen

4. Town Hall, Aachen, about 1903
Stadtarchiv Aachen

Aachen was a demonstrably successful provincial city of that ascendant age, a town on the one hand large enough to put on airs appropriate to the values of the time, on the other small enough to know its place in the larger national scheme of things, to be both typical and conservative, that is, and not to aspire strenuously to either cultural or political innovation. For anyone with the kind of ambition Mies's architectural promise had awakened by the time he mounted the train to Berlin, it was a perfect town in which to become sensible of the general rewards of upward mobility but to recognize that one's own specific goals must be pursued elsewhere.

What we know of Mies's home life and family background does more to confirm than to upset these speculations, although nothing in it seems encouraging to the growth of a singular artistic sensibility. As far back as we can trace the records—the late eighteenth century—his family on both parents' sides were Catholics of German stock who lived close to the *Dreiländereck*, the "three-country corner" where Holland, Belgium, and Germany meet and their respective cultures conjoin.[7] The fact that Ludwig's father, Michael Mies, was the first of either line to be born in Aachen proper (on 29 March 1851) suggests that his father in turn, Jakob, initially listed in the 1855 Aachen address book as a marble carver born in Blankenheim in the Eifel on 21 October 1814, moved to the city in the wave of urbanization that rose in the second third of the nineteenth century. Amalie Rohe, who married Michael Mies on 21 October 1876 (Jakob's sixty-second birthday), was almost eight years her husband's senior, having been born 14 April 1843, in Monschau, a picturesque suburb of Aachen.

During the 1870s Jakob Mies shared a "marble business and atelier" with his son Carl, Michael's older brother, at Adalbertstrasse

Aachen: Youth in Imperial Germany

5. Mayor's study in the Town
Hall, Aachen, about 1900
Stadtarchiv Aachen

116. Michael, who joined the business later, is mentioned in the address book as early as 1875, as a "marble worker." His name does not appear again until the edition of 1880. By then his marriage to Amalie had produced a male child, Ewald Philipp, born 13 October 1877 and thus the *Stammhalter* ("preserver of the stem"), first son and heir, a designation of considerable familial importance in nineteenth-century Germany.

Michael and Amalie now lived at Steinkaulstrasse 29, where their other four children came into the world; Carl Michael, second oldest, born 18 May 1879, died at age two, 9 November 1881, very likely in the pox epidemic that raged in Aachen for most of that year and part of the next; Anna Marie Elisabeth, born 16 September 1881; Maria Johanna Sophie, born 30 December 1883; and the youngest, Maria Ludwig Michael, who became Ludwig Mies van der Rohe only after World War I—for professional reasons—by the artifice of connecting his father's and mother's surnames with the invented "van der."

The Steinkaulstrasse is located outside and east of the limits of Aachen's ancient second wall (now replaced by streets), not far from the Adalbertsteinweg (earlier the Adalbertstrasse), where Michael, already listed as a master mason in 1883, and Carl, identified as a sculptor, took over the family business after the death of their father around

Aachen: Youth in Imperial Germany

6. Mies's parents, Michael Mies and Amalie, née Rohe, in 1921
Private collection

1888. This neighborhood was the fastest growing part of Aachen in the 1880s and 1890s. Rents were cheapest there. It was also located close to the city's established cemeteries, a factor of importance to any "marble business" that trafficked in gravestones.

The Mies family early on did not confine themselves to mortuary monuments. During the 1880s their business activities reflected the generally aggressive prosperity of Aachen as a whole: their chief product was the stone mantelpiece, a common feature of the fireplaces of the day, often carved in the rich neobaroque style favored among the bourgeoisie. The Mieses did well enough at this that labor was divided between Michael, who ran the studio, and Carl, who managed sales and traveled, frequently to Paris, occasionally even as far as the marble quarries of North Africa. Mies van der Rohe, who was an infant when the Mies atelier was most flourishing, recalled that old Jakob for a time "dominated the whole area from the Rhine to Brussels."[8] It was the closest his family would come to elevating themselves from the craftsman class to that of entrepreneur. Business shrank, however, during the 1890s. Carl died sometime between 1891 and 1893; moreover, cast-iron, coal-burning stoves more and more replaced the less efficient fireplaces and their accompanying mantelpieces. By 1893 two new cemeteries had opened on the west side of town, prompting Michael to establish a branch of his business there in 1895 and, apparently, to be content mostly with carving tombstones. By 1901 he and his eldest, twenty-four-year-old Ewald, both now listed as master masons, had moved family residence and studio alike to the Vaelserstrasse, the road to the Netherlands.

By then young Ludwig was fifteen years old. He had been born just as nation, city, and family were on an upswing that lasted long enough in his own house for him to remember and be affected by it, though even more consciously to recall his parents' reduced circumstances in the 1890s and thereafter. In short, his notion of the family's fixed position in society would have been that of middle-class—more exactly craftsman/middle-class—people, with the preindustrial implication of the term underscoring the fact that Michael Mies's children were most at home in an environment of things rather than ideas, artifacts rather than commerce. It had after all been Uncle Carl who was the salesman during the heady eighties. Father Michael was always happiest with the tools of the trade, an attitude he evidently communicated well enough that Mies van der Rohe's lifelong love of materials and his care in the detailed rendering of them must owe something to examples learned at home.

The 1968 interview Mies recorded with Dirk Lohan, himself an architect, is the chief source of what we know of early experiences pertinent to Mies's professional destiny:

> LOHAN: When you were very young, were you obliged to help in the family atelier?
> MIES: I did it for the fun of it. And always when we had vacations. I especially remember that on All Souls Day, when so many people wanted new monuments for the graves, our whole family pitched in. I did the lettering on the stones, my brother did the carving, and my sisters put the finishing touches on them, the gold leaf, and all that. I don't think we added very much to the process, but it probably was a little better for it.

Mies pictured his father as a craftsman reluctant to act the businessman but one who collided eventually and unavoidably with the changing values of changing times: "About the economics of capitalist speculation he understood nothing. 'To make this thing,' he would say to a customer, 'I need three weeks. And it will cost so and so much, to be paid when I deliver it.' That was the craftsman's way, not the merchant's. There was no room in it for flexibility, for consideration

Aachen: Youth in Imperial Germany

of long-term profits as opposed to short-term gains that could carry the business over hard times." On Mies's later visits home after he moved to Berlin, he listened to young Ewald debate old Michael. "My brother would say, 'Look, we can produce such and such an ornament without all that fuss, especially if it is way up high on a building facade where no one can look closely at it.' My father wanted no part of that. 'You're none of you stonemasons anymore!' he would say. 'You know the finial at the top of the spire of the cathedral at Cologne? Well, you can't crawl up there and get a good look at it, but it is carved as if you could. It was made for God.'"

Yet despite Michael's reverence for tradition, he could hardly afford to live locked in the past; the Industrial Revolution and the kaiser's new empire would see to that. Since the passing of the guild system, training in the crafts had increasingly taken place in the schools, which tended to add theory to rule of thumb, thus to educate as well as train. Ludwig, aged ten, was sent on from elementary school to the cathedral school—a move destined, whether Michael was aware of it or not, to sever the boy's connection with the family's tradition.

The cathedral school, which included Latin and Catholic instruction in its curriculum, was regarded as of higher rank than public elementary school and thus more likely to assure any of its students further advancement, say, to the *Gymnasium* if he aspired to loftier things or to the *Gewerbeschule* if proficiency in a trade were the limit of his ambition. Monsignor Erich Stephany, archivist of the Aachen Cathedral, has speculated that Michael had the latter in mind for Ludwig, firm in his notion that *Gymnasium* was too pretentious for a stonemason's son, while *Gewerbeschule* was a respectable, even appropriate alternative, especially if the son were neither *Stammhalter* nor certain to enter the family business. The cathedral school charged a small tuition, which Michael was probably able to manage for the full term of Ludwig's attendance there.[9]

That lasted three years, from 1896 to 1899. How good a student he was remains in doubt, since the institution's records were destroyed in World War II. We may surmise that since he was enrolled in a school that enjoyed substantial reputation throughout the Rhineland, he possessed above average intelligence. How much he learned is also uncertain, though he once told interviewer Peter Blake that he was "not very good," implying that his early gifts were more practical than intellectual.[10] Stephany is sure that neither his religious studies nor his reading in Latin brought him into contact with those two philosophers, Saint Augustine and Saint Thomas Aquinas, whom he cited often in his mature years and associated with his Catholic youth. He probably never even read Caesar.

The real encounter with philosophy came later. At thirteen he might have been finished with schooling altogether, had his father's willingness to help him with it been exhausted. It was not, not quite. True to Stephany's suppositions, Michael sent Ludwig on—as he had Ewald before him—but to *Gewerbeschule*, not to *Gymnasium*. Both boys spent two years there and no more, in consequence of their father's having sought and secured a full-tuition scholarship for each of them. So doing, he indicated his faith in their education according to the limits of the family's circumstances and history, while the sons in turn provided the first clear-cut clues available to us that they were talented in their own right. Otherwise, had Michael asked for financial assistance on grounds of need alone, the school in those pre-egalitarian days would surely never have offered it.

In view of his scholarship and the fact that he did not lose it, we may presume that Ludwig performed creditably as a student in the trade school. Again, records are lost. His daughter Georgia confesses to the vagueness of her recollection that he was specially awarded a full gallery to himself, that is, a one-person show within a group show, for the required exhibition of his school work on the occasion of graduation from the trade school.[11] We do know more certainly what he studied there, notably chemistry, physics, algebra, geometry, trigonometry, history, economics, geography, German, English, technical drawing, life drawing, and workshop. To this he himself added:

> The trade school was not the same as a crafts school [Handwerkerschule]. It offered the kind of two-year course that would enable a graduate to get a job in an office or a workshop. Great stress was laid on drawing, because it was something everybody had to know. You understand, the curriculum was no theoretically contrived program. It was based on experience, on the sort of thing tradesmen really had to use.

He added that Aachen had other technical schools of a "higher level," with four-year curricula, like the machine construction and building construction schools. He also mentioned the Hochschule, which offered the most theoretical program of all, but his heart clearly belonged to the practically trained folk: "They were flawless in their work habits. I would far rather have dealt with them than with anyone from the Hochschule. They could draw expertly—a roof frame, for example, that was perfect in detail. What you needed on a job; that is what they learned to do, masterfully."[12]

Mies was eighty-two when he uttered these words, and he had long since rationalized his own training. That he never matriculated at the Aachen Hochschule helps to explain both his impatience with the Beaux-Arts and his sympathy with an architectural education grounded in the elementary facts of building. If he had little formal education, he earned his own calluses, and he deeply valued the turn he did on the scaffolds following trade school. Signing on at fifteen, he worked for a year as an apprentice at local building sites and later, for four years, as a draftsman in several Aachen shops and ateliers. For Lohan's benefit he recalled in detail the way houses were put up in his youth:

> Someone dug the foundation and laid the mortar bed, slaked the lime and let it run down there. Then came the bricks. That's where we started. We didn't have concrete, at least not for these house foundations, which were made of brick, first laid dry, with no binder, then covered with mortar. We had to make our own mortar and carry it on shoulder boards shaped like half-cylinders. We loaded bricks and stones in them too, using one hand to hold the board pole steady, the other to help ourselves up the

ladders. Whoever could carry the most was cock of the walk.

Once you were there, on the wall, it was good. You learned to work slowly, not like some wild animal that gets tired after fifteen minutes, but quietly, for hours and hours. If you were really experienced, you knew how to do corners, which was very complicated. Mostly we laid the bricks in a cross bond, and now and then we'd make mistakes. The foreman would often just let us make them and carry on. Then we'd get the wall up a way and he would say, "O.K., that's wrong. Take the whole thing down!" Finally, when we were finished, the carpenters would show up, and we were shifted to the vital assignment of getting the water for the workmen's coffee.

We had little pots, and we could buy boiling water for them for two Pfennige. We'd put powdered coffee into the pot, pour the water over it and deliver it to the workers. We could also get sausage for five Pfennige. Or cheese. Cheese was the staple. Bread you brought from home. The Schnaps came later. At the end of the week, when people got paid, that's when you got your Schnaps, lots of it, five Pfennige a shot.

Clearly Mies was a child of an authoritarian system of rearing and training, and the habits he learned stayed with him. Students he taught decades later at the Bauhaus and in Chicago would recognize in his recollections the unelaborated critique, "Why don't you try it again." They would hear the origins of his lifelong love of brick, his fascination with the builder's ancient problem of turning the corner, the pleasure he took in solitude and the slow pace, and the consolation he sought in the cup that cheers.

In his narrative to Lohan, however, he had not yet reached his sixteenth birthday nor collected a day's pay for his labors. It was time, in his father's eyes, to declare an end to the boy's formal schooling, at least to the part paid for by the family. So Ludwig asked the supervisor of the apartment house project where he was working if he could be put on wages.

Of course the boss said no. He had had me for a year for nothing: why should he give me money now?

As it happened, I had a friend, a school chum, who knew of someone in town who needed a draftsman. I could draw: I had learned it at school. And I was good at lettering, with all that work on the tombstones behind me. So I applied to be a draftsman in a stucco factory run by a man named Max Fischer.

I got the job, though they put me in the office, not the atelier, and I had to keep the books and lick the postage stamps and get on a bicycle to take the wages to the workers at the construction sites. This I did for at least half a year.

Then the chief draftsman was called into the army and I got promoted to the drafting room. If I thought I knew how to draw before, I really learned now. We had huge drawing boards that went from floor to ceiling and stood vertically against the wall. You couldn't lean on or against them; you had to stand squarely in front of them and draw not just by turning your hand but by swinging your whole arm. We made drawings the size of an entire quarter of a room ceiling, which we could then send on to the modelmakers. I did this every day for two years. Even now I can draw cartouches with my eyes closed.

LOHAN: You worked in all styles?

MIES: All historic styles, plus modern. All conceivable ornaments.

LOHAN: Did you design any yourself?

MIES: When I was able—which is not as easy as it might sound.

LOHAN: Were those actually your first creative efforts?

MIES: I don't know that anymore.

This last answer was curt. Mies did not associate "creativity" with the plainness of his working life in Aachen. Less art and more of his own personality were evident in his departure from the stucco workshop, which happened suddenly one day when his boss, having taken him angrily to task over a drawing mistake, made an abrupt, unexpectedly threatening gesture at him. Mies stiffened. "Don't try that again," he warned the man, who backed off. Mies packed up his things and left the office. "Mind you," he told Lohan, "the man sent the police to haul me back, as if I were an apprentice and he owned me! But I was a novice draftsman. There is a difference!" Mies had his pride now. "My brother knew who I was as well as I, and when the cops arrived, he was there to tell them so, in no uncertain terms. 'Go home,' he said, and they went. Nothing more came of it. I was finished with the man and the job."

Youngest of his family, Mies had an ardent affection for his older brother, to whom he was at all times closer than to either of his parents or his sisters.[13] Ewald was guardian, spiritual counsellor, and fellow carouser, the two youths evidently having played as hard as they worked. Ludwig, a fierce amateur football player, was also something of a hell-raiser in his later teens, who once contrived to foul up the gas jets so thoroughly at the evening school where he was enrolled that classes throughout the building had to be dismissed until the following night. On another nocturnal occasion, well-fortified with spirits imbibed together with Ewald at a neighborhood saloon, he climbed the equestrian monument to Kaiser Wilhelm I at the Theaterplatz and had so raucous a good time sharing the saddle with the emperor that the constabulary was aroused and he was formally charged with insulting the national majesty.

He protested to the arresting officer that he could not get down from the statue, whereupon Ewald talked the law into helping him fetch a ladder from a nearby building site, and by the time the two men returned to Ludwig and the emperor, Ludwig had vanished.

The brothers' bond extended to shared talents; both were ambidextrous and possessed of equally keen vision. If Ludwig's eye has been celebrated by generations of architectural historians, Ewald's was held in awe among the stonemasons of Aachen. From a distance of two meters he could detect a misalignment of a millimeter in the lettering on a tombstone, and he was a designer of no small gift. The family monument in Aachen's Westfriedhof, which Ewald planned and executed in 1929, the year of Ludwig's great Barcelona Pavilion, is a masterpiece of modernist sans serif graphics, notable for the same understated refinement that marks the work of his more renowned brother.

Yet Ewald was content to remain in Aachen, unmarried, his whole life. Ludwig was ambitious, and as early as his tenure in the Fischer stucco workshops, he had put to rest any likelihood that he would return to Michael Mies's stoneyard and the family business. He had become a skilled draftsman at seventeen, suggesting that his eventual position, both socially and professionally, would rank higher than that of even the wealthiest stonemason. Between 1901 and 1905, according to his papers,[14] he worked for two architects in Aachen, the first identified only as "Architect Goebbels," the second as "Albert Schneider, Architect." The dates of these employments are not known. During the same four-year period he also attended what the papers list simply as "Evening and Sunday Vocational School" on nights and weekends while working full-time during the day and living with his parents and three siblings on the Vaelserstrasse.

"I somehow made contact," he told Lohan, "with the office of an architect [presumably Schneider] in Aachen who was designing a big department store downtown, a branch of the Tietz Company. He had conceived a highly ornamental facade for the building, but his reach was greater than his grasp; he couldn't draw it. He asked me if I could. I said, 'Yes.' He wanted to know how long it would take. I said, 'Do you need it this evening? Or do I have a little more time?' He looked at me as if I were either a fraud or a fool for promising to do it so fast. 'Give to it me tomorrow,' he said, and I did. Then he asked me to work for him."

Meanwhile Tietz had decided to turn control of the department store project over to the large Berlin architectural firm of Bossler and Knorr, demoting Mies's boss Schneider to the role of associate. Presently a small army of architects, engineers, and clerical workers from the German capital descended upon the Aachen office, and Mies found himself working and consorting daily with sophisticated invaders from the metropolis. His own efforts apparently were up to their standards.

> LOHAN: The story has it that someone in the office gave you the idea of moving to Berlin.
> MIES: It was an architect named Dülow, from Königsberg, an admirer of Schopenhauer. He invited me one evening for dinner. It was Schopenhauer's birthday. The fact is I was not very educated in that sort of thing.
> LOHAN: But you must have had some interest in it for him to invite you that way.
> MIES: Yes. Yes, I remember I did.

Enlarging on this in an interview with his daughter Georgia, he said: "On the day I was assigned a drawing table at Schneider's, I was cleaning it out when I came across a copy of *Die Zukunft* [The Future], a journal published by Maximilian Harden, plus an essay on one of Laplace's theories. I read both of them and both of them went quite over my head. But I couldn't help being interested. So every week thereafter, I got hold of *Die Zukunft* and read it as carefully as I could. That's when I think I started paying attention to spiritual things. Philosophy. And culture."[15]

There is nothing in his early life, no person, no event, no set of circumstances, to explain this sudden devotion to a subject that he understood so little at first and was academically so ill-prepared to study. We have to assume, lacking further evidence, that his interest in philosophy, which eventually affected his work more than that of any other major twentieth-century architect, grew from a source within himself.

Mies went on, talking to Lohan:

> In the course of the evening Dülow said to me, "Listen, why do you want to hang around here, in this tank town? Go to Berlin; that's where things are happening." I said, "That's easier said than done. I can't just buy a train ticket, head for Berlin and stand around the Potsdamer Bahnhof without the faintest idea of where to go."
>
> So he pulled an architectural journal, *Die Bauwelt* or some such, from his desk drawer. There were two classified ads in it, both looking for draftsmen, one for the new town hall in Rixdorf, the other for general work at the big Berlin firm of Reinhardt and Sössenguth. Send drawings, the ads said—nothing more, no diplomas, no recommendations. So I sent them a pile of things and got an offer from both places. The Rixdorf project promised two hundred Reichsmarks a month, forty less than the other one. But Dülow said, "Take Rixdorf; I have a good friend who is in charge of the project there. His name is Martens, a fine man, from the Baltic, painstaking architect . . . above all, an artist."[16]

Aachen was a closed chapter. It was time for the train to Berlin. What had been a craft had turned gradually into a calling; building had become architecture, a discipline that necessarily began on the earth, in solid materials soundly assembled, but ascended, Mies now recognized, no less urgently to a higher realm where somehow, in a way he did not yet comprehend, art was inextricably bound up with ideas.

Leaving Aachen he relinquished all claim to the family business. His brother assumed complete ownership following the deaths of Michael, in 1927, and Amalie five months later, in 1928. Over the years the Aachen address book regularly listed Ewald as a stonemason, though now and then he presumed to advertise himself as an architect. He had neither the license to warrant such a title nor any substantial formal training in the field; as late as the 1920s in Germany the mere act of hanging out a shingle was a legally acceptable way of identifying oneself as a professional designer of buildings. The tradition of the crafts died grudgingly.

As for the Mies women, it is consistent with the male domination of Wilhelmine society that they appear to us in retrospect only as indistinct forms. We know next to nothing about them. When Mies spoke of his mother, as he did in recalling visits with her to the Aachen cathedral, he was affectionate and respectful but vague, as if she were more a presence in his life than a force. His sisters Elise and Maria occupy a comparably neutral, not to say negligible, place in his recorded recollections. They were still single when they opened a grocery store on the Vaelserstrasse in 1911, just a few doors from the family residence. It survived as late as the 1950s. Elise eventually married one Johann Josef Blees, a widower with a teenage son; she was past fifty at the time. Maria was a lifelong spinster.

Whatever we make of this fragmentary record, none of it points to the blossoming of genius. Mies had native intelligence enough, though he was hardly brilliant, and the meagerness of his formal education gave him more cause to feel uncertain of his intellectual endowments than reason to be at ease about them. The chief source of justifiable confidence was his talent as a draftsman, a gift sufficient to impress all the professionals he met while he was still a teenager. Furthermore, he and his family were typical products of their soil, the Eifel district of Westphalia, whose Germans are a hard and independent lot, close to the Dutch, circumspect, exacting, not easily swayed, habitually acting on reflection rather than in haste.

Still, Mies's early life was nothing if not average in all respects. The one personal trait of his later years that quite overshadowed all the others of his youth, and without which the rest would hardly have led him to historic prominence, was a will of titanic proportions. We have thus far detected only a germ of it. To all appearances it was innate. The very fact that it developed slowly and gained force only cumulatively accounts for the fact that it was not especially evident in his green years. How Mies cultivated it and finally turned it into a creative force that altered the course of architectural history is the substance of this story.

Berlin: Problems of a New Century, 1905–18

Mies's arrival in Berlin coincided with a phase of fateful transition in the history of German architecture and design. Within a few years he would find himself working literally at the elbows of the men who did most to initiate it. Since he chose them as much as they chose him, we must presume he identified himself from the outset with the progressives. Yet he was no red-eyed rebel, nor were they. Being a more social art than painting, architecture responded at a slower pace and in a more complex way to the powerful pressures for change in the modern world. Painting had its secessionist wing, called the avant-garde, which was responsible to itself alone and thus had less to lose by rebelling extravagantly against middle-class tastes and values. The radically new came less readily to architecture, and only in respectful consideration of artistic and national traditions as well as the aspirations and whims of clients and the necessities of commerce. In view of this, Mies, by nature vastly more deliberate than impetuous, would himself take an exceptionally long time before his work broke through to the full-blown modernist manner. He was in his mid-thirties by the time he conceived the great Friedrichstrasse Office Building of 1921. Thus the years between 1905 and 1921—a period during which Germany advanced toward World War I, plunged headlong into it, and nearly drowned in the process—were the years of Mies's unhurried coming of professional age.

For now, he found himself in Rixdorf, recovered from his intestinal grief and working for the city building office. The assignment waiting for him was the detailing of the neo-Gothic design, already begun, of the wall panelling in the Council Chamber of the Town Hall. The program called for ample ornament, an exercise for which his endeavors in the Fischer studio had prepared him well at the graphic level. Nevertheless, as he later reminisced, the material he was given to work with was wood, and "for all the time I had already spent with stone and brick and mortar and all such, I had never properly learned to handle wood, neither in school nor at home nor during my apprentice year in Aachen."[1]

He did not add how well he managed under the circumstances, or whether he ever met Dülow's friend Martens, for his fledgling career was interrupted after several months by an unheroic but mercifully brief encounter with the German military. He was drafted into the kaiser's army.

"One day not long after induction," he recalled,

> we were ordered out onto the drill field for exercises. It was raining pitilessly, and the water kept rolling in torrents off our helmets—those comical old things with the spikes on them.

When we heard the command "Attention!" one of the poor recruits in the first row of our unit was thoughtless enough to reach up and wipe the water from his face. At this the drill sergeant flew into a rage. It was a breach of discipline, not to be tolerated. The company captain was equally furious, since it had happened in *his* outfit. So we were all ordered to do calisthenics in the pouring rain, for hour after hour until eight o'clock that night. It was utterly imbecilic, the whole thing, so much soldier nonsense, and its main effect was that next morning I was unable to get out of bed. I couldn't move. I was in terrible shape—not only me, but half a dozen others. We were all hauled off to the hospital, where it turned out I had developed a bad lung infection.

Since the army still had loads of healthy bodies and didn't really need us cripples, I was discharged as "unfit for service." I don't know what became of the others. I never went back to Rixdorf.

His military idyl could have lasted no more than a few months, since sometime late in 1905 or early in 1906 he found a way of learning about wood, and much more. He secured a connection, first as employee, later as student, with one of the most remarkable and multifaceted spirits in the German art world of the period, the first figure of any historic consequence to play a role in his life: Bruno Paul.

Just as the young Mies sought his fortunes in the capital city of Berlin, Paul, directly upon completion of his studies in Dresden about a decade earlier—in 1894—had moved to Munich, then Germany's most progressive art center.[2] The city was alive with artistic activity, much of it expressive of a gathering revolt against the imperialist-materialist values of late nineteenth-century urban civilization. For Paul's part, the way of the 1890s appeared to be the Jugendstil, the German equivalent of Art Nouveau, whose serpentine line and flat, abstracted patterns promised relief from the recycled fustian of the *Gründerzeit* and the 1880s, not just in painting and sculpture but in the utilitarian arts as well. From 1894 to 1907 the bold, protoexpressionist manner and vigorously liberal sentiments of the cartoons Paul drew for the Munich satirical journal *Simplicissimus* came to exemplify that periodical's irreverently antiestablishment image. At the same time, and no less energetically, he designed furniture and interiors, again in the Jugendstil, a style applicable to all the visual arts, thus a conscious response to the need—increasingly expressed in German vanguard circles—to upgrade standards of quality and workmanship in the artifacts of the total visual environment. This urgency had grown from an assimilation of the message of the English Arts and Crafts movement, whose organizers, William Morris and John Ruskin, a generation earlier deplored the cheapening, dehumanizing effect of modern machine production upon the handicrafts.

Thus Paul, like many of his Munich colleagues, turned his attention more and more from the fine arts to the applied arts and architecture. In the course of 1906 and 1907 he shifted his base of operations to Berlin. It was in fact a *Festdekoration*, executed in Munich, that earned him an invitation in 1907 to head both the School of Art of the Berlin

Museum of Industrial and Applied Art and the Academy of Arts, positions that carried no small authority within the German academic bureaucracy. An irony attaches to this, as to many another affiliation that grew out of the conjunction of radical and traditional forces in a time of cultural upheaval. The kaiser, if he professed appreciation of the arts, was an archconservative aesthetically as well as politically. Had he known of Paul's *Simplicissimus* cartoons, he would surely never have approved bringing him to Berlin. Paul, as aware of this as of the good fortune of his new official status and professorial position, continued to draw for *Simplicissimus* following his decision to move to Berlin, but under the alias of Kellermann.

In the meantime, together with most of his associates in the architectural vanguard, he quit the Jugendstil. In their eyes it had grown increasingly vulgarized in the first several years of the century, though, just as important, they saw it more and more as an exercise in self-conscious aestheticism and dreamy symbolist subjectivity—hardly the desired reduction of Wilhelmine formal excess. Thus they turned to harder, simpler forms, derived from cultures associated with more primitive, unsentimental tempers: the archaic Greek, the ancient Near East, the early medieval. Coolness and restraint took on the value of expressive moods more appropriate to the increasingly impinging realities of a modern industrial society. The new arts aspired to *Sachlichkeit*, a word whose meaning corresponds to a combination of matter-of-factness, objectivity, and sobriety. The yearning to be *sachlich* would recur over and over in the course of the twentieth century. In 1905 it gained its own language of form, its own iconography. Geometry replaced the soft, organic curve of Jugendstil; a stripped-down neoclassicism in the arts of design stood for the virtues of simplicity and restraint. This was the protomodern. Paul's own designs gravitated toward a rectilinear precision reminiscent of early nineteenth-century classical Biedermeier.

He proved to be a master at the new manner. In 1904, when the German design section of the St. Louis World's Fair won worldwide praise for the advanced look of its exhibits, Paul was mentioned as one of the most impressively represented members of the group. He distinguished himself further in 1906 with several crisply geometrized interiors at the Third German Industrial and Applied Arts Exhibition in Dresden. As his career prospered, he expanded his practice to include architecture. Thus young Mies, who was assigned to Paul's drafting tables while enrolled formally in his two Berlin schools, occupied something of a special place in the studio of the master, since he brought more building experience with him than anyone in Paul's decorative arts-oriented office.[3]

Still—and here Mies's Westphalian singlemindedness surfaced—[1] he tended to resist Paul's efforts to keep him on a regime of architectural projects, preferring to explore techniques and forms of expression he had never learned in Aachen. He took quickly and enthusiastically to furniture design and even tried printmaking. Ironically, it was through his encounter with the latter medium that his career as an independent architect had its start.

One day in 1906 while he was struggling over a woodcut in a studio supervised by an assistant to the well-known painter Emil Orlik, Mies observed a smartly dressed woman enter the room. She approached Orlik's teaching assistant, whose name Mies recalled simply as Popp,* and asked his help in the design of an ornamental birdbath for her lawn. Popp complied, evidently to her satisfaction, for some weeks later she returned with a more ambitious request. She and her husband, the philosopher Alois Riehl, a professor at Humboldt University in Berlin, wanted to build a house in the upper-class Berlin suburb of Neubabelsberg.[4] They were not interested, however, in an established designer; rather they hoped their commission would advance the career of some gifted neophyte. Popp promptly nominated Mies, already well regarded in the Paul office and all of twenty years old.

Introduced to Mies, Frau Riehl told him that she and her husband were entertaining guests that evening at a formal dinner. She asked him to join them.

Mies, recollecting again:

> So Popp informed me: "You'll have to wear a dinner jacket, of course."
> "A dinner jacket?!" I said. "I have no idea what that is."
> "You can buy one anywhere. Or rent one."
> I remember rushing around to all the desks in Paul's office, borrowing money from anyone I could find so that I might buy a frock coat. And once I had it, I didn't know what kind of cravat to wear with it. I ended up with some wild yellow thing, totally out of place.
> The evening came all too soon. I proceeded to the Riehls' apartment in Berlin, where a splendid-looking couple rode up the elevator with me, very fancily dressed, the man in tails and covered all over with medals. I figured they must be going where I was, so I let them get off first and followed them.
> The door opened and they glided, zumm zumm zumm, across the slick parquet, like a pair of expert figure skaters. For my own part, I was afraid I would break my neck. Now came the host Herr Professor, moving just as gracefully as the couple, floating from one person to the next.
> After dinner he invited me into the library, where he asked me a frightful lot of questions I can't remember in the least anymore. Finally he said to his wife, "Let's return to the guests. This one is going to build our house for us."
> It all happened too fast for Frau Riehl, who didn't trust her husband to such a decision. So she asked me over to her place again, the next day, and the first thing she wanted to know was what I had so far built on my own.
> "Nothing," I remember saying. "Nothing?" she replied.
> "Well," she said, "I really don't think we can afford to be guinea pigs in this case. It's a bit too risky. I mean expensive."
> "Just a moment," I said to her. "I *can* build a house. I've done it. I just haven't done it all by myself. What would life be like if

---

*This is very likely Joseph Popp, the later author of the monograph *Bruno Paul*.

everybody insisted you must have actually built such and such a thing by yourself? I'd be an old man and have nothing to show for the aging."

Well, she laughed at that. And I suggested further that she ask Bruno Paul about my abilities. She must have, because Paul later told me that she told *him*, "Your young Mies may be a genius, you know; but he's awfully young. Too young, I think."

Paul then suggested to me I might do the house in his office, with his help. I said no. And he asked, "How do you come by the nerve to say no to that?" You see, he just didn't understand. Well, I stood my ground, and I got the commission. I built the house. And in due course Paul asked me for photographs of it to use in one of his student exhibitions. I was told he later said to someone, "The house has only one thing wrong with it—that *I* didn't build it!" He was very decent to me, in no way small-minded.

Mies had as much cause to be grateful for Paul's generosity as Paul had to praise him. For the Riehl House, though a respectable effort, was a school piece, an amalgam of ideas from disparate sources that suggested its designer had yet to find his own personal way—even if parts of it pointed in that direction rather compellingly. Most of it reflected a debt to Bruno Paul's example.[5]

The exterior of the house in its original form offered its most conservative aspect. It was a simple brick structure covered in stucco, with a high-pitched roof surmounting a rectangular volume, the whole in keeping with the tradition of eighteenth-century small villas common to the Potsdam-Neubabelsberg area, while recalling to a degree the closed cubic masses of several houses, notably the Westend House and the House of Dr. B., that Paul was designing at about the same time.[6] A gable flanked by eyebrow windows sat symmetrically athwart the long side of the upper floor, directly above the main entrance.

To the east a veranda overlooked a lawn that fell easily away to a stand of trees, the first of a number of sloping sites for which Mies designed houses. The Riehls were thus afforded a view of a tree-lined lake beyond, the Griebnitzsee, chief topographic attraction of a palpably aristocratic landscape.

The plan was less conventional. An axial approach from the formal rose garden of the front yard led through the main portal and a small entry beyond into an exceptionally large *Halle,* or great room. Since it served as a common passage to the peripheral areas of the main floor, the *Halle* was clearly the most public space in the house, suited to receptions and formal dining. It gave onto the veranda through an arched pair of stately glazed double doors. Flanking the *Halle* and sharing a view of the veranda were two small doorless rooms, an informal dining nook and a study for Frau Riehl. Another study, notably larger and meant for the professor, was situated opposite the veranda, next to the family parlor. The kitchen and work area were on the cellar level, accessible from the east, since the slope on that side of the house provided it with a three-story elevation.[7]

Such a plan would suggest that the house, whose nickname *Klösterli* ("Little Cloister") was inscribed in its outer wall, was a country retreat, even perhaps a retirement cottage for the Riehls, who nevertheless meant it to accommodate formal parties. The upstairs plan, which featured four bedrooms and a bath approached from a common hall, would confirm that the couple, who had no children, frequently entertained overnight guests.

The interior detailing of the house, less dependent on tradition, re-

8. Riehl House from slope leading to Griebnitzsee

9. Bruno Paul, Westend House,
Berlin, about 1906
Joseph Popp, *Bruno Paul*

vealed more of Mies's awareness of the advanced styles of the day.
The panelled walls and squared tiles of the fireplace in the *Halle,* plus
the cozy sitting alcove in one of the bedrooms, recorded the impact,
felt by many designers in Germany, of contemporary English residential architecture. The emissary of that influence was Hermann Muthesius, the Berlin architect whose tenure as technical attaché in the
German embassy in London between 1896 and 1903 was spent in a
study that led to his monumental book of 1905, *Das englische Haus.*
There Muthesius argued that English domestic architecture was notable for functional comfort, economy of means, and a frequently picturesque informality, all virtues comparing favorably with the historicist ostentations of German house design during the flamboyant 1880s
and 1890s.

In the Riehl House Mies hardly treated either the walls or the
whole space of the *Halle* picturesquely. On the contrary, his manner
was formal, the plan of the room symmetrical, suggesting that if England was the indirect antecedent of the decor, a more immediate source
was the dining room Bruno Paul designed for the 1906 Dresden exhibition.

Mies followed his teacher's lead by panelling the walls below a wide
frieze and raising the lintel of his doors and windows to a level even

with the dividing line of panelling and frieze. All this reflected English usage, though more in detail than in mood, since Paul's symmetrical elevations and relatively tall ceilings recurred in the Riehl *Halle*, with the result that both rooms projected a classicizing sobriety. Elsewhere Mies continued to borrow: neo-Biedermeier wooden crossbars on the glazed cabinets sustained his debt to Paul, while his most obvious pattern-book derivation took the form of a swag over the front door.

Paul's Dresden frieze had been animated by luxurious reliefs; Mies decorated his own not at all. Yet even if we assume the professor took a bigger budget for granted, there remain elements of such willful austerity in the student's design that they must have originated more in his own head than in his clients' pocketbook—or in his teacher's example. (Mies tells us in any case that he quite characteristically overspent the Riehls' budget.) His omission of the dado from the walls of the *Halle*, together with his blank frieze, produced an abstract effect evocative of yet another style: Japanese houses, much admired and

10. Mies at Riehl House, about 1912
Private collection

Berlin: Problems of a New Century

11. *Halle* of the Riehl House

discussed among the European and American avant-gardes at the turn of the century, were notable for their use of a slender wooden lattice known as a shoji. The thin, brittle strips of Mies's wall were nearly as reminiscent of the Japanese idiom as they were of Paul's more generously dimensioned translations of English panelling.

In fact, the Riehl House, despite its overall eclecticism of parts, was united by a prevailing temper of cool reserve and a painstaking exactitude of expression. Its most distinctive features were clean, clipped, and severe to the point of chilliness, prefiguring the rock-hard lucidities of Mies's later efforts: the proportions of the windows and doors in the *Halle*; the bold scale and controlled positioning of the windows in the study; the razor-sharp indentations of the alcoves plus the precise rendition of their parts; the flat Paulesque exterior wall pilasters; above all, the south face, with its sure rhythms of square-sectioned columns (Paul's example again) and spaces along the veranda, together with the wall which seamlessly extended the facade outward into space, past and around the garden, a device premonitory of the podiums upon which a number of his later buildings would perch. Mies in 1907 was already committed to the classicist temperament that would remain with him for the rest of his life.

The Riehls, satisfied with their house, were just as content with its designer, judging from the fact that he was taken warmly into their social circle, where he remained a welcome guest for years. This seems to be early evidence of a natural personal attractiveness in Mies. It grew with the years and won the admiring recollections of countless people with whom he came into social and professional contact. The descriptions always agree: a quiet but dominating personality, a self-

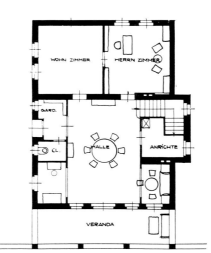

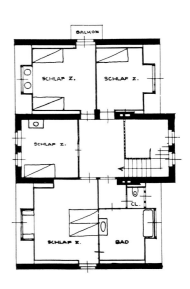

assurance bearing no trace of vanity, an emphatic masculinity in both looks and demeanor, engaging to both sexes. If Frau Riehl had earlier misgivings about his technical competence, they did not stand in the way of her husband's decision to send Mies to Italy, sometime in 1908. Popp went with him. Their trip included stops in Vicenza, Florence, and Rome and lasted between six weeks and three months; Mies's later recollections seem to have varied. Certainly it was meant in general to advance the education of an unschooled but promising artist, in particular to acquaint him with the classical culture at that time cresting to renewed popularity among the cultivated classes of Germany.

Mies was impressed and enriched by what he saw in Italy, after his own fashion. He found that he did not like the endless Mediterranean sun and he openly longed for the "gray heavens" of Germany, a response which may reveal something about his lifelong preference for neutral as opposed to bright colors.

"We were in Munich early in the trip," he told Lohan.

Frau Riehl had recommended an exhibition there which had a house in it that she liked, by [Richard] Riemerschmid.[8] I found it interesting. Popp, on the other hand, was constantly going to museums to look at pictures. Too often for my taste. He was after all a painter. So I just looked around the town, which turned out to be wonderful to see.

Then we passed over the Brenner, down to Bozen [Bolzano] and on to Vicenza, where Palladio built. We saw some of his finest country houses, not just the Rotonda, which is so formal, but others, much, much freer. They reminded me of a villa that Messel had done on the Wannsee, just outside Berlin.[9] I saw it when I was still working in Rixdorf. Excellent thing. Palladio detailed his buildings beautifully, but Messel was even better at that. Some people just have a feeling for such things, a sympathy.

In later public interviews Mies expressed his admiration for the Palazzo Pitti in Florence ("one of the strongest buildings . . . just huge stone walls with windows cut out . . . with how few means you can make architecture!") and for the ancient Roman aqueducts ("all of them were of the same character"), thus implying an early commitment to his well-known belief in achieving generalizing simplicity in architecture.[10] In talking with his grandson Dirk, his recollections of Italy were more personal. He recalled his own rather than the canonic view of Italy, his judgments, discoveries, tastes: an indifference to painting, for example, which lasted into his years at the Bauhaus, the early 1930s, much later in his life than his present-day reputation as a collector of Klee, Munch, and Schwitters would imply; his expression of admiration for the classical master Andrea Palladio, qualified by the distinction he drew between formal and free country houses, a contrast which would have significant bearing on his reconstitution of the classical villa in the 1910s and 1920s. His insistence that the Wilhelmine architect Alfred Messel was better at details than the great Palladio was based on personal observation, and Mies, as late as the day he offered this opinion in 1968 and as early as his weeks of working out the shape of the alcoves in the Riehl House, in 1907, had proved he had a right to judge architectural detail.

Evidently he had proved something else in the course of the Paul-Riehl period. "Just about the time the house was finished," he recalled, "Paul Thiersch came by. He was Bruno Paul's office manager. Earlier he had been with Behrens, and he told me Behrens once told him, 'Look, any time you see a talented youngster, let me know about him. Send him to me.' And Thiersch said to me, 'Now Behrens! There is a first-class man. *You* ought to look him up.' "[11]

Mies did and Behrens hired him, more evidence of the young Aachener's promise. For Peter Behrens, an architect more prominent in Berlin and the world than Bruno Paul, kept a small staff, appointing assistants neither on whim nor in quantity. As for Mies's motives, he knew, despite his success with the Riehl House, that it was still too early for an independent career. In the Behrens atelier he would be ideally situated to witness the most important architectural events of the day at close hand and to hear major issues debated by the most informed heads in Germany. In Behrens himself he would find an artist of talent, intelligence, and tortured complexity, whose work and thought exemplified the conflicts that both invigorated and confounded the arts in the first years of the new century. It is little wonder that Mies, with much to learn yet by nature given to simplifying perceptions rather than complicating them, would at first be greatly enriched by contact with Germany's leading architect, and later walk away from him.

In 1908 Behrens was forty years old.[12] At the crest of his powers and newly occupied with a group of exceptional industrial commissions in Berlin that would eventually prove the source of his most lasting fame, he had already gained sufficient experience during historically crucial years to be widely regarded as one of the several principal agents of the changes through which German architecture was passing on its way to modernity.

Parallels between his early career and Bruno Paul's are striking. Both men were trained in painting and the graphic arts, only later coming to architecture via the decorative arts, and mostly as autodidacts. Both spent much of the 1890s in Munich, where they met each other, and, following the spirit of time and place, finally turned away from painting and took up the cause of giving new life to the German crafts.

By 1900 Behrens's designs in glass, porcelain, and furniture, all rendered in the Jugendstil, had won him a substantial national reputation and a major exhibition in Darmstadt, the city which now aspired consciously to become the center of the German applied arts. It was there, on the Mathildenhöhe, a hill overlooking the town, that the historic Artists' Colony opened in 1901, with Behrens in a major role.

The fate of the Artists' Colony illustrates more aspects of the shift in values of the first decade. In particular, it demonstrated that specific remedial proposals varied widely, for the proposers often located the problem in different places. The Jugendstil, together with other variations of Art Nouveau allied with the symbolist aesthetic, had reacted against the exhausted academic styles, though just as surely against the materialist assumptions implicit in impressionism. Thus it sought to purify art, to aestheticize and abstract it, to make it ever more intensely artful. Yet almost concurrently a rationalist argument born of nineteenth-century positivist materialism rose up to contend that there was in a sense too much art already, that the excesses of late nineteenth-century culture now called for redress, for a dilution of "elitist" aestheticism and a greater awareness of social needs. Again, *Sachlichkeit.*

These differing reformist directions collided at Darmstadt, where a group of specially selected artists were charged with the responsibility of giving material expression to the renewed spirit in art, mostly through architecture and the "lesser arts," as Darmstadt publisher Alexander Koch had put it, citing as early as 1897 "the need for a complete integration of all artists, architects, sculptors, painters, and craftsmen."[13]

The dominant figure of the group was the gifted Austrian architect Josef Olbrich, who designed nearly all the buildings erected on the Mathildenhöhe. Most notable among these was the Ernst-Ludwig-Haus, an exposition hall that served as the showcase for the works, done in a variety of crafts-oriented media, by the artists in residence. The artists' private houses were put up nearby. The only one not built by Olbrich was the residence Peter Behrens designed for himself in the Jugendstil. It was the most expensive and lavish single residence on the Mathildenhöhe, and it proved to be as vulnerable as the rest of the colony to the attacks leveled by critics who complained that the whole affair was, at last, not the noble, socially minded enterprise it purported to be, but rather an extravagant gesture, meaningful to comfort rather than the commonweal. Michael Georg Conrad wrote: "In these rooms with their fairy-tale colors and magic-lantern quality, life is a holiday. It is more than a life among beauty—it is a life apart . . . For striving, careworn folk this is no home for everyday life. Here modern man can only pause fleetingly for the favor of a glimpse and a deep inward breath. Should he stay, he will degenerate into sick sensuality, living in a fool's paradise."[14]

Early in 1903 Behrens quit Darmstadt and effectively joined those who were moving ever closer to the rationalism that Conrad found wanting in the Artists' Colony. His first move was to Düsseldorf and the directorship of the School of Arts and Crafts, a post for which he was recommended by Muthesius. In the same year, 1903, another architect whose outlook bore heavily on the growing social consciousness of the time, Holland's Hendrik Petrus Berlage, finished the design of his Stock Exchange in Amsterdam, a work called "moral" by those who applauded the fact that it bypassed historical styles in favor of straightforwardness of construction and integrity in the use of materials, most prominently, brick.

Behrens invited Berlage to Düsseldorf and when the latter declined, appointed another Dutchman, J. L. M. Lauweriks, whose teaching method featured a system based on a modular rectilinear grid. Indeed, as early as 1902, Behrens had shown a dining room at the

Wertheim Department Store in Berlin, of which the critic Max Osborn wrote, "The fascination of the dining room set up in Wertheim's . . . lay in the manner in which a basic rectangular form was logically divided up into little squares and strips with a linear grid, which was extended all over, into the stencilled wall patterns, the carpet, the light fitting, the furniture and the crockery."[15] By 1904 all traces of the Jugendstil had vanished from Behrens's work. In their place geometry reigned.

While this shift may be interpreted as a symptom of the sobering mood of the mid-decade, it was more than that for Behrens. Some of the attitudes upon which it rested were not *sachlich* at all, but rather subtle reconstitutions of nineteenth-century idealism qualified, but only qualified, by twentieth-century rationalism. Behrens was a man caught between contending centuries.

Much of the four years he spent in Düsseldorf was given to reading and reflection, especially on the meaning of architecture and the relation of the artist to society. Such subjects drew Behrens irresistibly to the work and thought of Germany's premier architect of the nineteenth century, Karl Friedrich Schinkel.

Schinkel was a product of the exceptionally fruitful period in German cultural history that accompanied the ascendancy of his native Prussia following the Napoleonic wars.[16] The early revivalist temper was gathering momentum in architecture, and Schinkel, not surprisingly, developed a reverence for both antiquity and the Middle Ages, regarding them as the most nearly perfect passages of history and identifying the former with precepts of universal harmony, the latter with the loftiest phase of the German Christian past. A near-lifelong resident of the Prussian capital, Berlin, and a contemporary and friend of Wilhelm von Humboldt, he was powerfully affected by that great patron's efforts to improve education and cultural consciousness at the public level. He felt no less ardor for the philosopher Johann Gottlieb Fichte, who held to the moral principle—obviously in line with von Humboldt's position—that man was obliged to reconcile his individuality with a life consecrated to public action. All these influences combined to shape Schinkel's beliefs that the architect played a critical role in society and that, in view of the necessarily social nature of his endeavor, he was charged with more responsibility than all other artists to give clear and eloquent form to the best of public institutions and the noblest of collective cultural aspirations.

Like Schinkel, Behrens idealized the architect's social role, but in view of the events that had transpired between Schinkel's time and his own, he assigned a different weight to it. During the late nineteenth century the belief in a state based on voluntary conciliation between individual and collective consciousnesses—Schinkel's vision—had been threatened, if not hopelessly compromised. The headlong advance of science and technology, the growth of industry, the transformation of towns into cities and cities into megalopolises: these developments produced a world in which change was sudden, persistent, vast, and impersonal. An economy based on monopolistic capitalism only widened the distance between individual and collective and did nothing to nurture the hope that a culture of definable, shared

values was possible in a modern context. As early as the 1860s and
1870s, a generation after Schinkel, the artist had begun to react to
this new society by seceding from it, defensively, into Bohemia, and by
exalting himself, art, and the immaterial realm. The symbolist sensibility, of which Jugendstil was but one stylistic outgrowth, represented
a late extreme of this narcissistic reverie, and efforts followed—like
the Artists' Colony and Behrens's school in Düsseldorf—to effect a
rapprochement between the grievously divided interests of the proud,
troubled arts and a recklessly successful industrial society.

But these attempts could hardly be so tender in their assumptions
as those that Schinkel had entertained. Behrens was affected less by
Fichte and von Humboldt and more by the Viennese art historian Alois
Riegl, who stressed the role of will in both artistic and societal trans-
actions and who had less to say, or to take for granted, about com-
patibilities. Riegl argued a nineteenth-century determinist view that
the art forms of a given society are the reflections of that society's
social and religious preoccupation as well as technological condition—
its *Zeitgeist*.[17] Behrens took the *Zeitgeist* to be most instructively revealed in the art of architecture; thus it behooved the architect to
divine the *Zeitgeist* and know it, so that the buildings he designed
would be fitting and culturally enhancing reflections of it. But *his* own
will was a critical factor in the equation, one which, still resonant of
the symbolist faith, rose above and was independent of material fact.

For Behrens, then, as for Schinkel, the architect was obliged to
work with society, but in a relationship far tenser and more implicitly
confrontational than Schinkel envisioned in his still largely preindustrial world. Based as it was on the supposition of two great wills, the
one—society's—immense, roughly shaped, and urgent, the other—
the artist's—grandiose, compulsively form-giving, and self-exalting,
Behrens's view reflected the tragic cultural discordances of Western
civilization at the turn of the century as much as Schinkel's had the

relatively innocent hopes of a classical-romantic synthesis in the first half of the nineteenth century.

The hard geometries that Behrens imposed on the buildings of his 1903–7 Düsseldorf period were not, in a primary sense, rational responses to functional needs. On the contrary: in the exhibition pavilions of the Northwest German Art Exhibition in Oldenburg (1905) Behrens designed the most severely simplified geometrical prism, bold, generalized, smoothed-out, boxlike solids, almost pure architectural abstractions, in which he "celebrated the victory of his personal artist's will over the exigencies of material and purpose."[18] The cube was less a functional than a symbolic form.

Here was Riegl's *Kunstwollen* ("artistic will") at work, though Behrens recognized, as the symbolists in their rapture of introversion and the Arts and Crafts in their dogged nostalgia had chosen not to, that contemporary industrial society was an undeniable force in its own right, with which the artist would have to come to terms. Confrontation meant compromise.

Behrens's call from Berlin's Allgemeine Elektricitätsgesellschaft (AEG) came in 1907. Though first appointed as "artistic adviser," he was in full charge by late in 1908 of the invention of all the visual imagery associated with AEG: its advertising, product, even stationery design, plus its full architectural embodiment, which consisted of factories, exhibition halls, administration and ceremonial buildings. Moreover, he made a studious point of composing all these physical reflections of the AEG within a formally related program so that the corporation impressed itself upon the public as an institution of solidarity, size, and, of course, power. Behrens thus contributed signally to the early history of what we know as industrial design.

The AEG was one of the most spectacular corporate phenomena of the German industrializing period.[19] Founded in 1883 by Emil Rathenau, a skilled businessman as well as engineer, the firm enjoyed swift and robust growth. By 1908 it was a model at once of the strength of machine industry in general and of the excellence of modern German technology in particular.

Rathenau and his colleagues, most notably his son Walter, were by no means unconscious of this double identity, or of the interdependence of its parts. The significance of the AEG thus was political as well as economic: a sign of the ascendancy of the German nation as surely as of the advancement of modern industrial society. Moreover, in the years following 1900 a further recognition dawned on the Rathenaus that the visual arts could add a third, or cultural, component to the identity, producing a more complex but commensurately profitable symbiosis. For the arts would shape and solidify the image of AEG as a corporate entity, while the firm's reliance on the arts would establish it not only as a passive friend of culture but as an agency active in the reunion of art and life.

Then and there the visions and ideals of Behrens and the Rathenaus were joined. The AEG pavilion at the German Shipbuilding Exhibition of 1908, the architect's first major building for the firm, stood for the new corporation in common cause with the new culture, moreover with the old imperial order, which at once took the form of the New Empire. The kaiser must have been aware of these wondrous conjunctions when he appeared at the ceremonies inaugurating the building and conferred his blessing upon it. Behrens's world of the wills had apparently been confirmed: the artist had accepted the facts of his industrial age, given them meaningful form, and thus transmuted them into culture, all the while serving the ends of his people.

The record of the AEG building program in the years remaining before World War I bears all of this out. However much debate has been prompted by the construction system of the Turbine Factory of 1909—which does not, to cite one frequent criticism, depend for support on the corner pylons that appear to fulfill that function—it is a work that achieves quite precisely what Behrens wanted it to. In the unadorned expanse of its glass walls and the bold tapering steel stanchions that do hold up the arched girders of the roof, it conveys the power of industry with appropriate objective clarity, while the rustication of its pylons plus the allusion in the gable front to the classical pediment tie it to the tradition Behrens wanted consciously not to surrender.

One perceives the ambiguous "protomodernity" of the architecture of Behrens's time: its various double identities, its efforts to bridge the gaps between conservatisms of one sort, progressivisms of another. The AEG buildings as a group, though motivated by the lofty goals of making industry into architecture, were also meant as "temples of labor," where workers could turn from the new menace of socialism and identify instead with Germany's technology and culture, by extension with Germany's glory. One of the most progressive organizations in the history of the modern arts, the Deutscher Werkbund, which over the next several decades fought to upgrade standards of invention and craftsmanship in design and architecture, to reunite applied art and fine art, and to reform art education, was formed in no small measure out of nationalistically competitive motives.[20] Characterizing the rationale of Friedrich Naumann, one of the men most responsible for founding the Werkbund, Theodor Heuss wrote:

> The role of the Emperor is the unification and coronation of the national will to power and will to life—but how can this transpire when hostility and misunderstanding reign between the upper classes and the benighted masses? Devotion to the Nation can no longer involve *only* the external visage of the State . . . it must also possess an internal visage. The role of social-politics is *not* to be understood as a responsibility for social welfare, but rather as the realization by the State of an important new power through the development in the unpropertied classes of a freely held sentiment for the Fatherland. Democracy could be used to help these classes to learn to love the State as *their* State, to want to see the State great, strong and just.[21]

The unstable admixture of sentiments in this remarkable statement—egalitarian and paternalistic, democratic and nationalistic— points to some of the tensions that affected the German idealizing soul at the time the Werkbund was founded in 1907. That organization itself would shortly be turned into an arena where passionate loyalists to the Arts and Crafts cause, who cherished the individuality of the handmade work, would do battle with those pragmatic futurists who saw industry as part necessity, part blessing, but in the end all fact, and therefore the agency through which good art for the total environment could, that is to say must, be made by methods of standardization and mass production.

So much, then, for the issues that stimulated talk in the studio of which Mies was now a part. What he eventually made of such questions as will and fact and the relation of both to a potentially better world remains to be seen. Nor have we accounted for all sides of the story even yet. Other groups of intellectual consequence, less hopeful than the Werkbund, less comfortable than Behrens and well outside his ken, signified the more aggrieved aspects of the forces at work as the arts groped for a way of making sense out of the new century.

The reform movement, as Iain Boyd Whyte calls several "anarcho-socialist" associations of radical intellectuals, like the Choriner Kreis and the Deutsche Gartenstadtgesellschaft, was moved by a disenchantment with urban society and industrialism into a yearning for the decentralization of cities and a return to the land.[22] And the whole impassioned phenomenon of expressionism, though still only germinating in 1907, would shortly burst forth and grow ever more clamorous in the years before the Great War. "While the reform movement viewed contemporary society with profound dismay," writes Whyte, "the Expressionist avant-garde confronted it in a state of psychological

15. Behrens, AEG Turbine Factory, Berlin, 1909
AEG-Telefunken

shock. Black despair was the Leitmotiv of the movement, in all its manifestations. The Expressionist avant-garde felt itself to be alienated psychologically, socially, economically and stylistically from the affirmative, materialist culture of Wilhelmine Germany."[23]

In view of this tempest of movements and competing causes, we can readily believe Mies when he later remembered his early years with Behrens and especially his perplexity over the true nature and right direction of architecture. "I tried to understand what that task was," he said. "I asked Peter Behrens, but he couldn't give me an answer . . . Others said: 'What we build is architecture,' but we weren't satisfied with this answer; maybe they didn't understand the question. Since we knew that it was a question of the truth, we tried to find out what the truth really was . . . To find out what architecture really is took me fifty years—half a century."[24]

Mies entered Behrens's employ in October 1908, about a year after the master set up his chief working studio in a handsome old estate in Neubabelsberg. Already busy with the Turbine Factory by the time Mies hired on, Behrens had assembled a staff that included two other young architects destined for a place in history: Walter Gropius, then 25, and Adolf Meyer, 27, who within a few years would form a partnership of their own, achieving immediate and lasting fame for their design of a factory building more unqualifiedly modern than anything Behrens had done or would soon do: the Faguswerk, completed in 1911 in Alfeld-an-der-Leine.

That work was only the first dramatic constructed evidence of Gropius's precocity, sophistication, and generally forward-looking temperament, traits that had earlier won him the admiration of the highly influential industrialist, museum director, and patron of the contemporary arts-at-large, Karl Ernst Osthaus of Hagen, who recommended him enthusiastically to Behrens when the latter moved to Berlin. Gropius joined the Behrens office either late in 1907 or early in 1908 and was responsible for the detailing of Behrens's first AEG building, the pavilion at the German Shipbuilding Exhibition of 1908. By the time Behrens hired Mies, Gropius was chief lieutenant in the Neubabelsberg office.

Gropius's personal background, moreover, was almost the polar opposite of Mies's.[25] Born in 1883 into a distinguished Berlin family of long and solid upper-middle-class standing, he enjoyed all the benefits that wealth, status, family tradition, and the best of German education could bestow. His father Walther, a city building councillor, occupied an official position of considerable importance in Berlin, and his great-uncle Martin Gropius, celebrated among the architects of the mid to late nineteenth century, had been a devoted follower of Schinkel, designer of numerous villas and public commissions in Prussia, and principal of the very institution—the Berlin School of Arts and Crafts—that Mies had attended under Bruno Paul's guidance.

On the way to his *Abitur,* young Walter attended no fewer than four *Gymnasien.* He then enrolled in the *Technische Hochschule* in Munich, where he spent a term before returning to Berlin in response to the serious illness of a brother. There he stayed for a brief architectural apprenticeship before volunteering for a year of service with the famed and colorful Wandsbeck Hussar cavalry regiment—quite a different military experience from Mies's pitifully aborted stint as a common draftee—then continued his architectural studies at the *Technische Hochschule* of Berlin-Charlottenburg. A study year in Spain followed in 1907. There he met and attracted the attention of Osthaus.

The gap between his upbringing and Mies's speaks for itself. Mies even recalled that Gropius was the "gentleman chief" of the Behrens staff, which he had joined "just to learn. I don't believe he got any salary."[26]

There was natural cause for the two comparably gifted, ambitious young stalwarts eventually to develop a rivalry which over the course of their long lives would grow sharp enough at times to take on a real adversarial quality. For the time they were together in Neubabelsberg, however, less than two years, Gropius was clearly senior in all significant respects; thus an official distance automatically separated him from Mies. Moreover, the dual character of Behrens's practice tended further to ameliorate the competitiveness between the two.

If Behrens's industrial buildings for AEG tended to underplay historical ornament or to omit it altogether, his residential and ceremonial architecture was recognizably and consistently neoclassical in style. The difference, another illustration of his compromise between older and newer modes, was reflected in the division of labor within his office. Though Gropius worked on several of Behrens's classical villas (e.g., the 1909 Schroeder House and the 1909–10 Cuno House, both in Eppenhausen), he spent more time than Mies on industrial assignments and economic issues, designing some electrical appliances for the AEG shortly after he was hired by Behrens, and later, in 1910, addressing a statement to the Rathenaus on the merits of low-cost, mass-produced housing. His allegiance was to rationalism and functionalism; the historical styles interested him less and less.

We cannot say the same for Mies, whose experiences with Bruno Paul and the Riehls, plus a personal tendency toward classicism, disposed him toward the more formal designs emerging from the Behrens studio. He himself said that the only factory building he worked on seriously for AEG was the Kleinmotorenfabrik of 1910–13.

Gropius resigned from the atelier in June 1910 and set up his own office in Berlin, acting on the conviction that he was by then the equal of Behrens in talent and more advanced in his understanding of modernity.[27] Not content with reducing classical ornament to abstracted form, Gropius banished it from the Faguswerk altogether, leaving a pure geometric prism, a structure in which the floors are carried on a steel frame and the walls are sheer transparent glass whose non-supportive character is underscored by the absence of uprights at the corners. Here were the new materials of an industrial age expressed without the slightest regard for Behrensian spiritual tradition, the closest thing to an uncompromising embodiment of the rationalist outlook.

By comparison, Mies's position at the end of the decade was at once more conservative and closer to the mainstream progressive position in Germany. As that view was frequently rationalized, modernity was one thing, and rightly to be admired; of extremes, however, there had already been enough, whether in the form of historicism or its alleged antithesis of the 1890s, the Jugendstil. In 1910, just a year before Gropius completed the Faguswerk, critic Anton Jaumann wrote a review of Mies's Riehl House. Though the building was three years old at the time, it seemed to Jaumann to epitomize the architecture of the new generation, the "new growth," as he put it, which "is not motivated by an impulse to novelty or a striving to move ever ahead. On the contrary: their work, by contrast with that of the past decade [the 1890s], is reserved, even coolly critical. What do these young ones want? They seek resolution and balance, as surely as they avoid anything that smacks of radicalism. They prefer a 'golden' mean, between the old and the new."[28]

Of the full extent of Mies's assignments in the Behrens studio we are only partly certain. Those we know more than a little about date from the years 1911 and 1912, by which time he had gained a position of authority in the atelier. His activities during 1909 and 1910 are less

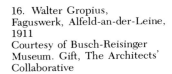

16. Walter Gropius, Faguswerk, Alfeld-an-der-Leine, 1911
Courtesy of Busch-Reisinger Museum. Gift, The Architects' Collaborative

Berlin: Problems of a New Century

clear. We noted earlier his own declaration that he was involved intimately with the design of only one of the AEG commissions, the Kleinmotorenfabrik, a building begun in 1910 and finished in 1913, with its first section completed in 1911. Mies apparently left the studio for a short time in 1909—exactly when, for how long, and under what conditions we cannot firmly establish.

The most reliable of all the fragmentary evidence available to us on this matter emerges from a document written in 1911 by one Salomon van Deventer, reporting a conversation he had just had with Mies. On 29 August, van Deventer, a chief assistant to the Dutch industrialist A. G. Kröller, for whom Behrens was at that time designing a residence near The Hague—with Mies as project supervisor—wrote a letter to Kröller's wife in which he remarked that professional animosity between Mies and an unnamed colleague on Behrens's staff had grown so sharp that Mies "left [the office] after a year. During the year in which he was separated from Behrens, however, he came to recognize the greatness in Behrens, and he decided that Behrens was the only man who could offer him something as an architect. So he put everything else away and returned to Behrens, where he has been now for three-quarters of a year."[29]

By this reckoning Mies, whose tenure with Behrens began late in 1908, would have quit his job late in 1909 and returned to it late in 1910. During this absence he would have had time to design the Perls House and the Bismarck monument project (figs. 26–27, 31–32) and to make a trip with the Deutsche Gartenstadtgesellschaft to England.[30] An absence in 1909–10 might also explain why he only dimly recalled any contact with the young French Swiss architect Charles Jeanneret (later Le Corbusier), who attached himself to the Behrens atelier sometime in the second half of 1910—after Gropius had left —and remained there less than half a year. Mies, in whose later life Le Corbusier would figure prominently, remembered him in 1910 only because "I ran into him once in the doorway of the office. He was on his way out, I was on my way in."[31]

If "on my way in," for what purpose, if Mies was not an employee? Yet by late in 1910 he might already have been rehired, assuming the accuracy of van Deventer's chronology. In any event Jeanneret was there on an independent research tour; he spent his time in Neubabelsberg more as an observer than as a designer. None of Behrens's work bears his imprint.

Tantalizing but inconclusive hints of Mies's hand appear in a pair of Behrens's industrial commissions from the 1910–12 period. The Frankfurter Gasgesellschaft (now Main-Gaswerke, in Frankfurt-Osthafen, 1910–12) is a factory group whose geometric massing prefigures expressionist architecture and whose brick detailing, especially in the use of the negative reveal (a narrow channel between window or door frame and adjacent wall surface), brings to mind Mies's later way with that material and that device in the buildings of his American period.[32] Similar treatments turn up in several passages of the Mannesmann Office Building in Düsseldorf (1911–12), notably in the elegantly precise entry hall and staircase, the detailing of which, according to one observer, Schneider-Esleben, was entrusted to Mies.[33]

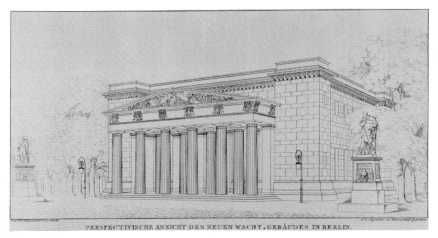

17. Karl Friedrich Schinkel, Royal Guard House, Berlin, 1816–18
Schinkel, *Sammlung architektonischer Entwürfe*

PERSPECTIVISCHE ANSICHT DES NEUEN WACHT-GEBÄUDES IN BERLIN.

But Behrens himself employed the negative reveal rather standardly in his work of those years, which leaves us unclear about the extent and sovereignty of Mies's responsibilities in these industrial buildings. The source of the device, in any case, can be traced to Schinkel.

Behrens's own reverence for Schinkel grew even stronger around 1910. In later years Mies recalled the occasions when he and the rest of the Neubabelsberg staff were conducted by their chief on pilgrimages through the Berlin area to visit Schinkel sites. The 1910–11 period, then, would seem to have been the likeliest time for those tours as well as the most opportune for Mies to immerse himself in Schinkel's work and thought. Aside from the lofty reputation the great contemporary of Hegel, Kleist, and Schelling had long enjoyed as an individual artist and public symbol of Prussian cultural glory, his architecture, particularly the neoclassical designs, was exactly suited to the aspirations of the Berlin protomodernists, not only to those designers accustomed to the newly subdued formal manners but to anyone taken with the rationalist frame of mind associated with industry: in short, to Behrens and all the members of his office. Schinkel's published writings and designs were easily available to Mies, who, influenced by his relationship with Professor Riehl, was reading seriously by 1910. Moreover, whenever Mies and his fellows took the train from Neubabelsberg to downtown Berlin, they could find several of Schinkel's best public structures within a few blocks of each other.

They might have begun on the majestic boulevard Unter den Linden, where Schinkel's first important completed building stood. The Royal Guard House, of 1816–18, was a single severe cube modified by four slightly higher angle blocks at its corners and a bold Grecian portico which emerged from its facade with stunning force and precision, all in all a vision more abstract than any actual Hellenic work, thus immensely appealing to the modernist eye. Mies in particular—given his lifelong devotion to exactitude of form—must have been struck by the blazing clarity with which Schinkel articulated part to whole in the Guard House.

A short distance to the south the Behrens group would have seen the substantially larger Schauspielhaus of 1818–21, which in the very complexity of its formal elements attested to Schinkel's command of geometric massing. Standing high on a basement story, or podium, it consisted of a main building containing theater and stage house in the central tract plus concert hall and rehearsal-storage spaces in the wings. The flanking masses were both unified and simplified by a screenlike system of entablatures and colossal, stripped corner pilasters that framed a rank of narrow windows. The windows were in turn separated by plain flat mullions—a device more classical in spirit than in historical usage but one which, again, must have been read with enthusiasm by moderns for whom the window band was an increasingly customary element in commercial buildings.

Possibly Schinkel's masterpiece among the major commissions he completed in the city was the Altes Museum of 1823–30, a work which, when we recall Mies's later way with the rhythms on the face of the Seagram Building (1958) as well as the placement of the latter work vis-à-vis a plaza on New York's Park Avenue, must have left the deepest of impressions on him. The Altes Museum conveys an image both grand and solemn, its classical vocabulary sparing but eloquent, its grammar, like that of the Guard House and the Schauspielhaus, more visual than archaeological in its fidelity to the antique. It surveys a broad square, facing beyond to the same great axial concourse on which the Guard House stands. This public space is addressed publicly, in the idiom of an Ionic colonnade whose regularity of march preserves the integrity of the building's stern geometric mass. Eighteen columns move in a prolonged but stately beat, though the effect of monotony is avoided as the cadence is arrested by spur walls resolved in antae which act as monumentally conclusive clamps to the facade. The long

18. Schinkel, Schauspielhaus, Berlin, 1818–21
Schinkel, *Sammlung architektonischer Entwürfe*

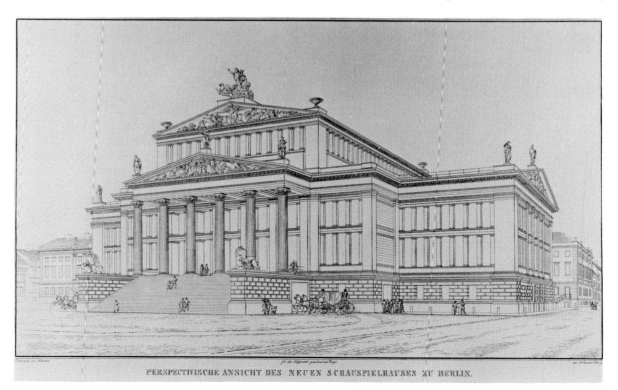

PERSPECTIVISCHE ANSICHT DES NEUEN SCHAUSPIELHAUSES ZU BERLIN.

　　　　Berlin: Problems of a New Century

low sweep of the Altes Museum is recapitulated in several of the pavilions of Mies's later years, chief among them Crown Hall in Chicago and the Berlin National Gallery.

Schinkel's formal authority was only one aspect of his attractiveness to the younger Berlin generation. His understanding of the needs, conditions, demands, and opportunities of a dawning industrial age was another. A study tour of England in 1826 introduced him to factory architecture there, to buildings constructed of unprepossessing vernacular brick walls and cast-iron roofs. This visit led him to a series of functional designs responsive to the data and values of an increasingly industrialized culture. *Sachlichkeit*, the matter-of-factness of attitude that Behrens, Muthesius, and the Deutscher Werkbund took as the expressive point of departure in their creative endeavors of the years just prior to World War I, was anticipated as early as the 1830s in Schinkel's work, or still earlier, if one recalls the series of pamphlets he published together with the Prussian official P. C. W. Beuth, *Vorbilder für Fabrikanten und Handwerker* (1821–30). This study detailed an assemblage of utilitarian objects and decorative ornament,

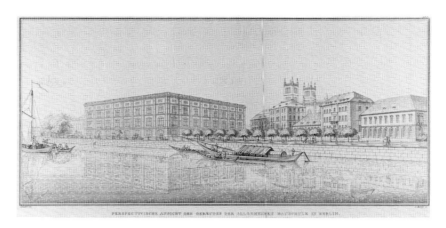

all designed by Schinkel and meant as a guide to public taste—thus a forerunner, by generations, of the efforts of the Arts and Crafts movement, the Werkbund, and the Bauhaus, among others, to unite the needs of life with the ideals of art in a modern context.

In 1827 Schinkel designed a *Kaufhaus*, or shopping center, for Unter den Linden, which, though never built, took the form of a building whose walls seemed almost dissolved in huge, high windows divided by brick columns. The result was an elevational grid derived from the axes of the interior supports. In his *Bauakademie*, or school of architecture, which was designed and constructed between 1831 and 1835, he pursued further the concept of the facade as a structural screen reflective of the building's actual structure. In these two works Schinkel arrived at architectural form not as a response to historical figuration but as the direct expression of a construction system. Such a treatment would hardly escape the notice of modern functionalists. For Mies it eventually became an article of faith.

Every bit as forceful in their potential influence on Mies as these various city buildings were those products of Schinkel's genius to be seen in the suburbs of Berlin and the surrounding countryside. Schloss Tegel, family seat of Wilhelm von Humboldt, was one of these, with its pair of heavy Doric columns dominating the foyer—features that would reappear in one of Mies's own residences from the middle of the second decade (see pp. 79–80). Surely Behrens's young assistant also saw the jewel of the Schlosspark Charlottenburg as well: an elegant little summer house whose flat roof, blond facade, and second story loggia are transferred in only slightly modified form to the first house Mies designed independently (see pp. 53–57) after hiring on with Behrens.

Though less inclined to copy medievalist devices, Mies may nonetheless have felt the subtle impress of another, less overt, aspect of the old Prussian's absorption with the Middle Ages. Schinkel was a painter of considerable accomplishment, and he left a series of brilliant landscapes in which buildings—usually Gothic churches—functioned as architectural incidents distinct within, yet unthinkable apart from, a vast panorama. In his design of architecture and in his painting of it he was as much a romantic as a classicist. Nature in all its mystery and grandeur enthralled him, yet he regarded it less for itself and more

Berlin: Problems of a New Century

22. Schinkel, *Cathedral over a City*, oil on canvas, 94.4 × 126.6 cm., after 1813 Munich, Neue Pinakothek

as the domain of man. Thus he was preoccupied with a differentiation of the built and the natural environments, at the same time with a commingling of the two in an ideal state of interdependence. Similarly, he saw man as the self-conscious observer of the world, yet compatible with it, the idealizing transformer of his universe. Goerd Peschken cites Schinkel's understanding that "architecture is the continuation of nature in her constructive activity."[34] The concept of continuation in the sense of process or of movement, characteristic of nineteenth-century thought and feeling, finds especially compelling expression in the villas and landed estates that Schinkel designed for the Berlin countryside. They were a ready antecedent for Mies's epochal efforts to break down the barrier between interior and exterior space in his own residential architecture. His 1923 project for a Concrete Country House (see pp. 109–13), in which radiating wings restlessly search out their surroundings, and his 1950 Farnsworth House (see pp. 252–59), whose inhabitant senses an infinity of space beyond his four glass walls, strongly suggest lessons derived from Schinkel's classical-romantic endeavor to express man's ideal relationship with his natural environment.

More of that relationship as Schinkel conceived it can be learned in the woods and meadows along the River Havel in the west end of Zehlendorf looking toward Potsdam. The pergolas of the Kasino of Schloss Glienicke are potent examples of the master's notion of a zone

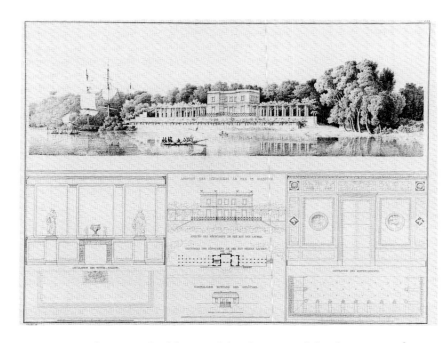

of transition between building and landscape, while the extraordinary
complex built in the late 1820s and early 1830s in the Charlottenhof,
a southern parcel of the royal grounds at Sanssouci near Potsdam, is
a mixture of classical and romantic elements that Mies in his own way
would follow in later works.

The patron of the Charlottenhof was Prince Friedrich Wilhelm IV,
himself an amateur architect whose sketches Schinkel gracefully translated into a complex marked by formality and informality, symmetry
and asymmetry, all in a delicately organized tension. The prince's
summer house, Schloss Charlottenhof, commands the grounds from
an eminence. It is designed as a Roman villa with a dignified Doric
portico, which straddles the cubic mass of the living quarters. Each
room has a view of the outdoors.

Unto itself the Schloss seems at first glance to be all severity, an
impression reinforced by the formal garden that follows the main axis
of the house to an exedra. On the other hand, the garden is flanked
to the side by a pergola which has the same effect already noted in
the Kasino: it connects the closed main block to the openness of nature, while comparably, to the other side, a geometrically shaped garden plane slopes downward, stopping at a less emphatically expressed
exedra, then moving through an asymmetrically situated pergola and
losing itself in an acreage as casual and rolling as an English garden.

This parkland, designed by P. J. Lenné, flows dreamily to a group
of buildings that not only relates contrapuntally to the Schloss but
relies, within its own confines, on the most picturesquely irregular,
cunningly balanced ordering of volumes and voids. This is the Gardener's Cottage together with a tea house and a replica of a Roman
bath, an architectural artifice typical of romanticism, but one in which
Schinkel preserves a winning discretion through his use of the classical
vocabulary. In fact, he employs the Tuscan vernacular, which, because

Berlin: Problems of a New Century

24. Schinkel, Charlottenhof,
Potsdam, 1926
Schinkel, *Sammlung
architektonischer Entwürfe*

it is a less formal manner than the Doric of the Schloss, not only acts
as a foil to it but encourages Schinkel to compose a quasi-cubistic assemblage of projections, towers, pergolas, trellises, round arches, flat
facades, gently sloping tiled roofs, and the spaces among them—ori-
enting the whole inward toward a formal garden court, outward toward
a meandering lagoon.

One cannot resist noting a single detail that follows from the informal Tuscan manner: a staircase leading from the garden to the podium
of the main building of the Gardener's Cottage. It is, however, not
oriented perpendicularly to that mass, not axially, that is, in obedient
classical fashion. Rather it slides up the side of it, parallel to it, in a
position that forces the pedestrian to turn to the right from the garden, double back to the left up the stairs, then turn again to the right
in order to enter the house. This passage has obliged him to take in
several necessarily shifting views on the way to his goal: an experience
more fluidly romantic than rigidly classical, and one which Mies, regardless of how consciously he ever took note of it, would repeat in
two famous staircases, one for the 1929 Barcelona Pavilion (see pp.
152–60), the other for the Tugendhat House of 1930 (see pp. 161–
71).

There is no more dramatic sign of Mies's serious study of Schinkel
during the Behrens years than a project which he designed independently in 1910. It has drawn only scant attention from those who have
written about Mies's early life, yet it is the first work of his career
which on more than cursory examination communicates signs of a first-
rate architectural talent, not merely a beguiling apprentice.

As we have already noted in our discussion of the headlong expansion of Mies's boyhood Aachen, Wilhelmine Germany had a passion
for monuments. In 1909, following two years of discussion, plans were
announced by the government in Berlin for a competition leading to

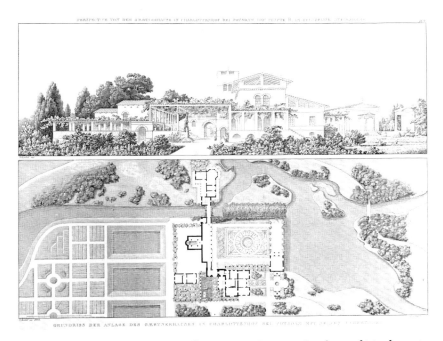

GRUNDRISS DER ANLAGE DES GÄRTNERHAUSES IN CHARLOTTENHOF BEI POTSDAM MIT SEINEN GÄRTEN

a monument to the memory of Otto von Bismarck, the political genius who had presided over the unification of the Fatherland and the establishment of the imperial German state. Hardly the first of its kind—Bismarck having become a memorialized cliché since his death in 1898—this one was nonetheless meant to be something out of the ordinary. The one hundredth anniversary of the late chancellor's birth was approaching in 1915; the planners took that as a target date for the unveiling of a work which would be meant as a demonstration of German unity, though in those days the line separating national aspiration from nationalistic anxiety was easily blurred, as can be read from the declaration of the presidium in charge of the enterprise "that a Bismarck monument must stand in those oft-embattled, much threatened yet faithfully defended borderlands of Germany."[35] There was no question this meant the Rhineland. It was a message addressed to the German people, but spoken loudly enough to be heard by the *Erbfeind*, the French.

The site of the monument was the Elisenhöhe, an imposing height overlooking the Rhine from its west bank at Bingen, close to the confluence of the Nahe.[36] The prospectus called for the monument to preside not only over the river below but, in an opposite direction, over a festival acre that was to be laid out on a plateau stretching away from the precipice. Mies's proposal recalled Schinkel both in its form and the relation to its setting. From a terrace meant to be built close to the river's edge a massive podium anchored in the hillside rose to lordly height. Mounted on it were five great interlocking masses, the longest of which consisted of two parallel walls built perpendicular to the river, enclosing a festival field on the plateau. Seen from the level of the river, they disappear into the foliage at the top of the hill. Openings were cut into these flat walls, at rhythmic intervals, creating the effect of an abstract colonnade with piers the same width as the

26. Exterior and elevation of
the Bismarck monument project,
Bingerbrück-Bingen, 1910

27. Bismarck monument project
from the festival field
Max Schmid, *Hundert
Entwürfe
aus dem Wettbewerb für das
Bismarck-National-Denkmal auf
der Elisenhöhe bei
Bingerbrück-Bingen*

spaces between them, the whole vigorously readable from a distance. At the river end of the inner face of the colonnades a pair of powerful, taller pylons joined them parallel, extending somewhat forward of them, then linking them securely to a semicylindrical wall, opened up with a similar columnar effect, which, like the prow of a great stone ship, contained the thrust of the entire mass toward the Rhine. Slim cornices capped each of the flat geometric masses, with the "prow" emboldened by a stronger cornice, or stringcourse, between the roofline and the top of the colonnade.

The festival field on top of the hill thus funneled into a forecourt approached up a flight of steps and flanked by the colonnades and the colossal pylons. At the far end, within the half-round, or exedra, and facing the forecourt, was a sculpture of the seated Bismarck, the sole figurative component of the monument. The grandeur that was considered suitable to such a medium of popular veneration (Mies named it *Deutschlands Dank*—"Germany's Gratitude") was evident enough from the analogy of forecourt, exedra, and statue to nave, altar, and icon.

28. Schinkel, Schloss Orianda project intended for the Crimea, 1838
Karl von Lorck, *Karl Friedrich Schinkel*

Mies clearly had studied history well enough to know what antecedents were appropriate to his project. The elevation of a temple on a podium was as old as Roman classicism. Schinkel was habituated to it, having paid special attention to the national monument to Frederick the Great, which the short-lived neoclassicist Friedrich Gilly designed in 1796. The decision at Bingen to hang a huge, symmetrical piece of classical architecture on a cliff overlooking an extravagantly romantic vista is traceable most specifically to Schinkel's published but unrealized Schloss Orianda of 1838, conceived as a pavilion for the Prussian royal family and meant for a panoramic site in the Crimea.[37]

Yet the clarity with which Mies established the identity of the interlocking masses of his Bismarck project while endowing them with monumental unity was proof that he was in command of his own invention, not simply obedient to Schinkel's recipes. A mastery of proportions was already evident, as was the conclusiveness with which Mies turned the flat planes of the walls into laconic but tautly dramatic colonnades. These various assets are clear from his perspective drawings of the monument, the earliest large presentation pieces of his to survive and the first tangible evidence of prowess in the art of drawing.*

The competition also provided him with an initial opportunity to design architecture on a monumental scale. At twenty-four, still barely known in professional circles, he could have had little expectation of winning so important a commission and thus, in what seems a characteristic gesture, he offered up a proposal distinctly more idealistic than practically feasible. He listed his own brother Ewald as the intended sculptor of the Bismarck image, even though there is no record of any serious sculptural work by Ewald and no certainty that he could have executed so ambitious a figure as the one suggested in the drawing. Moreover, while the competition jury, in a preliminary sitting of January 1911, included Mies's project among forty-one entries chosen

---

*A rendering of the monument now in the Mies van der Rohe Archive of the Museum of Modern Art is technically a collage composed of a photograph and pencil drawing. It proves that Mies was employing collage more than a decade before his well-known use of the technique in the early 1920s.

Berlin: Problems of a New Century

from a total of 380 submissions, they later rejected it, citing "obviously excessive building costs."

Mies, that is to say, appears to have done what he felt like doing, and we may conclude that his project was a reflection of his beliefs about architecture in 1910. It is perhaps just as well that he followed his intuitions in designing it, since the competition turned into an imbroglio all too typical of the conflicts between modern and traditional ideas that racked the arts in Germany during the first years of the century. Two founders of the progressive Deutscher Werkbund, Muthesius and Theodor Fischer, sat on the same jury with the patently conservative sculptor of animals, August Gaul. An entrepreneur, Walter Rathenau of the AEG, was among their colleagues, as were an aesthetician, Max Dessoir, and an art historian, identified as Professor Clemen. The panel, by a slim margin, awarded first prize to the proposal of architect German Bestelmeyer and sculptor Hermann Hahn, a remarkably restrained design of columns, trees, and a single statue of Siegfried, so modest, in fact, that a faction of the judges revolted

29. Behrens, Wiegand House, Berlin, 1910
Wolfram Hoepfner and Fritz Neumeyer, *Das Haus Wiegand von Peter Behrens in Berlin-Dahlem*

against the majority, complaining that the entry lacked the commanding force such a monument should exert over the landscape. The overseeing committee, after much quarreling, yielded to the rebels, reversed the jury's decision and granted top honors to the design of a colossal domed edifice flanked by a pair of giant eagles—"Faust"—the project of architect Wilhelm Kreis and sculptor Bruno Schmitz, two established favorites of the Wilhelmines. That one of the rebel jurors who favored the Kreis-Schmitz proposal was no less a champion of modernism than Muthesius testifies further to the contradictions and general turmoil of taste in prewar Germany. Plans for the Bismarck monument vanished in the fire and smoke of World War I.

The tendency to identify classicism with modernism, of which Mies's Bismarck project was an example, accelerated at the end of the decade. A wave of Hellenism swept German culture, as reports came home of successful German archaeological excavations in the Aegean area, especially those of Theodor Wiegand in Didyma, Samos, and Miletus. The kaiser himself bought a villa on Corfu in 1908. Upon Wiegand's appointment as director of antiquities of the Royal Prussian Museums in Berlin in 1910, he invited Peter Behrens to design a villa for him in Dahlem, one of the capital's most attractive neighborhoods.

We do not know if Mies, absent from the Behrens atelier at the time of the Wiegand commission, had anything to do with the design of the house. It was primarily Behrens's invention and one of his proudest, with the spirit of Schinkel informing nearly every aspect of it, down to the furniture and the appointments—all of those also designed by Behrens.[38] Yet Mies learned enough from it to affect several of his subsequent independent designs.

The house is a large cubic block of solemn gray limestone in cleanly joined ashlar, a prime example of reductionist classicism. It is entered through a massive Doric peristyle whose columns, unfluted and without entasis, are topped by capitals with only the severest indications of abacus and echinus. Passage from peristyle to house is gained through doors in each of the five bays. A long pergola binds one side of the garden. The floor plan is nearly symmetrical, with the main axis leading through the reception foyer to a drawing room flanked by a dining room and a library which extends equidistantly outward, in a U-shaped plan, to a formal garden. Thus the drawing room terrace functions as a shallow loggia. Similar plans appear in two other Behrens designs from the same period: the Schroeder House of 1909 and the Cuno House of 1910, both built in Eppenhausen, both featuring three side-by-side parallel rows of back-to-back rooms.

This recitation must recall Schinkelesque qualities—formality and restrained classicism—plus Schinkelesque devices—the axial plan relieved by asymmetry, the modular system of proportions, the building mass dissolving through the pergola into the natural surround. Mies must have known early in the planning stage a good deal about what the house would ultimately look like, since the image of it is reflected in his house for Hugo Perls.

It was during the summer of 1910, while Mies was independent of the Behrens office, that he met Perls. A well-to-do lawyer with a passion for contemporary art, Perls had turned his home in Berlin into

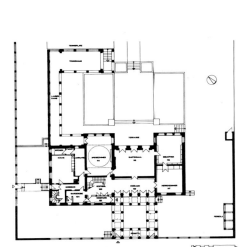

30. Behrens, Plan of the Wiegand House
Wasmuths Monatshefte für Baukunst 3, 1918/19

a gathering place for intellectuals. "Artists came" constantly, he later wrote in his autobiography; "Each would bring another with him. So it was, one evening, that Mies van der Rohe appeared."[39]

Mies was probably invited by another artist, though it has been suggested that that the two men were brought together by the Bruhns, an upper-middle-class Berlin family with their own cultural connections. Mies knew the Bruhns, whose daughter Ada he would later marry, through Professor and Frau Riehl. Regardless of his route of introduction, Mies was growing ever more inclined to seek out people of taste and influence like Perls. There was much he could could learn from them and not a little they could do for him. He had something of his own to offer in turn, as Perls's further recollections of his first evening with Mies attest:

> Van der Rohe spoke little, but whatever he had to say was manifestly illuminating. It seemed that a new era had begun in architecture. The better designers were at pains to keep their buildings free of all the superfluous embellishments, nooks, crannies, projections and other tacked-on ornaments of Romanticism. A new classicism had come alive. People were beginning to talk about "correctness" and "dignity" in building; it was van de Velde, after all, who had introduced the notion of morality in architecture . . .

> Van der Rohe had strong convictions . . . He wanted nothing to do with hand-me-down forms, though this didn't keep him from an appreciation of history and tradition in architecture. Thus he and I met on common ground through our shared delight in Schinkel. I think Schinkel was a unique phenomenon, by which I mean that no one before him or since could design Gothic one day and Greek the next and yet retain his own expressive personality.

> In any case Mies built our house, in Grünewald, near Krumme Lanke [i.e., in Zehlendorf]. My all-too-conservative tastes led to many a friendly skirmish between us, and I daresay the house probably could have been better, for Mies went on to become one of the great figures of modern architecture, a man well ahead of his time.[40]

The Perls House is a simple, rectilinear two-story prism of plastered brick, situated close and perpendicular to the street. Its flat hip roof, covered with pan tiles, rises from a clean, slender, molded cornice. Exterior walls are flat, free of stringcourses, pilasters or any other surface incident. The front facade, rigidly symmetrical, features a deep-set loggia on the ground floor through whose three bays, divided by square section columns topped by the thinnest, most abstracted suggestions of Doric capitals, narrow French windows offer triple access to the interior. Above the tripartite loggia is a rank of three short shuttered windows flanked by a pair of longer ones. The plan is axial, with an asymmetrical entrance-cum-foyer at the east corner. The loggia is entered from a formal garden on axis with the front facade, sunk just a step below ground floor level.

This prevailing "correctness" was in keeping not only with Mies's

31. Perls House, Berlin, 1910–11

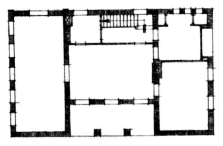

32. Plan of the Perls House
Photo courtesy of the Museum of Modern Art, New York

expressive temperament but with the wishes of a client who wanted the ground floor treated as a formal space in which his collections could be shown to best advantage. The three-part facade is echoed in the plan of the interior: on the ground level a large rectangular dining room, located exactly in the center of the house and accessible from the loggia, is flanked by a study and a library–music room. The lateral axis from the loggia is answered by a longitudinal one which originally extended with perfect symmetry across the study, through the dining room and, in A-B-A rhythm, once again across the library–music room.[41]

Mies's antecedents resonate everywhere. The indented three-part loggia flanked by single shuttered windows was a reprise, with levels inverted, of Schinkel's pavilion at Schloss Charlottenburg, just as the crossed axes were a favorite planning device of the master. The extension of the study and library–music room beyond the dining room in a U-shaped plan, plus the insertion of a fireplace in one of the short walls of the dining room, followed a similar usage in the interior of Behrens's Wiegand House. The planarity of the exterior walls and the abstracted cornice were traceable to both Schinkel and Behrens. So was the formal garden.

Berlin: Problems of a New Century

33. Alcove in the Riehl House showing radiator mantle

The Perls House was as derivative as was the Riehl House, with the noteworthy differences that its sources were fewer and more convincing in combination, its manner more discernibly classical-modern. Mies did cling to one decorative motif which appeared in the Riehl House, a radiator mantle made of wood, whose vertical bars, alternately square-sectioned and cylindrical (with exaggerated entasis), were enclosed in a frame with a projecting entablature of sorts, producing an effect sufficiently classical to fit as well in the Schinkelesque Perls interior as with the neo-Biedermeier decor of the Riehl House. All in all, the Perls residence was more internally consistent than the Riehl House, visibly better proportioned, carefully, even cannily planned, with the result that it evoked maximal classical dignity relative to its scale, which was that of a small suburban villa.

These qualities did not keep Perls from commissioning a set of unclassical decorations for one of the major interior spaces. The painter was Max Pechstein, one of the early expressionists, an original member of the Dresden movement Die Brücke, who moved to Berlin in 1911, the same year the Perls House was completed. Within months of Pechstein's arrival in the capital, he was directed by Perls to decorate the dining room with a group of murals on canvas which featured thirty-eight nudes in an arcadian landscape, the whole rendered in the nervous, glassily angular manner of Pechstein's Berlin period. Perls later gave these paintings to a friend as a birthday gift. They were transferred to the Berlin Nationalgalerie, but, as Perls reports,

34. Interior of the Perls House with murals by Max Pechstein, 1911
Courtesy of Ute Frank

"they disappeared soon after and I do not know what became of them." Pechstein also produced at least two expressionist designs for the metal screens covering radiators on the ground floor.

Whether Mies approved the invitation to Pechstein is not known. From photographs reproduced in a magazine of the 1920s, Pechstein's paintings were a striking group, hardly consistent in style with Mies's finely detailed classicism, but on that very account effective in contrast.[42]

The two Behrens projects in which Mies played his most prominent role as assistant also led to his permanent resignation from the office. The break was unfriendly, symptomatic not only of deepening differences between himself and his chief but of the younger man's growing sense of personal and artistic independence.

The first of the two designs was the German Imperial Embassy in St. Petersburg, a monumental edifice executed in the soberly opulent

35. Behrens, German Embassy, St. Petersburg, 1912
Bildarchiv Foto Marburg

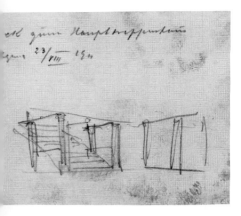

36. Sketch of the vestibule of the German Embassy, St. Petersburg, 1911
Auswärtiges Amt der Bundesrepublik Deutschland
Politisches Archiv
IB-Verwaltung: Das Botschaftshotel in St. Petersburg, Band 23

neoclassical manner characteristic of Behrens in 1912. Mies supervised the detailing of the interiors of the building and served between 1911 and 1912 as project manager at the St. Petersburg site.[43] It was there that he incurred Behrens's displeasure on two occasions, once when he secured substantially lower bids from local contractors than Behrens had been able to and later when he allowed his discussion of some of Behrens's plans for the interiors to be overheard by a journalist who published them in a newspaper article before German officials appropriate to the case could be formally advised.

Mies's involvement with the Kröller-Müller House was much deeper and lengthier, the conflicts with Behrens all the more nearly irreconcilable. In February 1911, while Behrens was occupied with the design of the embassy, he received a visit in Berlin from Mr. and Mrs. A. G. Kröller of Holland, who told him of their intention to build a villa on a large piece of country duneland they had lately purchased near Wassenaar, an affluent suburb of The Hague. The meeting was cordial and led to another a month later at the Kröller home in Scheveningen, where Behrens was formally awarded the commission to design the villa.

The names of Kröller and his wife, born Helene E. L. J. Müller, have come down to posterity chiefly on account of the formidable art collection they assembled and housed in the Kröller-Müller Museum and Sculpture Garden near Otterlo. The main building of the present-day complex was not built until 1938, by which time a convoluted history of both villa and museum, neither of them built by Behrens, had unfolded.

Kröller was a Dutch bourgeois who married into German wealth in 1888, took over his father-in-law's firm a year later, moved its headquarters from Düsseldorf to Rotterdam (later to The Hague), and turned it into an immensely successful enterprise with interests in shipping, mining, and heavy industry all over the world. A consummate entrepreneur, he was content to leave cultural concerns to his wife, who, in her middle years, developed a commitment to the arts and kindred secular spiritual matters that was as intense as her husband's dedication to commerce. In 1907 she met the art critic H. P. Bremmer, under whose tutelage she began an informal study of art which rapidly grew into a consuming passion. Bremmer became her guide, counsellor, mentor, intellectual pastor. When, in 1909, she began buying the work of the still controversial Vincent van Gogh, it was through the influence of Bremmer, who proceeded to advise her in all things pertinent to the refinement of her taste, her inclination toward the patronage of artists, the organization of a serious art collection, and the care and housing of it.

In 1910 Mrs. Kröller-Müller and her daughter traveled to Florence, where she was struck not only by the wealth of the art she saw there but by the role the Medici had played in its creation. They had been patrons, too, she reflected, and collectors—and commercial people, like herself and her husband. On her return to Holland, she was determined to build a new house for herself and Kröller at Ellenwoude, the name they gave to the parcel of land they had bought. It would be a country place where they could take their leisure sur-

Berlin: Problems of a New Century

37. Behrens, perspective of the
Kröller-Müller house project,
Wassenaar, 1911
Kröller-Müller Museum, Otterlo

rounded by their pictures. Further, since the collection was weighted
toward contemporary painting, the villa should be designed in the
modern manner. "I want no decorative embellishments," she wrote
Bremmer, and, in the same letter, "I prefer to build on the edge of
the dunes, so that I have a backdrop of the woods behind me and
great space in front of me, a large, spreading meadow," adding in later
correspondence, "the house [should] be long on its front, longer than
deep."[44]

Behrens took his new assignment seriously. He appointed Mies, by
now his most competent subordinate, as his chief assistant even though
the latter was already occupied with St. Petersburg. Over the course
of the next several months the master's concept of the villa took form.
In its final stage it consisted of a pair of two-story-high asymmetrical
wings joined by an entry fronted in turn by a loggia of square-sectioned stripped Doric columns.[45] This connecting piece rose slightly
higher than the wings.[46] All roofs were flat. A slender cornice was the
sole adornment of the exterior walls. The massing was sharply cubical,
the manner abstract-classical, the expressive effect discreet to the point
of understatement.

Obedient to Mrs. Kröller-Müller's prescription, the house was low-
lying and longer than it was deep. In one wing were the formal and
ceremonial spaces, in the other, the family rooms, dominated by the
generous chambers allocated to Mrs. Kröller-Müller. The paintings
were to be kept in the family wing, not simply as scattered decor, but
rather in a special exhibition gallery of their own, illuminated by a
skylight.

Why Mrs. Kröller-Müller was never content with Behrens's project
has not been fully or clearly explained. She was evidently uneasy about
his intentions as early as a few weeks after he took on the commission.
On 18 March 1911 she wrote Salomon van Deventer: Behrens "loves
long perspectives, and so he thinks he ought to make the house ever
so much larger. But I want to see it whole against a background, so
that it is contained, closed off."[47] Mr. Kröller, in an extravagant gesture meant to resolve his wife's doubts, arranged for a full-size mock-

up of the villa to be built on the Ellenwoude site in January 1912. It was constructed of wood and sailcloth, painted to match the intended final house color and set up on a system of rails so that it could be moved. Judging from photographs, the facade, though comfortably extended, hardly suggests the excessively "long perspectives" Mrs. Kröller-Müller had opposed. Moreover, the meadow appears to have spread away from the front of the house and the woods provided a backdrop to it—just as she wished. Still, her vague sense that Behrens was not attuned to the "life concept" she had in mind—whatever that meant—hardened into glum certainty. The project was rejected.

Meanwhile, young Mies was still very much on the scene, as he had been almost steadily since mid-1911. Over those months he was in frequent contact with Mrs. Kröller-Müller and had made a sufficiently deep impression on her that she found herself entertaining the possibility of turning the design of the house over to him, even as her confidence in Behrens waned. In turn Behrens himself had begun to suspect his assistant of coveting the commission.

Tensions rose in the home office, too. In the course of work on the Kröller project Mies had, judging from van Deventer's letter to Mrs. Kröller-Müller, been forced into a resumption of the intraoffice struggle with the colleague who aggrieved him before his 1909 departure from Behrens. (Van Deventer does not identify the man, save to say that he and Mies were the principals in Behrens's studio in 1911; this, however, would be enough to establish him as Jean Krämer.)[48]

At yet another point in the Kröller proceedings, Mies, conversing with Behrens, expressed his growing admiration for the Dutch ar-

38. Mies, model of the Kröller-Müller house project, 1912
Photo courtesy of the Museum of Modern Art, New York

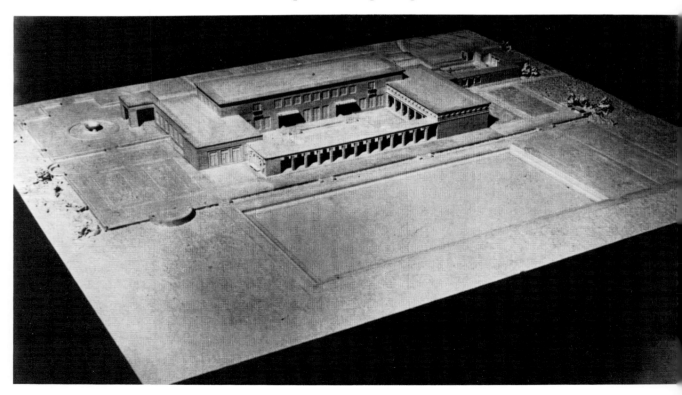

chitect H. P. Berlage, whose work he had recently come to know in Holland. Behrens replied that he found all of Berlage's work passé. "Perhaps," Mies said. Then he added drily, "assuming you are not simply deceiving yourself." Behrens wheeled on him angrily and looked, Mies reported later, as if "he would have liked nothing better than to give me one in the face."[49]

A rupture was now inevitable. Mies formally left Behrens's employ early in 1912, at about the same time Mrs. Kröller-Müller elected to turn the design of the villa over to him. Bremmer, on the other hand, took a dim view of the lady's decision. Not only did he doubt the capacity of an untested twenty-six-year-old to tackle so ambitious a project, he had in mind that Berlage himself, recently returned from a trip to the United States, might be available for it.

What ensued was, in effect, a competition between Mies, young, unknown, but championed vigorously by Mrs. Kröller-Müller, and Berlage, Bremmer's favorite, an established giant of European architecture, thirty years older than the rival who came more and more to revere him even as he worked to defeat him.

By spring, Mrs. Kröller-Müller had set Mies up in a studio in the company quarters at The Hague, a huge room, as he once said himself, typical of the outsized appetites of the Kröllers: "About fifty van Goghs were hanging there. I became a van Gogh expert in spite of myself; there was no way of avoiding the pictures."[50]

There he labored through most of the summer of 1912, in the course of which the Kröllers, to acquaint him with the environment, drove him all over the Dutch countryside. Every day Mrs. Kröller-Müller visited him in his studio, as her devotion to him deepened. Berlage carried on his own work in Amsterdam, calling on the family only sporadically.

By September Mies's design was completed. Despite his falling out with Behrens, much of the classical spirit of the master's earlier project had been incorporated in it; in fact the two designs look enough alike to have been occasionally confused in subsequent publications.[51] Each had the following in common with the other: a long, low profile with a longitudinal central block that rose above two laterally flanking wings, producing an I-shaped plan; flat-roofed masses organized axially and disposed around courts in a blend of symmetry and asymmetry that recalled Schinkelesque models; formal basins and axial approaching roadways. Similar details included square-sectioned stripped Doric columns, flat walls into which windows were cleanly cut, slender cornices just below the roofline.

Mies, however, made his central block by far the dominant element of his design. A pergola on the garden side connected the ends of the two wings, enclosing an inner court. Another pool, as long as the distance between the outer faces of the wings, lay to the rear of the house. On the front plane a portal stood at the corner of one wing, while from the far end of its counterpart a lower mass extended longitudinally outward, nestling a second court.

There is no known contemporaneous floor plan. Mies reconstructed one from memory about twenty years later, when he was teaching at the Bauhaus in Dessau.[52] According to this later drawing, the wing

39. Mies, perspective of the
Kröller-Müller house project,
1912
Kröller-Müller Museum, Otterlo

into which the portal led—the north wing—contained an entry, a *Halle*,
or reception area, and a formal dining room with a gallery beyond, to
the west. The two-story central block housed family rooms upstairs
and a corridor on the ground floor which served as an exhibition space
for porcelain. The latter passage led to the south wing: first to another
Halle, thence to several more galleries, including the windowless main
exhibition space and a room meant for prints. Extending still farther
to the south was a court bounded by a pergola and a conservatory.

All the masses of Mies's design were rigorously prismatic and often
interlocking, almost like elements of the constructivist compositions
which greatly influenced him in several of his post–World War I
residential projects. He himself later made the observation that the
Kröller villa, if stripped of its classical detail, would have borne a strong
resemblance to the abstracted cubic form of the works of the 1920s
modernists, himself included. And like his later projects, the villa,
though more centrally compact than the Behrens version, was spread
more expansively outward into the landscape, meeting it less abruptly.
Solids descended from the main block gradually, first to the flanking
wings, then, on the garden side, to the pergola-colonnade and on the
front side, to the conservatory pavilion. In all respects Mies's dimensions were generous. Photos of the model suggest the stateliest of country
houses, with an outward horizontal thrust that implied far longer perspectives than anything Mrs. Kröller-Müller had complained of in
Behrens's concept.

As we have noted, Schinkel could have provided the example
for such a transition from building to landscape, from artifice to nature, in the low, cubically pyramidal profile of his Gardener's Cottage
at Charlottenhof. "Nothing is piecemeal," the eminent critic Julius
Meier-Graefe wrote of Mies's design, "all the parts hang together and
are developed logically; the whole fits well the flat land for which it
is meant."

Meier-Graefe's words were addressed to Mies personally, in a letter from Paris, dated 13 November 1912. He went on: "I should like
to congratulate you. I see here an uncommonly felicitous solution to
the design of a house in which the essential problem has been to unite
liveableness with a rational display of art works. The need to preserve
the gallery's integrity could easily lead to its isolation. Your design has

happily avoided this. Instead, the gallery seems an essential part of the architectural whole, chiefly because of its handsome asymmetrical arrangement."[53]

Mies made a special trip to Paris to solicit this critique from Meier-Graefe, confident that an affirmation from so distinguished an authority would help him win the commission.[54] His supposition was never put to the test; Meier-Graefe's letter appears to have been written much too late. The Kröllers' moment of decision had come in September, when drawings and models prepared by both Mies and Berlage were assembled one evening in the company office in The Hague. Bremmer was called upon to render his judgment, which, given the abiding sway he held in the family councils, was delivered more in the form of a verdict. Van Deventer, who was present, reports the occasion: "Bremmer scrutinized the sketches and the maquettes long and thoughtfully. At last he motioned toward the Berlage pieces and said, 'That is art,' then to Mies's work: 'That is not.' He followed this with a torrent of argument in support of his view."[55]

Mrs. Kröller-Müller was destroyed. Bremmer, as certain of his authority as of his opinions, did not waver. In turn, Kröller, having broken one log jam, elected to use the same tactic on this one. The Mies project was translated into a full-scale wood-and-canvas version, as Behrens's had been. Trusting Bremmer's word, Kröller speculated that the weaknesses his hired critic had seen in Mies's design (they are not recorded) would be more visible if magnified. The strategem worked, rather as it had before. At any rate, Mrs. Kröller-Müller finally caved in. In January 1913 she wrote her husband: "Bremmer's judgment was the right one."[56]

The issue of a museum-house, seemingly troubled by demons more diverse than a wealthy client's irresolute temperament, continued inconclusively. Berlage's design, like those of Mies and Behrens, was never realized. Shortly after presenting it, he was retained as Kröller's resident architect and awarded several commissions relating to both company and family affairs. A condition of his contract was that he work for no one else. For six years he devoted his services exclusively to the Kröllers, though neither his original design for their villa-mu-

40. Mies, mock-up of the Kröller-Müller house project, 1912
Photo courtesy of the Museum of Modern Art, New York

41. Hendrik Berlage, model of
the Kröller-Müller house
project, 1912
Kröller-Müller Museum, Otterlo

seum nor several subsequent variations was ever built, partly because
he and Mrs. Kröller-Müller could not work harmoniously together. He
severed his relationship with the family and firm in 1919.

Within a year Mrs. Kröller-Müller had turned to yet another architect, whose Leuring House in The Hague ironically had triggered
her obsession with a modern villa in the first place: the renowned
Belgian Henri van de Velde. He, too, was now invited to produce a
plan for a museum, and he came up with one which, however, got
only as far as the construction stage before it was abandoned in the
anxieties of the 1922 international money crisis, which threatened the
very existence of the Kröller business itself. The structure that was
finally built in 1938, in Otterlo, after one more design by van de Velde,
was described as "temporary,"[57] though to this day it serves as the
quarters of the museum, the anticlimax of a star-crossed, frustrated
venture.

And how passionately Mies had wanted it for himself! If his special
visit to Meier-Graefe in Paris were not evidence enough, his letters
to Mrs. Kröller-Müller early in 1913, after her decision had gone against
him, indicate how much of himself he had invested in his labors, and
how grateful he remained to her for her support. "I hardly need to
tell you," he wrote,

> that your decision, though I expected it and though I accept it,
> came as a blow. I believe I allowed too much of my heart to be
> put into the assignment. I do understand the necessity of your
> decision.
>
> My feelings of admiration and appreciation, dear lady, for both
> you and your family, are not at all changed by the fact that my
> project was turned down. Indeed, the way you handled the
> matter and the concern you showed me only deepened these
> feelings.[58]

Despite his acute disappointment, however, Mies was hardly bereft. He had the project itself to show for his time in Holland, the most ambitious and mature design he had so far produced. Grandly conceived and elegantly detailed, the Kröller House project was a work which, for sheer monumental effect, was never surpassed in any of Mies's later residential designs.

Moreover, another and different form of profit accrued to him. Mies's first systematic reflections on the philosophical dimensions of architecture are traceable to the last years of his service with Behrens, and his thinking seems to have come into sharpest focus during his tenure with the Kröllers. If we accept his word, the man who did most to energize his thought was his own professional rival Berlage, with another designer, the American Frank Lloyd Wright, lately much celebrated in Germany, playing a more distant but not insignificant role. In the process Mies began to pay off his large debt to Peter Behrens.

Responding to an interviewer who asked him in 1964 what there was in Berlage's method that most suggested "modernity" to him, Mies put it this way: "It was chiefly a painstaking construction that was honest down to the very bone. That is what interested me the most, together with a spiritual character that had nothing to do with classicism, or with historicism. [Berlage's Amsterdam Stock Exchange of 1903] was a truly modern building."[59]

By 1912, then, Behrens, not Berlage, seems to have grown "passé" in Mies's eyes. Berlage, born in 1856 and trained in the tradition of such nineteenth-century rational theorists as Gottfried Semper and Viollet-le-Duc, was among the first Europeans at the turn of the twentieth century to subscribe to *Sachlichkeit* as an aesthetically appropriate, morally imperative creative attitude.[60] In itself this view did not distinguish him from Behrens or from many others of their time. But to Mies Berlage's views had the surpassing virtues of clarity and consistency and were not burdened by the convolutedness of Behrens's thought. Berlage was notably freer than Behrens of any residual symbolist trust in the *Kunstwollen* or in the *Volksgeist*. Persuaded that Christianity was a finished force, the Dutchman believed that science now provided the stimulus to a new moral standard which, moreover, was pertinent to no single nation but to the world. This supranationalist view, with its implications of universality, had its aesthetic corollary in his yearning for an objective "style," an embracing mode of expression deriving organically from a society based on principles of order and law. Proportion in geometry might furnish a formal means to reflect such order in architecture and would lead accordingly to that most desirable quality in the art of building, repose. This last was attainable at all levels, in Berlage's words, as "a charming repose in small works, a noble calm in great monumental architecture. Against this (i.e., ancient architecture), our current work gives the impression of being very unrestful. I might almost say that the two words 'style' and 'repose' are synonymous; that, as Repose equals Style, so Style equals Repose."[61]

The order Berlage saw as a condition necessary to "style" was not only potential in manmade law but actual in nature. He found the

42. Berlage, exterior of the Amsterdam Stock Exchange, 1903
Photo Bart Hofmeester, courtesy of the Royal Netherlands Embassy

43. Berlage, interior of the Amsterdam Stock Exchange, 1903
Historisch-Topografische Atlas, Gemeente Archief, Amsterdam

question of norms and types in the natural realm illuminated by Semper, whom he quoted:

> Just as nature is ever thrifty of motifs even in her endless abundance, constantly repeating her basic forms, but modifying them in a thousand different ways according to the condition of her creatures and their mode of life, stretching or curtailing some, hiding or revealing others—just as nature has her evolutionary processes, within whose limits old motifs continually reappear in new creations, so art lies within the scope of a few Norms or Types that derive from old tradition, each constantly reappearing in diverse forms, each with its own history, as in Nature. Nothing, therefore, is purely arbitrary, but all is governed by circumstances and relationship.[62]

What we know of Mies's mature thinking is in almost perfect accord with this summary of Berlagian theory. His offhandedly contemptuous remarks to Lohan about the German army signified as early as 1905–6 an indifference to patriotism which might have found Berlage's supranationalism more agreeable than Behrens's desire for a rapprochement with the *Volksgeist*. And Mies by the time he was a young professional had given up all formal connections with the church. Whether he was yet so committed to science as Berlage cannot be stated with certainty, but by the early 1920s he was a demonstrably avid student of morphology and would have been fully in sympathy with the sentiments expressed in the Semper quotation. His later efforts to reduce architecture to a minimum of structural and functional types attest to this. His disdain, moreover, for fantasy and caprice ("We don't invent a new architecture every Monday morning") was surely as firm as Berlage's own belief in an architecture derived from principles of order and law. Both men lamented the work of their respective contemporaries. Berlage called it "unrestful." Mies spoke of a "chaos of directions."[63] Even Berlage's distinction between "small works" and "great monumental architecture" was echoed in Mies's later citation of Saint Augustine's definition of order as the "distribution which allots things equal and unequal, each to its own place, and integrates an ensemble of parts in accord with an end."[64]

All this would seem to suggest that Mies, who had ample opportunity to read Berlage's published statements and to listen to his lectures, had assembled the foundation stones of his own architectural philosophy by the time he returned from Holland to Berlin in 1912. He would find Berlage's clarity and consistency preferable to the idealizing intricacies and historical ambiguities of Behrens's thought, though the concept of the *Zeitgeist* would be the one Behrensian legacy that proved most fruitful to Mies's developing worldview.

Yet the major fact that raises doubts about Mies's chronology of maturation and the part Berlage played in it—as he recalled both, over and over, in his American years—is the work he did directly following his term of service in The Hague. From then until as late as 1921 his designs showed no perceptible influence of Berlage's thinking and little change in manner from that which marked his output prior to 1912. Through the whole second decade of the century Mies remained a steadfast practitioner of classicism and historicism in architecture, the very attitudes he applauded Berlage for avoiding. There is, in fact, no evidence that he ever met Berlage personally, either early in Holland or late anywhere else.

The intent here is not to deny Berlage's influence on Mies—quite the contrary—but rather to suggest that Mies in recounting it in America, when he was celebrated as one of the founders of modernism, tried to make himself appear to have dismissed Behrens and accepted the more advanced, the more authentically modernist, position of Berlage more precociously than he really and finally did.

This chronological qualification would also apply to his acknowledgment of influence from Frank Lloyd Wright. Remembering what we said earlier about the hectic clash of viewpoints in European architecture during the century's first decade, we read Mies, who recalls seeing Wright's work for the first time in 1911 but writes of it in 1940, in America:

> We young architects found ourselves in painful inner discord . . . the potential vitality of the architectural idea of the period had by that time been lost . . .
> At this moment, so critical for us, the exhibition of the work of Frank Lloyd Wright came to Berlin.
> The work of this great master presented an architectural world of unexpected force, clarity of language, and disconcerting richness of form . . . Here again, at long last, genuine organic architecture flowered . . .
> So after this first encounter we followed the development of this rare man with wakeful hearts.[65]

But Mies, apparently, followed ever so cautiously, allowing years to pass between stimulus and response. His pre–World War I architecture offers no more inkling of homage to Wright than of reverence for Berlage.

The 1920s are another matter. There is ample evidence that the lessons Mies had learned from both men were urgent enough by then to be expressed in his own designs.

However much he owed both sources, then, he took his very unhurried time paying it back. As late as 1919, he was sufficiently proud of the Kröller project to submit the model of it to an exhibition organized by Walter Gropius, the director of the newly organized Bauhaur in Weimar.[66] Quite logically, it was rejected by Gropius, who had already committed himself to an anticlassicist modernism in 1911 with the Faguswerk, underscoring it in the 1914 Deutscher Werkbund exhibition at Cologne, where he showed a bravely abstract new model factory building. For the same occasion young Bruno Taut, at least as adventurous as Gropius, unveiled his expressionist vision of the future, the House of Glass.

Mies carried on with characteristic deliberateness. He did not join the Werkbund, and he did not go to Cologne. He returned at ease to Berlin, where he opened his own atelier in the suburb of Steglitz,

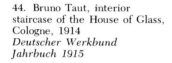

44. Bruno Taut, interior staircase of the House of Glass, Cologne, 1914
Deutscher Werkbund Jahrbuch 1915

married Ada Bruhn, and devoted himself almost exclusively to residential designs for the haute-bourgeoisie.

Professor and Frau Riehl, though childless, had a large company of nieces to whom their hospitality was forever extended. Since the Bruhns were close family friends, Ada knew the girls well and was herself a frequent guest at Klösterli. It was only a matter of time before she met the gifted young architect from Peter Behrens's office who had designed the Riehls' house. That first encounter probably took place in 1911 or 1912, during Mies's second tour of duty in Neubabelsberg.

It was equally likely that the two young people would find themselves more than casually attracted. Judging from early photographs, Mies was handsome, of slightly more than medium height, solidly, almost stockily, built. A high forehead crowned well-chiseled features, most pronounced among them sharp hazel eyes that must have been the chief agent of his commanding, if reserved, presence. Ada, born Adele Auguste Bruhn in Lübeck on 25 January 1885, was a bit more than a year older than Mies, thus at twenty-six or twenty-seven, a mature woman when she met him. She cut a stately figure and was, from all accounts, very good looking, tall, with long, straight brown hair, solemn eyes, and a Junoesque carriage.

She was also well fixed. Her father, Friedrich Wilhelm Gustav Bruhn, like the rest of her family a native North German (born also in Lübeck, 1853), was a tax inspector at the time of her birth. Later he became a manufacturer of small motors with holdings that eventually included a factory in London. He invented the taxi meter that was standard in Berlin cabs of the Wilhelmine period and an altimeter used in German military aircraft. As a personality he was exacting and stiff, hard to the point of brittleness. He is remembered by Ada and Mies's surviving daughters for having treated his own children with an authoritarian hand that all too inconsistently gave way to spasms of guilt, then to an expiatory lavishing of gifts, a textbook pattern for the encouragement of neurosis in his offspring. We can only conjecture how deeply these traits affected Ada; her lifelong bouts with somatic illnesses and depression are a matter of record.

Though Mies met her at the Riehls', he spent much of his courtship in the Dresden suburb of Hellerau, well known in the early twentieth century as a garden city planned and designed between 1909 and 1914, principally by Heinrich Tessenow, a leading architect of the German Garden City movement. The back-to-nature impulse that helped to create such communities made Hellerau an ideal place for the Swiss educator-composer Emile Jaques-Dalcroze to open his school of eurythmics in 1910. A form of dance based on gymnastics correlated with music, eurythmics shared with the Garden City idea the objective of a "natural," spiritually liberated human society. Appropriately, it was Tessenow who built the Jaques-Dalcroze Institute, between 1910 and 1912, in the abstract classicist manner of the day, and there Ada Bruhn enrolled herself as a student, presumably about the time the school began operations.

Ada shared a small house in Hellerau with two other young women who were destined to play either central or auxiliary roles in early

45. Mies, about 1912
Private collection

Berlin: Problems of a New Century

46. Ada Bruhn, 1903
Private collection

47. Ada Bruhn, 1907
Private collection

twentieth-century German cultural history. One was Mary Wigman, who became the most celebrated female exponent of the modern dance during the Weimar period; the other, whom Wigman described[67] as coming from a background even more comfortable than that of Ada Bruhn, was the Swiss Erna Hoffmann, later the wife of the psychiatrist Hans Prinzhorn, whose *Bildnerei der Geisteskranken* [The Art of Psychotics] was one of the major early studies of the relationship between art and psychopathology.

The trip from Berlin to Dresden was sufficiently rapid by rail to enable Mies to visit Ada frequently and, in the course of time, to get to know Wigman, Hoffmann, Prinzhorn, even the painter Emil Nolde, a friend of the elder Hoffmann's who occasionally accompanied them on visits to their daughter. According to Wigman, an easy cordiality developed among the whole small society. Their way of life was free, open, somewhat self-consciously modern—rather the sort of living style that became the norm among German liberal elements during the 1920s. In 1912 such a manner would have been considered quite advanced of middle-class mores, though for that very reason all the more attractive to young people with artistic and intellectual ambitions. For the value Mies brought to his relationship with Ada was the spiritual equivalent of her material wealth: he was talented and deeply committed to his art, assets which more than made up for his limited education and lack of inherited social standing.

And there was that air of mysterious profundity about him, surely another sign of the creative fires to which Ada, by her own presence at the Jaques-Dalcroze Institute, had indicated she was attracted. She had already been engaged to the renowned Heinrich Wölfflin, reigning art historian of his generation but in her view a man of thought and theory rather than of passion and invention. She had rejected him; he was twenty-one years older than herself, but mostly he bored her.

Mies, brooding and intense, did not bore her. She meanwhile brought to him, in addition to her family wealth, intelligence sufficient to his attentions, plus grace, comeliness, devotion, and social connections through which he could advance his career. He married her within a year of the opening of his own practice.

The Bruhns appear to have accepted him for some of the same reasons Ada found him worthy in her eyes: he looked like a man with a future. Their one recorded objection was to his unattractive name. In German *mies* means "wretched," "miserable," "out of sorts." "The weather is *mies*"; "I am feeling *mies*." A *Miesmacher* is a complainer. To the cultivated Bruhns, conscious of this sort of thing, "Ludwig Mies" hardly rang with the music of the spheres; "Ada Mies" grated further. "Ada Wölfflin" had a finer sound.

Nonetheless, that and any other parental objections came to nought. The couple were married in a Lutheran ceremony in Berlin-Wilmersdorf on 10 April 1913 and took up residence in the upper-middle-class suburb of Lichterfelde, west of town, not far from Dahlem, Zehlendorf, Potsdam, Neubabelsberg: Schinkel-Behrens country.

At the time, Mies was at work on the first commission of his independent career, a house in Zehlendorf for the engineer Ernst Wer-

Berlin: Problems of a New Century

48. Perspective of the Werner
House, 1912
Photo courtesy of
Dietrich von Beulwitz

ner, completed later in 1913.[68] Werner had inherited a piece of real
estate in Zehlendorf which abutted the very property on which the
Perls House stood. His daughter Renate's suspicion that Mies was
retained because her father greatly admired the Perls House is itself
suspect, since what Mies finally gave him seems in no way inspired
by that design. The Werner House is in fact the most schoolish piece
of Mies's prewar phase and, next to the Feldmann, Kempner, Eichstaedt, and Mosler houses of the early 1920s (see pp. 120–122), the
most stylistically retardataire work he ever produced. When he re-
visited the Perls House in 1965, he paid no attention whatever to the
Werner House,[69] even though the two buildings are separated by no
more than fifty yards, each quite visible from the other. It would appear he designed the Werner House more for bread and butter than
for high art, with future contacts in mind to which the Werners might
lead him. They had their own comfortable position in the Berlin cultural world, opening their home to artists and musicians much the
way Perls opened his. Mrs. Werner's father was a professor of drawing
in Dresden, her brother an art historian, and she herself a committed
patroness, subject of several portraits by well-reputed contemporary
painters, including one by the bright young expressionist August Macke.

The Werner family was deeply impressed by Mies—"an imposing,
forceful, vital man," in Renate Werner's words[70]—and altogether happy
with the house irrespective of its conservatism. Its exterior is even
more obedient to Prussian eighteenth-century precedent than that of
the Riehl House: a four-sided gambrel roof of pan tiles takes up twice
as much of the elevation as the stuccoed wall, beginning at the top of
the first story level with a pagodalike lip, then rising steeply past the
pedimented dormers of the second story, and breaking into a gentler
slope at the attic. Except for a forward-protruding service wing, the
house is rectangular in plan, overlooking a terrace toward the street.

The main entry is placed exactly in the center of the street facade, its shape and shutters repeated in the two French windows adjacent to it. An eyebrow window illuminates the attic.

Perpendicular to the service end of the rear facade is a roofed pergola that faces inward to a formal garden, the latter accessible from the house as well through three French doors exactly at ground level. Since the garden facade has no counterpart of the frontal ell and is flat except for a shallow two-story-high pedimented projection, its symmetry, underscored by the geometrically planned garden it surveys, gives it a more formal look than the street front.

Save perhaps for the precision of the relationships of their features, the elevations of the Werner House are less suggestive of Mies than of the pattern book. The pergola and garden are equally derivative, traceable directly to Behrens and indirectly to Schinkel. The plan is almost identical with that of Behrens's Wiegand House, which likewise features a frontal projection of the service wing toward the street and an entry to the right of that. The Werner House shows nothing so grand as the Wiegand peristyle; on the other hand the main axis of the ground floor, following Behrens's example, leads through a foyer into a living room, thence to the garden. A subordinate perpendicular axis runs from the foyer left to a stairwell and right to a salon. To the left of the living room is a dining room—leading to the pergola— and to the right, a study. This is exactly Behrens's plan at Wiegand, with only slightly different names for the functions of essentially the same types of rooms. Furthermore, it is the feature that most binds the Werner House to the otherwise dissimilar Perls House and also to the last residence Mies designed before the end of World War I, the Urbig House in Neubabelsberg (see pp. 77–80): a composition based on three parallel room depths governed by a main axis perpendicular to them that leads from street front to formal garden. Basically Schin-

50. Dining room of the Werner House with Mies's furniture, 1913
Renate Werner

kelesque and generically classical, it is the closest thing to a recipe to be found in the house plans of the protomodern Mies.

More arresting than the architecture of the Werner House is the furniture Mies designed for it. The dining room shows a round center table with arm and side chairs, a sofa, and a china cabinet. These pieces, plus a desk, still exist. The neoclassical manner common to the furniture of Schinkel and Behrens was dutifully employed here by Mies, who nonetheless brought to his task an exceptional assurance in the flow of line and the proportion of parts, as well as an overall mastery of detail.

The first surviving drawings of the Werner House date from late 1912, the last from mid-1913, the year it was completed.[71] The Mies-Bruhn wedding took place during this span. Very shortly thereafter the couple bought a large tract of land in Werder, a resort suburb west of Berlin. The property was abundant in cherry trees of a strain whose fruit was celebrated throughout the district. Mies either found or put up a modest weekend house on the grounds.

During World War I he and Ada were forced to give up this retreat, chiefly because they could not retain a caretaker for it. Until that time, however, they made good use of it. Mies was the first to seek it out, frequenting the lakeside taverns of Werder by himself, finding pleasure in them and drinking it up, so Mary Wigman tells us, as if it were a nectar that leaked from the first cracks in the vessel of his marriage.

By common agreement of all who knew him, Mies was not meant to be a responsible husband or, even after Ada bore three daughters in three years' time, a deeply caring father. "As a married man," Wigman recollected, "he was a caricature. . . . I lived through some pretty terrible times with the two of them, early in their marriage. I recall Ada, sometimes in the middle of the night, threatening to jump out of the window of their house, to get away from him, to leave him."[72]

As it was, he left her, not permanently—not yet—but often, on regular weekend excursions to Werder, where he struck up numerous casual liaisons, with little more motive than to have the best time possible.

"He had one girl there," recalled Wigman,

> who was known as The Horse, because she resembled one. "Yes, I know," he would say to me, "she's no beauty. But she's a dancer and we are fine together, and it is great fun. Furthermore, she is so open and spontaneous . . .!" He would go on for hours about his Horse.
>
> And remarkably, I have to tell you, it was somehow all right that way with him. I could never bring myself to say to him, "Ludwig, how *could* you?!" There was something about him that thrived on freedom, required exemption from convention. It was his way, and he blossomed. And dear Ada herself, after they were married a while, would say, "I want only to be a haven to him, a place he can come back to, and find peace." Is that a woman's nature, to be so yielding, so without rancor? I don't know. I do know the whole thing didn't work.

For a while, however, it had to work. Ada wanted it to, either de-

Berlin: Problems of a New Century

spite or because of the misery it caused her. Although she later moved out, she did not leave him. He remained, boon or burden, locked in her heart. Her daughters remember her with unqualified affection and pride, for she made a studied point of teaching them to tolerate and respect their father's need to be free. Mies was an artist, Ada would remind her children, who grew more excellent with the years, and required disencumbrance from the mean demands and humdrum distractions of bourgeois life. Mies would have agreed with her.

The birth of a daughter on 2 March 1914 prompted Ada herself to spend more time in the country at Werder. The child's name, Dorothea, is thought by the family to have been taken from Goethe's *Hermann und Dorothea*, a curious source since it is a long and highly sentimental love poem, the sort of literary work that the young moderns of Germany, soured as they were on romanticism, would not readily espouse. Was Dorothea a symbol of the hopeful reaffirmation of Ada's and Ludwig's love? There is reason to suspect as much, in view of Ada's notebooks, written between 1914 and 1919, which are as full of adoring references to Mies as they are devoid of any hint of the marital stress Mary Wigman observed.[73] Mies himself devoted no more time to any building project of 1914 than to the house he conceived for himself, and presumably for his family, on the Werder site.

Our only documentary evidence of this work consists of a pair of drawings, each showing the house in different form, tersely but clearly enough to prompt some engaging conclusions. Both sketches are aerial perspectives in which Mies seems to have been interested less in delineating the actual building than in establishing its relationship with a surrounding landscape. Each design is unmistakably Schinkelesque in its prismatic geometry. Both are radically simplified. One consists of a long mass with two wings extending forward to embrace a forecourt. The roof of the house is as flat as its wall, which in turn appears free of any incident except a discreet cornice molding and long, widely spaced, sharply incised windows reaching to the ground. The Kröller villa comes to mind along with Mies's remark that if freed of classical ornament that project resembled a house of the 1920s. The same is true of both designs for the Werder house. The second sketch shows the house divided into two prisms at right angles, one sliding slightly forward of the rear plane of the other. As with the interlocking blocks of the Kröller villa, such a treatment prefigures Mies's constructivist designs of a decade later. A more telling asymmetry, reinforcing this one, appears in both designs in the garden extending forward and away from the forecourt. A flight of steps leads down perpendicularly to a broad walk below which, accessible by another staircase, lies a rose garden sited well to the left of the axis running into and through the main house block. The sunken garden is in effect a negative volume which, related to the masses of the house, creates a remarkably informal, rectilinearly geometric organization, again suggestive of a considerably later period in European residential architecture.

Both drawings show several similarly asymmetrical but formally composed stands of trees, likely the famous cherry trees of Werder, which flank the house. Though both sketches are quite summary, it is clear Mies regarded the architectural problem as embracing more than the house alone. By itself this is unremarkable, especially in view of the lessons Schinkel taught about building in concert with nature, yet Mies's composition is more boldly simplified and abstracted than the Gardener's Cottage at Charlottenhof. The breakdown of the barrier between architecture and nature takes on characteristic twentieth-century form.

One suspects, then, that his progress toward modernism might have appeared swifter had the Urbig family accepted the first proposal he offered them after they commissioned a house from him in 1914 or early in 1915, to be built in Neubabelsberg. According to Renate Petras, his initial idea "provided for a one-story neoclassical villa which bore a close resemblance to the plans for [Mies's] own residence in Werder, likewise not carried out."[74]

Frau Urbig knew of Mies through her friends the Riehls. She liked the Riehl House, she liked Schinkel, and she liked Mies. When she and her husband Fritz, a prominent Berlin banker, elected to build a home fronting the Griebnitzsee just a short walk from Klösterli, she had hoped for a Schinkelesque design. This Mies gave her. Herr Urbig, however, balked at the flat roof, whereupon Mies produced a quite different solution which was accepted. Construction was begun late in 1915 and completed in November 1917.

The house proved to be as conventional and eclectic in concept as it was rich in exterior aspect and lavish in the appointments of its rooms. The facade, again suggesting Mies's early willingness to build more conservatively than he thought, looks back to the eighteenth century in its symmetrical, seven-bay-long front which rises two stories to an attic under a hip roof and five dormers. The round arch over the main entry is literally overshadowed by a balcony whose richly decorated wrought-iron railing climaxes the rhythm set up by the elaborate medallion reliefs over the six flanking French windows. Flat pilasters mark the bay divisions. Mies relies again on the planning device, already noted, of three room depths, side by side, leading to

52. Street facade of the Urbig House, Neubabelsberg (Potsdam), 1914/15–17

a garden. However, just as a pergola projects from the rear facade of the Werner House, embracing a garden, the dining room of the Urbig House juts out, partially enclosing a terrace. A travertine staircase then leads downward to a garden level, whence another stair, at right angles to the first and perpendicular to the rear facade, descends to a lawn that flows gently downward to the waterfront. From this green-

53. View of the Urbig House from the garden

sward the view of the house is animated by terrace, balustrade, and retaining walls.

The interiors are classical in style, chilly in temper. Passage from the spacious entry, via the main axis into a hall at right angles to it, thence to a music room, is punctuated by two formidable fluted Doric columns, reminiscent of the pair Schinkel used at Schloss Tegel. The corridor leads to a salon and a study at one end of the main floor, from which a single bronze standing figure on the garden parapet is visible through the French windows, and to a staircase plus an entry to the dining room at the other. There is a plenitude of classical ornament: ceiling reliefs, modillions, moldings, panels, round arches, all recalling Mies's days at the drawing board of the Fischer stucco workshop in Aachen.

The Urbig House, though elaborate to the point of pomposity, is neither an original nor an inspired work. Still, it is technically quite assured, testifying to its designer's evident mastery of planning, construction and decorative program. Mies probably earned a generous fee from it, enough, when taken together with the support that was always available from the Bruhn family if needed, to enable him and Ada to live comfortably without hastening after other commissions during the first two years of the Great War.[75]

Mies was not drafted into the army immediately. Too old for the first round of conscription in 1914, as a family man he was free, even in October of 1915, to move with his pregnant wife and their little daughter to an address in the Tiergarten district of Berlin: Am Karlsbad 24. He maintained this abode for the remainder of his life in Germany up to 1938. It was an apartment on the second floor of a typical central Berlin townhouse built probably between 1860 and 1870. All the rooms connected with a long central corridor: on the street side, living room, studio, suite of two small bedrooms (one most likely for

Berlin: Problems of a New Century

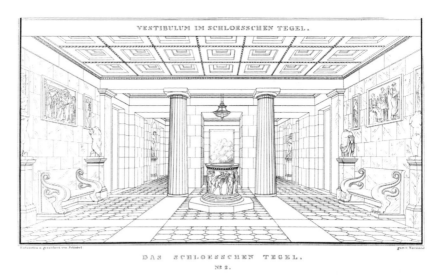

the children, the other for a maid), and balcony; on the rear side, master bedroom, bath, kitchen, and stair entry.

Ada's notebooks depict the period immediately following the move to Am Karlsbad, notwithstanding occasional discommodations, as the happiest of her married life. The bad times seemed past. Nineteen-month-old Dorothea, nicknamed Muck, doted on her father "now that she has moved to Berlin after a summer in which she saw so little of him." On 25 October her mother wrote that Mies "has to leave for the army, and the happy atmosphere of the family will be given up for a while. Muck looks everywhere in the apartment for her daddy, and is over and over again disappointed."

Several weeks later, on 12 November, when a second girl child was born to Ada, Mies was in Hanau, near Frankfurt, assigned to an army railroad detail. Lacking a university education or its equivalent, he was obliged to remain in noncommissioned rank for the rest of the war. In December, Ada wrote: "His first greeting after my news of his second daughter was, 'I am grateful to you, and joyful over Marianne!' (it was he who gave her that name)."

If Ada's account of Mies's movements is accurate, he was back in Berlin by the spring of 1916. She had taken the children to Werder for Easter, and upon their return to the city she found him incapacitated with appendicitis. He promptly underwent a serious appendectomy and spent the next two months hospitalized. Convalescence was fitful and slow. His military duties, which had meanwhile shifted to clerical work in a regimental headquarters in Berlin, were interrupted again in September. "He is not at all well," Ada wrote. "His nerves are in the worst shape." Packing the children off with their governess, she joined Mies for a fourteen-day rehabilitation leave in Eisenach, where, quite probably, a third child was conceived. "It is October," her next entry reads, "and we are all together as a family on Karlsbad. Pappi is enjoying a deep contentment."

In the meantime—probably no earlier than the beginning of 1915— Mies had struck up another close relationship, with the sculptor Wilhelm Lehmbruck, who moved to Berlin from Cologne the preceding

November. According to Lehmbruck's son Manfred, the two men and their families saw each other frequently during 1915 and 1916, exchanging visits in Berlin and Werder.

By all accounts the friendship was one of the deepest of Mies's young adulthood, perhaps of his whole life. Lehmbruck was a native Rhinelander like himself, with a similar working-family background (mining). He was five years older than Mies and by the time the two met, in Paris, during Mies's 1912 trip there, Lehmbruck had a decade of worldly experience and singular professional success behind him, including several sojourns in Italy, four years of residence in Paris, and a trip to New York, where he participated in the epochal 1913 Armory Show, sold a major work, and established himself as a sculptor of international repute.

Lehmbruck stood for the kind of aesthetic figure whose company Mies preferred to that of the utilitarians he could have consorted with in the architectural world. "Whenever Mies came over to our place," Manfred Lehmbruck recollects, "he could deliver the obligatory incantation without delay: 'Lehmbruck, open up the battery!' [the bar]. To that love Mies was eternally true! Of course the two of them knew each other's work and they talked endlessly, until late in the night. Often they discussed philosophical issues."[76]

If they talked of the war, it is certain they expressed no love for it. Lehmbruck himself resisted conscription, managing to work as a medical orderly in Berlin before fleeing to Zurich late in 1916, at a time when Germany as a whole was wearying of the interminable and debilitating struggle. Though he spent most of the remainder of the war in Switzerland, he suffered recurring bouts of depression and finally, in the spring of 1919, several months after the armistice, took his own life.

Mies himself saw no combat in World War I, but early in 1917 he was ordered to quit the regimental offices in Berlin. He was sent to a field assignment in Rumania. "That trip took fourteen days by rail," Ada reported in her daybook. "Twelve men in each barely heated fourth-class coach. With no straw to sleep on." On arrival in the Balkans Mies was attached to a company of bridge engineers and road builders. He is reported by a later associate to have quarreled with a sergeant and ended up in "an outlying region guarding railway sidings. At that time he had a love affair with a gypsy woman, who provided him with food, of which he sent a lot to his daughters in Germany."[77]

In Mies's absence, Ada confessed, "we are melancholy. There is no coal here, so we have moved in with the grandparents [the Bruhns], where the cold persists anyhow. A real affliction, this horrid winter; how hard on all the people, everywhere."

On 15 June 1917 Ada delivered her third daughter, born like Marianne in Mies's absence. Her name, Waltraut, rich in overtones of Wagner and nineteenth-century German national romanticism, seems as implausible as Dorothea, given the modernist tastes of her parents. Still, it should be noted that Ada spent much of her young marriage alone with her girls or in the house of her parents, who could not be expected to encourage her more progressive attitudes. During the waning months of the war, she may have found a measure of comfort in the uses of tradition.[78] Then, on the occasion of Mies's last army leave, she exulted:

> July 21: When Waltraut was five weeks old, her beloved father returned, in the midst of a wild rainstorm, fresh and cheerful, like a real soldier. He has spent twelve days in our little house in the sun.
>
> On the 27th, Waltraut's baptism. A country church procession, through a lovely old stone gate, always under sunshine. Our two big sisters there too, festively done up, dear, proud, so well-behaved. An hour or two at a cafe followed, then a long walk. Pride in the baptismal child. Supper and a moonlight cruise on the lake.

Ada's renewed spirits survived her own appendectomy and subsequent intestinal misery in early 1918, as well as the prolonged lung infection Marianne suffered during the international influenza epidemic of that spring.

On 22 November, with the war over, Mies returned from Rumania, and by early January 1919 he was once again with his family in Berlin. Ada offers no evidence of his reaction to Germany's catastrophe. She herself was preoccupied with other things, including her own stomach distress. During the spring she wrote of "the severe illness of my mother, followed by an operation. I had to care for her until the middle of May. But *then at last* we all moved to Karlsbad. It is now an indescribably beautiful, harmonious time; the blossoming chestnuts fill our room with light, and in their own little corner the children are lost in their own happy little world."

3 Europe out of the Ashes: Response to the Modernist Challenge, 1919–25

During the very period of the greatest ferment in the German arts of the twentieth century, we know the least about Mies's professional actions and thought, and not much more about his personal life. The concentrated energy with which German artists responded to their country's defeat was in striking contrast to the demoralization that gripped the citizenry at large. Between 1918 and 1923 the national economy was in an almost steadily desperate condition, while the apparatus of central government sputtered in confusion and futility. Yet painters, writers, architects, and critics fell to their tasks with such a force of invention that their efforts set the pace for the modernist culture that dominated the Weimar Republic until it was brought low by the Nazis in 1933.

The chief reason for the difference between the depressed quality of life in postarmistice Germany and the vigor of creative expression there was that legions of artists and intellectuals were swept along by the spirit of revolt that rose up in reaction to a bloody and terrible war. Revolutionary attitudes ranged from anger and disillusionment to futuristic optimism, but they were united on two points: the conviction that an oppressive imperialist order was responsible for the war and Germany's ensuing misery, and a belief that modernist idioms of expression were the most appropriate vehicles for antiestablishment sentiments.

To infer Mies's reaction to this postwar mood we are obliged to make the most of fragmentary evidence. Many of his files of the years 1918–21 are lost, and it is not unthinkable that he later destroyed a portion of them himself—as one of his assistants has claimed—in an effort to simplify history's impression of his embrace of modernism.[1] He did not, however, give himself to the revolution either so promptly or so wholeheartedly as some others around him. Until as late as the mid-1920s he designed and built works in manners as traditional as anything in his prewar catalog. Yet at the very same time he was offering these concoctions to rich clients of the sort he had cultivated earlier, he was busy with a set of radical projects whose ultimate importance to the development of modern architecture was fundamental.

To a degree he must have felt the need to keep his options open in a period of economic and political turbulence. He had a family to support, though this practical necessity was ameliorated by his sustained access to the substantial means of Ada's parents. She had no money in her own name; whatever came from the Bruhns went effectively to him, who as the man and head of the house directed its outlay. Indeed he had no reason not to resume the comforts, to the extent they were available in 1919 and 1920, which he and Ada had known prior to the war. He could afford vacations, in the course of which he took up skiing and learned to ride.

Moreover, his society with the Bruhns kept him in close touch with people who would pay him well to build their houses. Surely Mies sensed that the values and traditions of Hohenzollern Germany were at the point of eclipse even as he produced residential monuments to them; doing so, however, only gave him more independence to reflect upon another society, that of the revolutionists. They were a complicated lot in their own right, standing for a wide spectrum of attitudes that called for the kind of circumspect study to which he was naturally inclined.

The spirit of revolution had already grown unruly during Mies's protracted absence from Berlin. As the dream of German victory turned to nightmare, antiwar views were aired with increasing vehemence in *Die Aktion* and other journals and reflected in the visual arts as well. Max Beckmann, who served on both the eastern and the western fronts, was demobilized after an emotional breakdown and sought to purge himself of the horror he had seen by translating it as early as 1917 into concrete images, cold, ruthlessly exacting parables of pathos and violence. The Berlin dadaists, including Huelsenbeck, Hausmann, and Baader—those who returned from Zurich where they first fled the war—relied not at all on myth or allegory but on expressions of bellicose irrationality and sheer impulse, as if aesthetic anarchy were the most fitting way of showing contempt for the values of bourgeois society. George Grosz in turn, though part of the early dada group, took up the leftist political cudgel and a more directly representational manner of communicating his abhorrence of a social, economic, and political system which seemed to him, even after the republic was established in Weimar in 1919, irreversibly corrupted. Otto Dix went even further in narrative realism, recalling the terror of the trenches and dwelling, at times with morbid fascination, on the avarice and carnality that were common to Berlin life in the early 1920s. Mies's late friend Lehmbruck himself had written with pained fervor in January 1918, nearly a year before the end of the war: "Who stayed behind after these murders / Who survived this bloody sea? . . . You, who prepared so much death / Have you no death for me?"[2]

Yet such expressions of bitterness and defeat hardly made up the whole of the German arts at the end of the war. For many, the overthrow of the Hohenzollern regime was seen less as a ratification of hopelessness and more as a stroke of good fortune which cleared the air, awakening hopes as well as underscoring the necessity for an altogether new world. To the formation of that world the arts could make signal contribution. The republican government, despite its stops, starts, and general disorder, held out the promise of a political environment in which such aspirations could eventually be realized. It was capable, in theory, of initiating enlightened patronage as well as stimulating a wholesome way of life in tune with the best in culture; moreover, its socialist sympathies were rooted in a tradition of internationalism, not in the hidebound patriotism associated with the German state during the imperial years. Hence, since many of the modernist movements all over Europe had already begun to push in the direction of revolution in the arts before the war, their postwar representatives would be welcome in the circles of the German van. The German arts, isolated from the world scene since 1914, had much to learn from them.

Such social optimism, with its emphasis on collective action, was more often associated with the social arts: architecture, the crafts, and sister disciplines. At the same time, since the publicness of architecture left it at the mercy of an economy more often than not moribund, it was the art in which the least amount of actual work was produced. During the first years following the war, architects and designers were left to root about the ruins by day, as it were, and by night to speculate and fantasize or congregate and talk. The major German architectural achievements of 1919 took the form of projects imagined and associations organized. The prevailing mood was tentative and expectant, and in lieu of commissions and similar practical engagements, it inspired dreams and manifestos whose proposals were as yet more rhetorical than substantive. Mies was not the only member of his profession who spent many hours in thought at the turn of the 1920s.

There was more to think about than the choice between hope and despair. The form in which either of those states of mind was expressed was also important; thus aesthetics were at issue as surely as world view, however much the two were intertwined. When Mies returned to Berlin the dominant manner in the German arts was expressionism, which had gained preeminence among the painters, sculptors, and writers of the avant-garde in the years just prior to 1914. By inertia alone expressionism could be expected to sustain a strong following after the armistice, especially since contacts with other countries and alternative stylistic modes were largely lost.

Perhaps more important, however, the emphasis expressionism placed on highly charged subjective states and on the artist's role as mystically favored conveyor and mediator of those states was precisely suited to the mood of many German artists after the war. No single figure produced more fantastic visions than Bruno Taut.[3] Even before the end of 1918 he had concocted a series of schemes, published in his *Alpine Architecture* (1919), in which he proposed the transformation of vast mountain landscapes by cutting clefts into existing peaks and planting them with enormous spears of colored glass, decorating glaciers with precious stones and vitreous panes meant to reflect and magnify the sun's rays, embellishing alpine lakes with still more crystalline floating elements. In all their shimmering transparency and abstracted geometric form, these mountains of glass were metaphors for the transfiguration of the world and man.

Contemporaneous with Taut's grandiosities were various related developments. Nietzscheanism flourished again, as it had in the days of the Jugendstil. Expressionists often identified their creative personalities and philosophical points of view with the image of the sage Zarathustra, who harbored no love for urban life, perceiving the city as a concentration of mean-mindedness and rot. A mass longing for a return to the land was reawakened with the end of military conflict. The elemental, the primitive, the organic were once again exalted in

Der
Kristallberg

Der Fels ist
oberhalb der
Vegetations-
zone behauen
und geglättet
zu vielfachen
kristallinischen
Formen.

Die hinteren
Schneekuppen
sind mit
Glasbögen-
architektur
bebaut.

Vorne Kristall-
nadelpyra-
miden

Über dem Ab-
grund eine
Brückenver-
gitterung aus
Glas

56. Taut, The Crystal Mountain
Alpine Architecture, 1919.
Courtesy of the Museum
of Modern Art, New York

57. Taut, The Valley as a
Blossom
Alpine Architecture, 1919.
Courtesy of the Museum
of Modern Art, New York

the abstract and given specific expression in the renewed emphasis on the handicrafts. Taut designed his own ideal settlements, relying not only on the Garden City concept of decentralization, but on symbols and meaning drawn from archaic and exotic sources: Indian and Gothic architecture, for example. At the core of the most famous of his zoned towns was the *Stadtkrone,* or crown of the city, center of cultural and spiritual life, and rising from the middle of that, the *Kristallhaus,* the house of crystal, which, as Taut wrote, "contains nothing apart from an incredibly beautiful room," and whose panes of colored glass reflect a radiance "over everything, like a sparkling diamond."[4]

The crystal was the central metaphor of expressionist architecture. It seemed an ideal unity of iconography and form: its trinity of solidity, transparency, and reflectiveness suggested a universality of meaning, a concentration of all things in one that touched again on the mystical, while that same multiplicity of properties was compelling in strictly architectural terms. For crystal was close to glass, and glass as a building material had been earning its own mystique at least as early as Gropius's Faguswerk and Taut's Glass House in Cologne.

The power of the expressionist aesthetic attests to the widespread zeal with which the postwar generation sought to conjure utopia. Even at the old Kunstgewerbeschule of Weimar, newly named the Staatliche Bauhaus and reopened in April 1919 under the direction of that erstwhile *sachlich* functionalist Gropius, the spirit was more passionate than rational. The final sentence of Gropius's manifesto for the school read: "Let us together, then, will, conceive, and create the new building of the future, which will encompass architecture *and* sculpture *and* painting in *one unity* and which will rise eventually toward heaven, from the hands of a million craftsmen, as the crystal symbol of a coming new faith."[5]

Europe out of the Ashes

Given the romantic fervor of expressionism, it is only reasonable to presume the ascendancy of countermovements in the postarmistice years. The dadaists, who had gained strength from their perception of the war as the ultimate failure of Western civilization, were impatient with aesthetics of any kind and especially with those of the expressionists. George Grosz spoke contemptuously of the artist who "lives in a filthy studio and dreams of higher things."[6] Nevertheless dada, offering no positive program of its own for the future, played an increasingly marginal role as the 1920s unfolded. Much of its energy was transferred to other collective endeavors which, though hardly millenarian in their faith, sought to cope with the world rather than reject it outright. These movements had in common the conviction that the world was not likely to be moved, much less transformed, by the mystical yearnings of the expressionists. Postwar reality was brutal, to be sure, but the very fact of its reality weighed more than any idealizing response to it. Thus any art made or action taken in the face of quotidian fact must be based on the soberest acceptance of that fact.

In a sense it was 1905 all over again. As in the first decade of the century the mysticized aesthetic of symbolism gave way to *Sachlichkeit*, the romance of expressionism was now challenged by a *neue Sachlichkeit*.[7] This "new factuality" inspired art of widely differing temperaments: the savage social criticism of Grosz and Dix on the one hand and on the other a hopefully socialized architecture which, making the most of modern machine technology, began to produce mass housing for the German public by the mid-1920s. Yet "realism" was the point of departure common to these two strains of *neue Sachlichkeit*, just as, in formal terms, they were both given to an impersonal exactitude in the handling of their respective media. Grosz and Dix painted in a dry, linear manner stripped of the expressionist painterly gesture, while the new architects cleansed their work of ornament or other idealizing historical references, seeking to be straightforwardly functional and reducing their working vocabulary to forms whose geometric precision called to mind the production techniques of the machine.

The *neue Sachlichkeit* was destined to win the day in Germany. It was in fact related to a larger movement gaining ground everywhere on the Continent, a tendency away from the riot of dada, the antiart of the futurists, and the subjective indulgence of expressionism, toward a cooler, more exacting, and order-conscious mood in all the arts. By 1923 Igor Stravinsky was composing in an astringent neoclassical style and Arnold Schönberg had produced his first dodecaphonic scores. Picasso had turned from his cubist experiments of the mid-1910s to a classicizing figuration. Strenuous antiromantic movements like de Stijl in Holland and constructivism in Russia were seeking once again to effect a détente, based on the rule of reason, between art and the machine, while in Paris Charles Jeanneret, now called Le Corbusier, the Swiss architect whom Mies had encountered in the doorway of Peter Behrens's Neubabelsberg studio more than a decade earlier, was promoting a *rappel à l'ordre* in design on the pages of the journal *L'Esprit nouveau*.

Ludwig Mies, stonecutter's son, assistant to Bruno Paul and Peter Behrens, disciple of Schinkel and admirer of Hendrik Berlage, was by training and temperament ill-suited to either expressionism or dada. Furthermore, he must have known finally that to continue serving conservative clients could only leave him in a cul-de-sac. The future belonged to the aesthetic left, where, among the doctrinal choices open to him, *Sachlichkeit* was the most congenial. Whatever conclusions he drew from these reflections, he put them into action during 1921, the most decisive year of his life following his move to Berlin at the age of nineteen. His resumption of sustained design and the effective dissolution of his marriage occurred within months of each other, in the latter half of that year, though both events presupposed other decisions that are traceable to several crucial personal relationships formed about the same time or shortly before.

The most catalytic of these was his friendship with Hans Richter, an artist of varied talents and interests who personified the adventurous mood of the German arts in the wake of the war. Richter had been part of the dada group in Zurich before returning late in 1919 to his native Berlin. There he collaborated with the Swedish artist Viking Eggeling in abstract "scroll pictures," which evolved by the next year into abstract films. The two men joined the Novembergruppe, a radical new society devoted to forwarding the revolutionary cause through the arts. Richter formed an especially close bond with those members whom we will, for now, call simply antiexpressionist, since at the turn of the decade de Stijl, constructivism, and Die neue Sachlichkeit were not yet organized as positive programmatic forces in Germany.

This condition was soon to change. By the end of 1920 Theo van Doesburg, prime evangelist of de Stijl, had arrived in Berlin. Less than a year later the constructivist El Lissitzky was there, too, and in contact with van Doesburg. Thus the most persuasive individual spokesmen of two of the liveliest new movements in European art converged on the German capital within a few months of each other.

It was through Richter that Mies met van Doesburg and Lissitzky, both of whom frequently turned up at Richter's atelier, a favorite meeting place and forum of argument for a company of international artists, poets, and critics who had come to Berlin to enjoy an atmosphere of intellectual freedom unique among European capitals of culture.

"This circle," Richter wrote, "included [Hans] Arp, [Tristan] Tzara, [Ludwig] Hilberseimer, [Theo van] Doesburg, but soon also Mies van der Rohe, [El] Lissitzky, [Naum] Gabo, [Anton] Pevszner [*sic*], [Frederick] Kiesler, Man Ray, [Philippe] Soupault, [Walter] Benjamin, [Raoul] Hausmann, etc."[8] The bracing cosmopolitanism of the new Berlin is apparent from even the few names Richter lists. De Stijlists consorted regularly with constructivists, ex-neoclassicists with dadaists, Russians with Germans, Dutchmen with Rumanians, painters and writers with sculptors and architects, etc.

Van Doesburg, Lissitzky, Richter, and Mies saw a good deal of each other in the next two to three years. Mies was initially much impressed by the fearlessness with which van Doesburg and Lissitzky and other members of their respective movements had carried forward the efforts of his own prewar generation: the expunging of naturalistic references from painting and sculpture and historical references from architecture. Such a process of abstraction, of paring away superficialities in order to reveal essences, struck Mies as the crucial method of arriving at vital form in the new arts, and the apparent purity of geometric form in both de Stijl and constructivism appealed to him more than the shaggy, capricious, crystalline angularities of expressionism. For geometry seemed the most rational product of abstraction, which was itself a rational mode of creative expression. Moreover, no Germans had carried geometric abstraction to such sophisticated and rationalized lengths as had the members of de Stijl and constructivism, since both movements had begun before the war ended and had had time meanwhile to refine their thinking and their work.

Their thinking nonetheless was not monolithic; differences of opinion among members of both movements were sometimes sharp. Still, Mies must have found much in the published statements of van Doesburg to accept, and a good deal to learn from. The very title of van Doesburg's lecture, "The Will to Style," delivered in Berlin and other places during 1921 and 1922, reflected a debt to Berlage, and its sentiments were as opposed to expressionism as they were accepting of some aspects of *Sachlichkeit:* "All that we used to designate as Magic, Spirit, and Love will now be efficiently accomplished. The idea of the Miraculous, that primitive man made so free with, will now be realized simply through electric current, mechanical control of light and water, the technological conquest of space and time."[9] In turn van Doesburg's cordiality with the constructivists can be made out from one of Alexander Rodchenko's constructivist aphorisms: "Consciousness, experiment . . . function, construction, technology, mathematics—these are the brothers of the art of our age."[10]

The "age" was a special preoccupation of modernist artists of nearly all styles and persuasions in the third decade of a young and self-conscious century. No one was more obsessed with it than the constructivists and the members of de Stijl, especially van Doesburg. Both movements were more utopian in outlook than Die neue Sachlichkeit, convinced as they were that the arts were vital components in the necessary remaking of the world. Such a vast reconstitution, however, required the sober—*sachlich*—rejection of all articles of past faith that appeared inconsistent with the instruments of modernity as de Stijl and constructivism measured them. The materialist bias of the new Soviet intelligentsia undergirded the Foundation Manifesto of the Constructivist International of 1922, which affirmed that "this International is not the result of some humanitarian, idealistic, or political sentiment, but of that amoral and elementary principle on which science and technology are based."[11] Though van Doesburg was always too much the conscious aesthete to accept the highly socialized and mechanistic position of the constructivists, he had already written in the first manifesto of de Stijl in 1918:

1. There is an old and a new consciousness of the age. The old

one is directed toward the individual. The new one is directed toward the universal . . .

. . . .

    3. The new art has revealed the substance of the new consciousness of the age: an equal balance between the universal and the individual.

    4. The new consciousness is ready to be realized in everything, including the everyday things of life.[12]

Mies's own sympathetic response to these intentionally *sachlich* viewpoints as they were discussed among van Doesburg, Lissitzky, Richter, and himself in the several years following 1921 is evident from his own famous statement of 1924: "We are concerned today with questions of a general nature. The individual is losing significance, his destiny is no longer what interests us."[13]

By 1923 the four men found themselves close enough in their opinions to collaborate in the publication of a journal called *G*. Mies contributed several pieces of writing to it, all quite representative of the uncompromising *Sachlichkeit* with which *G* later became identified. Nor were the lessons he learned from de Stijl and constructivism confined to ideas. Formal affinities with the work of both movements were apparent in Mies's designs throughout the 1920s, and to a diminished extent later than that, as we shall see.

At the same time, even as he consorted with van Doesburg, Lissitzky, and Richter and sounded a lot like them, he was forming his own world view, which in both theoretical sense and formal realization eventually separated him from them. In view of what he later designed and wrote, we are obliged to look for stimuli upon him which had little to do directly with anyone we have so far mentioned.

It was Arthur Drexler who suggested an influence to which scholars had previously given little if any consideration.[14] During a conversation in the 1960s that revolved around the question of the *Zeitgeist* in architecture, Drexler asked Mies if he had ever read Oswald Spengler. Mies's immediate response was a broad smile, followed by a moment's reflection and an answer in the negative. He acknowledged, however, that he knew a good deal about Spengler's point of view, and he delivered so skillful a paraphrase of Spengler's central theses that Drexler suspected that he had learned them from the original, not some secondary source.

As already noted, Mies became a serious reader before World War I, his special interest in philosophy having been encouraged by his first client, Professor Alois Riehl. He amassed a substantial private library, about 700 entries of which survive.[15] These reveal a far larger number of titles published in the late teens and early 1920s than in the earlier years, leading us to speculate that he increased his reading considerably after returning from the war.

The fact is, he owned a first edition of *The Decline of the West*, the two volumes of which were published in 1918 and 1922. Mies's marginal markings indicate he read most if not all of the book, and his own later writings suggest that he took Spengler greatly to heart, effectively, more, in fact, than any major architect of his generation.

He was, of course, not alone among his countrymen in his familiarity with Spengler's gloomy vision.[16] *The Decline of the West* exerted an immediate and terrific impact on intellectual circles in Germany; 100,000 copies had been sold by 1926. Part of Spengler's appeal lay in his oracular tone and the conviction of his grim message, delivered at the grimmest of times, to an audience caught between a ruinous war and an anxious peace.

Spengler contended that according to the nature of things, great cultures of the world go through life cycles; history is thus, within limits, predictable, like the morphology of living things or the rhythm of the seasons. The first phase of a given culture he saw as heroic, bursting with seminal vigor, expressing itself in the form of religious myths and epic works. In the West—the "Faustian" culture—this would have been coeval with the High Middle Ages; in the Greco-Roman—the "Apollinian"—with the Homeric period. Faustian visual art is predicated on dynamic movement in space, quintessentially realized in the Gothic cathedral, while the Apollinian counterpart was the static, self-contained form of the Greek temple.

A cultural "summer" would follow this germinating phase, producing a secular aristocracy and a circumscribed company of great individual geniuses who take the place of their nameless springtime ancestors. Here Spengler mentions Galileo, Michelangelo, Shakespeare. Autumn then brings maturity, the golden fulfillment of the culture's personality which, again in the West, is most eloquently offered up in the poetry of Goethe and the music of Mozart. At the same time philosophy commences to threaten religion; the first signs of decline are manifest. It is the Enlightenment, the eighteenth century.

In the protracted winter, cities, long since separated from the life-giving land, extend themselves into sprawling megalopolises, "deserts of stone," as Spengler called them; art turns inward and grows abstruse; materialism flourishes, along with political tyranny on a global scale, and imperialism, and constant warfare. The vital spirit of the culture ebbs away, to be replaced by "civilization," in which administrative tasks beckon more urgently than high creative ones, and technology supersedes science.

All this was irreversible, Spengler decided. Time was running out for the West, and however apocalyptic he made that prospect sound, he also wrote as if it were a matter of incontrovertible fact:

> We are civilized, not Gothic, or Rococo, people; we have to reckon with the hard cold facts of a late life, to which the parallel is to be found not in Pericles' Athens but in Caesar's Rome. Of great painting or great music there can no longer be, for Western people, any question . . . Only *extensive* possibilities are open to them.
>
> . . . we cannot help it if we are born as men of the early winter . . . Everything depends on our seeing our own position, or destiny, clearly, on our realizing that though we may lie to ourselves about it, we cannot evade it.
>
> . . . .
>
> For me the test of value to be applied to a thinker is his eye

for the great facts of his own time. Only this can settle whether he is merely a clever architect of systems and principles, versed in definitions and analyses, or whether it is the very soul of his time that speaks in his works and in his intuitions.[17]

The proximity of several of Mies's best-known statements to Spenglerian concepts and even locutions is so noteworthy that, together with the evidence of the two well-worn volumes in his library, we are led to believe that the melancholy historian-philosopher was on Mies's mind even as he was getting to know the members of Richter's atelier group.

A year after the publication of the second volume of *The Decline of the West*, Mies wrote: "Architecture is the will of an epoch translated into space"; "Not yesterday, not tomorrow, only today can be given form"; and "Create form out of the nature of our tasks with the methods of our time. This is our task."[18] As late as 1930 he added: "The new era is a fact; it exists, irrespective of our 'yes' or 'no.' "[19] And in 1964: "My definition of civilization is an order in the material realm; and culture is the order in the spiritual realm—or rather the harmonious expression of order in the spiritual realm . . . We speak of the Roman *Civilization* and the Greek *Culture*; and this is how I see it."[20]

The reference in this last, late statement to "civilization" and "culture" is traceable certainly to Spengler, though it is more the cold-blooded tone of Mies's earlier remarks that rings with the sentiments of *The Decline of the West*, even as it points to his ultimate differences with de Stijl and the constructivists.

Indeed Mies's own preoccupation with the *Zeitgeist* suggests not only his early debt to Peter Behrens but his later reasons for breaking with him. We have reported that Mies turned away from Behrens's symbolism-tainted *Kunstwollen* out of a higher regard for the tough-minded scientism of Berlage. It is worth noting that Spengler himself, in his profound fatalism, gave little place in his world view to the *Kunstwollen*, believing that creative activity in the modern age was narrowly circumscribed by the facts of modern history. He was not much moved by the power of art to change modern life. In this regard he was neither the utopian nor the aesthete van Doesburg was, nor did he look to sociopolitical ideologies to provide ways out of modern dilemmas, as the constructivists did. Mies's own maturing outlook was closer to Spengler's than to that of any of the artists he knew personally. In fact his differences with de Stijl and the constructivists became only more apparent as the 1920s passed.

Yet before the decade was over he began a serious reinterpretation of the Spenglerian lessons, and here we must cite another philosophical influence upon him which is recalled by the distinction he drew between the "material" implications of "civilization" and the "spiritual" dimensions of "culture." During the early 1920s he was already reading Saint Thomas Aquinas, among other ancient philosophers, and the writings of the great Scholasticist whose name he had been taught to revere since childhood slowly revealed to him the signs of a system he could make his own.

Saint Thomas saw divine order reflected in but transcending the material world on which Spengler concentrated his attentions. Mies, we submit, consented to Spengler's morphological understanding of history, cleaving most intently to the view that a great thinker—or architect—was he and he alone through whose works and intuitions the very soul of an epoch spoke. However bleak the epoch might be, it was real; there was no escaping that. All a citizen could do was strive to clarify his intuitions and—herewith Saint Thomas—elevate them from material fact to spiritual expression within the discipline of an idealizing order. For Mies, Spengler confirmed the unassailable facts of the material world while Aquinas posited a spiritual realm—of which fact was an earthly manifestation—through which a higher truth might be reached and, by the artist, conveyed.

By the late 1920s the functionalist position associated with Die neue Sachlichkeit in architecture, like the materialism of the constructivists, seemed to Mies barren, devoid of a spiritual purpose. On the other hand, van Doesburg's insistence that aesthetics be given final preference to the logic of hard fact was as unacceptable to him as Behrens's residual symbolist aestheticism had been a decade and a half earlier. For Mies, then, *Sachlichkeit* was a necessary condition, though, lacking in spirituality, an insufficient one. It remains to be seen how these various aspects of Mies's thought developed in detail, and how they related to his own building. As of the fateful year of 1921, they were still in an early stage.

There is little evidence of the exact order of events in 1921, but by the fall of the year, most certainly, Mies's life had taken a new course. His contacts with the Richter circle have been reported; moreover, we know that by the onset of winter he was sharing the working space in his Am Karlsbad studio with another architect, the Swabian Hugo Häring.

It is unclear just when and how, relative to all this, his marriage to Ada came apart. Sometime in the latter half of 1921 she moved with the children to an apartment in the suburb of Bornstedt, near Potsdam. She and Mies did not divorce, nor was their separation dramatic. The very coolness with which their decision to live apart was made seems as symptomatic of a growing emphasis among Weimar moderns on individual freedom at the expense of antiquated matrimonial restraints as of any irreconcilable personal differences. To be sure, there were enough of the latter, if we accept the recollections of the daughters, or even if we trust our inferences. For in reading Ada's notebooks, we must find it hard to believe that so coolly self-absorbed a man as Mies could have lived either long or comfortably with a woman who was endlessly attentive to him and yet constantly infirm in his presence.

The daughters insist nevertheless that their parents more nearly drifted than split apart. From time to time Mies visited Bornstedt, at first on weekends, later with decreasing regularity. He began to work again, putting his family gradually out of his mind. He made the Berlin apartment over into a bachelor's atelier, converting the connubial chamber into a guest room, the dining room into a drafting

58. Elevation and plan of
Mies's atelier-apartment,
Am Karlsbad 24, Berlin
Drawn by Sergius Ruegenberg

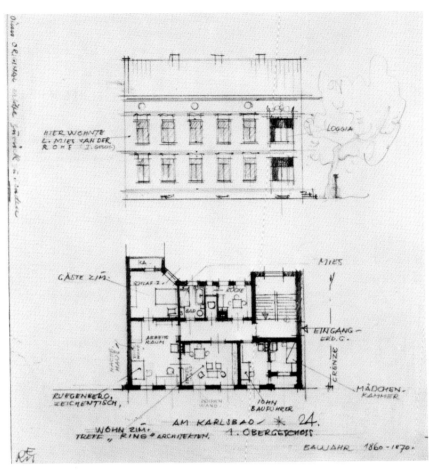

room, and moving his own bed into the bathroom—not so bizarre a notion as it might sound, since in typical nineteenth-century Berlin flats, the bathroom was the size of a boudoir, roughly three by four meters, while the water closet was located in a separate room.

"Muck" and Marianne, the two older girls, alternated between private tutors and public school in Bornstedt. Sometime during 1922 the American dancer Isadora Duncan opened her own academy in a *Kavalierhaus* on the grounds of the sumptuous Neues Palais, near Sanssouci, in Potsdam. Ada, who regarded Duncan's freely expressive form of dance as the very essence of modernity and much akin to what she herself had studied at Hellerau, enrolled all three children in the new school. They had spent something less than a year there when a restlessness descended upon their mother. Ada quit Bornstedt and, with the girls, began a long and lonely journey of fitful residential stops in Switzerland, the Tyrol, and Bavaria, which did not end until the 1930s, when her daughters were nearly grown.

Mies now put his own priorities in order. He would stay married, at a discreet distance; any alternative meant either a limitation of personal freedom or the loss of a large part of his means of support. These decisions made, he proceeded to work, moreover with as much will and drive as were apparently suppressed during the previous several

Europe out of the Ashes

years. In fact his initial major postwar effort, submitted to an architectural competition, was only the first of five altogether uncommon projects, which vaulted him to the forefront of the German vanguard by 1924. Within three years, Mies turned from moderation to radicalism in design and took his place among the seminal figures of twentieth-century architecture.

As early as 1912 the *Berliner Morgenpost* had issued an open letter to the mayor of the city, proposing the erection of tall buildings downtown as a means of bringing visual life and a more effective concentration of business activities to the urban center. The war retarded but did not defeat the idea; despite the postarmistice economic distress it was revived with enthusiasm in 1921. The Germans were greatly impressed with the example of the American skyscraper, not to mention America itself. "The land of unlimited possibilities," as it was commonly called, seemed to dramatize the new world for which so many Weimar intellectuals strove, and the skyscraper was one of America's most telling symbols. "In my opinion," said Walter Rathenau, earlier of the AEG and for a time following the war the German foreign minister, "nothing since the Middle Ages is as architecturally imposing as New York City."[21]

Late in 1921 the Berlin Turmbaugesellschaft sponsored a competition for a tall office building to be put up on a triangular downtown site bordered by the Friedrichstrasse, a huge railroad station, and the Spree River. The prospectus of the competition placed fairly strict and specific conditions on the entries.[22] Of highest priority was the concern that the neighborhood be enhanced, not brutalized, by a design whose suggested height would not exceed eighty meters. Differentiated functions throughout the building (offices, studios, public establishments) called for detailed individual floor plans. The ground floor was to include a variety of shops, plus garages, a cafe, and a movie theater.

Most of the 145 submissions proposed solutions in which a main tower was set back from flanking wings or stepped back from low-rise elements. Expectably, the dominant style was expressionism: frequent use was made of acute angles, spiky forms, and massive blocks disposed against each other. (The triangular site encouraged this.) Yet *Sachlichkeit* as a motivating factor was also apparent in more than a few of the projects. Critic Adolf Behne was gratified that "our architects knew quite precisely that antique columns do nothing for a skyscraper," then, commenting on one individual design, added this antiexpressionist aside: "It is treated like a place for offices and businesses . . . and it does nothing to conjure any particular emotion."[23] And Max Berg, in praise of an entry known by the code name "Honeycomb," noted that it "strives for the highest simplicity . . . the broadest concept . . . it is an enriching effort to master the fundamental problem of a tall building."[24]

Honeycomb was Mies's design, and Berg was right about it. He was also right, however, in scoring the work for features that help to explain why the jury declined to award it an official mention. Mies flouted

59. Ada Mies, 1921
Private collection

60. Marianne, Dorothea, and Waltraut, about 1920

nearly all the rules of the prospectus pertaining to the function and setting of the building. He did not submit differentiated individual floor plans above ground level, since he conceived all floors as identical. He designed a nearly symmetrical grouping of three obliquely angular prismatic towers, twenty stories in height, which rose from street to roof with no setbacks. Located at the corners of the triangle, the towers were connected by corridors leading to a common circular core of elevators, staircases and lavatories. The whole mass was thus oriented outward, so that the walled inner court, more nearly typical of American skyscrapers, was avoided. A steel skeleton with cantilevered floor slabs was sheathed completely in glass. On each side of the triangular site two sides of the prismatic masses were adjacent, separated by deep vertical notches and subdivided by shallower ones into two more flat surfaces that were bent slightly inward toward each other. "The plan," Berg complained, "corresponds not at all with the image of a building of manifold function. Only if it were meant as a warehouse would there be some excuse for the great depth of the

61. Ada with the children, Marianne (seated), Waltraut, and Dorothea (right), Montana, Switzerland, 1924

63. Plan of the Friedrichstrasse
Office Building

rooms and the exceptional amount of light that would surely come through such large expanses of glass."[25]

Again Berg was correct, though he evidently did not or could not recognize why Mies had done what he did. Suspecting reasonably enough that national economics would prevent his design from being built even if it had won first prize in the competition, Mies offered it more as a manifesto than as a practical piece of architecture. It was meant to be all of and no more than what Berg had called it: "an

enriching effort *to master the fundamental problem* of a tall building" (italics mine). As early, then, as his first major postwar project, Mies sought to reduce a building problem to what he regarded as its morphological essentials and to endow its solution with universal applicability and significance. There is no characteristic more fundamental to all of Mies's later endeavors than that achieved in his first modernist work.

No less remarkable, and again indicative of the deliberateness of thought that must have filled his two and one half years of willful inactivity following the war, were the visual impressiveness of Honeycomb and its fidelity to Mies's theoretical purposes. The abstractness of its form lent it an unexampled monumentality. Steep as a cliff, its volumetric variations occurring in plan rather than in elevation, it rose with a radically simplified upward thrust that had no precedent in tall buildings except in the works of Louis Sullivan and his colleagues of the early Chicago school. Even these it surpassed in its reductivist mass, since all hint of the perforations in traditional window framing—not to mention Sullivan's tripartite division of the elevation— was submerged in the vast smooth reticulated uniformity of its glass surfaces. At the same time Mies's use of glass not only insured the building's simplicity of form but took maximum advantage of that very

Europe out of the Ashes

material, which gained in reflectivity through an elegant and lively juxtaposition of acute and obtuse angles on the surfaces of the facade and razor sharp corners on the three towers.

The angularity of the Friedrichstrasse Office Building and the exuberance with which Mies exploited the potential of glass suggest the influence of expressionism and crystal-worship. While there seems no denying that he was at least somewhat open to the light from both sources, and while he wrote about Honeycomb in the summer issue of *Frühlicht*, a magazine published by Bruno Taut, he sounded like something other than an expressionist:

> Only in the course of their construction do skyscrapers show their bold, structural character, and then the impression made by their soaring skeletal frames is overwhelming. On the other hand, when the facades are later covered with masonry this impression is destroyed and the constructive character denied, along with the very principle fundamental to artistic conceptualization. These factors become overpowered by a senseless and trivial chaos of forms. The best that can be said for such buildings is that they have great size; yet they should be more than a manifestation of our technical ability. Above all we must try not to solve new problems with traditional forms; it is far better to derive new forms from the essence, the very nature of the new problem. The structural principle of these buildings becomes clear when one uses glass to cover nonloadbearing walls. The use of glass forces us to new ways.[26]

Mies's antiexpressionist bias seems implicit in his rejection of "a senseless and trivial chaos of forms," suggesting that whatever influence he felt from that movement was largely unconscious. What he was consciously after was a rational method, and insofar as he called for the derivation of the building from its "nature," he set his theoretical course for the duration of his life. Still, however much he emphasized "structural character" and rationalized his use of glass—which "forces us to new ways"—he was evidently so taken with that material for itself that in drawing the perspectives and plans of Honeycomb he featured the shimmering expanse of wall at the expense of any instructive demonstration of the building's structure.

Much the same characterization fits the project which rapidly followed it, an equally untraditional tall building known in the literature as the Glass Skyscraper—partly to distinguish it from the competition entry of which it is a companion piece, partly because it was an even more dramatic image of soaring transparency, a veritable apotheosis of glass.

No client, specific function, or actual site has been established for the Glass Skyscraper, leading us to presume that Mies, having already produced one project indifferent to the Friedrichstrasse rules, now designed another, an even bolder abstraction, primarily to learn for himself how far and how freely he could carry the idea of a glass-sheathed tower.

And a tower it is: at thirty stories, half again as high as Honeycomb and perceptibly slenderer, it is meant to stand on an irregular five-sided block located near the convergence of two broad avenues. There Mies laid out a remarkably free-form plan consisting of three curvilinear shapes, each scalloped by lobes of unequal size. The plan looks like a pool of spilled milk, save for the end of one of the shapes, which resolves itself into a straight line and a pointed corner. The three shapes are separated from each other by deep clefts, in two of which nestle entries that lead to a large foyer, again brazenly irregular in plan, plus two circular elevator-staircase-lavatory cores (as compared with one in the Friedrichstrasse design) and quarters for a custodian. The plan deals with function no more specifically than that; all floors are inferentially identical, although one curious drawing of a floor plan, which shows three entries leading to a circular foyer girded by elevators, indicates the location of the columns of the frame.

This last is a most unconvincing effort, in which a geometric system of piers is forced to take root in an amoeboid plan. The geometry itself collapses into irregularity and all trace of rational order is lost. The sketch seems nothing but a casual postulation, lending further weight to the presumption that Mies at this point in his career was less interested in working out structure than in declaring the theoretical importance of it. Moreover, the beauty of the model he constructed of the building depends on features that would have made the final work virtually impossible to build. The floor slabs are implausibly thin and there is no indication of a solution to the problem of ventilation. (Air conditioning systems in 1921 would hardly have been equal to the assignment.) In the Glass Skyscraper Mies was preoccupied less with structure than with form.

Specifically he was fascinated by the strictly aesthetic possibilities of glass. Throughout his life he would always be prepared to qualify his fundamental commitment to rationality, his admiration for technology, his abiding faith in philosophy, with a simple yet powerful passion for materials—a sensibility we must trace to his years in a stonemason's yard. In his *Frühlicht* article he devoted almost all of his further remarks to the effect that glass made upon the exterior: "My efforts with an actual glass model helped me to recognize that the most important thing about using glass is not the effects of light and shadow, but of the rich play of reflection." He then added, however, as if once more to downplay any connection with expressionism: "A superficial examination might suggest that the curved outline of the plan is arbitrary. This was determined, however, by a concern for the illumination of the interior, for the massing of the building as viewed from the street and for the play of reflections. The only fixed points of the plan are adjusted to the needs of the building and designed to be carried out in glass."

One feels no need to take issue with these remarks; on the other hand, the rhapsodic license of Mies's plan suggests that he gave quite free rein to subjective motives. The foyer, not to mention the contour of the whole exterior, is very nearly as informal in plan as the fantastic expressionist sketches Hermann Finsterlin executed in 1919–20. Further, the effect of the amoeboid sculpture of Hans Arp—who was part of the Richter circle in 1921/22—has been frequently noted, though it is likelier that Mies was affected more than even in Honeycomb by

64. Model of the Glass
Skyscraper project, Berlin, 1922

the company he kept with Hugo Häring. Häring's own project for the Friedrichstrasse competition, which was probably worked out simultaneously with Mies's, is notable for fat, rolling exterior curves that readily bring the undulating volumes of Mies's second project to mind. Häring was a believer in organic form in architecture, a generalization hardly applicable to Mies over the years, yet there is nothing in the latter's catalog that comes closer to biomorphism than the plan of the Glass Skyscraper.

65. Plan of the Glass
Skyscraper

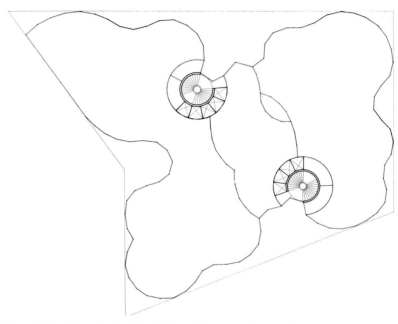

66. Preliminary sketch of the plan for the Glass Skyscraper Collection, Mies van der Rohe Archive, the Museum of Modern Art, New York. Gift of Ludwig Mies van der Rohe

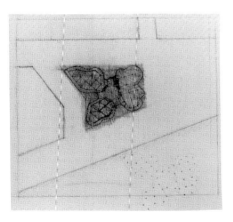

If by 1922 Mies had allied himself with the modernist movement, at least in his theoretical endeavors, he was still working to secure his own channel within it. Even so, this did not prevent him from designing brilliantly in the process. His Glass Skyscraper is at once more daring and discreet than Häring's Friedrichstrasse project, and especially compelling for the disciplined manner in which the rich outward proliferation of the massing is united with the severely regular upward sweep of the whole structure. For sheer rarefaction it goes beyond even Honeycomb. Indeed it is doubtful that either project could have been built, or, if built, would have achieved the diaphanous quality Mies drew into them. As a pair, they remain superb paper concepts, as close to platonic form as any architectural efforts of the twentieth century. Mies was very likely reading Plato at the time he did them,[27] which leads us to conjecture that glass, if it had great meaning to him as a material, was paradoxically no less important for its dematerializing qualities. We are reminded again of the crucial relationship which Mies, the older he grew, saw between material fact and immaterial spirit, between the thing and its essence.[28]

With the resumption of active work in design, Mies broadened the scope of his social activity. He cultivated friendships within the Berlin dada circle, notably with Hannah Höch, Raoul Hausmann, and Kurt Schwitters. He joined the Novembergruppe, though his reasons appear to have been primarily artistic, since much of that organization's original political motivation had been lost by 1922 and it functioned chiefly as an exhibition agency.[29] It was in the Novembergruppe section of the Great Berlin Art Exhibit of 1922 that the Glass Skyscraper was first displayed. Shortly thereafter, Mies was appointed director of the architectural department of all Novembergruppe exhibitions.

His own presentation pieces were huge—one of his later Novembergruppe drawings (see fig. 67) measures more than nine feet—not least because the structures they depicted were usually meant to be exhibited rather than built. Paper architecture was still the rule of the day, the economy being what it was; thus architects had only other architects, and other artists, to talk to. Like Dornröschen, the clients slept.

In this atmosphere Mies found it appropriate to assume a professional name. Exactly when he began to call himself Ludwig Mies van der Rohe is not certain, though typically, he never troubled himself to make the change legal or otherwise official. The presumption is that he decided on the pseudonym in 1921, the year of his marital separation and his entry into the Friedrichstrasse competition. (Charles Jeanneret's decision to become Le Corbusier was made the previous year.) The first appearance of "Mies van der Rohe" in print seems to have been the aforementioned review of Honeycomb by Max Berg in *Die Bauwelt* of May 1922.

Thus Mies joined his father's name to his mother's maiden name by the artificial linkage "van der." Coming from Aachen, he had long admired things Dutch, and Holland's popular reputation for orderly living and sober good sense sat well with Germans of the Weimar years. He would not have dared to assume a designation of real German nobility, like "von," but "van der" was permissible; it sounded faintly elegant to the German ear though it was common enough to the Dutch. In a further effort to muffle the disagreeable connotation of *Mies*, he took to printing an umlaut over the *e:* Miës, to be pronounced *myess*, monosyllabically. He persisted with this strained invention until the 1930s, though with increasing desultoriness. It never quite worked. Most people continued to address him as Herr Mies, or Herr Mies van der Rohe, or, if they were personally close, simply as Mies. "Ludwig" and its variants, including "Louis," became vestigial for all but family and a few childhood and prewar friends.

Meanwhile throughout Europe, as building activity languished in the postwar slump, theoretical exertions redoubled themselves, providing a major outlet for pent-up creative energies. Arriving in Berlin late in 1921, the Russian novelist Ilya Ehrenburg joined forces with his countryman, the ubiquitous El Lissitzky, to publish the periodical *Veshch*, which would "acquaint creative workers in Russia with the latest Western art [and] inform Western Europe about Russian art and literature." It would stand for "constructive art, whose task," in Lissitzky's words, "is not to decorate our life but to organize it." Similar sentiments issued from the Hungarian journal *MA* in the words of László

Moholy-Nagy, himself now also in Berlin: "Constructivism is pure substance. It is not confined to the picture frame and pedestal. It expands into industry and architecture, into objects and relationships. Constructivism is the socialism of wisdom."[30]

In Paris the new direction toward an architecture of sobriety expressed in rectilinear abstract form was discernible not only in the pages of *L'Esprit nouveau* but in Le Corbusier's epochal book *Vers une architecture*. Published in 1923, it quickly established itself as the most significant summary statement of the modernist position to appear anywhere since the war. With the momentum swinging to the constructivist/*Sachlichkeit* view across the Continent, the restless van Doesburg now carried the battle to the Bauhaus in Weimar. Uninvited by Gropius and less than welcome in the official sight of the school, van Doesburg presented a series of off-campus lectures in 1921 and again in 1922, each time inveighing against the crafts-expressionist emphasis which—witness Gropius's original manifesto—had dominated the thinking of the school since its opening in 1919 and inspired the teaching of its most influential faculty member, Johannes Itten.

With the momentum of the times on van Doesburg's side, change would probably have overtaken Weimar whether he had been there or not. By the end of 1923 Itten was gone, replaced by Moholy-Nagy, who became the chief faculty promoter of the constructivist ideals that guided the school through most of the remainder of the decade. Gropius in fact had begun his own personal retreat from expressionism even before Moholy arrived, as is evident from the constructivist design he and Adolf Meyer submitted to the 1922 Chicago Tribune Tower competition. Bruno Taut's magic dreams began to evaporate as his appointment to the directorship of municipal building in Magdeburg forced him closer to practical solutions and a position of *Sachlichkeit*. Within a few years he would be talking affirmatively of the relationship of architecture to the machine and industrial production.

And Mies himself, never one for debates, found himself at last obliged to enter into the polemical fray. Ideology was the order of the day; there was no other route to acceptance in the world with which he had allied himself. Over the next decade he would see to it that his thoughts found their way continuously into print.

According to Richter, the magazine *G* was conceived as early as 1920, when van Doesburg, on his first visit to Berlin, urged Richter and Eggeling to put together a journal of opinion on the arts.[31] "Beginning 1922," Richter wrote,

> we had finally enough material for two numbers. But that moment the money was already gone and besides that, Eggeling and I had separated; and only towards the end of 1922 I got [a] small amount of money which allowed me at least to start . . .
>
> The title "G" was given 1922 by Lissitzky as an abbreviation of G-estaltung [roughly "formation," "forming," or "creative organization"], for which he became member of the editing staff. To honour Doesburg's co-foundership we put a square behind the letter G [G□].[32]

The first issue of *G*, which appeared in July 1923 under the editorship of Richter, Lissitzky, and the disaffected young ex-Bauhaus student Werner Graeff, announced its hostility toward romance and subjectivity in art in terms as harsh as any thus far heard in Europe. Closer in sense to Lissitzky's constructivism than to van Doesburg's de Stijl, the statements on the cover page sounded uncompromisingly materialist and impatient of any sort of individualized aesthetics, though they were expressed in the exalted and abstract terms of a cafe manifesto:

> The basic demand of creative organization [*Gestaltung*] is economy. Pure relationship of power and material. This depends on fundamental [*elementare*] means and a total command of means. Fundamental [*elementare*] order. Regularity.
> We have no need for the sort of beauty that attaches itself like tinsel to our very being; rather we need [to realize] the internal order of our being.

The authors of these words, which define ends more exactly than means, are listed as Richter and Graeff. Mies contributed a statement to the same issue. In context it was consistent with the views he expressed in *Frühlicht*, but now he wasted no time in argument. His manner was brusque and confrontational:

> We reject all aesthetic speculation, all doctrine, all formalism . . .
> Create form out of the nature of our tasks, with the methods of our time.
> This is our task.

He was no less challenging in the second issue of *G*, published later in 1923:

> We refuse to recognize problems of form, but only problems of building.
> Form is not the aim of our work, but only the result.
> Form, by itself, does not exist.
> Form as an aim is formalism, and that we reject . . .
> Essentially our task is to free the practice of building from the control of aesthetic speculators and restore it to what it should exclusively be: Building.

G appeared in three more issues, and Mies went so far in his commitment to its hard line that he personally financed the magazine's third issue in 1924, evidently at considerable cost, since it included the assembly of a full sans serif type font which, in Graeff's words, "was 'elemental,' for it alone reveals clearly that it is constructed, whereas the customary printing types, even though constructed, imitate the character of handwriting."[33]

Mies designed one major work, the Concrete Office Building, sometime between late 1922 and early 1923, the period during which the first issue of *G* was being prepared. Among the famous five projects of 1921–24, it is the most neutral in character, the least hospitable to subjective nuance, the closest to the *sachlich* tone of the writing

67. Perspective of the Concrete
Office Building, 1923

in G. It was a right-angled, flat-roofed office block in reinforced concrete, eight stories high (including a sunken ground floor) and of considerable though, judging from the drawing, indeterminate length, thus
horizontal in effect. The floor slabs, cantilevered outward from a grid
system of beams supported by tapered posts, turn upward at their
outer edges to form continuous parapet walls. These walls are thick
and high enough to accommodate cabinets, an arrangement which frees
much of the interior floor spaces, while the windows, continuous bands
of glass recessed behind the broad parapets, alternate with the walls
in a vigorous play of light and shadow which animates the facade and
underscores the fact that the walls bear none of the structural load.
Entry to the building is gained by an interruption of the first parapet,
through which a stately flight of steps leads to the landing of the first
floor. Seldom noted in previous discussions is the fact that each story
extends ever so slightly beyond the one below it. The resultant overall
mass is a subtly inverted trapezoidal prism.

Like the Glass Skyscraper, the Concrete Office Building appears
to have been a visionary production. All we know of it derives from
the spectacular nine-foot drawing displayed at the Great Berlin Art
Exhibition of 1923, and from a statement published over Mies's byline
in the second issue of G, dated September 1923, and written in the
gruff, matter-of-fact G style:

> The office is a building   of work   of organization
> of clarity   of economy.
> Bright open work spaces, distinct and unbroken, articulated
> like the business organism itself. Maximum effect with a
> minimum of means.
> The materials are   Concrete   Steel   Glass.
> Reinforced concrete buildings are by nature skeletal

constructions. No macaroni [*Teigwaren*], no armored towers. With columns and girders, no loadbearing walls. That is to say, skin and bones building.

Mies proceeds to discuss layout, measurements, and other specifics of the Concrete Office Building, leaving further interpretations to us. His one overtly editorial remark—a curt dismissal of "macaroni" and "armored towers"—is aimed, respectively, at historical ornamentation and expressionist spikery. Positive motivation, on the other hand, is limited to the recognizably constructivist ends of producing the most reductively functional type of modern urban office building possible, a rational construction devoid of all blandishments, any quirks of subjectivity.

Yet if it is demonstrably an exercise in functionalist engineering, it is no less a piece of considered architecture whose subtle refinements elevate it to a level significantly above mere parts assembly. There is as much art to it as cold fact, and even more history than a doctrinaire and unqualified functionalist would have been content with.

Mies's way with both outer wall and entry illustrates this. By recessing the fenestration behind the parapets he created a bold three-dimensional rhythm on the facade and avoided the papery planar monotony to which the ribbon window has all too often led in subsequent uses. By opening the lowermost parapet and guiding a wide staircase up and into the resulting space with its four very visible piers, he arrived at a direct and uncomplicated solution to the entry problem while at the same time dramatizing the experience of approaching the building. The powerful concrete columns are unmistakably modern elements, but the staircase ascends to the first floor with the gravity and pronounced axiality of Schinkel's work at its best. In the Concrete Office Building, then, Mies's *Sachlichkeit* was not without overtones of the classical temper, however freely he expressed it in the language of modern abstraction. Indeed he told an interviewer on a later occasion that his design for it was "a little inspired by the Palazzo Pitti, for I wanted to see if we could make something of a similar strength with our means and our purposes."[34]

A further backward glance brings Berlage's Amsterdam Stock Exchange to mind, with its vast interior that Mies remembered and so admired, and yet another previous work, which impressed Berlage himself and must thus have become known to Mies: the 1904 Larkin Building in Buffalo, by Frank Lloyd Wright, which not only showed a wide, deep, high inner office space but offered the precedent of storage cases tucked in the outer walls.

Mies deviated from the example of both these earlier edifices by opening up the exterior of the Concrete Office Building and indicating its structural system far more explicitly than he had in the 1921/22 skyscrapers. Since the days of Berlage and the young Wright, glass had gained the potential of a major building material, and Mies's commitment to it, first evident in the dramatic effects he evoked in the skyscrapers, is in no way diminished by the neutral temper it took on within the rectilinear generality of the Concrete Office Building.

The inner space also recalls the past, while pointing as well to the

68. Frank Lloyd Wright,
general office interior of the
Larkin Administration Building,
Buffalo, 1904
Photo courtesy of the Museum
of Modern Art, New York

future. Even if Mies never read the letter Peter Behrens wrote to a Berlin newspaper in 1912, he would have been familiar with its author's sentiments.

Responding to the *Berliner Morgenpost*'s invitation to comment on the quality of commercial building during those years of the city's wildfire growth, Behrens began by lamenting a widespread weakness for "romantic ostentation." Then he called upon architects to "regard the office building as an artistic challenge" and, when designing one, to provide "maximum entry of light into the interior spaces, adaptability to future changes in their sizes, unobstructed communication among, and full use of, all floor areas."[35] There is no simpler and likely no earlier affirmation of the assets of "universal space," a concept Mies later—after emigrating to the U.S. in the 1930s—developed into one of the central objectives of his architecture. The design of the Concrete Office Building, added to what Max Berg had noted in Honeycomb as "the great depth of the rooms and the exceptional amount of light that would surely come through such huge expanses of glass," suggests that Mies was consciously treating space as a generalized element in his architecture as early as the early 1920s. Thus he often argued with Hugo Häring, who labored earnestly over the solution of the most specific needs in his buildings. "Make your spaces big enough, man," Mies would urge Häring, "that you can walk around in them freely, and not just in one predetermined direction! Or are you all that sure of how they will be used? We don't know at all whether people will do with them what we expect them to. Functions are not so clear or so constant; they change faster than the building."[36]

At roughly the same time Mies designed the Concrete Office Building, he returned to a genre which until 1921 had occupied his creative attentions almost exclusively: the private residence. The last two of his aforementioned five projects of the early 1920s were country houses, one in concrete, the other in brick. Each proved as important as his three preceding large commercial structures both in originality—with implications for the future—and in intrinsic quality.

It has been observed that among all forms of European and American architecture since the Industrial Revolution, the villa has had the most powerful influence on the general theory of architecture.[37] While the nineteenth and twentieth centuries have required a far greater variety of building forms and functions than previous ages did, nearly all the most brilliant architectural talents of modern times have addressed themselves seriously to the question of the house, especially the kind a wealthy bourgeois might put up for himself in a comfortably countrified setting. Some of the building art's most innovative concepts and forms have emerged from residential designs; in this century it is enough to recall the inventions of Wright, Le Corbusier, *and* Mies, as the last of these proved never more emphatically than in his two great villa projects of the early Weimar years. Again, just as we learned from the Friedrichstrasse Office Building and the Glass Skyscraper, these country houses suggest that Mies in 1923 and 1924, despite his famous *Frühlicht* statement—not to mention his subsequent American reputation—was not inclined, or perhaps not yet in a position, to pursue the matter of structure which he seemed to hold in such high

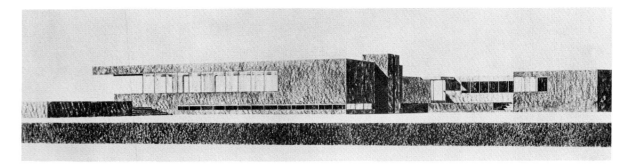

69. Perspective of the Concrete Country House, 1923

theoretical esteem. Instead, the surpassing contribution of the two houses in question was a revolutionary approach to space.

Of the Concrete Country House, which dates probably from the early months of 1923, no floor plans are known to exist. There are several perspective drawings, all rendered from the same vantage point. Two photographs of a now lost model leave a whole side—insofar as we can speak of a side of this multibranched house—almost totally undisclosed.

Still fewer documents survive from the Brick Country House, which Mies appears to have designed either late in 1923 or early in 1924. One perspective drawing and the plan of the ground floor are extant—in photographs only. There is no trace of the arrangement of the upper story.[38]

In the same Great Berlin Art Exhibition of 1923 that included Mies's drawing for the Concrete Country House, El Lissitzky showed an environmental piece called *Proun Space:* a three-walled room, around whose vertical surfaces was spread an integrated composition of painted and raised geometric elements.[39] Despite obvious differences in media, the two productions bore several important formal similarities. Both were based on the play of large rectilinear units with subordinate geometric component forms passing by or anchored in them. Most of Lissitzky's painted forms were planar while Mies's prisms were three-dimensional, yet the works they comprised intruded searchingly into ambient space. Instead of the compact form of the traditional house,

70. Model of the Concrete Country House from the street side

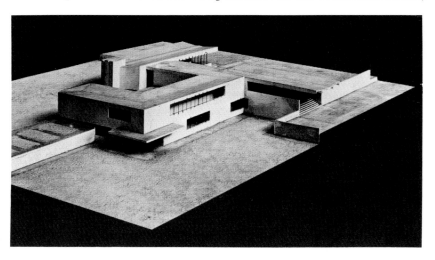

71. Model of the Concrete Country House from the garden side

Mies's villa spread asymmetrically from a central core into three hooked, flat-roofed prismatic masses, presumed to contain living room, dining room-entry, and bedroom-service wing. Lissitzky's composition, whose bright colors reflected the influence of de Stijl, literally surrounded the viewer, so that the whole could be apprehended only in the act of moving around within it. The Mies house could also be taken in only from a variety of vantage points. If Cubism had destroyed the authority of the vanishing point, the works of Lissitzky and Mies in their own ways advanced the idea of a free space without a center or a single favored perspective, thus without hierarchical order. No less evident, especially in the pinwheel composition of the Concrete Country House, were lessons learned from Frank Lloyd Wright's habit of extending wings outward from the central core of his prairie houses. Mies's building penetrated space as space passed among its asymmetrical masses, creating a play of solid and void in which neither was quite free of the other.

Is there reason to suppose that he was consciously striving for an architectural design that expressed such a fluidly dynamic, characteristically modern relationship between man and the world? His own remarks do little to encourage any such presumption. True to the doggedly functionalist implications of his writings of 1923, he restricts himself to practical considerations:

> The chief advantage in the use of reinforced concrete as I see it is the opportunity to save a great amount of material. In order to realize this in a dwelling it is necessary to concentrate the bearing and supporting forces on only a few points in the structure. The disadvantage of reinforced concrete is its inefficiency as an insulator and its being a great conductor of sound. Therefore it is necessary to provide special insulation as a

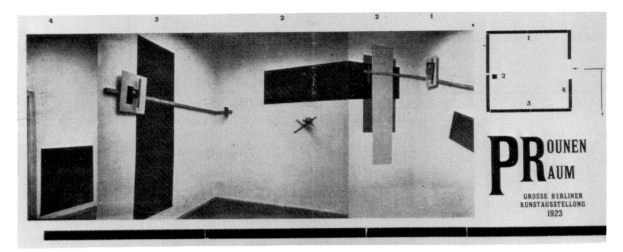

72. El Lissitzky, *Proun Space*, 1923
Stedelijk Van Abbemuseum, Eindhoven

barrier against outside temperatures. The simplest method of dealing with nuisance of sound conduction seems to me to be the elimination of everything that generates noise; I am thinking more of rubberized flooring, sliding windows and doors, and other similar precautions, but then, too, of spaciousness in the ground-floor layout.[40]

To these practical considerations Mies added nothing about expressive significance. Yet there is no contradiction between his stated attempts to solve technical problems and any unstated efforts at articulating a uniquely modern spatial relationship between the built and the natural environments. Since the Concrete Country House was carried on point supports, its windows could be made large and placed where the architect wanted them, thus affording fullest views of the outdoors and freest access to outdoor light. Visual passage to exterior space was thus unburdened, while the interior itself took on comparable spatial freedom and fluidity. The open plan, one of modern architecture's proudest achievements, clearly exists in germinal form in the Concrete Country House.

Were these various effects nothing more than by-products of technique? "Is it not rather," writes Wolf Tegethoff, "that changing personal and artistic needs require the exploitation of existing materials and methods and the application of new ones?"[41]

Certainly there was less in the new technology of reinforced concrete and more of Mies's own subjectively expressive intent to account for the pinwheel thrust of the three wings of the house into space. Compared with the relatively closed volumes employed by such advanced architects as Le Corbusier, Mendelsohn, and Gropius as late as 1923, Mies's villa is without architectural precedent in Europe. Even the sliding planes of the most famous de Stijl house design of the period, Gerrit Rietveld's 1923 Schroeder House in Utrecht, do not search out space so aggressively. With the Concrete Country House, the modern house becomes more filter than fortress, with the best of the outdoors invited inside, the worst locked out. One senses a prefiguration of the German devotion of the 1920s and early 1930s to hygiene and sport, a disposition whose architectural resonance took the form of picture windows, which promised sunshine, fresh air, and good health while assuring fluid passage between inner and outer environments.

If radical in these respects, the Concrete Country House again illustrates Mies's debt to history. Like the Kröller-Müller villa, whose comfortably horizontal profile it seems to have transformed into the modernist idiom, it looks back to Schinkel in another way: in the nineteenth-century master's romantic-classical attempt to bring man into concert with nature. The interplay of the Concrete Country House with the green space around it is more than a little romantic in its own right.

Was Mies's client here none other than himself? It is hard to imagine, even with his relative financial security, that he would undertake so patently costly a commission during the hard times of 1923. On the other hand, if we remember how diligently he sought to relate the 1914 project for his own house in Werder to its natural environment, and if we keep in mind an incorrigible habit of living beyond his means, it is indeed conceivable that he had the villa in mind for himself. Mixed in with all the letters of 1923–24 in which he advertised himself to potential clients is correspondence that indicates he was trying to purchase land in the high-priced environs of Potsdam-Neubabelsberg, for the purpose of building a house for himself.[42]

Last of the famous five projects, the Brick Country House was both a catalog of the influences that turned Mies into a modernist during the early 1920s, and a prefiguration of several of his own most important spatial and organizational concepts. By the time he finished it, either shortly before or shortly after the end of 1923, he was utilizing what he learned earlier—but apparently did not act upon—from Berlage and Wright. Had the villa been realized, it would have been constructed in brick, a material out of favor among the machine aestheticians of the time, but one which Mies felt comfortable with when he was still an apprentice in Aachen and admired all the more deeply when he saw what Berlage did with it in the Amsterdam Stock Exchange. Now Mies was sufficiently confident of himself to use it in a palpably modern design. He was no less prepared to carry Wright's treatment of space beyond the limits the American had set on it, and he did so with what appears to be the help of models taken from van Doesburg. The result of all this, seen from the outside, was an asymmetrical grouping of rectangular prismatic masses clearly indebted to the interlocking sculptures of the constructivists.

The plan of the Brick Country House is its most arresting feature. It resembles a de Stijl painting, and one of the reasons it has gained great fame since it was first exhibited in drawn form at the Great Berlin Art Exhibition of 1924 is that it is possessed of nearly as much pictorial potency as architectural meaning. Much has been alleged about its kinship with one work in particular, by van Doesburg, *Rhythm of a Russian Dance*, executed about 1918. In the painting lean, straight bars of color, all the same width, rectilinearly disposed and asymmetrically organized, activate movement not only among themselves but in the spaces that flow restlessly through and around them in labyrinthine fashion. It is easy to imagine that Mies, who was familiar with van Doesburg's work, might associate this configuration with a floor plan, the more so since the edges of the pastel areas of color, where flush with the long and short edges of the dark bars, could bring to mind glass partitions. The painting might also recall a real architectural antecedent: Wright's decellularized interior spaces, which Mies had studied as early as the 1911 Wasmuth exhibition in Berlin and to which, we presume, he was now ready creatively to respond. As early as 1889 the American master had begun his famous alteration of the plan of the traditional house by breaking down wall boundaries between rooms so that the space of one cubicle flowed unimpeded into that of another.

Around 1904 Wright left this idea pretty much at the stage to which he had brought it by then: however much his rooms flowed, rooms they remained. In the Brick Country House Mies radically advanced the Wrightian notion of an open plan. By erecting freestanding walls that neither enclosed rooms nor even suggested roomlike areas but

73. Perspective and plan of the Brick Country House, 1924

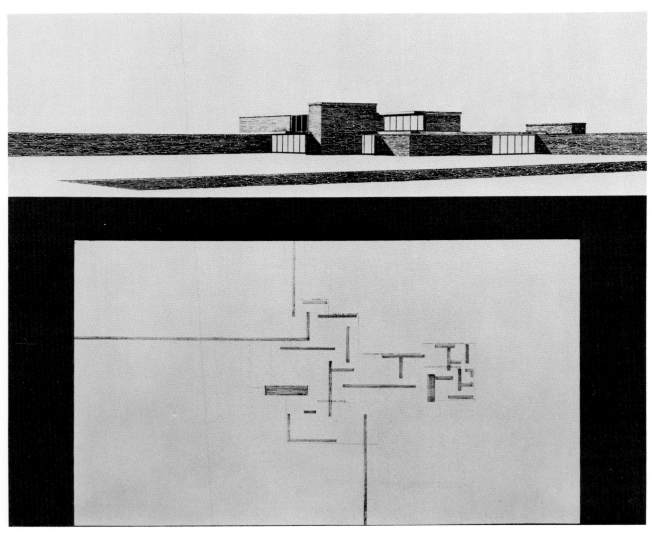

Europe out of the Ashes

74. Theo van Doesburg,
Rhythm of a Russian Dance,
1918. Oil on canvas, 135.9 ×
61.6 cm.
Collection of the Museum of
Modern Art, New York.
Acquired through the
Lillie P. Bliss Bequest

only directed movement among spaces that melted into each other, he transformed the interior into a dynamic spatial unity. He himself identified the parts of his floor plan no more specifically than "living spaces" (*Wohnräume*) and "service spaces" (*Wirtschaftsräume*). His powerful drive toward universality had produced an unprecedentedly generalized open plan.

He did more with the walls than use them to organize interior space. He extended three of them into the space surrounding the house, each in a long line that went fully off the page of the drawing, as if to imply that the architectural entity was carried to infinity. So doing, he advanced the emulsification of interior and exterior space that he had begun in the Concrete Country House. The two now interpenetrated so markedly that, if we study the plan, the house ceases to function as a traditional enclosure of space.

We get a different notion of it from the perspective drawing. Seen from outside, the house does not look like the delicate series of membranous planes the plan makes it seem. It is a grouping of cubic masses, and even where the outer brick walls are interrupted by glass walls of floor-to-ceiling height, the latter appear as opaque as the former. Seen from inside, of course, those same glass walls against bright daylight disappear, and a distinction between interior and exterior seems to dissolve. Mies thus appears to have relied on extended walls to slide from under the roof into the landscape, and on roof slabs to extend outward to become visible through the glass walls, thus to achieve a mediation in the interior between a sense of enclosure and a feeling of freedom.[43]

Walls and slabs as planar elements functioning three-dimensionally were destined to play an increasingly important role in Mies's later treatment of the relation of structure to space. Space will gradually make way for structure, as in the Barcelona Pavilion of 1929, where a grid of supporting columns balances the free flow of interior areas. In the Brick Country House, whose walls support the roof as well as define the interior space, a subjectively organized movement is still virtually unimpeded. The earlier project, then, is a transitional work as well as a revolutionary one. Moreover, it looks back in time as well as ahead. The case has been made that it is a simplified reconstitution of the Concrete Country House, with its "living spaces" and "service spaces" developing respectively out of the living, dining, and entry wing and the bedroom-service wing of the latter. Together with the Concrete Country House it also recalls Spengler again, particularly his contrast of the Apollinian concept of space—finite, bounded, localized—and the Faustian—searching, conscious of distant perspectives, and forever reaching out to act within them. In Mies's copy of *The Decline of the West*, he underlined this sentence: "In analogizing the horizon with the future, our age identifies itself with the 'third dimension' of experienced space."[44]

The swift pace of events in the early 1920s in Germany may be measured by Mies's personal relationships as well as by changes in his work and outlook. These were years of polemics and politics, egos and ideals, a period of individuals and groups seeking attention, jockeying for position, colliding, and conspiring. From among the *G* group van Doesburg emerged as Mies's closest comrade in thought—for a time.[45] Never quite comfortable in his relationship with his former colleague, the suavely aristocratic Gropius, Mies sided with van Doesburg when the latter attacked the Bauhaus. Mies perceived Gropius—and rationalized the perception, for he was not a little jealous—as a weather vane rather than as a man of conviction. Mies remained unimpressed when Gropius shifted from an expressionist to a constructivist position in 1922/23. The post-Itten reform at Weimar, Mies wrote van Doesburg, had led not to an "authentically constructive" approach to design but to an arty formalism, a "juggling of constructivistic [in the sense of pseudo-constructivist] form."[46]

Yet during the very time Mies was criticizing Gropius to van Doesburg, he was carrying on an altogether cordial correspondence with the director of the Bauhaus. Gropius, who had declined to accept Mies's Kröller-Müller project for an exhibition in 1919, now asked him to participate in a show at the Bauhaus—a review of the best of the new European architecture. Mies promptly consented and sent several postwar pieces.[47]

Ambivalence marked Mies's relationship with van Doesburg himself. In the March 1923 issue of *De Stijl*—published during the high tide of *G*, of which van Doesburg was one of the founders—he referred to painting as "the most advanced form of art," which "indicates the path leading toward modern architecture."[48] This was probably meant as a critical reproach to the antiaesthetic ideology of *G*. Surely Mies, in his longstanding indifference to painting, could hardly have found much to like in van Doesburg's elevation of aesthetics above constructive logic. Indeed, Mies's statement in *G* of May 1923, "We reject all aesthetic speculation, all doctrine, all formalism," was intended as a rebuttal to van Doesburg.[49]

Yet two months later, van Doesburg invited Mies to show his work in a fall exhibition at Leonce Rosenberg's L'Effort moderne gallery in Paris, and Mies eagerly accepted. A still further sign of the mixed allegiances of the day was the curious composition of that show. It was devoted to the architecture of de Stijl, though Mies alone among the exhibitors was not a member of the movement. And van Doesburg specifically encouraged him to submit a model of the Glass Skyscraper, a work more illustrative of expressionist form than of the principles of de Stijl.

Lissitzky left Berlin in 1923 to recuperate from tuberculosis in Locarno. Before long Mies began to soften the edges of the constructivist materialism which had been the driving force of *G*. More and more as the 1920s progressed he was content to seek his ideological way on the pages of the philosophy books in his own growing library. By 1924 he was finished with professional tutelage.

The time was appropriate. During 1924 and 1925 the Weimar Republic enjoyed a hopeful reversal of political and economic fortunes. Late in 1923 the French occupation of the Ruhr, begun when Germany was held in default of her war reparations payments, ended after Chancellor Gustav Stresemann agreed to put a stop to his countrymen's passive resistance to the French forces. Violent efforts at revolution from the German right and left alike, brought on by prolonged internal socioeconomic miseries, were crushed, with the result that the central government in Berlin emerged stronger than before. Early in 1924 the Dawes Plan went into effect, whereby Germany secured a large loan from her former enemies for the purpose of paying them reparations. The murderous spiral of inflation tailed off. In the wake of these developments the nation began an upward swing toward a prosperity and stability it had not known since the Hohenzollern days.

The effect on architecture was immediate, since that art stood to gain more than its sister disciplines from subsidization programs enacted by national, provincial, and municipal governments. At long last modern building became buildable, on a scale, moreover, destined to be augmented over the next four years. An acute housing shortage, combined with the activated patronage of a progressive socialist government, made for a set of circumstances in which the vision of the New Architecture could realistically hope to be brought to collective physical fact.

Unsurprisingly, as the opportunity to advance the modernist cause arose, so did resistance to it, in the form of conservative agencies and individuals opposed to so substantial a change in traditional German architecture. Mies responded by throwing himself into the ensuing debate. Now fully committed to the modernist position, he became one of its most vigorous and tireless spokesmen.[50] He lectured, argued, and corresponded, organized and participated in exhibitions, promoted and juried competitions. Having earlier shied from joining progressive organizations, he now entered their councils with a will. Following the 1923 shows at L'Effort moderne in Paris and the Bauhaus in Weimar, he was included in displays in Jena, Gera, Mannheim, Düsseldorf, and Wiesbaden, even in Poland, Italy, and Russia—only, however, when the exhibitions specifically promoted the cause of the New Architecture. He further restricted his entries to the major recent projects: the Glass Skyscraper, the Concrete Office Building, the Concrete Country House, and now and then the Brick Country House. He welcomed publication of these works as well, though he preferred them to appear in avant-garde journals: *Die Baugilde* and *Die Form*, organs, respectively, of the Bund deutscher Architekten and the Deutscher Werkbund, plus *Querschnitt*, *Qualität*, and *Merz* in Germany, *L'Esprit nouveau* in France. More and more he consorted with practicing architects, less with theoreticians. A member of the Bund deutscher Architekten since the summer of 1923, he shortly joined with the younger vanguardists of that organization to form a subdivision called the Ring, which proved to be one of the most activist groups in behalf of the New Architecture in Berlin during the remainder of the 1920s.

Only nine men made up the Ring at first, which called itself later and variously the Zwölferring and the Zehnerring, depending on the number of its members at any given time. It was founded on 14 April 1924, just a fortnight after 72-year-old Ludwig Hoffmann stepped down as Berlin's building commissioner. Hoffmann's retirement, as the younger architects saw it, had occurred at a critical moment. The position was central to city planning in general and to the approval of individual building commissions in particular. A veteran architect whose roots reached down to Wilhelmine soil, Hoffmann was conservative by 1920s standards and the younger architects despised him. Sensing that his departure, coincident with the promising new economic conditions, added up to an opportunity to reshape municipal architectural policy, the Ring promptly issued a statement to the press which included four demands for reforms in the commissioner's office: greater creative freedom for individual architects, elimination of political favoritism in the judging of new designs, quicker approval of projects, better-qualified judges and competition jurors.[51]

A noisy and prolonged conflict followed in which the conservatives of the Bund deutscher Architekten (BdA) sought to dissociate themselves from the Ring, and vice versa. Months passed without a replacement for Hoffmann. Mies, whose atelier had served as a regular meeting place for the Ring and who was one of the most forceful proponents of the vanguard position, finally resigned from the BdA in January 1926. Within weeks the Ring was initiating efforts to form a nationwide organization of progressive architects, an objective reached at last in November, at just about the same time Martin Wagner, a founding member of the Ring and a confirmed progressive, was appointed building commissioner of Berlin.

The modernist cause thus leaped still further ahead, as it had in other ways throughout Germany in the months following the stabilization of the economy. Cooperative, limited-profit building societies in several major German cities, subsidized largely by state loans, began to produce sorely needed housing projects on a huge scale, in the process providing many progressive architects with important commissions. More often than not, these were designed in the functionalist-geometric manner that was gradually becoming the hallmark of the New Architecture. Individual names—Ernst May, Bruno Taut, Walter Gropius, Erich Mendelsohn, not to mention Mies—drew increased public attention even as they excited a proportional amount of hostility from the opponents of modernism. The most advanced and controversial architecture in the world was now coming out of Germany, encouraged by the atmosphere of experimentation and radical theorizing that had risen from the very ashes of a discredited prewar tradition.

Mies's activism was not restricted to the BdA. Roughly at the time he helped form the Ring—the spring of 1924—he accepted an invitation to join the Deutscher Werkbund, reasoning that that organization was ready, as he put it, for a "transfusion of new blood."[52] Historically the Werkbund had stood above all for quality in visual design, and to that end had avoided endorsing any one movement or style. Now, however, in 1924, with the hope of an artistic revival under the leadership of architecture livelier than ever, the membership began to throw its weight behind the architects of *Sachlichkeit* with whom Mies was politically allied.

This development he himself traced largely to the efforts of the radical sculptor Paul Henning, who as a member of the Werkbund had been arguing that quality was altogether attainable through elementarist construction (*Elementare Gestaltung*): "In place of formal qual-

75. Perspective of Haus K., 1919

ity, the most important task for us is the design ideal of originality, self-evidence, and purity of construction."[53] The words, at the time, could very nearly have been Mies's own. Henning and Mies lectured to the Werkbund on elementarist-construction in mid-1924, with Mies thereafter exercising more and more personal sway over the younger members. In 1926 he was named vice-president of the Werkbund, and though he insisted that Peter Bruckmann, honored elder statesman of the Werkbund and symbol of organizational solidarity, occupy the presidency, it was clear to all that Mies at the age of forty had become the most powerful figure in the most firmly established technical society in Germany.

In later years when Mies was enjoying his greatest fame in America, he was known as the silent Mies, profound and taciturn, who expressed himself in works rather than in words. "Build, don't talk," was the charge his admiring students often attributed to him. The image is quite at odds with what we have written of his active and skillful politicking within the profession in Germany during the mid-1920s. Yet consistent with his biography, he was slow to build, more precisely, a long time in seeing his modern ideology realized in modern work. During and for several years after the period of the five projects, indeed after his historic labors at the Weissenhofsiedlung in Stuttgart in 1927, notably more of his designs were unbuilt than built. And among those that were constructed, several were so traditional in manner, so much nearer his prewar work than the five projects, that by 1925 it could be said of him that he talked substantially more modern architecture than he made.

In view of the incompleteness of his files, we are not yet sure of the nature of his first post–World War I commission. It may have been nothing more auspicious than the tombstone he designed for the grave of Hugo Perls's mother Laura, who died in 1919. An illustration in a magazine article of 1927 ascribed to Mies a flat-roofed Schinkelesque villa identified only as "Haus K."[54] It is dated 1919. This is our sole evidence of what may, or may not, have been a preliminary stage of a house for Frau Franziska Kempner, which, however, was completed as late as April 1922, from a considerably different design. The latter was submitted for the approval of the Berlin building authorities in the summer of 1921, the year Mies apparently resumed his practice in earnest. By the following November he had also conceived a residence for the industrialist Cuno Feldmann, which was finished in June 1922. Stylistically close to one another, the Kempner and Feldmann houses had a faintly Georgian look about their austere brick exteriors: each was composed of a long flat-faced, two-story mass flanked by wings and surmounted by a decidedly *un*modern steep hip roof. ("Haus K." meanwhile remains a mystery.) The Kempner House, which was built in Berlin-Charlottenburg, was demolished in 1952. The Feldmann House still stands in Berlin-Grünewald, though in much altered condition.[55] The Eichstaedt House of 1922, which survives in Berlin-Zehlendorf, is a hip-roofed, square-planned villa in stucco that bows to the local vernacular, while the last of Mies's anachronistic designs, the 1924 Mosler House in Neubabelsberg, recalls the Kempner and Feldmann features: a long rectilinear brick mass with a steep hip roof.

Mies did nothing to encourage critical attention to these traditional houses, and even today little has been written about them. They were all conservatively attractive abodes and respectably executed, though without the foreknowledge that they were designed by a master, one would probably not be inclined to give any of them much more than a second glance. Mies's tendency to incise windows cleanly into walls and his gift for proportioning them in neatly regular rows on the facade are apparent in the Kempner, Feldmann, and Mosler houses, as is the origin of such concerns in Schinkel's work. The Feldmann House appears to have been the most successfully integrated of the lot, and the Eichstaedt House, oddly for Mies, projects a downright cozy aspect. Nonetheless, pending further research, we are disposed to conclude that all of these houses, which owed more to formula than invention, were relics of a transitional period in their maker's career. Perhaps the most intriguing thing about them is that they show a side of Mies to which we are not accustomed: he was anything but serenely unidirectional in his thought processes during the early 1920s. In a solicitation to a client written in 1924, he cited the Kempner, Urbig, and Mosler houses as examples of his work by which his competence and promise might be judged. Yet in the same year he wrote the

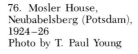

76. Mosler House,
Neubabelsberg (Potsdam),
1924–26
Photo by T. Paul Young

following in a vanguard journal: "It is hopeless to try to use the forms of the past in our architecture. Even the strongest artistic talent must fail in this attempt. Again and again we see talented architects who fall short because their work is not in tune with their age. In the last analysis, in spite of their great gifts, they are dilettantes."[56] And even as he continued to design in traditional manners for some clients in the early 1920s, he offered more modernist forms to others, including the problematical Petermann and Lessing houses of 1921 and 1923, respectively, both meant for Neubabelsberg, and the 1923 Ryder House in Wiesbaden.

Construction on the last of these was begun but never finished, because of depletion of the client's funds. No reliable explanation has come down to us for the failure of the Petermann and Lessing houses to materialize. In many instances Mies's projects came to nought because fate, pure and simple, worked against them in a variety of ways. Yet he himself, with his unhurried and often unhurriable pace, was capable of taxing a client's patience quite beyond endurance. The most notorious example of this was an assignment which Mies's office later knew as "L'Affaire Dexel."

Being a painter in his own right as well as the director of the Jena Kunstverein, where Mies had already shown his work, Walter Dexel might have been expected to deal more efficiently with Mies, though it is possible he overestimated the importance of the opportunity he had to offer. On 7 January 1925, just four days after Mies was invited to design Dexel's house, the latter was prodding him for proposals to be shown as early as a week later to Dexel's father-in-law, a partial financier of the project. "Please either keep to our agreement and come on Thursday for certain," Dexel directed Mies, "or even better plan your stay in such a way that we will have time to come to enough of an agreement right away about the exterior layout and the floor plan."

Dexel's deadlines were severe by any standards; by Mies's they were next to unthinkable. Had the house been a major rather than a modest commission, Mies, who knew the difference, might have responded more promptly, even to Dexel's brusque instructions. But Mies tarried, and when Dexel grew sarcastic ("Perhaps you will prove the rule of not writing and not coming with an exception? Everything doesn't have to be straightforward, but for once something could be!"), his case was as good as lost. Mies was a devout believer in *die schöpferische Pause,* or creative pause to reflect, as a requisite of artistic accomplishment. Doubtless he often turned this rationale of creativity into a rationalization of procrastination, and we must suspect that the Dexel matter was one such occasion. The sardonic tone of Dexel's early letters later changed to rage and finally to helplessness as Mies more often than not simply neglected to reply to him. The commission was cancelled in the spring of 1925.[57]

Mies's uncommonly long persistence with the use of traditional forms ended at mid-decade, following which his work bore a steadfastly modern stamp. He did not, however, go the way of the social functionalists, who began to dominate German architecture as the country's economic miseries abated. Only once did he venture into the realm of low-cost housing. His apartment building on the Afrikan-ischestrasse in Berlin was commissioned by the municipal authorities and built in 1926/27. Tightly compressed into a rectangular prism containing three blocks of flats, with taut skin and flush windows, it was a typical example of the leanly functional architecture of the *Existenzminimum*, identifiable as his own only in the exactitude of the proportions of the fenestration.

Mies was normally not interested in social programs as such. Ironically, it was a housing project—the Weissenhofsiedlung, in which he played the lead role—that did the most to lift his reputation from a national to an international level. Yet by the time he gave himself to it, he had already begun to turn away from the strenuously antiaesthetic position of his *G* period, and he approached the Weissenhofsiedlung as if it were art rather than sociology. Moreover, between the time he began work on it in 1925 and the time he finished it in 1927, he saw two of his designs realized in the modern manner to which he was now at last unequivocally committed.

The earlier of the pair was a rich man's house in Guben, on the Neisse River. Though destroyed in World War II, in its original form it was fairly well documented.[58] The client, Erich Wolf, commissioned it in late January or early February 1925, about the time when Walter Dexel was growing irritated with Mies. That Wolf managed to get his own house built may be due to the fact that it was more ambitious, which is to say more expensive, than Dexel's, though in surviving correspondence Wolf appears a far more patient man. He evidently had to be; Mies dawdled on this piece of work, too, not completing it until 1927.

The Wolf House was built on a hill athwart a narrow lot. Following the lead of Mies's two great country house projects of the early 1920s, it spread asymmetrically outward into space. The elevation, similarly informal, was composed of cubic volumes with hard flat walls and flat roofs. Windows were cut sharply into the brick walls, and slab overhangs, one sheltering a door leading from the topmost terrace that served the house, the other supporting a balcony at the northwest corner, were faint reminders of the slotted articulations of de Stijl architecture, just as the interlocking volumes recalled constructivism. The centrifugal composition of the plan suggested Mies's continuing homage to Wright.

Photographs indicate that Mies's handling of the bonding of the brick was as sensitive as anything one might have expected from his revered Berlage. This is most apparent in the uppermost terrace, from which Mies's organization of exterior volumes and spaces appears most felicitous. Also notable at that level is a long retaining wall that can be traced to antecedents as early as the Riehl House, as recent as the Brick Country House project. Though the ends of several interior walls were freestanding, the plan treated room spaces as fundamentally cellular. In short, the Wolf House, in some respect still more summary than prophecy, was chiefly noteworthy for having freed Mies from the ranks of the paper architects.

Mies's other realized structure of 1926 was no less exceptional, though substantially more impressive. It is even singular among his entire corpus, not alone because he never did anything else quite like it but because it emerged from an implausible mixture of capitalist wealth, Marxist communist ambition, the intent of the old arts, and the manner of the new.

If Mies had abandoned historical styles by 1926, he retained his interest in clients of means. He knew that the Hugo Perls House, one of his own early designs, had been purchased by the celebrated and wealthy historian Eduard Fuchs, author of the mammoth *History of Morals,* a work nearly as familiar to the wider reading public as to the intellectual community. Knowing, too, that Fuchs had used his money to put together an art collection, as Erich Wolf had in Guben, Mies hoped to meet Fuchs and persuade him to build a new house in the same modern manner, with a similar exhibition space, as he had used in his design for Wolf.

Fuchs had dreams of his own—not of a new house but of a wing added to his old one. Nevertheless he knew of Mies, whom he already had in mind as his architect. Chance thus turned to purpose, and Fuchs one evening entertained Mies for dinner and conversation.

We do not know when Mies decided to join the Society of Friends of the New Russia, but since his membership card was issued in January 1926,[59] it seems reasonable to assume the affiliation had something to do with his meeting and subsequent friendship with Fuchs. For his potential client was not only a rich bourgeois but a high-ranking member of the German Communist party, and Mies, despite a lifelong indifference to politics except within the circles of his profession, may have rationalized his membership in the society by associ-

77. Wolf House, Guben, 1925–27 (now destroyed)

ating it with the many vanguard groups in Berlin in the mid-1920s. In any case, there is no record of his later activity in its behalf.

Mies did produce an addition to the Fuchs-Perls House, but it had to wait two years. "After discussing his house problem" at dinner, Mies later recalled, "Mr. Fuchs then said he wanted to show us something. . . . a photograph of a model for a monument to Karl Liebknecht and Rosa Luxemburg."[60]

The party had asked Fuchs to see to the execution of a design for a memorial to the martyrs of the ill-fated Spartacist uprising in 1919. Several years earlier, it appears, party official Wilhelm Pieck had proposed such a monument, and in July 1925 he claimed to have secured a model of it, the central element of which was a sculpture by Rodin.[61] Why this plan was never carried out is unclear, but Mies remembered that Fuchs, on the occasion of their first dinner together, showed him an elaborate neoclassical creation with Doric columns and medallions of Luxemburg and Liebknecht. "When I saw it," said Mies, "I started to laugh and told [Fuchs] it would be a fine monument for a banker."

Fuchs was not amused. Still, he telephoned Mies next morning to ask what *he* would propose.

"I hadn't the slightest idea," Mies said he told Fuchs, "but as most of these people were shot in front of a wall, a brick wall would be what I would build . . . A few days later I showed him my sketch . . . He was still skeptical about it and particularly when I showed him the bricks I would like to use. In fact, he had the greatest trouble to gain permission from his friends who were to build the monument."[62]

What Mies evidently showed Fuchs, and finally built in the Friedrichsfelde cemetery in Berlin, was essentially what he had promised: a brick wall, more exactly a huge, rectilinearly geometric sculpture in brick, 6 meters high, 12 meters long, 4 meters wide.[63] It consisted of

79. Liebknecht-Luxemburg
Monument, Berlin, 1926
Photo courtesy of Mies van der
Rohe Archive, the Museum of
Modern Art, New York

a series of long, low rectangular prisms arranged horizontally in staggered layers, each prism functioning vaguely like a single enormous Roman brick within a comparably outsized wall section, bonded, however, in the asymmetrical manner of constructivist sculpture, here extruded, there retracted. A more architectural simile would relate the composition to Frank Lloyd Wright's habitual use of interlocking volumes, though Mies's stern geometry seems to have anticipated the stereometric counterpoint of Wright's Kaufmann House by nearly a decade.

The brick was purplish clinker brick, rough and burnt, retrieved from demolished buildings. It had the double effect of keeping the cost down and heightening the desired coarseness of an executioner's wall. The proportioning of the prismatic layers, in contrast, was exacting, and the bonding as refined as any part of the terrace of the Wolf House. This disparity, instead of producing expressive conflict, endowed the whole work with a rude but unimpeachable dignity that bordered on the tragic. The Liebknecht-Luxemburg monument is perhaps the closest Mies ever came to an architecture of overt psychological content. One cannot resist noting the posthumous irony of a remark made before World War I by Liebknecht himself to Hugo Perls. "Your architect," he said to Perls, "seems a most capable man. When the Independent Socialists [as opposed to the Social Democrats] take over the government, we will keep him busy."[64]

By comparison with the stoic mood of Mies's abstract masses, the symbolic star with the hammer and sickle is almost a superfluous literalism, though without it the monument might suffer an excess of formal severity. Whether Mies actively wanted it or acceded to party insistence is not known. The inscription "Ich bin, ich war, ich werde sein" (I am, I was, I will be), superimposed on one of the left-hand

Europe out of the Ashes

layer faces, appears in an early photograph, but was evidently removed by 1931, for reasons as yet unclear.[65] Mies took special pains to obtain the star, which was made of stainless steel two meters in diameter, an object much too large to be entrusted to a neighborhood forge. At first the Krupp Steelworks refused outright to fabricate a symbol for a radical leftist group, whereupon Mies ordered five identical diamond-shaped plates, which Krupp provided. When they arrived in Berlin, he assembled them to form the star that hung in place when the Communists, led by Ernst Thälmann and Wilhelm Pieck, unveiled the monument on Rosa Luxemburg's birthday, 13 June.[66]

The memorial, which Hugo Perls called "the most splendid of our time," was demolished by the Nazis in 1933.[67]

By the time the Luxemburg-Liebknecht monument was completed, Mies had been living the artist-bachelor's life for five years. Contacts with his family were confined to his own vacation trips and to visits the girls paid him in Berlin, sometimes with, sometimes without, their mother. Ada seems to have accepted her joyless marital condition as permanent, deriving her satisfaction principally from the care of her brood and the conviction that a genteel martyrdom was the best she could offer a husband she loved even if she could not possess.

At the end of the 1922–23 school year she and her daughters left Bornstedt and made their way to the Wallis district of French-speaking Switzerland. There, at a sanitarium in the resort town of Montana they visited Elsa Knupfer, a friend from Ada's Hellerau days, who was suffering from tuberculosis of the spine. Ada spent the summer close by her side, while "Knüpferlein" gave lessons in French to the oldest Mies daughter, Muck. In 1924 Ada moved the children and herself to Zuoz in the Swiss Engadin, where they joined another old Hellerau chum, Erna Hoffmann Prinzhorn and her family. The Mies girls were enrolled in a private German-language school. With their mother they spent the better part of a year in Zuoz, the four departing Switzerland in the spring of 1925, then pressing on to the South Tyrol, newly a part of Italy though still steeped in a prewar Austrian heritage. They rented a patrician town house in the village of Mariahimmelfahrt overlooking Bozen, halfway up the mountain to Oberbozen.

Life was materially comfortable, though Ada's health remained as fragile as ever. She loved the mountains but was gradually forced to curtail her hiking as she began to suffer more and more from a fear of heights. Precisely when she sought psychiatric help is not certain, nor do we know quite why. Her surviving daughters claim she was not in any special distress, that she entered psychoanalysis chiefly because it was the modish thing to do in the 1920s, though a letter dated 15 June 1925, to Mies from Prinzhorn (who was himself practicing psychiatry in Frankfurt), suggests a more serious and enduring problem: "I hear from [Karl] Fahrenkamp [a Stuttgart heart specialist] that Ada has managed a recovery, through Coué. That would be *wonderful,* not just for the end of it, but thanks to all the subterranean work of years."[68]

Ada received more counseling later, in the early 1930s, from Heinrich Meng, an analyst high in the Freudian circles of Frankfurt, where she was living at the time. In view of this the recovery which Fahrenkamp claimed had been effected with the help of another famous therapist, Emile Coué of Nancy, must be regarded with a measure of doubt. Meng's widow, *née* Mathilde Köhler, who knew Ada personally and regarded her as a friend, recalled that her psychic pain was longlasting, with origins traceable to the harshly inconsistent treatment—Mrs. Meng called it sadistic—she received at the hands of her father.

In view of Wigman's recollection of Mies's pronounced need of personal freedom, it is hard to imagine that he would have extended much sympathy or solicitude to a woman from whom he was more than content to be separated in the first place. His companion of his later years in Chicago, Lora Marx, reports that he was, at least when she knew him, antagonistic toward psychotherapy of any kind. His exchanges with Prinzhorn, whom he knew primarily as a friend, skirted the subject of psychiatry in all respects but those which touched upon the arts.

Nonetheless, this left a lot to draw both men together. Mies saw to the publication of an article by Prinzhorn in *G* on the latter's well-known research topic, the art of psychotics. In turn Prinzhorn, who in 1925 was planning to produce an enormous "encyclopedia of living knowledge," was confident that Mies would contribute the text for one entire volume, on the subject of architecture.

Ironically, Prinzhorn misjudged the mental makeup of his friend. If Mies was slow to design buildings, he could be even slower in composing so much as a letter. Still, since Mies did write more in the mid-1920s than at any other time of his life, Prinzhorn's error may be understood to a degree, and more so since Walter Gropius also asked Mies to write an essay for the *Bauhausbücher,* which had begun to appear in 1925. Not surprisingly, Mies came up with nothing for either petitioner.

Mies's relations with Gropius grew friendlier as the decade passed midpoint. From time to time and usually in a private note to a colleague, Mies would repeat his misgivings about the "formalism" at the Bauhaus, of which he complained to van Doesburg in 1923/24. Yet the correspondence between Mies and Gropius during 1925 grew trusting, even protective. When Mies was approached late in 1925 by leading citizens of Magdeburg who asked him to make himself available for the post of city building commissioner, which Bruno Taut had lately given up in that city, he received the following from Gropius:

> Of course I urgently counselled them to get you. I heard about the position several days ago, in Halle, and I was asked at that time what you had had to do earlier with Behrens. Apparently somebody in Magdeburg—I can guess who—has spoken out against you, suggesting you were dishonorably discharged by Behrens, or some such thing. I rejected that notion outright, without knowing any other details, simply because I know Behrens myself, well enough. Nevertheless, I would suggest to you confidentially that you keep your eyes open for the signs of burrowing moles.[69]

Mies's reply includes a reference to the same unnamed (and yet unknown) enemy: "he has no idea how closely we work with Behrens today. In any case I thank you for your recommendation."[70]

Evidently, then, Mies regarded his comradeship with both Gropius and Behrens in the struggle for the New Architecture to count for more than the quarrels and disagreements he may have had with each of them personally—even though those differences were taken no less seriously unto themselves. Such an interpretation of his conduct toward both men might further explain his ambivalent attitude toward van Doesburg (with whom he was still corresponding warmly in 1925) or with Mendelsohn (whose work he disliked for its excessive plasticity). Mendelsohn was no fonder of Mies's designs, finding them excessively hard in their angularity, but Mies included him, as he did Gropius and Behrens, in several of the Novembergruppe exhibitions he organized in the mid-1920s.

Whatever Mies's motives in the politics of the German architectural world in 1925, he had become a force in his own right and he knew it. Persuaded finally that the Magdeburg authorities were looking for an *apparatchik* rather than someone of independent judgment, he advised the industrialist G. W. Farenholtz, who had earlier sought to interest him in the position, that he was not Magdeburg's man:

> If it is not possible for me to pursue the objectives I have set for myself in my own work, I have no intention of going there; Magdeburg must decide whether it wants to entrust the office to a *Routinier* or to a man of spiritual values.
>   . . . It is being bruited about here that I am interested in Magdeburg because I want to be called a commissioner. The degree of my title mania is best measured by the record, namely, that I turned down the [directorship of the] Magdeburg [industrial design] school as well as professorships in Breslau and Dresden. No more words need be wasted over this.[71]

Mies resisted all of Magdeburg's later efforts to placate him. He was, after all, too well ensconced in Berlin by the end of 1925, close to the contacts a cosmopolis could provide his steadily growing reputation, and enjoying the society that went with art and expanding renown. Above all, he had a far more important assignment in Stuttgart than anything Magdeburg could offer.

Mies's supervision of the housing colony known as the Weissenhof-siedlung, completed in 1927 under the auspices of the Deutscher Werkbund, was his most important professional accomplishment following the five projects of the early 1920s. It focused unprecedented attention on the New Architecture as a whole and on his own understanding of the movement. In his capacity as artistic director at Weissenhof he assembled an international company of designers of such talent, scope, and record that the buildings they put on a hill overlooking Stuttgart certified, as nothing previously had, the triumph of modernism in building. His overall plan for the project together with the apartment block he contributed to it, plus his design of the so-called Glass Room for an affiliated exhibition, were embodiments of major principles which he and others of his generation had earlier only postulated. Hardly less important, he resumed an interest cultivated during his youthful days with Bruno Paul—the design of furniture—and he rapidly became one of the leading figures in the conversion of that art into modernist idiom.

By 1927 housing projects sponsored by municipal and state governments and cooperative building societies had been designed by some of the most gifted architects of the German vanguard: by Otto Haesler in Celle, by Ernst May in Frankfurt, by Walter Gropius in Dessau, by Martin Wagner, Bruno Taut, and Hugo Häring in Berlin. The Deutscher Werkbund not only took notice of this development but actively promoted it. More and more persuaded that architecture derived from machine technology and machine form was the key to a revival of the arts in society, the membership gave itself over to the leaders of the radical Ring: Häring and Adolf Rading were elected to the executive in 1926, Ludwig Hilberseimer in 1927. Meanwhile, the association's journal *Die Form* became so preoccupied with the modernist idiom that by 1927 it had become the unofficial organ of the New Architecture.

The Werkbund exhibition following the 1923 inflationary crisis was titled Form ohne Ornament (Form without Ornament). It was organized by the Württemberg chapter of the association and mounted in Stuttgart in 1924. In March 1925 the Werkbund proposed another exhibition for the following year with the intention of fashioning it into the organization's most important collective effort since Cologne in 1914. Stuttgart was again chosen as the site, due largely to the progressivism of the Württemberg branch, especially its director, Gustav Stotz. The theme was to be the modern home, and plans were laid to include interiors and furnishings as well as a colony of houses by designers from all over Europe. "Only those architects," declared

Werkbund president Peter Bruckmann, "who work in the spirit of a progressive artistic style [*Form*] suited to today's conditions, and who are familiar with the appropriate technical equipment for house construction, will be invited."[1]

That the Werkbund executive appointed Mies van der Rohe artistic director of the exhibition—largely at Stotz's behest—was hardly surprising. Just a year before his appointment to Weissenhof he had written in *G*: "I consider the industrialization of building methods the key problem of the day for architects and builders. Our technologists must and will succeed in inventing a material which can be industrially manufactured and processed . . . All the parts will be made in a factory and the work at the site will consist only of assemblage, requiring extremely few man-hours. This will greatly reduce building costs. Then the new architecture will come into its own."[2]

At first, then, Weissenhof must have seemed a perfect vehicle for the advancement of these ends, as nearly ideal for Mies as he for it. Indeed, the program was distinguished from the rationales of most other housing projects of the day largely by its encouragement of experimentation in construction techniques and by an intention to accommodate a variety of house types to an assortment of living needs. All efforts were to be guided by considerations of economy.

What was finally presented to the world at Stuttgart followed this functionalist line, but not consistently. The deviation must be attributed to Mies's gradually developing ambition to achieve something else and something more at Weissenhof than what he had affirmed in *G*. To some degree this could be inferred even from his first proposed list of participating architects. Late in September 1925, Stotz, who became Mies's most trusted associate at Stuttgart, had submitted the following names for Mies's approval: Peter Behrens, Paul Bonatz, Richard Döcker, Theo van Doesburg, Josef Frank, Walter Gropius, Hugo Häring, Richard Herre, Ludwig Hilberseimer, Hugo Keuerleber, Ferdinand Kramer, Le Corbusier, Adolf Loos, Erich Mendelsohn, Mies van der Rohe, J. J. P. Oud, Hans Poelzig, Adolf Schneck, Mart Stam, Bruno Taut, and Heinrich Tessenow.[3] A reply from Mies's office dropped the names of Herre, Keuerleber, and Bonatz—all Stuttgarters—plus Loos and Frank, and added Henri van de Velde, Hendrik Berlage, Otto Bartning, Arthur Korn, Wassily Luckhardt, Alfred Gellhorn, and Hans Scharoun.[4]

Mies's edited roster leads us to suppose that he preferred designers he knew in Berlin, or in the Ring, to those he didn't in Stuttgart. More important, the presence of such figures as van de Velde and Berlage, both of whom retained elements of the craft tradition in their work, suggests that he felt no obligation to stick closely to a rationale of machine technology. He seems simply to have admired van de Velde and Berlage as artists rather than as adherents to a doctrine.

Something of the same willfulness is evident in his own model of the site plan that he sent Stotz several weeks earlier, a strikingly original piece of work not altogether consistent with factors of economy and functionalism. It completely avoided the customary arrangement of 1920s German housing projects, in which units were laid out exactingly, in rows parallel to streets and often separated to allow for

81. Model of the original plan for the Weissenhof housing project, Stuttgart, 1925

free admission of sunlight and ventilation. Instead Mies conceived a long, low-profiled assembly of interconnected cubic house forms arranged informally in weaving terraces. Walkways free of automobile traffic were meant to carry the complex upward to a plaza surrounded and dominated by several larger though comparably horizontal structures. These last were reminiscent of Bruno Taut's *Stadtkrone* (closer to expressionist lore than to *Sachlichkeit*), while the whole layout bore a resemblance, as does the Liebknecht-Luxemburg monument, to the asymmetrical, interlocked massing of constructivist sculpture. It was an unprecedented concept in town planning, though remarkable more for its formal invention than for its functionalism.

Much has been made of Mies's generous insistence that all the contributing architects be free to design as they pleased with the sole proviso that they employ flat roofs and white exteriors, both devices identified by most modernists with the precision and generality of classical form and abstract cubic geometry. Still, the comments he made to Stotz about his model indicate a stratagem meant to guarantee that corporate unity would not be sacrificed to individual liberty: "I have striven for an interconnected layout because I believe it *artistically desirable* [my italics], but also because we will not be so dependent on the individual collaborators. I have the presumptuous idea of inviting all the architects of the [artistic] left, which I believe would be an unheard-of success as an exhibition strategy. By this means the colony would achieve a significance equal to that which the Mathildenhöhe in Darmstadt won in its time."[5]

These words convey none of the uncompromising determinism that chilled the pages of *G;* Mies sounds not only like an artist—again, after several years of seeming to keep a distance from art—but like an impresario with an ear cocked to the plaudits of history. He remains loyal to his emphasis on generality and unity in architecture, and hostile toward individuality, yet he assumes the individualistic right to define and interpret that generality and that unity. He sees no conflict in this; he is much too sure of his perceptions to entertain the notion that they, like art, might owe something to subjectivity.

Still, he soon suffered opprobrium for loosening the bonds of *Sach-lichkeit*, and the attacks would come from right and left alike. The angriest criticisms were delivered from a pair of professors at the local *Hochschule*, Paul Bonatz and Paul Schmitthenner, leaders of the so-called Stuttgart school of architecture. Demonstrably more conservative than the new architects but possessed of a proud tradition of their own, Bonatz and Schmitthenner published newspaper articles, in Stuttgart and Munich respectively, which accused Mies of the very offenses he had condemned in others.[6] Schmitthenner called his plan "formalistic" and "romantic," while Bonatz denounced it as *unsachlich* and "dilettantish," describing it as "a heap of flat cubes, arranged in manifold horizontal terraces, [that] pushes narrowly and uncomfortably up the slope; the whole thing bears more resemblance to a suburb of Jerusalem than to a group of houses in Stuttgart."

Bonatz's remarks dug to the roots of the antagonism toward the New Architecture which was growing among conservatives in Germany as fast as the New Architecture prospered. The cubic masses Mies perceived as a purification of architectural form Bonatz saw as not only technically impractical but culturally destructive of the historic German pitched roof.* The Stuttgarter went on to associate the free-flowing community plan with the tight, box-lined alleys of Near Eastern towns, a criticism easily understood by the rallying antimodernists of 1926 as the sign of another cultural surrender, this time to inferior ethnic traditions.

Mies had more than Bonatz to contend with in seeing his plan through, though he answered all antagonists with a bluntness that was free of any trace of self-doubt. His own fellow modernist and confrere within the progressive circles of Stuttgart architecture, Richard Döcker, wrote him that he had intended to reproach Bonatz until he saw photographs of Mies's model. "I was taken aback, having expected something quite different," wrote Döcker, who went on to question whether the plan Mies seemed to have in mind was at all reasonable: "The attempt, for example, to mix the one-, two-, and three-story blocks together as you have, is unorganic, in plan at best only partially possible, and thus *unsachlich*."[7]

Mies answered acidly: "I must decline your good efforts to be helpful . . . The model, let me make it clear, was meant to provide a representation of a general idea, not to indicate [actual] house sizes and the like . . . I didn't receive the final space specifications until the middle of May [1926] anyway . . . [and] do you really believe I would design rooms without light and air? . . . You seem to understand a plan only in the old sense, as so many separate building parcels . . . I think it necessary at Weissenhof to strike a new course. I believe that the new dwelling must have an effect beyond its four walls."[8]

This last remark seems a conscious expression of the attitude toward extensive space which we inferred from Mies's designs of the concrete

---

*In 1932–33 Paul Bonatz and Paul Schmitthenner led in the organization and design of a housing colony built on principles opposed to those that animated the Weissenhofsiedlung. They called this project Am Kochenhof. Built a few blocks away from the Weissenhof, the dwellings of Am Kochenhof featured devices far more traditional to the German house, most notably the pitched roof.

and brick country houses of 1923 and 1924. Nevertheless, his hopes of realizing any such objectives at Stuttgart were frustrated when the city decided its economy was not equal to his concept: the exhibition houses, once finished, would be sold to private owners and thoroughfares would be built to accommodate auto traffic in their midst. Thus "separate parcels" would have to be the rule.

The colony opened to the public on 23 July 1927, and while that date represents a year's delay in the original schedule (the project was cancelled outright for a time in early 1926), it is surprising that Weissenhof was readied even by then. To Mies's running battles with local political officials, exhibition functionaries, and his own presumed cohorts, not to mention a legion of avowed enemies, must be added his own tendency to procrastinate. Mia Seeger, who assisted Werner Graeff in the Weissenhof press department, called him "colossally slow"[9] and recalled that it took him days to write a paragraph-long introduction to the exhibition catalog. He did not approach Le Corbusier with an invitation to participate in the exhibition until 5 October 1926,[10] and as late as the following February, Max Taut, brother of Bruno—the two of them now among the Weissenhof designers—wrote Döcker: "My brother and I are shocked that the Stuttgart matter progresses no faster than it does. We find it incomprehensible that our colleagues are so far behind in their work . . . Is there no way to get them moving, for that matter to press the city of Stuttgart to some conclusion about the direction it wants to take?"[11]

Construction on the project began at last and in earnest a month later, in March. It proceeded quickly, in some cases much too hastily, as later cases of technical error and slapdash construction vouchsafed. The list of architects, moreover, had changed numerous times, with the final group of sixteen representing five countries: Mies, Gropius, Scharoun, Döcker, Behrens, Poelzig, Hilberseimer, Schneck, Adolf Rading, and the Tauts, all from Germany; Oud and Stam from the Netherlands; Frank from Austria; Le Corbusier from France; and Victor Bourgeois from Belgium. The very large crowds that regularly attended the show that summer and early fall (forcing its extension from 9 October to 31 October) were drawn to some degree by the notoriety of the contentious debate that the project generated, a debate which to this day has not subsided.

Yet there is no gainsaying the historic impact of the exhibition.[12] The twenty-one separate structures comprising sixty dwellings proved to be astonishingly unified in their clean, unarticulated, shimmering white rectilinear facades, flat roofs, and ship's-railing balconies. The various strains of architectural theorizing had apparently merged into the reality of a single International Style—the name by which modern architecture as a whole later came to be known. Here, at Weissenhof, was the fullest communal realization of the new art of building in concert with progressive politics, the closest thing to the brave new world which modernism had dreamed of since the war. Mies's original plan, however altered and adulterated, was still perceptible in the graceful arcs with which the houses followed informally curving streets, and in the slow rise of the complex to a height dominated by his own three-story apartment block, the vestige of his earlier *Stadtkrone*. Anchor-outcroppings at both ends of his 1925 plan now took the form of a pair of houses by Le Corbusier (done in tandem with his cousin Pierre Jeanneret) at the south end, and the twelve-family apartment house by Peter Behrens at the north. Gropius's two houses stood a few feet from Le Corbusier's. The old Neubabelsberg atelier had its reunion, and the New Architecture its most compelling corporate incarnation, in 1927, on the slopes of the Killesberg hill.

Quite aside from the secure proportions of its facade and the advantage granted it by its size and placement within the whole colony, Mies's apartment building was notable for the use he made of structural technique in the service of space. This was the first time he employed skeletal steel construction in a building, a method which not only led to perceptibly lighter walls and larger areas for windows but, more significantly, enabled him to leave the interiors free of bearing walls. Thus the size, shape, and placement of rooms could be defined by moveable partitions at the discretion of the tenant. The concept of open and flexible space, which Mies had proposed as early as the Friedrichstrasse Office Building and which Behrens had rationalized in his 1912 statement (see p. 109), was at last achieved, within Mies's own oeuvre, at Stuttgart.

Still, by comparison with his later work or with Le Corbusier's in the same exposition, Mies's Weissenhof apartments were a somewhat cautious endeavor. Not only was the principal living-dining area of Le Corbusier's single-family house left almost totally open in plan, with space circulating freely around a central hearth stack, it was vertically unimpeded too, rising two stories and interrupted only by the floor

82. Aerial view of the Weissenhof housing project

slab of the boudoir which extended into and overlooked the room below. Of all the Weissenhof projects it contained the most visually arresting interior space.

Sergius Ruegenberg reports that Mies was immensely impressed by Le Corbusier's design and by the great Swiss himself, whom he met for the second time in his life in Stuttgart in November 1926, on an occasion far more memorable to both men than the chance encounter in a doorway of Peter Behrens's Neubabelsberg studio in 1910.[13] We have no record of their conversations at the Werkbund exhibition and are left only to suspect that Mies's gathering doubts about the virtues of pure functionalism were fed by his contact with an architect who as early as 1923, the year he published *Vers une architecture*, had made it clear that functionalism was the province of the engineer and that the architect's role was to respect that province but to raise his own efforts above it, to the level of art.

Mies's own foreword to the catalog of the Weissenhofsiedlung is nearly a paraphrase of Le Corbusier: "the problem of the modern dwelling is an architectural [*baukünstlerisches*] problem, with all due respect to its technical and economic aspects. It is a complex problem, thus to be solved by creative powers, not simply by calculation and organization. Based on this belief and despite such commonplaces as 'rationalization' and 'standardization,' I held it imperative to keep the atmosphere at Stuttgart free of one-sided and doctrinaire viewpoints."

Mies expressed his intentions even more pointedly in a statement written for a special issue of *Die Form* in 1927, when the "problem" he had earlier called "architectural" he now called "spiritual" (*geis-*

83. Mies and Le Corbusier, Stuttgart, 1926

84. Gustav Stotz, Le Corbusier, and Mies, Stuttgart, 1926
Private collection

85. "Arab Village," a tricked-up anonymous photograph of the Weissenhof housing project, 1934
Photo courtesy of Mies van der Rohe Archive, the Museum of Modern Art, New York

tig).[14] There is no easy way to reconcile such a view with what we have said about the Neue Sachlichkeit's emphasis on fact unless fact, like form, be regarded as a reality necessarily dependent upon and derivable from a higher truth than outward appearance. And that is what Mies seemed to be saying, again in 1927: "The leaders of the modern movement must recognize and come to terms with the spiritual and material forces of our time and, without prejudice, draw the

86. Apartment House,
Weissenhof, 1927

necessary conclusions from them. For only when architecture derives from the material forces of a time can it activate its spiritual decisions."[15]

Herewith Mies affirmed the importance of spirit in architecture, a factor he had seldom made a point of underscoring in his writings. More and more he would do so toward 1930, leading us to recall again his growing debt to Saint Thomas and other Catholic philosophers. The distance between him and the functionalists progressively widened. To the extent that the functional capacity of the New Architecture was one of the objectives at Stuttgart, it is hard to defend the stunning rapidity with which most of the houses deteriorated, within as little as one or two years. In short, Weissenhof was less a triumph of *Sachlichkeit* and functionalism than of the *image*—or in Mies's terms, the spirit—of modernism.

Meanwhile, Mies's experience at Weissenhof included a good deal more than the planning of the colony and the design of his own building for it. We are not sure when he met Lilly Reich for the first time. As early as 1925 she was in correspondence with him from Frankfurt, writing in a tone more professional than personal but indicative of an established acquaintance.[16] Prior to 1923 she had lived in Berlin, where she was born in 1885, and she might have gotten to know him in the postwar hurly-burly. Lacking any record of that, we must presume their relationship began in the mid-1920s out of a common involvement in the affairs of the Werkbund. She had belonged to the organization for at least a decade and before World War I had worked under Josef Hoffmann in the Wiener Werkstätte. A designer of textiles and women's apparel, she was already of sufficient reputation and rank to have been put in charge of a Werkbund fashion show in Berlin in 1915. She was thirty at the time, a year older than Mies.

Reich occupied a singular position in Mies's life and career. She was the only woman with whom he ever developed a close, even dependent, professional rapport. That she was his lover as well hardly qualified her as unique. But the length and character of her relationship with him did. She was Mies's constant companion from about 1925/26 until he emigrated to the U.S. in 1938, and he entertained her on her visit to Chicago in 1939. She continued thereafter to care for the office he left in Berlin, maintaining it throughout World War II and even as late as the year of her death, 1947. Mia Seeger, who was close enough to know and reliable enough to be believed, has reported that Mies and Reich shared a small apartment in Stuttgart during the preparations for Weissenhof, in which they were both professionally involved. In all of his life following the breakup of his marriage, Reich was the only woman except his daughters with whom he lived under the same roof. Even when he resumed full-time residence in Berlin and she took a studio there, they lived apart.

Mies's reputation for being partial to good-looking women hardly rested on his relationship with Lilly Reich. Physically plain, she might have appeared coarse, except that she kept herself as carefully groomed as one might expect of a professional couturière. Nevertheless, in the liberal circles of Weimar Germany, where a taste for the mannish female was commonplace, she pointedly disdained all suggestion of flounce. When Mies's daughters traveled from Zuoz to Berlin to spend time with him, Reich was quick to express disapproval even of the understated manner in which Ada had them turned out. They would be hauled off to Braun's and there costumed strictly and expensively, according to Reich's preferences, with Mies's approval—and what was left of Ada's family money. The girls did not appreciate such pains. All three of them rather cordially disliked Reich, finding her cold and hard even by the antiromantic standards of the time and Mies's world.

It did not matter to her. Correctness mattered. She was a consummate professional, intelligent, disciplined, and endowed with a sensibility as keen as Mies's own. She bowed to his authority—in this sole respect she played the traditional European woman's role—leaving the larger concepts to him while tending to refinements and details, compulsively, even in his personal life. Her professional thoroughness, turned by love for him into personal solicitude, finally caused him to retreat from her. Mies cherished nothing in his life more devoutly than his independence, and when he emigrated to the U.S. he closed her out of his life. She suffered in spirit for it, and it can be argued that he never found a later collaborator who rounded out his own formative talents as effectively as she did.

Yet during the years of their closeness his natural proclivity toward elegance and subtlety of style was sharpened, and in his work of the Weissenhof period and thereafter, a demonstrable authority over architectural fundamentals was amplified by increasing attention to the appointments of his interiors.

Reich's own chief assignment at Weissenhof was the organization and installation of an exhibition of the latest articles of furnishings and appliances, held at the Gewerbehalle Stadtgarten in downtown Stuttgart. In concert with her, Mies began to recognize and react to a condition which Weissenhof as a whole had made apparent: in the great drive toward modernism architecture had outdistanced furniture design. Pioneering efforts in the latter art, by Frank Lloyd Wright and Charles Mackintosh in the first decade of the century and by Gerrit Rietveld of de Stijl in the second, had been significantly advanced only as late as 1925, by the designers of the Bauhaus. In that year Marcel Breuer, inspired by the handlebars of the new Adler bicycle he rode around Dessau (where the Bauhaus had relocated), fashioned the first tubular steel chair, naming it the Wassily, after his famed Bauhaus colleague Kandinsky, who had expressed admiration for it. The Wassily was a landmark, not only a radically effective reductionist abstraction of the traditional heavy four-legged lounge chair but one which achieved its dematerialized modern look by hewing to the cubic geometry which the *Bauhäusler* now, in mid-decade, practiced collectively. Moreover, perhaps most important, it utilized a material, steel, chrome-plated and gleaming, which was handsomely expressive of the new machine technology and the aesthetic of standardization so beloved of the avant-garde.

It remained, however, for a step to be taken beyond the Wassily: the cantilever chair, whose seat would rest suspended on the continuous loop of the tubular frame: a symbolically weightless form for an age that had already escaped gravity. In 1926 the Dutchman Mart Stam, one of the architects invited to Stuttgart, produced what is customarily regarded as the first modern cantilever chair, a rigid, slightly ungainly object made of gas pipes and fittings but quite true to the simplified vanguard mode. He exhibited an improved version of this chair in his house at the Weissenhofsiedlung. Mies in turn unveiled a similar design of his own at Stuttgart.[17] Examples with arms and without were shown in several rooms of his apartment block. He acknowledged that his creation postdated Stam's, and we presume that he learned of the latter's idea when Stam discussed it at a meeting in Stuttgart in November 1926. Given Mies's limited prior knowledge of the tubular steel production process, he must have carried out his design with a minimum of his usual procrastination, but with typical thoroughness. For his own chair, unlike Stam's, proved to be not only resilient—thus earning him a patent in August 1927—but distinctly superior in the assurance of its form.

Known standardly as the MR Chair, it is as demonstrative and characteristic of Mies's gifts as is the best of his architecture. The differentiation of the metal frame from the leather seat and back supports is classically lucid and the proportional relation of curves to straights a model of fluidly disciplined movement in space. It is in fact memorable more for the refinement of its geometry than for its workability, since in its original form it had a notorious tendency, since corrected, to pitch the sitter involuntarily forward when he rose from it. We are reminded that Mies designed other furniture for Weissenhof that had less to do with machine theory than with art, most notably several wooden Parsons-type tables covered in luxurious veneers, as reductionist in form as his MR Chair but prompted more by a sensitivity to material than by any loyalty to advanced 1920s technology. One senses a renewed debt to the craft tradition he had learned in his father's stone yard.

This is not to say that he turned from his efforts to achieve a concordance of modern materials and significant modern form. Ample proof of that shone forth from his Glass Room at Stuttgart, a work which prefigured, even more than his Weissenhof apartment block, the fully mature phase of his European architecture which would follow at the end of the 1920s.

The industry and craft exhibition at the Stuttgart Stadtgarten, for which Lilly Reich organized her own furnishings and appliances show, included one hall which Mies divided into three areas, each identified by its sparse furnishings with a residential function: living room, dining room, working room. These three subspaces were united into a single large flowing space articulated by fixed, freestanding walls of glass—Mies's most dramatic physical exploration up to that time of the spatially dynamic plan which he had earlier proposed in the Brick Country House of 1924. One of the walls had the effect of an exterior wall, with a view of what might have been the outdoors or at least a winter garden. The ceiling was nothing but a series of strips of stretched fabric permeable to the outdoor light that was the sole source of illumination. The floors were covered with linoleum in separate areas

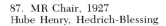

87. MR Chair, 1927
Hube Henry, Hedrich-Blessing

88. The Glass Room, Stuttgart, 1927
Photo courtesy of Mies van der Rohe Archive, the Museum of Modern Art, New York

of white, gray, and red which almost corresponded with their respective "rooms" but not quite, so that resultant "transition zones" reinforced the effect of spatial flow. The glass likewise varied, in color and texture (mouse gray, olive green, etched) as well as in degree of clarity ranging from full transparency to milky opacity. The viewer entered a vestibule perpendicularly to its length. There he could glance to his right and see, behind the glass wall of the only sealed-in area of the ensemble, a sculpture of a female torso by Mies's late comrade Wilhelm Lehmbruck, then turn to his left, where he was invited to follow the curve of space around the end of the vestibule wall in a movement reminiscent of Frank Lloyd Wright's spatial dynamics, into the living area and thence to a full tour of the Glass Room. He exited through another vestibule exactly opposite the entry.

As a show piece the Glass Room was more an abstraction of a residential space than a real example of one. It was not practical in any respect except as prestige advertising for the German glass industries that commissioned it. In that sense, however, it was as visually compelling as it was theoretically important in its unification of two established ways of rationalizing architecture in glass, expressionist romance and Constructivist elementarism, with Mies's own unique determination to elevate material fact to the level of immaterial aesthetic truth.

During the summer of 1927 Mies gave up his apartment in Stuttgart, returning to full-time residence and work in Berlin. With evidence mounting of Weissenhof's international success, his own reputation grew in all respects as well: as designer, planner, organizer, theoretician, and centrally as one of the several most prominent architectural talents of his generation.

These were the headiest of the Weimar years, yet even as the vanguard spirit thrived, the signs of reversal were no less visible. We have encountered some of them already in the ethnocentric complaints that Paul Bonatz lodged against Mies's "suburb of Jerusalem" at Weissenhof. The forces of German right-wing nationalism, stymied by the success of Chancellor Stresemann's pragmatic politics, never made their peace with him, neither forgave nor forgot. The yearning to avenge Versailles was the bacillus of the German soul, waiting to be activated more by national adversity than by national good fortune. In 1925 Adolf Hitler published volume one of *Mein Kampf* and reorganized the Nazi party that had been discredited two years earlier in the failure of his Munich *Putsch*. This rebirth, at the very outset of Weimar prosperity, was matched by reaction within the architectural profession too. Paul Schultze-Naumburg, who before World War I had been an architect of progressive stamp, in the later 1920s led a crusade against the New Architecture, at first arguing that it was an impractical way of building but later, with increasing vehemence, associating it with "un-German culture" and tracing its roots to the vile soil of bolshevism. And Schultze-Naumburg had his allies, including Konrad Nonn, who attacked the Bauhaus in the pages of his journal the *Zentralblatt der Bauverwaltung*, and Emil Högg of the Dresden *Hochschule*, who published equally shrill denunciations of the Ring.[18]

Eventually, despite its alliance with the dominant Social-Democratic politics of the late 1920s, the New Architecture built less than it dreamed of building. The list of Mies's own unrealized projects bears this out. By the time the Weissenhof exhibition opened he was forty-one, with a professional career of exactly two decades' length, yet he had seen but fourteen of his architectural schemes completed, among which only six—the Wolf House, the Luxemburg-Liebknecht monument, the Afrikanischestrasse apartments, the revised Weissenhof plan plus apartment block and Glass Room—were executed in the manner of the New Architecture. One of the wonders of the movement is that it went on, however modified, to conquer the world following World War II, a generation after it had been crushed under the Nazi boot in Germany and thrown into doubt throughout the rest of the world.

In the later 1920s Mies behaved as if he could not or would not wait for a social architecture. He was never a convinced utopian, and lately his reawakened devotion to art had led him to elevate the value of material effects in his work. Surely Lilly Reich's influence is evident here. For the fashion exhibition Exposition de la mode, staged in Berlin's Funkturmhalle in September 1927, Mies and Reich together designed the Silk and Velvet Cafe, a single passage of space within the larger show where visitors could relax over coffee, seated in Mies's MR chairs at tables also conceived originally for Weissenhof, and sur-

rounded by lengths of tall draperies suspended with elegant simplicity from slender metal rods. The partitions thus formed curved gracefully past each other, further evidence of Mies's maturing concept of an endlessly flowing space. The materials themselves were no less important to the effect of the ensemble: hangings done in black, orange and red velvet and black and lemon yellow silk reflected Reich's exceptional way with textiles as well as her vivid, opulent sense of color. Indeed it was a silken trail that led Mies to his next important architectural commission.

Conflicting accounts trace the origins of his relationship with Josef Esters and Hermann Lange, the two managing directors of the Verseidag, the silk weaving mills in the Rhenish city of Krefeld. One source suggests the connection was Lilly Reich but other reports refer to earlier contacts, perhaps between the Langes, who were avid art collectors, and the modernist group as a whole in Berlin, or between the Krefeld Museum and either Peter Behrens or museum officials in nearby Duisburg, where Mies had exhibited in 1925.[19]

The assignment yielded more lasting results than most of Mies's efforts of the 1920s: two finished buildings demonstrably related to each other. Most obviously they are outgrowths of the Wolf House, each an asymmetrical composition of joined cubic volumes whose flat walls, capped by the slenderest cornices, are perforated cleanly by large windows or bands of windows. For all their modernity of form, this description is enough to suggest how much they still owe Schinkel's example. Furthermore, as with the Wolf House, their faultless execution in brick is crucial to the impact they make, even as it offers another sign of Mies's continuing respect for the craft tradition. For had the Esters and Lange houses been rendered in the putatively up-to-date stucco of the Weissenhof International Style, they would have lost much of the monumentality their solid brick walls give them. Thus the impression they leave, standing side by side on the tree-lined concourse of Krefeld's Wilhelmshofallee, in the city's aristocratic quarter, is one of austerity. This is especially true of the bluff Esters facade, notwithstanding the sure proportions of its windows and the alleviating mass of a northeast wing with its projecting one-story-high roof that extends from service entrance to main entrance. The front of the Lange House is almost a duplicate of that of the Esters, except for a setback in the middle of the second story which creates the more active impression of a three-part division.

It is in the garden sides of both houses, opposite the facades, that they come most impressively alive. Here Mies incised sharp-edged windows into the hard brick. From within, these openings offer spectacularly generous views of the parklike estates to the south. Still, if the rear elevations save both structures from a formal chilliness, an examination of two preliminary pastel sketches of the Esters House in perspective suggests that that building might have been more impressive than it is if Mies had persisted with his concept of almost completely glazed running walls on the garden facade instead of keeping the windows discrete, and if he had preserved the interlocking volumes of varying heights on the north which lend animation to plan as well as to elevation. These drawings recall the audacious massing of the Brick Country House as well as the promise of glass as immaterial substance that was advanced in the Glass Room at Stuttgart. In a comparably early stage of the plan of the Esters House Mies even suggested an area of flowing, uncubicular space, again echoing earlier such proposals. When the houses were finally built, these forward-looking inventions were abandoned, even, we presume from Mies's own recall, proscribed. "I wanted to make this house much more in glass," he said, "but the client did not like that. I had great trouble."[20]

90. Street facade of the Josef Esters House, Krefeld, 1927–30 Photo courtesy of Mies van der Rohe Archive, the Museum of Modern Art, New York

91. View from the garden of
the Esters House
Photo courtesy of Mies van der
Rohe Archive, the Museum of
Modern Art, New York

During 1928 and 1929 Mies produced four designs for large urban projects. Known as the Adam Building, the Stuttgart Bank, the second Friedrichstrasse Office Building, and the plan for the Alexanderplatz, they have attracted relatively little attention among students, probably because of the surpassing excellence of several residential designs executed by him at about the same time. Indeed, the four works, which were never built, are not among his most compelling or original efforts; nonetheless, they are important to this study chiefly because of their implications for his American period.

Since 1923 Mies had busied himself mostly with works of small scale in which he sought to explore the dynamism of space by breaking down barriers between interior space and exterior space and by relating interior spaces more closely to each other. Glass and the freestanding wall became his primary means of achieving these ends, which, moreover, in one- and two-story houses encouraged a treatment of masses reaching out into ambient space. In large, multistory buildings such subjective planning was less feasible. As early as the first Friedrichstrasse Office Building he had proposed a glass wall that minimized the distinction between inside and outside, but the stacking of stories called for a regular plan based on a structural framework. In the subsequent Glass Skyscraper the framework seems to have been compromised in its clarity and rationality, largely because of an informal plan, and Mies thereafter chose to impose a more rigorously objective than subjective order on his multistoried buildings.

The objective order would eventually dominate Mies's architecture as a whole in the United States. Indeed the play of subjective and objective orders would take on the character of a critical struggle in his work of the 1930s. This dichotomy, like so many other germinal factors in Mies's modernist architecture, had its origins in the great five projects of the early 1920s. As the open plan of the Glass Room grew from the Brick Country House, the disciplined regularity of the four 1928–29 projects evolved from the Concrete Office Building.

We are not certain which of the four Mies designed first. The Adam Building, a proposal for a department store in downtown Berlin on which he was at work early in 1928, and the Stuttgart Bank, a competition piece of the same year, are most typical of the group, at least from a structural standpoint. Each was a single rectangular prism, presumably metal-framed, its cantilevered floor slabs and mullions flush with an uninterrupted sheath of glass and the windows of the ground floor set back behind the piers. The two designs featured Mies's first use of a curtain wall on a rectangular prism, the clearest prefiguration from the 1920s of his American high-rise buildings. "Neither wall nor window but something else again, quite new," said Curt Gravenkamp of the Adam Building. "It achieves the ultimate possibilities of a material [glass] already millennia old . . . modern architecture weds a building to the landscape, binds the interior with the space of the street."[21]

Thus in a metal-framed commercial project Mies gained some of the same effect he had with the freer planning of his low-slung villas. The modular structure of the multistoried composition, however, suggested a far more neutral, generalized character to him. Indeed, as he "dissolved" the wall in the Adam Building and the Stuttgart Bank, he likewise carried further his favored concept of the "universal," functionally flexible space: "The exceptional variability of uses to which your building would be put," he wrote the Adam Company in Berlin, "requires maximally open spaces on all floors."[22] The Stuttgart Bank was very likely treated similarly, as we infer from his later montage of the building bearing the Brenninkmeyer department store sign.

92. Mies working on a drawing of the Esters House
Private collection

93. Perspective with collage of
the Adam Building project,
Berlin, 1928

Mies was further encouraged to pursue the architecture of abstraction in two competitions whose very nature was speculative. One was the Alexanderplatz preliminary competition of 1928, an enterprise meant to elicit the ideas of its participants, not to promise them any final building commission. Mies nevertheless proceeded as if he were designing the conditions of the event, not just a plan that might satisfy them, even though conditions had already been laid down by the sponsoring agency, the Traffic Authority of Berlin, in response to a pressing need to reconstitute one of the city's largest, densest, and busiest traffic centers. The prospectus affirmed that the Alexanderplatz was no village square based on an arrangement of buildings, but a metropolitan plaza necessarily organized by, and, ideally, shaped to accommodate, heavy modern vehicular traffic.

Mies was one of six individual architects and firms invited to the competition. His entry placed last. The jury maintained that it quite fully ignored the competition requirements and appeared, to no one's surprise, far too costly to carry out.

Indeed the first place design was notable for the way the Luckhardt Brothers and Anker sculpted an ensemble of buildings to fit the prevailing traffic patterns, rather than vice versa. Mies's plan was no less remarkable for the near-total independence of both components: a group of slablike buildings arranged asymmetrically and dominated by one seventeen-story high-rise, addressed themselves to the circular core of the Alexanderplatz, almost as if the relation of architecture to thoroughfares were accidental. The structures themselves were austerely stereometric, curtain-walled outgrowths again of the Concrete Office Building, while their overall composition recalled in three dimensions the loose organization of tightly shaped polygons in Malevich's suprematist paintings of a decade earlier.

A more immediate influence, however, was the city planning of Ludwig Hilberseimer, by this time one of Mies's close friends. The two men had met at Richter's in the early 1920s and worked together at G, though Hilberseimer remained truer longer to the tough functionalist line. Indeed, when Gropius, who resigned the directorship at the Bauhaus in 1928, was replaced by Hannes Meyer, a left-wing architect with previous connections to the Swiss functionalist group ABC, Hilberseimer joined the faculty at Dessau. His book on city planning, *Architecture of the Metropolis*, represented *Sachlichkeit* at its most exalted.[23] Le Corbusier's ideal of a city consisting of separated tall buildings surrounded by greenswards and elevated above traffic—thus cleansed of the ancient "mess" of streets, lanes, and alleys with their thrown-together tenements and clotted courtyards—was translated by Hilberseimer into drawings that showed perspectives of infinite length and chilling emptiness.

There is much of that overpowering antisepsis in Mies's Alexanderplatz project, especially in the six nearly identical buildings to the south whose ruthless march toward the horizon is an embodiment of the "endless boulevards and languid streets" that Spengler saw in the modern city. That part of Mies's project is a disquieting prefiguration of some of the public architecture he designed in the 1930s (see pp. 195–97) and, worse still, of the urban districts (New York's Sixth Avenue for one) that rose in ill-advised tribute to him and Le Corbusier

94. Collage of the Stuttgart Bank project (with accommodation for Brenninkmeyer Clothiers), 1928

95. Aerial view and perspective with collage of the Alexanderplatz project, Berlin, 1928

in all too many parts of America following World War II. What rescues Mies in this effort of 1929 is his fundamental sensitivity to the articulation of volumes in space, which lends his proposed Berlin cityscape an elegance of abstract form if not a humanizing scale.

Hilberseimer, who saw things differently, was Mies's staunchest defender in the press. Accusing the managers of the Alexanderplatz competition of seeking a design that closed the plaza and created "an effect reminiscent of classicism," he maintained that "Mies van der Rohe's project is the only one of the designs submitted which breaks through this rigid system and attempts to organize the square as an

96. Perspective with collage of the Alexanderplatz, 1928

independent shape. The traffic lanes retain the circular form, yet Mies has designed the square by grouping freestanding buildings according to architectural principles alone. By opening the streets wide, he achieves a new spaciousness which all the other projects lack."[24]

Much the same struggle between idealization of form and specificity of function marks the proposal Mies designed, for the second time in his career, to fill the triangular space on the Friedrichstrasse between the train station of that name and the Spree River. The competition organized in 1929 by the Traffic Stock Holding Company of Berlin was in many respects a reprise of the 1921 contest for which Mies produced Honeycomb. Once again the officially stated objective was a tall building of manifold function that would add a variety of commercial and recreational services to downtown Berlin without overpowering the neighborhood or creating unmanageable congestion. Once again Mies's project was easily distinguishable from the other entries in its generalizing regularity. (Once again none of the submissions was built.) Whereas the architects who split the top prize, Erich Men-

97. Perspective with collage of the Friedrichstrasse Office Building project 2, Berlin, 1929 Photo courtesy of Mies van der Rohe Archive, the Museum of Modern Art, New York

delsohn and the team of Paul Mebes and Paul Emmerich, proposed complexes in each of which a tall four-sided tower rose from a ground-hugging, more or less three-sided base, Mies's solution was formally far more unified: three identical curved prisms created the effect of a single trihedral mass around a central core. The whole ascended without indentation to a flat roof on which a structure resembling a roof garden was set. Judging from titles he lettered on the plan, he thought in more differentiating terms in this project than he had in Honeycomb. Still, as in each of his large-scale projects of the 1920s, all functions indicated were made consonant with the building form, rather than vice versa. The evidence of the American Mies, of the architect in his later period, is discernible in these four large projects of 1927–28, though before they were turned from sign to concretion, he constructed several buildings that had the effect of climaxing his German career and summarizing 1920s modernism as a whole.

The culminating moment of Mies's European years occurred on 26 May 1929, when King Alfonso XIII and Queen Eugenia Victoria of Spain entered the newly completed German Pavilion of the Barcelona International Exposition and affixed their signatures to a golden book. Presiding over the opening of the building, they took formal recognition of one of the most important architectural accomplishments of the twentieth century. The Barcelona Pavilion is Mies's European masterpiece and quite possibly the capstone of his life's work. Its consequence to the New Architecture has been often and amply demonstrated; that it belongs among a select few works of the modern movement to stand comparison with the greatest architecture of the past is a judgment of comparable historical accord.[25]

Despite Mies's unrealized projects of the 1920s and his growing determination at the end of the decade to build only as he saw fit, he was sufficiently well-known and highly regarded that the German government appointed him to supervise the design and installation of all German exhibits at the Barcelona fair. His indifference to standard functionalist doctrine made him, if anything, more attractive to the government, not less. In the ten years since the war Germany had remodeled herself into a peaceful, prosperous, culturally productive, and international-minded society. It was appropriate that any image she conveyed to the world be consistent with her new values. Mies's uncompromising commitment to architecture as a high art made him a natural choice to play a major role in the Barcelona fair. In a speech marking the opening of the German exhibition at Barcelona, Commissar General of the Reich Georg von Schnitzler said: "We wished here to show what we can do, what we are, how we feel today and see. We do not want anything but clarity, simplicity, honesty."[26]

Having received the commission some time around the first of July 1928, Mies responded with atypical speed and decisiveness. Even under the most concentrated of normal conditions he was wont to fuss endlessly over a project, forever revising, leaving a trail of hundreds of sketches. He did plenty of drawing for Barcelona anyhow, yet the basic shape of the entire German contribution to the fair, including the plans for the exhibition halls representing various German industries, was sufficiently determined by October that he hired on a complement of assistants at that time, obviously to execute ideas already formed.

Some of the explanation for this alacrity rests with Lilly Reich, whose responsibility for the exhibition halls relieved Mies of much of the burden of organizing and outfitting them. Thus he could devote his energies mostly to the pavilion, which he must have approached with a special eagerness, traceable partly to the circumstances. The July 1928 minutes of the Werkbund refer to the official request at Barcelona for a German *Repräsentationsraum*, a word best translated as a space of formal or ceremonial purpose as distinct from utilitarian function. There surely could have been nothing closer to Mies's heart at the time than an assignment so free of practical limitations that he could make pure architecture of it.

His first formative decision was the siting of the pavilion. Extending up the north inclination of the hill known as Montjuich, the Barcelona fair grounds were composed in classic Beaux-Arts manner. They date

98. Aerial view of the International Exposition, Barcelona, 1929, with the German Pavilion (far left). Photo courtesy of Mies van der Rohe Archive, the Museum of Modern Art, New York

99. View from the street of the Barcelona Pavilion

from 1915, when they were built by the Catalonian architect Josep Puig y Cadafalch for an exposition that was delayed by a variety of economic factors until 1929. The main axis of the grounds, culminating in the domed National Palace, was flanked mostly by large exhibition buildings and crossed at about halfway point by a transverse axis both wide and long enough to function as a grand central plaza. It was at the west end of this secondary concourse that Mies erected his pavilion. Longer on its front than on its sides, it stood perpendicular to the plaza, facing past formal arrangements of trees, fountains, and freestanding classical columns to another pavilion, representing the city of Barcelona, at the distant far end. Behind the German pavilion a gentle slope rich in embracing shrubbery rose to the Spanish Village. Immediately to the south stood the massive bluff walls of the palace of Alfonso XIII, its roughly identical counterpart, named after Eugenia Victoria, sitting opposite it across the main axis. Mies was initially scheduled to build his pavilion in the space between these two huge structures and across the axis from the French pavilion. His decision to change this location to the final site was advantageous in several respects. "[It appears] virtually obvious," wrote the critic Walter Genzmer, "that the main orientation of the pavilion should be perpendicular to the palace wall, that in contrast to the considerable height of that wall the pavilion be quite low, and that in contrast to the calm unbroken surface of the wall it be kept open and airy."[27] Thus the pavilion enjoyed a placement more isolatedly visible, especially in its greenery, and more commanding in its long approach.

The foundation of the pavilion seen from its axial approach had the effect of a Roman podium, so that the horizontally-oriented, flat-roofed structure it supported might have seemed the counterpart of a Roman temple were it not for the asymmetry of the freestanding walls beneath the roof—marble and glass planes that appeared to slide past each other, under and out from under the roof, in an altogether unclassical kind of movement. Moreover, rising from the south end of the podium was another section of wall in travertine, again an element with no classical counterpart. Only by making a further unclassical gesture of his own, by departing from the axis to his right, could the visitor see that that wall turned the corner as if to enclose the podium at the southern end. He now also perceived that the front of the podium was recessed to the west and that from the jog forming the recess, a staircase rose. To ascend the eight steps thus required another turn, 180 degrees to the left. Bit by bit a travertine terrace and a large reflecting pool lined in green glass came into view directly before him. It was this open area that the tall travertine wall enclosed. As he mounted the stairs, however, his attention was also drawn to his right, where he could make out an interior space beneath the roof, revealed yet closed off by a transparent glass wall.

Access to the interior required still another 180 degree turn to the right. As he entered he may have noticed amid the prevailing asymmetry one feature of striking regularity: in front of the vert antique wall leading inside, a row of slender, X-sectioned chrome-plated col-

100. Barcelona Pavilion with interior space in distance

101. Secondary preliminary
scheme of the plan for the
Barcelona Pavilion
Collection, Mies van der Rohe
Archive, the Museum of
Modern Art, New York

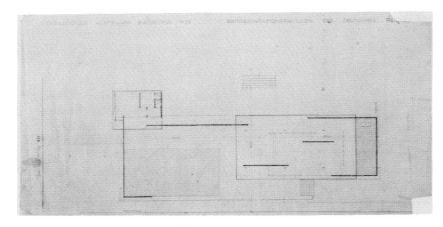

umns, equidistantly placed like ceremonial guards attending the sar-
abande of the wall planes. Proceeding deeper into the roofed area, he
might easily have forgotten to inquire the function of these columns
as he found himself in a central space dominated by a single element:
a freestanding wall roughly ten feet high and eighteen feet wide made
of a ravishing and rare marble called onyx dorée, golden, with a vena-
tion that ranged from dark gold to white. To the left of the onyx wall
as he faced it was a milk-glass wall lit from within; in front of the
onyx, a table that bore the king's golden book and to the right of it,
a pair of metal-framed lounge chairs set side by side, each with rectangular cushions in white kid.

These materials all around the visitor, not least among them the
black carpet on which he was standing and the scarlet drapery that
covered a portion of the glass wall behind him, were without exception sumptuous. Thus to the physical impression of free-flowing space
was added the visual sensation of rich color and opulent surface, plus
another, deriving from the dazzling play of reflections given off by
the polished marbles and the glass. The reflections shifted as he moved,
mirroring what he had seen or adding to the promise of something
yet to come. Through the bottle-green glass wall behind the chairs he
could make out the standing bronze figure of a woman, reachable by
a left turn behind the green glass to a platform at the edge of a second
pool, smaller than the first and lined with black glass. The figure,
Evening, by Mies's contemporary Georg Kolbe, seemed to rise out of
the water at the far end, thus encouraging the visitor to advance toward it, laterally across the pavilion.[28] The Tinian marble wall enclosing the pool slid out from under the roof and acted like a clamp
to the whole north end of the structure, informally balancing the travertine wall at the south end. Following this Tinian wall the visitor
made his way back again, southward, along the west side of the pavilion, whence he could either reenter the central space past and around
the rear of the onyx wall or continue, between a dark gray glass plane
and a small garden immediately to the west of the podium, into the
terraced area. Or he could simply exit onto the garden path and follow
a staircase upward to the Spanish Village. No matter how he visited
the pavilion and even if he bypassed the central space, he was obliged
to describe a circuitous route.

Thus movement was a factor central to the concept of form and space in the Barcelona Pavilion. All that Mies had postulated in the Brick Country House about the dynamic interaction of inner and outer space was now fulfilled, moreover in a built work. His debts to both Frank Lloyd Wright and Theo van Doesburg were manifest in his union of the American's concept of free-flowing interior space with the de Stijl precedent of sliding geometric planes. A passionate feeling for materials was traceable to his own family's craft tradition. Other influences were at work as well: from Reich, the bold color scheme, from Le Corbusier—specifically from the entry to the first floor of the single family house at Weissenhof—the device of the revelatory 180 degree turn at the top of the staircase. Indeed, in that same passage there was a reverberation of Schinkel's use of a parallel exterior staircase in the Gardener's Cottage at Charlottenhof.

The podium itself has been cited as a further reflection of the old Prussian master's classicism, yet the pavilion as a whole owes more to Schinkel the child of early romanticism. The freedom with which

102. View toward Georg Kolbe sculpture, *Evening*, in the small pool of the Barcelona Pavilion

Mies organized masses and spaces at Barcelona brings Charlottenhof to mind, as if he had abstracted the forms of the Gardener's Cottage, then exploded them.

But he rang in a containing element: the columns, eight of them, ranged quite formally in longitudinal rows of four. Part of their purpose was to hold up the roof independent of the walls, which, unlike those in the Brick Country House, were now freed of this assignment. For the first time Mies separated the function of support in a building from the definition of space. He had something else in mind as well. Frank Lloyd Wright, who greatly admired the pavilion, once declared, "Some day let's persuade Mies to get rid of those damned little steel posts that look so dangerous and interfering in his lovely designs."[29] Wright recognized that Mies could have achieved the same spatial flow by requiring the walls to support the roof; doing so would not have relieved the walls of their space-defining role or deprived the pavilion of its spatial dynamism. However, Mies's intention for the columns was not the functional use of structure but rather the expressive use of ordered structure. In the Barcelona Pavilion the contention of objective and subjective orders was held in equipoise.

At the time it was designed, the whole Barcelona enterprise seemed alive with happy auguries. The exhibition halls, which Mies supervised, but which were carried out by Lilly Reich, with graphics executed by Mies's childhood friend Gerhard Severain, were further demonstrations of the high level to which Mies and Reich had carried the art of exhibition design by the end of the 1920s.

Among the varied achievements at Barcelona, none proved as last-

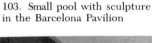

103. Small pool with sculpture in the Barcelona Pavilion

104. Interior of the Barcelona Pavilion

ing in a physical sense as the two chairs in the interior of the pavilion. The building was demolished when the fair came down; the chairs, though the originals were lost, were later reproduced, and even today are manufactured in quantity. The first two examples were intended to accommodate the king and queen of Spain at the inaugural reception, which is to say the Barcelona Chair was designed as a royal throne. Its metal bar frame consisted of two curving elements, one a long arc, the other a somewhat shorter ess, which crossed, forming a junction of seat and back. They were joined just above the junction, at the front of the ess and at the top of the arc, by three transverse bars. Two welted leather cushions, one for the seat, resting on the top end of the ess, the other for the back, leaning against the top of the arc, provided comfort. An overall resemblance to the curule chairs of ancient Rome as revived by the early nineteenth-century neoclassicists has been noted.[30]

The graceful lines, ample dimensions, and understated luxury of the Barcelona Chair have secured for it as honored a place in the history of twentieth-century furniture design as the pavilion enjoys in the annals of modern architecture. It was as becoming to royal privilege in Barcelona as the reject bricks in the Liebknecht-Luxemburg

monument were appropriate to the militantly antimonarchic left of Berlin. If ever proof were needed to show that Mies's devotion to art was proportional to his indifference to politics, these two works, separated by only three years, would suffice.

The last days of the Barcelona fair were notably less felicitous than the first. The exposition closed in January 1930 and the pavilion was promptly disassembled, its steel framing sold on the spot, its marbles, chrome-plated columns, and various other salvageables sent back to Germany in hopes that they could be utilized by the firms that supplied them.

What had intervened was the world financial crisis of October 1929. Already a worsening economic situation in Germany had caused budgetary cutbacks that several times threatened the whole national enterprise at Barcelona, especially the luxurious pavilion. These storms appeared to have been weathered by the time the fair opened; indeed spirits soared when international critical response to the German contribution, above all to the pavilion, proved almost unanimously enthusiastic. Even as late as the end of October the prospects were lively for saving the pavilion by selling it as it stood. But the crisis only deepened; a little more than half a year after the building was put up, it was taken down.

Weimar at the Flood

The days of the republic were numbered and with them, ultimately, those of Mies's personal good fortune. Nonetheless, when the Barcelona fair closed, he was still caught up in the busiest period of his life, laboring most seriously on the commission for a residence in Czechoslovakia which had come to him indirectly through the agency of Eduard Fuchs. In 1928, when Mies built the addition to the Fuchs House which the two men had discussed a couple of years earlier, Fuchs was in close contact with a young Czech couple, Fritz and Grete Tugendhat, well-born, newly married. The bride's father had promised her the wedding gift of a new house in Brno, to be built by an architect of her choice. Even before her marriage she had been a frequent guest in Fuchs's house, which, despite its overall traditional character, had impressed her with its lucid arrangement of spaces and the ease of passage, through three great glass doors, between living room and garden. It had been designed by Mies van der Rohe, she learned, the same man who supervised the celebrated Weissenhof-siedlung. "I always wanted a modern house with generous spaces and

106. Mies, in a top hat, at the opening ceremony for the Barcelona Exposition, 1929

161

107. Departure of the King and Queen of Spain from Barcelona Exposition's opening ceremony (Mies in top hat center right, striding away from pavilion)

clear, simple forms," she later recalled. "My husband for his own part retained a horror of the doilies and knickknacks that overflowed every room of the houses of his childhood."[31]

Mies was invited to meet with the Tugendhats, who reacted to him as countless others before them: "From the first moment," Mrs. Tugendhat said, "it was certain he was our man, so impressed were we with his personality and the quiet assurance of his way of talking about his buildings. We knew we were in the same room with an artist."

In September 1928 Mies traveled to Brno to inspect the Tugendhat site, a sharply sloping lot on a hillside which inspired him with its commanding view of the city and the hallowed old Spielberg castle across the valley. He returned to Berlin where he fell to work on the house even as he continued his labors on Barcelona.

"Toward the end of the year," Mrs. Tugendhat reported, "Mies told us his plan was ready. Somewhat breathlessly we met with him the afternoon of December 31. We had a New Year's Eve date that evening, but we cancelled it. The three of us talked until one in the morning. What seized our attentions most in the plan was a great giant space that contained just one round wall and one rectangular wall.

"Then we noticed little crosses in the drawing, spaced about five

meters apart. What are these, we asked, and Mies answered, as if it were self-evident, 'They are the steel columns that carry the building.'" Clearly, the use of a skeletal framework at Barcelona was to be repeated at Brno with the same ends in mind: on the one hand, the walls were allowed unimpeded freedom in defining space; on the other, their movement unfolded within a regular, objectively justifiable structural order.

Mies responded to the Tugendhat site by placing the public side of the house in a one-story elevation paralleling the Schwarzfeldgasse on the top of the hill.[32] Since the house was tucked into the descending slope, it was two stories high on the garden side. The street facade, less dramatic than its more private counterpart, was divided into a larger residential wing to the east and a smaller service wing to the west. The latter contained a chauffeur's apartment on the upper level and a kitchen plus servants' quarters downstairs. Topside the space between the two plaster-surfaced wings, through which the Spielberg was visible, was roofed over by a slab that had the effect

109. View of the Tugendhat
House from the garden

110. Interior of the Tugendhat
House looking toward the
winter garden

of uniting two buildings into one. The residential wing was punctuated
by a perpendicular chimney that separated a long flat wall to the east
from a milk-glass wall that rose from the travertine forecourt to the
roof slab. The latter wall curved 180 degrees inward to reveal a recessed entryway leading to a vestibule. The top story of the residential
wing was divided into two blocks of bedrooms parallel to the street,
one containing a pair of children's rooms plus a guest room, the other
the individual bedrooms of the parents. Vaguely reminiscent of de Stijl
composition, the two blocks slid almost but not quite past each other,
so that the vestibule was connected to an open terrace (the roof of
the first floor) by a short corridor. Between the blocks all bedrooms
opened onto the terrace and a southern view.

The curved glass wall housed a round staircase that led downward
to the large living space that Mrs. Tugendhat described as containing
"just one round wall and one rectangular wall." Though reachable from
within by the staircase, it could be entered from the outdoors as well,
at the southwest corner. The latter route would again awaken memories of Barcelona. From the garden, as from the axial street in front
of the pavilion, one would mount a staircase parallel to the long build-

ing mass and, while ascending, be drawn by the view to the right, through a long glass wall, into the interior. This last could be entered only by making a 180 degree turn from the travertine terrace at the top of the steps and passing through the entry door. The first identifiable subspace within the large space was a dining area, sequestered by the rich striped black and light brown macassar ebony wall that described slightly more than a half-circle in plan. Though its counterpart at Barcelona was a straight wall, Mies placed a translucent light wall perpendicular to each element in each building. The pavilion was most emphatically recalled by the central area of the Tugendhat space, dominated as it was by another splendid wall of onyx dorée, longitudinally placed. In front of it stood several pieces of Mies's furniture, again specially designed for the occasion and underscoring as the chairs did at Barcelona the symbolic function of the onyx wall as an abstracted fireplace or domestic altar.

At the east end of the space, another glass wall extending nearly the whole width of the building revealed a winter garden in a place equivalent to the pavilion's smaller reflecting pool. Comparably again, one piece of sculpture stood in the Tugendhat House, relieving the prevailing geometry: a female torso by Wilhelm Lehmbruck. This piece, which appears in some though not in all photographs of the house, was situated at the end of the onyx wall.

In addition to this conversation area and the "dining room," three other passages in the great space could be identified according to function, though they were distinguished from one another as much by furniture and furniture placement as by architectural elements. Be-

111. Interior of the Tugendhat House looking toward the dining area

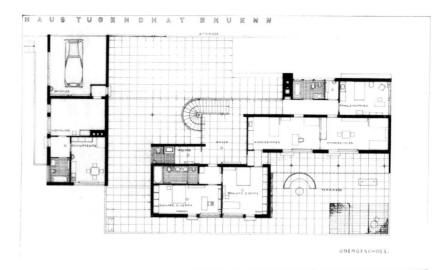

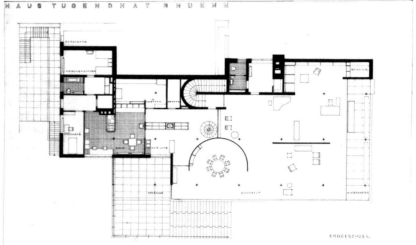

hind the onyx wall to the north were a study and a library, the one
giving way to the other at the point where two stubby wall extensions
protruded into the large space. Separated from both by a long cabinet
was an area containing a grand piano, implicitly a music room.

Such differentiations did no more than qualify the fundamental
perception of a single interior space. While the onyx and macassar
walls, not to mention the furniture, broke this openness into elegantly
proportioned units, they did not create quite so dynamically flowing
a space as had "happened" under—and out from under—the roof at
the pavilion. One was more aware of the whole contained space at
once than of a kinetic space perceptible only in parcels. Moreover,
since this was a real house, not a "representative" abstraction thereof,
it had to be enclosed, so that inner space was kept more demonstrably
distinct from outer space.

Nevertheless, the virtually uninterrupted glass walls on the east
and the south functioned only as membranes, and in some places not
even as those. The glass wall on the east, roughly fifty-five feet in

length, gave onto a winter garden. The south wall, about eighty feet long, overlooked the garden. The floor-to-ceiling windows that made up these walls were huge—fifteen feet of sheer glass between frames—and every other one of them on the south could be lowered electrically into the ground. Thus the large living space was almost as much an outdoor terrace during warm weather as was the upper patio.

It was the rhapsodic freedom of space that made the first floor of the Tugendhat House so immediately arresting, though its excellence

113. Window of the Tugendhat House with electrically retractable panes
Photo courtesy of Mies van der Rohe Archive, the Museum of Modern Art, New York

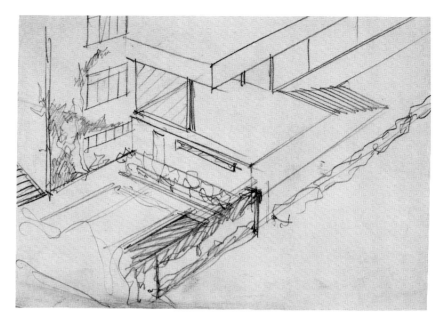

114. Drawing of the exterior staircase of the Tugendhat House
Photo courtesy of Mies van der Rohe Archive, the Museum of Modern Art, New York

finally depended as surely on Mies's strictly disciplined spatial proportions and the cool order of the columnar system. At the same time, the care with which the appointments were selected and the furniture designed was of only a little less importance. Mies chose white linoleum as a floor covering, so that the impression of a seamless area that "mirrored" the ceiling might be preserved. Before the onyx wall lay

115. Tugendhat Chair, 1930

a handwoven carpet of natural wool, behind it, in the study, one of brown wool. Draperies—black raw silk and black velvet on the winter garden wall and beige raw silk on the south wall—could be drawn so as to seclude the entire space from the outdoors, thus reinforcing the sense of containment. Curtains on tracks could also close off any one of the subspaces from the larger whole.

With the generosity and cooperation of the Tugendhats, the house became a classic proving ground for Mies's ideas about modern furniture design as well as architecture. He produced more new pieces at Brno than in any other assignment of his career. Two previous designs, the MR Chair used in the study and the Barcelona Chair in the conversation area, demonstrated Mies's belief in the interchangeability of good design. Nevertheless, in order to provide a lounge chair that might be as comfortable as traditional overstuffed examples, he created the so-called Tugendhat Chair, by applying the cantilever principle to a flat bar frame, which gave resilience, and adding cushions much like those of the Barcelona Chair. To improve on the workability of the MR side chair with arms as a table side chair, he designed the Brno Chair, which featured a shallower convex curve from arm to floor, thus enabling the sitter to get closer to the table. The Tugendhats could place twenty-four of these chairs at their dining room table, itself designed by Mies as a circular black disk of pear-wood supported by a single length of X-sectioned column. Another table, which proved eventually far more famous, was the X coffee table, a cross of four bar angles upon which a square piece of unframed glass twenty millimeters (13/16 inches) thick rested. In all of these objects, most strikingly in the emerald green leather, ruby-red velvet, and white vellum on stools and chairs, the influence of Lilly Reich was evident.[33]

The Tugendhat House was the last large residence that Mies built in Europe. The family left Brno just a year before Hitler's 1939 take-over of Czechoslovakia, following which one depredation after another befell the building. Though the Nazis had no place in their aesthetic for so modernist a work, they did not raze it. In fact, it was inhabited for a time by no less a panjandrum of the Third Reich than Albert Messerschmitt, the aircraft manufacturer. During the collapse of the Wehrmacht on the Eastern front, troops of the Red Army took charge of the house. The year was 1944. The Russians rode their horses up and down the travertine garden staircase and roasted oxen on a spit set up in front of the onyx wall—ironically turning what had been an abstracted fireplace into an all too real one. The macassar wall disappeared during the war years. So did the Lehmbruck torso. Though the house still stands, it was one of the most grievous casualties suffered by the modern movement during its post-1933 extremity.[34]

Even before the Nazis took power it was a subject of vigorous controversy. Justus Bier, in an article in *Die Form* titled "Can One Live in the Tugendhat House?" offered a substantially negative answer.[35] It was, he maintained, a showpiece, not a home, and as such its "precious" spaces and ostentatious furnishings suppressed both intimacy and individuality.

Die Form published rebuttals by the Tugendhats themselves, the upshot of which was not so much that the house was more functional than Bier contended. Rather, in Mrs. Tugendhat's words, "I have . . . never felt the spaces as being precious, but rather as being austere and grand—but not in a way that oppresses, but rather liberates."[36] To this Mr. Tugendhat added: "It is true that one cannot hang any pictures in the main space, in the same way that one cannot introduce a piece of furniture that would destroy the stylish uniformity of the original furnishings—but is our 'personal life repressed' for that reason? The incomparable patterning of the marble and the natural graining of the wood do not take the place of art, but rather they participate in the art, in the space, which is here art."[37]

The Tugendhats' defense of their house together with other passages of Bier's critique provide further clues to the position Mies had taken vis-à-vis the New Architecture by 1930. Their disagreements notwithstanding, all discussants were at one with Mies himself in granting highest priority to the spiritual component of architecture, an attitude Mies had been emphasizing at least since the Weissenhofsiedlung. Bier regretted that Mies was not working on projects "that engage his

117. X table, 1930
Photo courtesy of the Museum
of Modern Art, New York

ability, which is equal to the highest tasks of architecture, in the proper place, namely, where it is intended to build a home for the spirit, and not where the necessity of living, sleeping, and eating requires a quieter, more muted idiom."[38] Mrs. Tugendhat claimed that Mies was in fact "doing justice to the primarily spiritual sense of life of each and every one of us as opposed to mere necessity."

Mrs. Tugendhat went on: "To what degree this [spiritual sense] is proper or possible in a home . . . is a social question that Herr Mies cannot resolve."[39] So saying, she lent implicit support to another of Mies's distinguishing marks, an indifference to social issues for which the architectural left had long scolded him. It is true enough that he had next to no interest in architecture as an instrument of political therapy in the standard socialist sense. Earlier in the year he delivered a speech to the Werkbund in Vienna which could not have been less compromising on the subject:

> The new era is a fact: it exists, irrespective of our "yes" or
> "no." Yet it is neither better nor worse than any other era. It is
> pure datum, in itself without value content . . .
> Let us accept changed economic and social conditions as a fact
> . . .
> Here the problems of the spirit begin. The important question

to ask is not "what" but "how." What goods we produce or what tools we use are not questions of spiritual value.

How the question of skyscrapers versus low buildings is settled, whether we build of steel and glass, are unimportant questions from the point of view of spirit . . .

Yet it is just the question of value that is decisive.

We must set up new values, fix our ultimate goals so that we may establish standards.[40]

This is the statement that is held most unforgivingly against Mies by those who remember that he made it at a time when the fragile republic, staggering under the weight of the Depression, was increasingly endangered by extremists of both right and left. The anti-Mies argument is that there was no excuse for his frosty neutrality, that the arts like the citizenry at large did have a choice between democracy and totalitarianism, plus the responsibility to exercise it.

The meaning Mies assigned the words "spiritual" and "value" requires clarification. The implications of the aesthetic are unavoidable, given his talk of the "how" as opposed to the "what" and his insistence on "standards." Yet he can hardly have meant spiritual as exactly synonymous with aesthetic. He had always harbored an antipathy toward formalism in art which he had sought to rationalize in one way or another. In 1922 in *Frühlicht* he had called for the derivation of "new forms from the essence, the very nature of the problem."[41] In *G* two years later he said the goal was to "create form out of the nature of our tasks with the methods of our time."[42]

A sense of the actual, the imperative, and the inevitable mingle in both statements with the search for the essence, the generalizing truth. Mies labored to unite these two positions, to regard them as compatible. Moreover, when, in the later 1920s, the concept of the spiritual became commonplace in his pronouncements, it seems to have been due more to his reading of Saint Thomas than to any other source.[43] Apropos essence, form, and truth, Mies's obsessive concerns, here is Aquinas in the *Summa Theologica:*

> Now we do not judge of a thing by what is in it accidentally, but by what is in it essentially. Hence, everything is said to be true absolutely in so far as it is related to the intellect from which it depends; and thus it is that artificial things are said to be true as being related to our intellect. For a house is said to be true that expresses the likeness of the form in the architect's mind, and words are said to be true in so far as they are signs of truth in the intellect. In the same way natural things are said to be true in so far as they express the likeness of the species that are in the divine mind. For a stone is called true, because it expresses the nature proper to a stone, according to the preconception in the divine intellect. Thus, then, truth is principally in the intellect, and secondarily in things according as they are related to the intellect as their principle . . .
>
> Now since everything is true according as it has the form proper to its nature, the intellect, in so far as it is knowing, must be true so far as it has the likeness of the thing known,

which is its form in so far as it is knowing. For this reason *truth is defined by the conformity of the intellect and thing* [my italics], and hence to know this conformity is to know truth.[44]

Clearly Mies knew these passages, or knew of them: "In my opinion," he said years later, "only a relationship which touches the essence of the time can be real. This relation I like to call a truth relation. Truth in the sense of Thomas Aquinas, as the *'adequatio rei et intellectus.'* Or, as a modern philosopher expresses it in the language of today: *'Truth is the significance of facts.'*" The "modern philosopher" to whom Mies was referring was Max Scheler, whose definition of truth Mies translated as "der Sinngehalt eines Sachverhaltes,"[45] or, the significance of facts, which is not quite what Aquinas meant. Still, since Mies was not a trained philosopher, he evidently found the two statements close enough to his own view to be effectively identical. "The conformity of intellect and thing" becomes in German "die Übereinstimmung des Geistlichen und des Sachlichen," with "geistlich" referring to spirit as surely as to intellect. "Spirit" for Mies, then, was indeed bound up with the aesthetic, with art, that is, thus with architecture, but it took on an elevated quality that reached fully to the divine.

We can understand why he often labored so infuriatingly long on a project, and why he frequently spent hours at a time, immobilized, "t'inking," as he put it to his mystified American students. Nor can we forget in this connection his famous remark, "I don't want to be interesting; I want to be good."[46]

The argument has been advanced that Mies in seeking to raise fact to spirit in the modern world was uncritical of *those* facts—the rise of Nazism, for one—whose effect was to destroy modernism and finally to bring himself to personal and professional misfortune. This seems nonetheless to have been the measure of the man. If he really accepted Spengler, he would have reasoned that "the decline" consisted precisely of the sort of horrific events that were unfolding in the late 1920s with the Depression and the 1930s with the flourishing of totalitarianism. He would have preferred, like Spengler's Roman soldier, to endure the chaos stoically and, like a Christian ascetic, to place himself—and his art—spiritually above it. Yet soldier, ascetic, or whatever—epicurean, not least—he still had to eat. And however much he sought to elevate architecture to the realm of spirit, it remained intractably a material and social art which would never quite allow him to escape quotidian reality. In 1930 he accepted an appointment to the directorship of the Bauhaus.

5   Depression, Collectivization, and the Crisis of Art, 1929–36

In the summer of the year the school was sorely beset. Despite its international renown, or perhaps because of it, there had been hardly a moment in its eleven-year history that it had not been under some manner of attack from within or without, whether on aesthetic or political grounds and either from conservatives or radicals.[1] Van Doesburg had assailed its expressionist tendencies in the early 1920s, following which Johannes Itten was supplanted by László Moholy-Nagy as the leader of the faculty and spearhead of the newly adopted machine aesthetic. Right-wing elements in Weimar had forced it to quit that city in 1925. Thereafter it found a home in Dessau, with sanction and support from a liberal municipal administration, but less than three years later wrangling within the faculty together with mounting hostility from local nationalists, directed especially against Walter Gropius, had prompted him to an extreme decision. Hoping that the Bauhaus might find peace if it were free of his controversial personal image, Gropius resigned the directorship in the spring of 1928. The position was offered to Mies, clearly a less incendiary political figure. He turned it down.[2] Gropius then nominated the Swiss Hannes Meyer, who had been brought to Dessau in 1927 to head a newly formed department of architecture. Meyer accepted, and Gropius returned to private practice in Berlin.

It is the consensus of historians that the spirit of search and discovery that marked the glory years of the Bauhaus ended when Meyer took over. Gropius's resignation was swiftly followed by those of three of his stalwarts, Moholy-Nagy, Marcel Breuer, and Herbert Bayer. Meyer, an avowed functionalist, concentrated his energies on the architecture department while emphasizing practical as opposed to speculative endeavor. Not only did he stand for the severest form of *Sachlichkeit*; he was a political leftist who preferred collective solutions to personal experimentation. Hilberseimer was appointed to supervise projects in mass housing and city planning. Walter Peterhans was put in charge of the new courses in photography. Fate would later see to it that these last two men found their way to Chicago and a major role in Mies's life.

Meanwhile, Meyer's two-year tenure, like so much of the Bauhaus' achievement, ended in institutional frustration. His radical functionalist aesthetic alienated the artist-teachers, though not so much as his unrelenting Marxism and his tendency to insinuate sociology into all Bauhaus activities, thus pushing the school further and further from its original purposes. Oskar Schlemmer quit the faculty in 1929, while Josef Albers, Wassily Kandinsky, and Paul Klee suffered the progressive isolation of the fine arts from the curriculum. In 1930 Meyer was at last obliged to step down following charges that he had given money to striking miners in the name of the Bauhaus. Hostilities erupted all over again, this time with attacks coming from the left—supportive of Meyer—as well as from the right. Midway through the year Mayor Hesse, following the weary recommendation of Gropius, approached Mies and again offered him the directorship of the school. This time Mies accepted.

Hesse's strategy was apparent. Mies was a man neither of the right nor the left, nor even of the center; he was an artist. Thus he could be expected to keep the political dogs at bay without compromising the progressive standards of the school. He was widely identified with the design of glamorous homes for rich men and known to care more for beauty than for utility. But there was no question about his talent or his integrity as a designer.

In fact Mies in Berlin had continued to cultivate the image of the Grand Seigneur to which he had aspired ever since he saw Peter Behrens act the part so convincingly. He dressed as he always had, conservatively but impeccably, with a preference for dark suits set off by bowlers and homburgs and now and then even by spats. For a brief, ill-considered spell he wore a monocle. His natural reserve deepened, one should say grew, into a magisterial aloofness, but with the familiar effect of impressing people with the monumentality of his personality. And of his person: in his mid-forties a naturally ample physique had become thick-set. "When you see from the distance two men approaching," said Selman Selmanagic, one of his later Bauhaus students, "and nearer to you there is only one man, you will be sure it is Mies."[3]

Needless to say, Mies would run the school differently from Hannes Meyer. Almost as predictably, given the reflexive quarrelsomeness of the Bauhaus, his persona produced an angry response from the students. Meyer's supporters festered: the traditionally democratic, politically conscious atmosphere of the Bauhaus had been invaded by an elitist taskmaster who, once he arrived, proceeded to behave like one. In noisy mass meetings in the school cafeteria the students voiced their indignation at the dismissal of Meyer while demanding that Mies descend from his office fastness and defend himself in person.

They had clearly challenged the wrong man. Summarily Mies called in the Dessau police and directed them to throw the students out of the building. Mayor Fritz Hesse closed the Bauhaus for several weeks. According to Selmanagic, Mies officially expelled all the students, with the offer to accept any back who, in painstaking individual interviews with him, expressed the desire to rematriculate. Thus, presumably, the most radical elements would be flushed out. About 180 of the roughly 200 students at the Bauhaus returned to work.[4]

And work it was, under Mies's solemn, stolid direction. The Bauhaus was turned into something approaching a school of architecture that operated with little of its former rambunctiousness but much midnight oil. The crafts workshops lost a measure of their erstwhile autonomy as Mies redirected their activities toward the central discipline of interior decoration. Klee resigned to take a professorship in Düsseldorf. Kandinsky stayed on, having quarreled about the curric-

Depression, Collectivization, and the Crisis of Art

ulum with Mies, who agreed to retain fine arts though only in reduced form. Mies proved to be closer in some policies to Meyer than either of them was to Gropius, though more than the other two, he ran the institution with a personally autocratic hand. Hilberseimer's influence within the faculty grew. Lilly Reich was appointed to head the weaving workshop. She and Mies shared an apartment at the Bauhaus, spending three days a week there, the rest in Berlin. Hilberseimer, who like Mies was married but had a mistress, Otti Berger (Reich's workshop assistant), at Dessau, took charge of the school when Mies was away.

All the records and anecdotes pertaining to Mies at the Bauhaus fit the portrait we have painted of him as a man.[5] He took reluctantly to administrative tasks, leaving most of them to Reich, and he made no conciliatory efforts to mediate internal institutional arguments. He restricted his teaching to advanced students, whom he drove through endless revisions of such apparently simple assignments as a single-bedroom house or a house facing a walled garden. The latter notion he himself wrestled with over and over in the famed court-house designs of the 1930s (see pp. 189–93). "The very simplicity of these houses," wrote his student Howard Dearstyne in justification of Mies's teaching approach, "is their chief difficulty. It is much easier to do a complicated affair than something clear and simple."[6] Mies was more likely to tell a student "Versuchen Sie es wieder" (try it again) than to criticize—or encourage—in detail, though he was not incapable of illustrating his points with pith. Disdainful as he was of Meyer's doctrine of architectural functionalism, he once objected to an awkward

118. Mies with students at Bauhaus, Dessau, about 1930 (Selman Selmanagic, far right) Private collection

passage in a design Selmanagic claimed to have made perfectly workable: "Come now, Selman, if you meet twin sisters who are equally healthy, intelligent, and wealthy and both can bear children, but one is ugly, the other beautiful, which one would you marry?"[7] Nor did Mies conceal from his students his negative judgment of Gropius as an architect, which had apparently not changed much since the early 1920s, no matter how cordial the two men had been in correspondence.

Mies remained head of the Dessau Bauhaus until 1932, when it was dissolved as a state institution. He reopened it the same year as his own private school in Berlin, though it closed again, during the summer of 1933. The Bauhaus succumbed in both cities from fundamentally the same illness: the ascendancy of Nazism. In retrospect the Berlin Bauhaus was little more than a holding action, since Mies's hopes to regain eventual state sponsorship were crushed quickly enough by what, in 1933, had become an altogether inhospitable state.

It is not surprising that Mies's directorship has won mixed reviews from critics and historians, since their judgments have been conditioned by their own visions of what the Bauhaus should have been. The "old" guard, most prominently the Gropius circle, decided Mies was at least as much an outsider as Hannes Meyer had been and, moreover, one who never lived by the *Geben und Nehmen* (give and take) spirit that guided the early Bauhaus. Those few students who stayed with him until the end in Dessau were almost unanimous in their reverence of him as an artist and their affection for him as a man, though it is clear they saw him more as a godhead than as a fellow searcher. Mies approached education much the way he took on architecture, with a drive to abstract it, to distill its ends and means to indivisible, unarguable essentials. Thus he taught his one-bedroom house projects with excruciating thoroughness; thus he had no more tolerance for administrative chores than he had for the specifics of the prospectuses of all those competitions he had entered earlier in his life—and lost. Thus, too, his own declaration that "the reasons for the great influence on the Bauhaus all over the world lay in the fact that the Bauhaus was an idea."[8]

An idea and a word: "The best thing Gropius has done," he declared late in life—as surely in criticism as in praise—"was to invent the name Bauhaus."[9]

In 1929, before Mies became involved with the Barcelona commission, he designed a house in Zehlendorf for Emil Nolde, the expressionist painter whom he knew before World War I when both men frequented the little Jaques-Dalcroze circle in Hellerau (see pp. 70–71). The Nolde House was yet another unfinished project. The painter's letters to the architect complain about the latter's dilatoriness, though out of a sense of loss as much as of exasperation: "[cancellation of your services] would disappoint me most especially, since I value you highly as an artist."[10] Other documents indicate that Mies finished the design by the deadline, but that financial difficulties rose up to block the completion of building. Much the same fate was in store for the plans Mies drew up in 1930 in response to an invitation to participate in a limited competition for the design of the Krefeld Golf Club. That the club later asked for a second, more modest proposal is presumed to be consequent to the straitened economic circumstances of the time. Mies did not submit a second design, and this project too wasted away.

Neither the Nolde House nor the Krefeld Club was a pivotal work in itself, though each in its own way foreshadowed his residential projects of the mid-1930s. The remodeling of the interior of Schinkel's Neue Wache (see p. 42) into a memorial to the fallen of the Great War, was the goal of a 1930 competition which Mies also lost. Nevertheless, in a site so fundamentally somber and ceremonial, his own proposal of a simple, Tinian-lined space containing a horizontal black slab and dedicated, in his own typically generalizing formulation,[11] to "To the Dead" (Den Toten) was both appropriate and moving. Of his minor completed projects in 1930, the most remarkable feature of the addition to the Henke House in Essen was its 25-foot-long retractable window in a single sheet of glass.[12] The Hess and Crous apartments in Berlin and the Johnson apartment in New York were bread-and-butter propositions.

The client who commissioned the last of these was a twenty-four-year-old American named Philip Cortelyou Johnson, Cleveland-born, Harvard-educated, precocious, opinionated, and newly appointed director of the department of architecture at New York's Museum of Modern Art. Johnson was touring Europe in the summer of 1930, devoting most of his time to a firsthand study of the New Architecture, a subject known hardly at all in the United States. One of his chief sources of information was Gustav Platz's book *Baukunst der neuesten Zeit*. There for the first time he saw the work of Mies, who he decided was an even better architect than Le Corbusier or Oud, the two modernists favored by Johnson's friend, the architectural historian Henry-Russell Hitchcock. Just a year earlier, in 1929, Hitchcock had published his own book, *Modern Architecture*, and two years later, in 1932, Johnson and Hitchcock together organized the Museum of Modern Art's epochal first exhibition of international modern architecture. Mies made his initial public appearance in America in that show.

Thus Johnson was the man who effectively introduced him to the New World. For the next four decades the two men would carry on a relationship marked alternately by warmth and polar chill, intellectual accord and personal animosity, but one as lively and vital to the history of twentieth-century architecture as any on record. The germ of it was the genuine admiration felt by a bright, rising young man of privilege for a brilliant, accomplished older one lately in danger of eclipse. Johnson stood for wealth and institutional authority in a land of boundless material resources; Mies had risen from modest origins to high professional rank by virtue of his own uncommon talents, in a country which by 1930 seemed to have moved all too rapidly from the paralysis of military defeat to the impotence of economic depression. Surely, then, Johnson engaged Mies's attention largely because Mies had always gravitated toward cultural power, especially if it gravitated toward him in return. At the same time Mies's colossal pride must have counseled him to keep his brash young admirer at

119. Perspective drawing for
the remodeling project of the
interior of Schinkel's Neue
Wache, Berlin, 1930

arm's length. There was plenty of cause for both attraction and conflict in the relationship that began in the summer of 1930 and grew
more turbulent in 1931.

"We used to go to Schlichter's all the time," Johnson recalled, "and
I'd pay for him. It was frightfully expensive and he had no means of
support that I could see. In 1930 he had only my apartment to do.
He did it as if it were six skyscrapers—the amount of work he put
into that apartment was incredible."[13]

One allows for some hyperbole from Johnson. Mies was on salary
from the Bauhaus and, despite the evaporation of the Bruhn money
on account of the Depression, he was not quite so poor nor quite so
idle, not yet. Still, Johnson's recollections are too vivid and he is too
skilled a reporter to be ignored:

[Mies] loved to drive in the country. That was one way I knew
I could get to see him . . . and I had a Cord, naturally, a Cord
. . . And his favorite buildings were the *Hallenkirchen*, up north
toward Stettin, up toward Lübeck . . . The *Backsteingotik* was
where he felt most at home, in the *Hallen*, in the tall churches.
I didn't understand German Gothic. I was brought up on Ile de
France Gothic. It was a little strange, the tall halls done in
brick.

Depression, Collectivization, and the Crisis of Art

I used to try to get him to talk about Schinkel. But he would just say yes, if I got enthusiastic, and would never really discuss it, even though he did that early thing [the Perls-Fuchs House] that looks like the Persius house. When I first found that I jumped for joy and said: "Oh, you know Persius." He didn't. Not by name. It was hard to know what Mies had seen, and what not.[14]

Whatever Johnson's frustrations with the man, his admiration for the architect apparently only grew. He made certain Mies was given a major place in the Museum of Modern Art's exhibition and even invited him personally to install the show. Here one senses the esteem in which Mies was held by MoMA's director as well, Alfred H. Barr, Jr., who also visited Berlin in 1930 and who must have done a lot to solicit the assistance of one of the museum's most important benefactors, Mrs. John D. Rockefeller, Jr. Early in 1931 Johnson wrote her from Berlin: "It is extremely encouraging to know that when the time arrives, probably in September, for the show to be designed, that [sic] we can have the greatest architect do it. Your cooperation and interest mean a great deal to us, especially in this preliminary period."[15]

Mies's own attitude toward Johnson's attention in general and the exhibition in particular seems to have vacillated between cordiality and the loftiest indifference, judging from Johnson's correspondence with Barr in New York. In July, complaining about the great man's all-too-frequent inaccessibility, Johnson wrote: "Mies is having a fit of being very hard to get hold of, and there is just nothing to be done. Repeated calls only make him mad."[16] Days later, on the other hand, Johnson found him, "I must say, very eager to design a new house especially for us."[17]

Did Mies really behave toward Johnson, not to mention the Museum of Modern Art, with such apparent caprice? What we know of him suggests he may have. He was fully capable of hauteur, especially toward a young man who may have pressed him too closely. Yet we have little evidence beyond Johnson's irrepressibly gossipy letters of what may have been going on in Mies's head during the darkening days of 1931. In what respects was the Bauhaus "falling apart rather badly," as Johnson said?[18] Why did Mies never go ahead with his design of a house for the MoMA show after "absolutely promising to send the model from Berlin by October 15"?[19]

"More modest show," Johnson wrote tersely on the margin of a memo late in 1931. "Mies not coming, no installation."[20] Again, reduced ambitions point to shrunken financial means all around, though it seems possible that Mies in his infinite capacity for the phlegmatic behavior he rationalized as *die schöpferische Pause* would find the familiar uncertainty of Berlin preferable to the unfamiliar uncertainty of New York.

What other reason might there be, except a slow withdrawal into himself during the early 1930s, a response, perhaps, to his perception of a darkening world? Johnson had good reason to presume that Mies would be more available toward the end of 1931 than toward the beginning. His expectation that the master would come to the U.S. in September to install the MoMA exhibition is consonant with the August closing of the one event of the year on which he, Mies, had labored earnestly.

It may overdramatize facts to suggest that the Berlin Building Exposition was Mies's swan song in Germany. Nevertheless, the house for a childless couple which he introduced in 1931 at the Berlin Fair Grounds on the Reichskanzlerplatz was the final work that reflected in built form his manner of the 1920s: that approach of flowing, searching, subjectively organized space most closely identified with the early country house projects as well as the Barcelona Pavilion and the Tugendhat House. Not even in his vigorously active second life in America did he do anything quite like it. Further, while it was not without intimation of the future, being yet another prefiguration of the mid-1930s court houses, the latter were never realized. As the final public demonstration of Mies the Weimar modernist, then, his exposition house was his formal if unwitting farewell gesture to a time, a place, a world view.

In turn, the exposition as a whole was his last major organizational assignment as a spokesman for the New Architecture. It was meant as a study of international city planning, architecture, furniture, and construction materials, with Mies in charge of the section devoted to "The Dwelling in Our Time." Unlike the Weissenhofsiedlung, which treated the same theme, his show in Berlin was an indoor display contained within a single very large hall. Nevertheless, Mies chose the architect-participants and designed the arrangement of their in-

120. View of the hall of the Berlin Building Exposition House, with the house by Mies, 1931

dividual contributions, just as he had at Stuttgart. Houses by the Luckhardt brothers, Hugo Häring, Marcel Breuer, and Lilly Reich were featured along with apartments by such as Walter Gropius, Ludwig Hilberseimer, and Otto Haesler and some rooms outfitted by Josef Albers and even Wassily Kandinsky. On a balcony that ringed the whole hall, the materials exhibition organized by Lilly Reich was shown.

Mies's own one-story house meant for a childless couple derived its support from the same system of regularly spaced columns that he first employed at Barcelona.[21] The walls were freestanding, of course, and almost all of them extended outward from the interior, for the most part paralleling the main, or longitudinal, axis but penetrating exterior space in all directions, as dynamically as in any design he had produced since the Brick Country House. Interior space was comparably free-flowing and unimpeded. Only the bathroom and the service rooms were closed in, and the latter alone looked out through conventional windows. The living-dining area was surrounded on three sides by glass walls, one of which, presumably to the west, could be lowered electrically into the ground, allowing indoors to merge literally with outdoors at that point. The living-dining area was further enlivened by a longitudinal wooden partition whose placement, and the spatial movement it engendered, recalled the use of the onyx walls in Barcelona and Brno. While one had to turn 180 degrees around the east wall of the living area to reach the bedroom area, there was no partition separating the two spaces, nor any wall between the bedrooms themselves (one for the husband, the other for the wife). Similarly in principle of free passage, the bedrooms, like the living-dining area, looked through great glass walls onto a terrace marked by another sculpture of a standing female figure by Georg Kolbe. Plaster walls which surrounded the bedroom terrace and separated it from a shallow pool had the effect of creating an enclosing court rather in the manner the travertine and Tinian walls at Barcelona had "clamped" the entire structure there. In Berlin, however, the walls split apart, making for an asymmetrical interplay of inner and outer space that was unprecedented for Mies in his completed work. The one long wall that escaped from under the flat roof and moved west to connect with Reich's house—and to create a garden area between the two struc-

121. Preliminary plan of the house for Berlin Building Exposition House

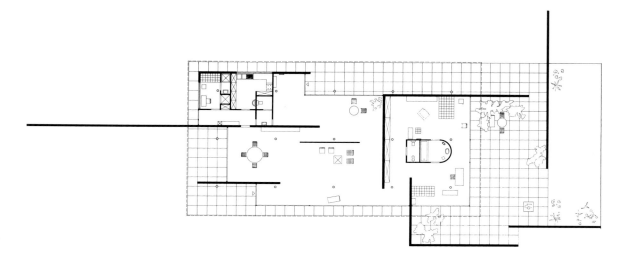

tures—was reminiscent of the walls darting off to infinity in the Brick Country House.

If the Exposition House was to prove the last example of its kind, it was also the most radical. None of the blockiness resulting from the contained spaces of the Tugendhat and Nolde houses is evident in it; it appears to explode its material confines more even than the Barcelona Pavilion did. Clearly it was an exhibition piece, in which Mies could fulfill his yearning for controlled fluid space more than he might have if he had had to cope with real tenants. Yet he would never again, even in his dreams, indulge himself quite so freely as he did here. The 1920s were over; the thirties had begun. If this was a last hurrah, he delivered it like a valedictory.

Both Johnson and Hitchcock wrote critical reviews of the Berlin Building Exposition and both agreed that Mies's house together with his furnishing of a bachelor's flat in one of the apartment houses easily constituted the most successful individual entries in the show.[22] The Americans also affirmed, however, that the whole exposition was dominated by the International Style, a term evidently invented by Hitchcock, which they took to be synonymous with the New Architecture. It was this that they made the focus of their international exhibition at the Museum of Modern Art. Titled "Modern Architecture: International Exhibition," the show ran from 9 February through 23 March 1932. Johnson installed it. More than fifty architects were included, and a catalog was published under the supervision of Barr, Hitchcock, and Johnson. It featured essays on the major Europeans, Le Corbusier, Oud, Gropius, and Mies, as well as on such vanguard Americans as Raymond Hood, Howe and Lescaze, the Austrian-born Richard Neutra, and Frank Lloyd Wright. Mies was represented by the Barcelona Pavilion, the Tugendhat House, and the Lange House.

The exhibition aroused terrific controversy in New York, where the New Architecture as a corpus was seen for the first time. Controversy, to be sure, meant attention: Edward Durell Stone, who later (1939) designed the building that now houses the Museum of Modern Art, said the Johnson-Hitchcock effort "did for architecture what the famous Armory Show had done for painting."[23] Johnson and Hitchcock followed their success with a book bearing the title *The International Style*, in which they identified three hallmarks of the "style": "There is, first, a new conception of architecture as volume rather than as mass. Secondly, regularity rather than axial symmetry serves as the chief means of ordering design. These two principles, with a third proscribing arbitrary applied decoration, mark the productions of the international style."[24]

In 1966, some thirty-four years later, Hitchcock reflected on the term and the definition and recognized that neither fitted quite so neatly as he and Johnson had hoped all the work they included in the show—not the least of that Mies's distinctly unvolumetric Barcelona Pavilion—or all the able designers they downplayed or simply omitted. "At least, however," he concluded, "the book [represented] an account by young and enthusiastic contemporaries of the new architecture of the twenties at the moment when it had reached its peak of achievement at the opening of the next decade."[25]

Depression, Collectivization, and the Crisis of Art

Sometime in 1926 Ada Bruhn Mies and her three girls, aged twelve, eleven, and nine, left the Tyrol for southern Germany, where they spent the winter in Garmisch-Partenkirchen, at the pension owned and operated by Ada's divorced sister. Early in 1927 they moved again, to Icking, a comfortable Bavarian village where all three daughters attended private school. In 1930 Muck enrolled at Salem, Germany's most exclusive country *Gymnasium*, where she earned her *Abitur* in 1933.

Marianne remembers her four years at Icking, during which she grew to adolescence, as a happy and untrammeled time. Ada probably saw them differently. For one thing, her illnesses did not relent; she continued under the care of Dr. Fahrenkamp in Stuttgart and in 1928 underwent a serious abdominal operation that almost took her life. For another, the dwindling supply of family money in the midst of the Depression forced a more austere regime upon her and her daughters. In 1931, with Waltraut and Marianne in tow, she moved again, to Frankfurt.

Mies during these years of the late 1920s and the early 1930s rarely made more than annual visits, and slowly Ada's little female compound itself began to break up. Muck aspired to the dance, took a stage name—Georgia—studied with Mary Wigman, and presently joined her troupe. Marianne quit school just a year short of her *Abitur* and left for Sweden, pursuing a new-found passion for Nordic literature.

That was in the spring of 1932. The condition of the German economy had grown grave enough by then to awaken memories of the worst postarmistice days of 1919. Street fighting was commonplace again; politics became increasingly polarized. In the national elections of 31 July, to which an unprecedented number of citizens responded, more than half the electorate endorsed parties expressly committed to the overthrow of the republic.

The Dessau Bauhaus spun toward its doom. Blows rained upon it from the forces of the architectural right, led by Paul Schultze-Naumburg, and from the local Nazis, who demanded not only the closing of the school but the demolition of the Gropius buildings that housed it. Under pressure from the national government, worried Dessau Social Democrats abstained from a crucial city council vote in the summer of 1932. The Nazis won the day.

Seeking, nonetheless, to cultivate the appearance of fairness, the victors announced that a committee of experts would visit the school's regular end-of-term exhibition and judge formally and finally whether the Bauhaus warranted more funding from Dessau. The left-wing students and faculty rejected the idea. Mies, whose behavior seems to have been naïve or headstrong or both, insisted on proceeding with the show but persuaded only a few of his own students to participate in it. With Schultze-Naumburg at its head, the committee took the few minutes needed to view the pitifully small display Mies put together, then rendered its fatal judgment with comparable dispatch.

The Bauhaus was shut down on 1 October. Mies and Mayor Hesse nonetheless—and in this case not at all naïvely—managed to negotiate a legal agreement the effect of which was to keep the school alive as a private institution. Mies's full salary would be guaranteed until 31 March 1933 and half of it thereafter until 31 March 1935. Similar arrangements were made with other instructors. Since it was Mies's intention to move the school to Berlin, the city of Dessau gave up its rights to the name "Bauhaus," thus securing it to Mies as director. Patents and equipment were likewise turned over to him.

In late October the Bauhaus reopened in Berlin-Steglitz, with a faculty consisting of Albers, Hilberseimer, Kandinsky, Peterhans, Reich, Friedrich Engemann, Hinnerk Scheper, and Alcar Rudelt. Their quarters were humble, an abandoned telephone factory in an unprepossessing neighborhood on the southern edge of the city. Mies's efforts at renovation were confined to painting the interior entirely in white. He claimed, even late in life, that he and his colleagues liked the place better than they had the Dessau Bauhaus, a recollection attributable more to his dogged pride than to his fairminded reporting. Though he succeeded in reopening the school as early as 25 October, enrollment fell short of the one hundred students he had hoped for. He reinstated the Dessau curriculum as best he could under the circumstances, and a measure of calm descended until shortly after Hitler's accession to power on 30 January 1933. Thereupon someone raised a swastika in front of the Bauhaus and Mies summarily had it hauled down.[26]

It was now only a matter of time before all breath was out of the beast. Significantly, those who are old enough to retain affirmative memories of the Berlin Bauhaus recall one event more than all others: the Fasching (Carnival) costume ball of 18 February, for which students and faculty made a great show of redecorating the building with gaudy colors and lights. In retrospect it was a little like a jazz funeral, Basin Street on Birkbuschstrasse.

The new government lost no time in getting down to business. Less than two months after the ball, on the morning of 11 April, Mies arrived at the school to find the portal locked and the building cordoned off by police. The Nazis had taken over the premises in a search for documents that might show links between the school and the Communist party. Mies himself later recounted the incident: " 'Stop!' I said. 'What's the idea? This is my school; it belongs to me.' But there were the Gestapo searching the premises. They were looking for the foundation deeds of the Bauhaus so as to take proceedings against the Mayor of Dessau. We had, of course, nothing to do with it all. They regarded us as perfectly harmless—and so we were. Then they interrogated me for hours."[27]

Mies was now getting his first close-on glimpse of another aspect of the "new era" which three years earlier he had called "neither better nor worse than any other."[28] He made an appointment with Alfred Rosenberg, the busy new Minister of Culture, who could not see him until late in the evening of the day following the Bauhaus closing. Mies said he wanted the Bauhaus reopened. He insisted it was a school with an idea, and the idea was not related to politics but to the aesthetics of technology and industrial development. Rosenberg answered that he was himself a trained architect, and he knew about these things. "Then we will understand each other," Mies replied. "What do you expect me to do?" protested Rosenberg. "The Bauhaus is supported by forces fighting our forces!"[29]

Mies persisted. "For any cultural effort," he said, "one needs peace, and I would like to know whether we will have that peace."

"Are you hampered in your work?" Rosenberg asked.

And Mies replied, "Hampered is not the correct term. Our house has been sealed, and I would be grateful to you if you could look into this matter."[30]

Rosenberg agreed to do so, according to Mies, who meanwhile appealed elsewhere, making several visits of entreaty per week for several months to Gestapo headquarters. At last all efforts seemed unavailing. By mid-July no official word from the authorities had been received. Half the dispirited students had decided to make other plans for their futures. The money was gone. On 20 July Mies wrote the Gestapo "that the faculty of the Bauhaus at a meeting yesterday saw itself compelled, in view of the economic difficulties which have arisen from the shutdown of the Institute, to dissolve the Bauhaus Berlin."[31]

This letter was crossed in the mails by another, dated 21 July, from the Gestapo to Mies, in which permission to reopen the school was granted—conditional, however, on two main concessions. Hilberseimer and Kandinsky must be replaced "by individuals who guarantee to support the principles of the National Socialist ideology," and a new curriculum satisfactory to "the demands of the new State" must be submitted to the Prussian minister of culture.[32]

The prospect of such a compromise added to an already desperate fiscal condition was more than Mies and the faculty could bear. Sometime late in July they met again, and he asked them to join him in a champagne toast. "And now I make a proposition and I hope you will agree with me," he later recalled telling them. "I will send a telegram to the Gestapo saying 'Thank you very much for the permission to open the school again, but the faculty has decided to close it.' . . . That was the end of the Bauhaus."[33]

On 10 August Mies so notified the students.

The character of the 1920s was determined by 1924 and that of the 1930s almost exactly one decade later. Modernism had based its high hopes for a new world upon an aesthetic of the machine that was doctrinally broad enough to make room for functionalists like Hannes Meyer and artists like Mies van der Rohe, but that proved to be so impotent at the level of practical economics and politics that the new utopia eventually took up little more real estate than could be measured out on the pages of the intellectual tabloids. The Depression quickly demonstrated how much at the mercy of cold economic reality the warmest artistic dreams were; worse still, the totalitarian regimes that "saved" their citizenries from the privation of the turn of the thirties regarded the modern arts more often with open hostility than affection or even indifference.

Nowhere did conditions finally grow more hellish than in Germany, though Nazi policy was seldom simple or clear-cut, a fact that only added vexation to diabolism. Right-wing *völkisch* sentiment saw the modern arts as pernicious and pathological, the expressions of a rootless *undeutsch* urbanism for which the International Jew was made the most readily fitting symbol. Yet Nazi thought could just as easily identify itself with modernity, with science, and with advanced technology. One has only to recall how, in Leni Riefenstahl's classic film *Triumph of the Will*, bands of fresh-faced youngsters camped in grassy fields gazed awestruck into the sky at the gleaming new German airplanes headed for the 1934 Nazi party congress in Nuremberg. Among all the arts architecture was the one gripped most tightly in a vise of contradiction. The Nazis fumed over Gropius's Bauhaus in Dessau, threatening alternately to tear it down and to raise a pitched roof over it. Yet they also built the superbly efficient Autobahn. Hitler's personal preferences ran to a neoclassicism reminiscent of the pre–World War I years, while Hermann Goering commissioned buildings for the air force that were indistinguishable from the most *sachlich* of 1920s modernist works.[34]

Every German architect was obliged to adjust to the changed conditions that came first with the Depression and later with Hitler. Mies, who just lately had become a famous and celebrated man, saw his future threatened by economic and political forces with which he was psychologically ill-equipped to cope. Even with Weissenhof he had begun to retreat from the community of the vanguard, into himself. Now external events drove him into a more pronounced solitariness. He alternated between concentrated effort and sluggish indecisiveness. Between 1930 and 1937 he both affirmed common cause with world modernism and drew back from it. At the end of the twenties he had joined the Congrès Internationaux d'Architecture Moderne (CIAM), the newest and probably the most hopeful global instrumentality of the New Architecture. Yet he kept his distance from it, at times consenting to participate in its efforts, then bowing out of them altogether. To be sure, he liked recognition and sought it at the official level: he was elected to the Prussian Academy of Arts in 1931; at the same time, his files of the early 1930s are filled with bids to show in far-flung exhibitions of modern architecture—bids he repeatedly turned down in letters that project a state of mind bordering on lethargy.

The cultural barbarism of the 1930s did not settle upon Germany only with the formal Nazi takeover of the central government in 1933. Undoubtedly the right wing opposed modernism by consensus and meant to throttle it as a central driving force in the arts. Yet modernism succumbed not at once but gradually, and never quite completely. Here and there aspects of it were absorbed by Hitler's state and utilized in fragmented, adulterated, or distorted form, both by accident and calculation. Moreover, many of the modernists themselves were unable early on to perceive, and reluctant later on to believe, that their careers could not be sustained in the very country that had been so hospitable to vanguard art in the 1920s. Their efforts to stay in Germany and go on working as they had ranged from outright resistance through attempts at accommodation to work done in privacy or in secret. Those who nursed the hope that the "progressive" spirit of Nazism might eventually tolerate or even encourage their kind of art, averted their eyes from the unregenerate Nazi doctrines—especially those pertaining to race and ethnicity—about which there was never any doubt from the start. Mies's own attitude was a conflicted patchwork of indifference toward national politics in general, hostility toward Nazi philistinism in particular, dedication to architectural principle, and desire to build regardless of who asked him. Moreover, like many Germans during the first years of Nazi domination, he was not prepared to believe that Hitler was there to stay. Given these mixed feelings, his attempts to cope covered a spectrum of visionary projects and built works, some freer and more inventive than others, some more political in implication, some less, yet only few clearly correlated in quality with political intent.

As a group, his house designs of the 1930s are his most creatively significant endeavors, though their realization was almost constantly frustrated. Between 1931, when he finished the house for the Berlin Building Exposition, and 1938, his last active year in Germany, he worked on perhaps as many as a dozen separately identifiable houses, of which the only two completed—the 1932 Lemke House in Berlin and the 1933 Severain House[35] in Wiesbaden—were easily the least ambitious and in final form the least interesting.

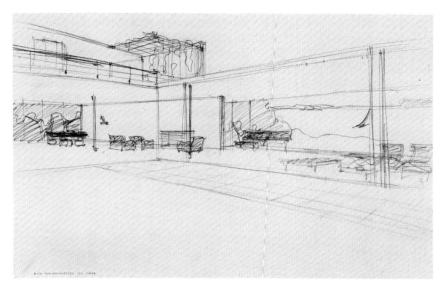

123. Perspective drawing of the Gericke House project, Berlin, 1932

One of the most arresting, though never built, was designed in less than a month's time during the summer of 1932, at just about the time the Nazis were intensifying their attacks on the Dessau Bauhaus. The client, Herbert Gericke, director of the German Academy in Rome, had taken the unusual step—for a private citizen—of initiating a competition for the design of a house he meant to build on a site overlooking Berlin's Wannsee. Several weeks after Mies submitted his proposal, he was informed that Gericke had rejected it. Mies never received an answer to his subsequent offer to rework the project at no extra cost.

Had the house been built, it very likely would have rivaled the Tugendhat House and the two villas of the early 1920s, if not in luxury, surely in the imaginativeness of its design.[36] It was in fact a cousin of the house in Brno in that the upper story, at street level, was given over to children's and governess' rooms, with a passage separating them, while the living area on the ground floor was reached by a circular stair. The whole house, however, spread generously outward, its plan less compact than that of the Tugendhat House and more reminiscent of the radiating wings of the Krefeld Golf Club. The living area was, in effect, bounded on all four sides by glass walls that granted anyone inside an exceptionally rich view of the outdoors. A large number of drawings of the project survive, including perspectives notable not only for Mies's surpassing draftsmanship but for his equally uncommon interest in the interdependence of house and natural surround. That abiding concern for the subtly sensuous experience of distinguishing interior from exterior through the near-immateriality of glass is rarely matched in any of the graphic representations he made of his architecture.

As a building type, no less as a vessel of meaning, the court house is Mies's most compelling architectural accomplishment of the 1930s.[37] We mentioned earlier (see pp. 176–77) that Mies required his Bauhaus students to design simple houses which looked out on courts and gardens surrounded by walls. This fact has led to the presumption that

Depression, Collectivization, and the Crisis of Art

his own designs of such buildings commenced about 1931. We are not sure of this, however; they may not have begun in earnest before 1934.[38] In a sense there can be no exact starting point, since Mies had been moving toward the "pure" court house—in which there is a fully enclosing wall—ever since his "clamping" of the ends of the Barcelona Pavilion within travertine and Tinian walls. In the Nolde House of the same period, Mies used angled walls to suggest the containment of space. This device was carried forward in the Berlin Building Exposition House of 1931, in which walls nearly closed off completely the terrace outside the bedrooms. Thus the walls, in sliding, asymmetrical order, permitted moments of visual access to the outside, while continuing to act as Mies's walls had ever since the Brick Country House, namely, to extend the whole structure searchingly out into space.

In the House with Three Courts, a drawing of which (presumably the preliminary plan) dates probably from 1934 or 1935, the court house idea is fully developed. Mies postulates a complete rectangular enclosure in masonry. A narrow entrance on one of the long sides leads onto a transverse terrace bounded by a garden on the right, the long side of the house on the left. The house is roughly T-shaped in plan, with the stem of the T flanked by two other, smaller courts.

This is the simplest account of the layout, though a more fitting description would begin from within rather than from without. Interior space is altogether free-flowing except for service rooms. In both the preliminary and the supposed final plan, the living and dining areas occupy a single space in the bar of the T more distant from the entrance. That space turns into the bedroom, in the stem of the T.

124. Plan of the Gericke House

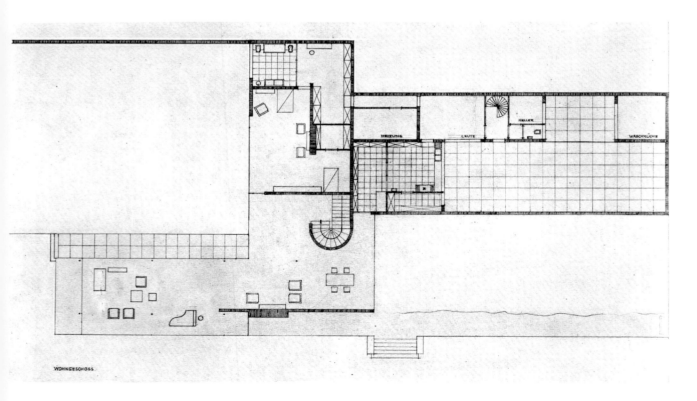

Depression, Collectivization, and the Crisis of Art

125. Perspective of a row house project with interior court, from living room, about 1934 (studio drawing c. 1939)

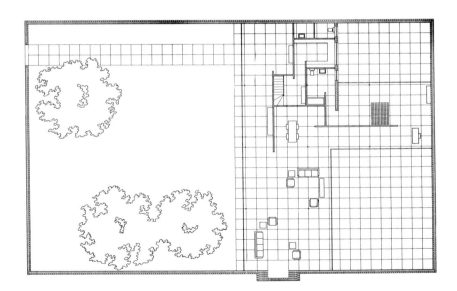

126. Plan and elevation of the House with Three Courts project, about 1934 (studio drawing c. 1939)

Depression, Collectivization, and the Crisis of Art

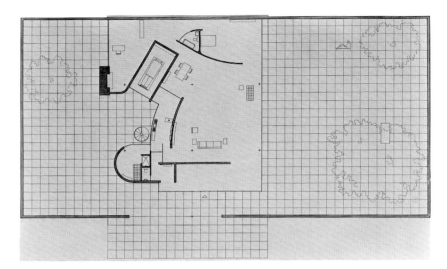

Freestanding walls define spaces and views, blocking but not closing them off. The flat roof, as is customary in all of Mies's house designs by now, rests on a grid of columns that provides support as well as a rational system within which space may move at the subjective discretion of the planner.

To this extent the house is typical of Mies's 1920s work, with, however, a substantial twofold difference. All outside walls except those of the service rooms are of glass; thus the exterior is maximally dematerialized, the house nearly pure membrane. Yet the courtyard wall acts as a tough sheath, protecting the membrane, rather in the sense of an exoskeleton.

Mies thus maximized the exchange, the mixture, the interplay of inner and outer space at the expense of a reach into infinity, which is here most decisively arrested. Material and immaterial elements are separated as surely as inner and outer spaces are emulsified. Movement within the compound is restlessly free, while the compound from outside is closed and compacted, perceptible as a dense, introverted mass.

One can do little more than guess about the motives and implications of this change. Mies may have had nothing in mind more profound than the practical transformation of a country house into a town house: guaranteeing the glassy freedom of the Gericke House by sequestering it within a walled residence marshalled by the rectangular lot of a city street. The House with Three Courts may be the germ of an elegant urban tract development. Or, for the very reason that his court-house designs seem to have no client, they may have been purely visionary endeavors in which he extended, evolved, refined his concept of space for its own sake. There seems to be no accounting for the Court House with Curved Wall Elements beyond the apparent wish to push subjective space well beyond the rectilinear guidelines of the column grid, further into the implicitly romantic realm of diagonals and curves than he ever went.

Yet one cannot help wondering, at least, to what extent his own inner drive toward essence and abstraction collided with the outer constraints of freedom imposed by the rough economic and political conditions in Germany during the 1930s. Was the vitreous interior of the House with Three Courts his architectural approximation of spiritual form and was the wall hard material fact? Or was the wall the public face, the interior Mies's personal "liberation," as Fichte might have put it? Correspondingly, can one read the nautiluslike court houses as an effort to arrive at the "conformity of intellect and thing"—truth, as Saint Thomas saw it?

Two major projects of the 1930s, neither of them built, were carried sufficiently far to suggest how the purposes of specific tenants might qualify the general concept of the court house. Frau Margarete Hubbe asked Mies to build a house for her on an island in the Elbe River at Magdeburg, the commission dating most likely from the early months of 1935. Mies acknowledged the challenge of the site, commenting on "the broad panorama of the Elbe" visible from it, but adding that

> the lovely view lay to the east, whereas to the south the view was utterly without charm, almost a disturbance . . .
>
> Therefore I extended the living area of the house toward the south by means of a garden courtyard surrounded by walls, thus obstructing this view while at the same time preserving all of the sunlight. Downstream, on the other hand, the house is completely open, flowing freely over into the garden.
>
> In so doing I not only followed the site conditions, but achieved a nice contrast of quiet seclusion and open expanse as well.[39]

128. Perspective of the Hubbe House project, Magdeburg, 1935

Depression, Collectivization, and the Crisis of Art

The idea of enclosing the whole, court house fashion, developed only in the course of the planning. As in the House with Three Courts, a T-shaped volume whose stem includes living-dining area and bedroom walled in glass is apparent in the final drawings, though openings in the girding wall to both east and west are wide enough to disclose the broad and distant vistas that Mies found so attractive in that particular place. Closer views give onto a pair of partially enclosed courts. In these respects the Hubbe House is a variation of the theme most strictly followed in the House with Three Courts. As with the Gericke House, the surviving perspective drawings emphasize the natural setting as much as they do the architecture. Moreover Mies, as he often did in the 1930s, treats perspective in a singular manner that intensifies a sense of deep, almost telescoped space. All rooms, terraces, even window surfaces appear vaster and recede more rapidly than the eye would see, suggesting that Mies, more in the early 1930s than at any time in his career, luxuriated in the very perception of space as defined and shaped by the formative mind.

"Sadly," Lilly Reich reported in a letter of 12 February 1936 to J. J. P. Oud, the Hubbe House "was not built, for the lady client sold the property. Another small project for Krefeld has also had to be abandoned. All of this is not easy for us; I myself only have a few small jobs, but for M. it is especially difficult."[40]

The Krefeld project to which Reich referred is the Ulrich Lange House, intended for the newly married son of Hermann and commissioned more or less contemporaneously with the Hubbe House. Neither enterprise was really "small," judging from the numerous revisions Mies rang on each, including the nearly total reconstitution of preliminary plans. In final form the Lange House would have resembled the Hubbe House in its T-shaped plan, which featured a glazed living-dining area that looked onto an enclosed court and through a substantial opening in the outer wall to a distant view. Opposite the terraced court was a service court containing a garage. The space-defining element so familiar in Mies's living room areas, a freestanding partition (in this case screening off a kitchen), was unusually shaped in an S-curve.

129. Elevation of the Ulrich Lange House project, Krefeld, 1935

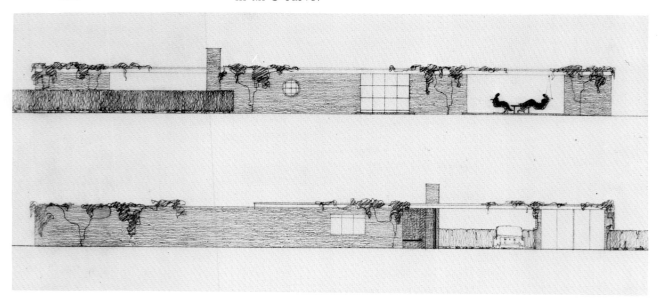

Reich's letter to Oud did not divulge the reason why this design was never built. The local authorities, hewing to the Nazi antimodernist line, refused Mies the necessary building permit unless the house was concealed from street view by the construction of an earth berm. Mies reportedly was so disturbed by this condition that he declined to abide by it and the whole endeavor collapsed.[41]

That, however, was as late as 1936, by which time he had had ample opportunity to recognize how little affection the Nazis felt for him. It was a lesson he had to learn the hard way. In the three years since Hitler took power in 1933, Mies's history of encounters with Nazi policy was sufficiently tangled and tortured to require careful discussion here and painstaking assessment.

Two projects, both of major dimensions, dominate the record. On 9 February 1933, less than two weeks after Hitler's accession, Mies was invited by the board of the Reichsbank (Imperial Bank) to participate in a competition for an addition to the main bank building in downtown Berlin. The most notable fact about the list of people associated with this enterprise is that they represented the full range of viewpoints current in the German arts. The invited architects included Gropius, Otto Haesler, and the conservative Wilhelm Kreis. Behrens served on the jury alongside Mies's old Weissenhof nemesis Paul Bonatz. The six final award-winning projects, Mies's among them, tended toward a cautious, modified modernism. Mies's clearly stood out: it was the simplest in profile, the most rigorously symmetrical in plan. It was also by far the most monumental in effect: a ten-story-high block with a massive, unornamented convex facade. Three unparallel wings grew out of the rear of this element, converging toward the Spree River. Elevations were fenestrated by rows of unbroken ribbon windows. A two-story light on the front disclosed an immense 50-by-350-foot entrance hall behind, surely the most overpowering single passage Mies had designed for a building since his neoclassical days. Several press critics praised his project for its simplicity and generosity of form, while complaining of its failure to harmonize with the older buildings of the neighborhood. There is no record of comment about its Germanness or lack thereof, or about any other aspect of it that might touch upon Nazi doctrine.

We must conclude that Mies's Reichsbank design proves next to nothing about his acceptance or rejection of the tastes of the new regime, if for no other reason than that those tastes seem to have been undeterminable from the whole episode. Hitler's own love of the "heroic" was not so vital a factor in German public architecture as it would be after Albert Speer became his trusted architectural deputy, in 1934. The Reichsbank, then, largely because it is both abstract in form and enormous in scale, appears ambiguous in motive. If it tells us anything significant about Mies's public buildings in the 1930s, it is that the three cubic wings on the Spree River side are derived as much from the huge slabs of his own 1928 Alexanderplatz project as from any Nazi standards. Beyond that debt to himself, the trend of which the Reichsbank is symptomatic is no less international than national. Modernism as we have discussed it became blurred everywhere in the desperate and combative 1930s; more exactly, world public architec-

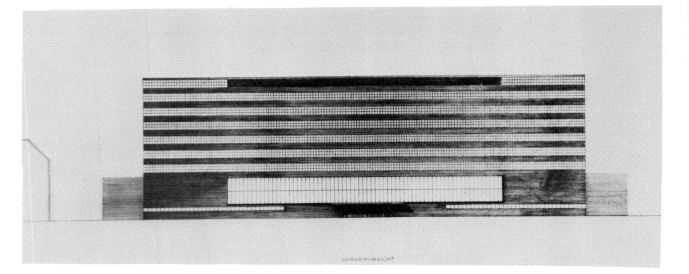

VORDERANSICHT

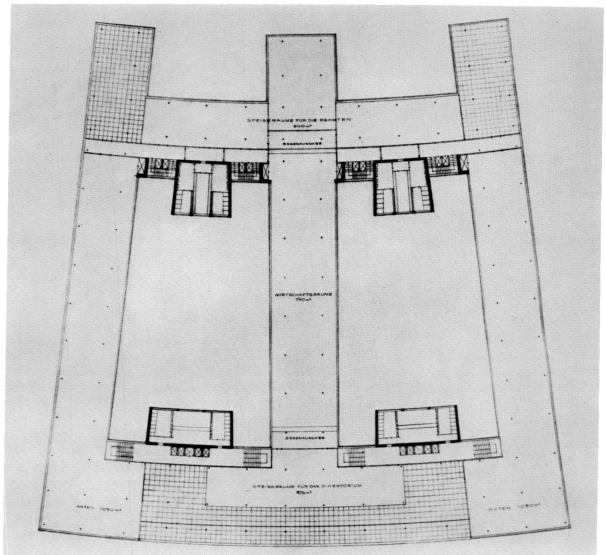

ture shrank from the radical modes of the twenties in which the spirit of internationalism was equated with and symbolized by abstract form, and to which the vanguard designers of Germany were emphatically committed. What came to the fore everywhere were either historicist revivals of classicism or the more conservative "moderne" of Art Deco — styles in any case whose traditional vocabularies of figurative ornament could be used symbolically to advance patriotic causes in popularly familiar terms. It is enough to recall the monumental columned and corniced government buildings put up by the Roosevelt administration, not to mention the widespread turn to social realist painting and sculpture throughout the democracies as well as the dictatorships. The axiality and immense scale of Mies's Reichsbank may have reflected some of this cold new nationalist classicism, but it retained more modernism than most public edifices of its time, either in Germany or elsewhere.

Mindful of this as well as of the incoherence of Nazi policy, Philip Johnson pondered the architectural future of Germany in an article,

"Architecture in Third Reich," published in the fall of 1933. "What [its] new buildings will look like," he said, "is as yet completely unknown."[42] Then, reviewing the factions vying for the attentions of the party — the conservatives (Schultze-Naumburg, Paul Erwin Troost), the "half-moderns" (Schmitthenner) and "the young men in the party, the students and revolutionaries who are ready to fight for modern art," Johnson went on,

> there is only one man whom even the young men can defend and that is Mies van der Rohe. Two factors especially make Mies' acceptance as the new architect possible. First Mies is respected by the conservatives . . . Secondly Mies has just won (with four [*sic*] others) a competition for the new buildings of the

Reichsbank. If (and it may be a long if) Mies should build this building it would clinch his position.

A good modern Reichsbank would satisfy the new craving for monumentality, but above all it would prove to the German intellectuals and to foreign countries that the new Germany is not bent on destroying all the splendid modern arts which have been built up in recent years.

Johnson has lived long enough to regret his overly optimistic view of the Nazis. And Mies must have been embarrassed by his own apparent slowness to learn from the new government's purge of the progressive municipal building administrations in Berlin and Frankfurt, which took place even as the Bauhaus was being shut down.

Yet building societies had been customarily more radical than schools,[43] and Mies, obdurate as ever, persisted in waiting out a decision on his own institution.* Indeed, with the further passage of time he might well have entertained more, not less, hope that he

*Both Ise Gropius in a personal conversation of July 1979 and Sibyl Moholy-Nagy in a reply to Howard Dearstyne (*Journal of the Society of Architectural Historians* 24 [October 1965]: 255–56) claimed that Mies was among the signers of a formal appeal issued in June 1933 to German intellectuals and artists by Schultze-Naumburg in behalf of the new *völkische Kulturpolitik*. This document has never been found.

133. Lilly Reich, at Lugano, 1933
Courtesy T. Paul Young

134. Mies and Lilly Reich on
an excursion boat on the
Wannsee, 1933
Photo courtesy of Mies van der
Rohe Archive, the Museum of
Modern Art, New York

would be able to build as he wanted. Late in 1933 a body called the Reichskulturkammer was established at the behest of Propaganda Minister Josef Goebbels.[44] Mies joined it.[45] During the previous year Goebbels had made a point of publicly opposing the militantly intolerant attitude toward the modern arts for which Alfred Rosenberg's Kampfbund für deutsche Kultur stood. The Reichskulturkammer was assembled largely to advance Goebbels's position. In his speech at the 16 November 1933 inauguration of the organization, he attacked conservatism, declaring, "German art needs fresh blood. We live in a young era. Its supporters are young, and their ideas are young. They have nothing more in common with the past, which we have left behind us. The artist who seeks to give expression to this age must also be young. He must create new forms."[46]

There was enough implicit encouragement of the modern arts in that statement to hearten their champions. As matters developed, Goebbels, a consummate opportunist, neglected to fight for the ideals he claimed to embrace. Nevertheless, for a time, mostly in 1934, Mies could have rationalized his membership in the Reichskulturkammer, which imposed no stylistic restriction on him (though it required proof of "racial purity") and even provided him with an invitation to participate in another competition, for another exposition pavilion.

This project was meant to represent Germany at the Brussels World's Fair in 1935. Now the Nazis sought to make their position explicit in the exposition guidelines, though again, ambiguously enough apparently to prompt Mies to accommodate himself to it. The most intriguing paragraph of the prospectus began on an aggressive nationalistic note: "The exhibition building must express the will of National-Socialist Germany through an imposing form; it must act as the symbol of . . . National-Socialist fighting strength and heroic will." There followed, however, a curious, faintly modernist echo of *Sachlichkeit*, no less nationalistic: "These thoughts must be expressed both in the layout of the buildings and, above all, in the exterior design, which must stand in opposition to the *somewhat pompous aspect of the Belgian buildings* [my italics]."[47]

On 3 July Mies wrote a statement that appears to have accompanied the submission of the drawings and model of his design to the Ministry of Propaganda and Enlightenment of the People:

> During the last years, Germany has developed a form for its expositions that more and more . . . progressed from exterior embellishment to the essential, to what an exposition should be, to a factual [*sachlich*] but effective visual display of things, to a real picture of German achievements . . .
>
> This clear and striking language corresponds to the essence of German work . . .
>
> Upon entering the German section, one reaches the hall of honor through a forecourt. This hall of honor, defined as it is by freestanding marble walls, serves to accommodate the national emblems and the representation of the Reich. It opens out into a court of honor, which will receive the best German works of art.[48]

Depression, Collectivization, and the Crisis of Art

If in the case of the Reichsbank competition there is some question about Mies's efforts to accommodate himself consciously to a Nazi position, there can be no doubt of the intent of his rationalizing remarks about the Brussels pavilion. He was clearly doing what he could to gain the commission. One cannot help remarking something pathetic in his statement, in the strained efforts of a highly accomplished artist to be true to his philosophy of order and rationality while trying to make the words sound acceptable to a Nazi's ear. Yet Mies was not alone in expressing himself as he did. Gropius also sought in 1934 to identify the New Architecture with the German spirit ("I myself see this new style as the way in which we in our country can finally achieve a valid union of the two great spiritual heritages of the classical and the Gothic traditions"),[49] while Hitler himself acknowledged the popularity of the slogan "Deutsch sein heisst klar sein," explaining it as "to be German means to be logical, above all to be truthful."[50]

There is further evidence in the very design of the pavilion of Mies's attempt to live up to nationalist expectations while remaining faithful to his principles. Though he had declined to affix the imperial German eagle to the walls of the Barcelona Pavilion, he sketched one, ever so abstractly, over the entrance to the Brussels project in one of his drawings for it. A swastika appears in another. Meanwhile, in yielding somewhat to the classicizing, symmetrizing trends of the day, he also and for the most part offered a free plan akin to those he had designed in the 1920s. The visitor to the building was meant to enter the "hall of honor" through two massive parallel walls of marble. Once past that axial passage, he moved through a space made up of typically Miesian asymmetrical freestanding walls and open courts. And the rectilinearity of the exterior elevation was as uncompromisingly severe as anything he had ever done.

The Brussels Pavilion was never built, since the necessary funding for the German participation in the exposition could not be obtained. Thereafter, Mies was granted only one commission traceable with certainty to the government, the design of an exhibition for the Deutsches Volk/Deutsche Arbeit Exposition in Berlin in 1934. This endeavor, too, proved ill-destined. Sergius Ruegenberg reports that the Nazi au-

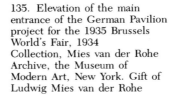

135. Elevation of the main entrance of the German Pavilion project for the 1935 Brussels World's Fair, 1934
Collection, Mies van der Rohe Archive, the Museum of Modern Art, New York. Gift of Ludwig Mies van der Rohe

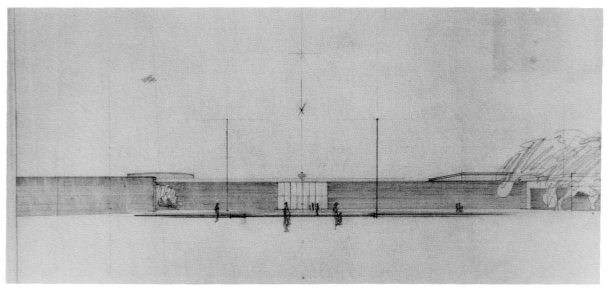

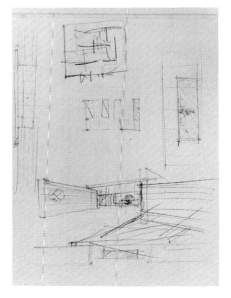

136. Interior perspective of the German Pavilion
Collection, Mies van der Rohe Archive, the Museum of Modern Art, New York. Gift of Ludwig Mies van der Rohe

137. Sheet of sketches for the German pavilion
Collection, Mies van der Rohe Archive, the Museum of Modern Art, New York. Gift of Ludwig Mies van der Rohe

thorities allowed him to carry out his design, but finding its modernist look offensive, omitted his name from the exhibition catalog.[51]

In retrospect Mies's several efforts at conciliation with a Nazi arts policy that was no less brutal than it was capricious served only to make him look foolish, if not distinctly unheroic. In view of the catastrophe that engulfed Germany in the years after the Brussels project, there is nothing to gain by picturing Mies as some of his admirers have tried, namely, as a staunch opponent of Nazism. This was, after all, a man who within eight years' time had designed a monument to a pair of Communist martyrs, a throne for a Spanish king, a pavilion for a moderate socialist government, and another for a militantly right-wing totalitarian state! Politically Mies was a passive soul; his active moral energies were turned toward his art and away from practically all else. Yet if we acknowledge that much about him, in fairness we must also remember that many more politically alert heads than his could not have known more certainly in 1934 than he that there would be no union of any fruitful kind between modernism and Nazi policy. And, indeed, after his experience with the Deutsches Volk/Deutsche Arbeit Exposition, he made no further recorded attempts at obtaining government patronage.

He sat, a man constitutionally loath to move. He had lived in Berlin for three decades, in the same apartment for two. He found the idea of leaving his homeland extreme, even if he was no patriot. German was the only language he knew, and Germany the sole cultural context; despite his elevated tastes he was an Aachener burgher at heart, no real citizen of the world. While he surely could have asked the Americans who already admired him to help him initiate emigration

Depression, Collectivization, and the Crisis of Art

procedures, he seems to have lacked either the desire or the practical resourcefulness to do so. Two radical changes in governmental structure in Germany had occurred in his lifetime: from the fall of the empire to the rise of the republic and from the collapse of the republic to the establishment of the new Reich. For someone naturally slow to action in any case, one might readily expect him to have supposed, at least to have hoped, that yet another change of political climate was likely and with it, the restoration of his fortunes. Meanwhile, he gazed listlessly out the window at the gray streets.[52]

Since the closing of the Bauhaus and the dissolution of most of the Bruhn money in the Depression, he had made his living the best way he could, which was none too cleverly. In 1933 he and Lilly Reich took the train to Switzerland and set up quarters in Lugano, where they were joined by five apprentices who paid Mies for architectural instruction. This arrangement lasted only a few months in the fall of the year. During the early and mid-1930s he was dependent mostly on royalties from the sale of his furniture, which since 1931 had been manufactured in quantity. For a time he did well enough with this. But the Nazis progressively made a point of deploring modern furniture, just as they grew gradually more hostile to the modern arts as a whole. As the decade passed the midway point, court battles over furniture patent rights and contractual obligations together with his own thoughtless way with money left Mies in a continually precarious financial state.

From his drawing board in 1934 came sketches of a trio of houses, the so-called Mountain House for the Architect, the House on a Ter-

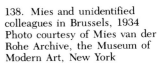

138. Mies and unidentified colleagues in Brussels, 1934
Photo courtesy of Mies van der Rohe Archive, the Museum of Modern Art, New York

139. Exhibition of glass half-cylinders showing the latest in German technology at the Deutsches Volk/Deutsche Arbeit Exposition, 1934

race, and the Glass House on a Hillside. All three were apparently visionary. The last, a perfect rectangular prism on stilts, set the stage for the Resor House of 1937–38 plus other American projects. In early 1937 he designed an apartment in the Berlin suburb of Rathenow for his daughter Marianne and her new husband, the *Gymnasium* professor Wolfgang Lohan. The only work of any size that he realized during the early Nazi years was an addition to the factory of the Verseidag silk company of Krefeld. As early as 1931 he had put up a shed structure, a two-story plant and a one-story connecting block on the company grounds, adding two stories to the plant in 1935. The effort was done in a mixture of factory vernacular and International Style detailing—Mies at his most tepidly workmanlike.

Idleness settled over him as the 1930s wore on. His business manager of the 1920s, Hermann John, had quit as early as 1931. Sergius Ruegenberg, who spent several tours of duty with Mies starting in 1924, was gone for good by 1934, as was Friedrich Hirz, who had worked on the Barcelona Pavilion and the Tugendhat and Nolde houses. Ruegenberg and Hirz both agree that there was simply too little work to keep them and other assistants busy. Only Herbert Hirche, who had studied at the Dessau Bauhaus, was taken on as a regular during

Depression, Collectivization, and the Crisis of Art

the Depression years, at a time when hopes for the Reichsbank were still alive.[53]

Now and then the old bunch would briefly return to Am Karlsbad 24, as individuals for the rare free-lance assignment, en masse for social get-togethers. In March 1936 Mies's friends chipped in enough money to send Hirche off to the studio of Max Beckmann, who was then living in Berlin. From Beckmann Hirche purchased an oil painting of a reclining nude which was presented with earnest if somewhat threadbare ceremony to Mies on 27 March, his fiftieth birthday. It was the first painting of any importance that he owned and he seems to have cared enough for it to display it prominently in both his Berlin and Chicago apartments.

It was now 1936. His last design efforts repeatedly miscarried, as the debacle of the Ulrich Lange House attests. The Perls, Wolfs and Fuchses, of yesteryear, wealthy, liberal clients, were nowhere to be found, and the new breed of German patron had something other than the New Architecture on his mind. The Messerschmitt people talked to Mies about designing the interior of a small airplane, conversations that led nowhere but to Mies's first plane ride, a quick spin above the streets of Berlin, from which he returned, Hirche remembered, visibly green. He was frustrated one more time when a commission from the textile industry to put together an exhibition in Berlin was taken from him as a result of Hermann Goering's assumption of control of the show. Hirche was present at a subsequent meeting when Ernst Sagebiel, designer of the Tempelhof Airport and much in favor with the Nazis, more or less formally took over the commission from Mies. "Sagebiel was the very image of the triumphant field marshal," Hirche said. "He treated Mies with caricatured respect, making remarks like '. . . that is, if Herr Mies is not *opposed* to such an idea.' "[54] The incident, throughout which Mies remained stonily silent, is worth recounting because it must have occurred at about the time Mies was beginning to get messages from an assortment of Americans who expressed interest in his professional services.

Almost coincident with his fiftieth birthday celebration Mies received a letter dated 20 March from John A. Holabird of the architectural firm of Holabird and Root in Chicago. The writer identified himself as the head of a search committee that was looking for a head of the architecture school of the Armour Institute of Technology, "with the idea of making it the finest school in the Country."[1] Holabird said he had already asked the recommendations of "various Americans who might consider this position. Amongst others I wrote to Richard Neutra in Los Angeles. He suggested the possibility of interesting Walter Gropius or Josef Emanuel Margold as he felt that the best was none too good for Chicago. He added that he had sent a copy of my letter to Mr. Gropius and Mr. Margold.

"In talking the matter over with the Advisory Committee, I thought that as we were considering the possibility of a European . . . I would like to ask if you would, under any conditions, consider such an appointment . . . if we are to consider the best I would naturally turn to you first."[2]

To this Mies replied by wire, on 20 April: "Thanks for the letter. Am interested. Letter follows."[3]

Such a response seems only reasonable. Other artists and architects of progressive stamp, Gropius, Mendelsohn, and Breuer among them, had already decided that their future in Germany was bleak enough to warrant their flight from it once and for all. But matters developed differently for Mies, and the reasons lay largely in his convoluted, even conflicted, perceptions of what he had, what he wanted, and what risks he was willing to take to narrow the gap between the two.

His letter to Holabird on 4 May reiterated his interest in the Armour position but appended conditions that he be free to give the school a "basically new form" and to continue his own private practice in Chicago.[4] A week later, probably without having yet received this message from Mies, Holabird wrote again: "I sincerely hope that you can arrange to take this position . . . With you as head, this should be the finest school in America."[5] On the following day, 12 May, Armour president Willard E. Hotchkiss added his own letter to Mies, declaring that he was "very glad to note your interest," acknowledging only that a definite offer could not be made "without the authority of the Board of Trustees."[6]

Mies should have understood that this last qualification was a matter of form that did not change Armour's otherwise affirmative posture. Yet his next communication was abruptly negative in tone. He declined the Armour proposal, sounding like the curt and uncompromising Mies of the pre-Weissenhof days: "A change of curriculum would have to be so fundamental as to extend beyond the present framework of [your] architecture department."[7]

Hotchkiss answered him, patiently and courteously, offering assurances of good intentions but allowing that only Mies's personal acquaintance with the Chicago situation would be properly instructive. Would Mies consent, then, to give a course of lectures at Armour in the fall or winter? "You would then be in a better position to decide whether we have here the kind of opportunity for creative work which would attract you."[8]

This last is dated 2 July. Mies did not answer it until three months later, and Armour was left hanging. For in the meantime a series of encounters with other solicitous Americans transpired, though these, too, eventually led nowhere, partly because fate itself, like Mies, seemed stuck on dead center.

Even before Hotchkiss's letter of 2 July, Alfred Barr of New York had shown up again in the German capital, this time for the purpose of discussing with Mies his possible role in the design of a new building for the Museum of Modern Art. Now Mies responded with unequivocal enthusiasm. "Your museum plans interest me," he wrote Barr once the latter had left Berlin; "it could be a rare and wonderful assignment."[9]

It turned out yet another will-o'-the-wisp. Barr was forced to withdraw his offer as early as 19 July, when he wrote Mies from Paris: "I have tried very hard to have our museum bring you to America as collaborating architect on our new building but I am afraid I shall not succeed. Believe me, I am very disappointed in my defeat. It has been a hard battle." As it turned out, the MoMA trustees, feeling less generous than Barr, were in no mood to offer the job to a foreigner.

"In any case," Barr continued, "I hope most sincerely for a favorable outcome to your conversation with Dean Hudnut."[10]

Joseph Hudnut was the distinguished dean of the Faculty of Architecture of Harvard University. On 21 July he wrote Mies: "I am greatly pleased to learn from [Barr] that you are interested in the possibility of accepting a Chair in Harvard University . . . I look forward . . . to seeing you in Berlin on about the sixteenth of August."[11]

If Mies had his doubts about Chicago, plus a new disappointment out of New York, could he really also question Harvard? Surely there could be no better agency for turning the increasing prospect of emigration from uncertainty to hopeful anticipation. The meeting with Hudnut apparently went well, judging from the letter he sent Mies on 3 September, from London.

"I should like as soon as I reach Cambridge," he wrote,

to make a final request to the President of the University in respect to the appointment of a Professor of Design. I hope that I may receive from you a letter telling me that you are able to consider favourably the acceptance of a chair should this be offered you by the President . . .

It would be foolish to pretend that there will not be opposition to the appointment of a modern architect as Professor of Design. In Berlin I tried to make clear to you the cause of this opposition—which is based in part on ignorance and in part on a difference in principles—and since my visit to Berlin, I have received letters which promise an opposition even more serious than I expected.

The President, however, has assured me of his sympathy with my plans and I have every reason to suppose that I can successfully carry them out.

The President suggests that my chance of success may be improved if he is able to present to the Senate at least two names, each of which is acceptable to me. This is a customary procedure at Harvard, where the Board of Overseers expects always the privilege of considering an alternate.[12]

Most of this was on page one. The first paragraph of page two read: "I should like, therefore, to propose not only your name but also that of Mr. Gropius. If for any reason this does not meet with your approval, I hope that you will tell me so frankly."

Hudnut was not prepared for Mies's reply:

Your letter from London has taken me aback. It forces me to the unpleasant decision to cut back [*einschränken*] the agreements I made to you in my letter of September 2.

I am willing to accept an appointment, but not to make myself a candidate for a chair. If you stand by your intention to submit several names to the President of the University, kindly omit mine.

I trust I am not adding a burden to your efforts.

I would be grateful if you were to advise of further plans.[13]

Mies's ambivalent attitude toward Gropius, whom he regarded as more privileged and socially adroit than himself but patently inferior as an artist, had apparently escaped Hudnut. Still, the American persevered. He promised not to list Mies as a "candidate"; rather he would endeavor to secure the post for him on his merits alone. Hudnut took pains to learn how various state laws of architectural licensing pertained to foreigners wishing to design in America. Massachusetts and New York, in the dean's view "the two most important states in the Union in respect to the practice of architecture," were far more restrictive than "the third state," Illinois, where—ironically, in view of Armour's suit—qualified foreigners had often been registered and permitted to practice.[14]

As Hudnut continued to struggle on his behalf, Mies received two letters from yet another American. This was Michael van Beuren of New Jersey, a former student at the Bauhaus who, apprised of the Armour and Harvard offers, took it upon himself to look into both and report his findings to his mentor:

I saw Rodgers and Priestley [two more ex-*Bauhäusler*] in New York . . . They both believe it is better for you in Chicago than in Boston. The people [in Chicago] have more initiative; they get more naturally and directly to the point of things. Here [in New York] as well as in Boston issues are far more theorized and more influenced, through personalities and tradition, by *unsachlicher* politics.

At Armour . . . you could do what you want . . . the people [there] repeated their promise of absolute freedom to the department head, plus assistants to take over administrative work if he wants more time for himself . . .

But the school is small, as yet insignificant, no stature. And the location is miserable [*mies*(!)]. You should see what an example it is of America's fantastic inconsistencies. Chicago's "grandest" building, its great temple of art, the Art Institute . . . is an ostentatious relic of the cultural ambition of the last century . . . But in the school of the Art Institute everyone works in tunnels beneath the temple . . . while the Armour school of architecture sits on the roof of the temple . . . The studios snake along under the skylights of the attic . . . In the summer, you roast. On the other hand, Boston:

Boston, self-anointed "hub of the universe," has allowed New York to fracture some of its spokes in the last fifty years. Lately it is a proud, "foin" city, which all in all does not love our century . . .

[About Harvard]: the location, the spaces, the whole school, all are elegant; the entire layout looks well-to-do. You can work comfortably there.

[But] the difficulties . . . ridiculous . . . and serious. All the big shots, among them worthy gray heads who haven't had a chance to design a palace since the Depression, have their own recommendations for the professor's chair. Hudnut is young and new at his post . . . arrayed against him are all the cranks who smell something—they want "no more foreigners." . . . About Gropius Hudnut tells me honestly that he likes him, that Gropius has so many "ideas" . . . but above all he [Hudnut] wants you . . . he has limited his list to your name and intends to stick with that . . . He admits that the fame of Gropius' Bauhaus is great and that it counts with the opposition . . . he's no great fighter, and would rather use persuasion on an opponent . . . but if the opponent understands too little, and will not listen . . . ?[15]

On 16 November Hudnut wrote Mies: "I am sorry . . . that I have not been successful in my plans . . . it will be impracticable to invite you at the present time to accept a Chair at Harvard . . . it will be necessary for me to consider now what other men may be available for appointment as Professor of Design . . . I am very greatly disappointed . . . please be assured of my continued esteem."[16]

Lacking any other letters, even further replies to Hudnut or van Beuren, we are left with an image of Mies alone and immobilized in Berlin in 1936, victim of circumstance but no less of his own contributions to circumstance.

He paid the price of his hermitage stoically, though for him it was hardly a new way of coping with the world. He abstracted life into thought as he did architecture into art, and he took refuge in the knowledge that in his studio he was an artist of first magnitude who built his art on truth. Personal feelings would not count, as he implied whenever he cited the saying of William of Orange which he learned even before World War I and quoted for the rest of his life: "To begin without the need of hope; to persevere without the expectation of success."

Alfred Barr was constituted differently. As late as 1937 he nursed hopes that he could obtain a commission for Mies to design at least the facade of the new Museum of Modern Art. According to Johnson, who noted this with understandable perplexity in view of all Mies had said about organic building, Mies was willing to go along with Barr's notion.[17] Following the miscarriage even of this enterprise, Barr succeeded in another—at long last—which ultimately had the effect of cancelling out very nearly all the failures.

He persuaded Mrs. Stanley Resor, a trustee of MoMA and a highly placed executive in a large Manhattan advertising agency of which her husband was president, to commission Mies to design a summer house for them in Wyoming. The Resors were promptly in touch with Mies, who bestirred himself sufficiently to meet them in Paris during the summer of 1937. Following congenial discussions, he was invited to come to the U.S. as their guest, and to make the trip as soon as possible. With uncommon dispatch, he returned to Berlin, packed his trunks, and in a matter of days was on board the SS *Berengaria*, disembarking in New York City on 20 August.

If Mies had any intention of communicating with Armour Institute of Technology while he was in the U.S., he showed no sign of it. On 2 September 1936 he had written President Hotchkiss in Chicago to say that he was in negotiation with "another American university," and would not be in a position to deliver even a lecture course at Armour.[18]

Even when Harvard hired Gropius in 1937, Mies gave no indication of second thoughts about Chicago. It appears that he had also been approached by the Vienna Academy, sometime in 1937, with the likelihood of an offer of the post lately vacated by Peter Behrens. Reports from Vienna suggest that he liked the idea (did he or was he simply covering his American tracks?) but that it evaporated when the Nazis marched into Austria in 1938.[19]

On his arrival in New York he was greeted by John Barney Rodgers, a young German-speaking American architect who with his partner William Priestley had studied at the Berlin Bauhaus. Rodgers was available to the Resors as an interpreter and Priestley also made himself useful. He was working on a commission in Chicago at the time Mies arrived in New York, and it was through him that Armour learned of the master's presence in the States.

Mies tarried only briefly in New York before entraining west, with Mrs. Resor, to study the building site in Jackson Hole at the foot of the Grand Tetons. During a day-long layover in Chicago, he was met by Priestley and two young architect friends, Gilmer Black and yet another ex-*Bauhäusler*, Bertrand Goldberg. The three "showed [Mies] all the Richardson, Sullivan, and Wright he could find," Priestley recalled, adding, "I talked to John Holabird who was most anxious to see him when he returned" from Wyoming.[20]

When Mies made his way to the Resor family ranch, he found a portion of a house already begun but later abandoned. The architect had been Philip Goodwin, the very man whose membership on the Board of Trustees of the Museum of Modern Art had worked to the disadvantage of Mies's commission to design a new museum building. The Resors had lately had a falling out with Goodwin, but only after enough of his structure was up that Mies was called upon to adjust his own design to it. After several weeks of constant sketching done for the most part in silence, since neither of his hosts spoke German nor he a word of English, he returned to New York to continue working out his concept of the house.

Once again Priestley and Goldberg, both of them modestly competent in German, met him in Chicago when he made the necessary change of trains. They took him on a brief auto tour of the Frank Lloyd Wright houses in Oak Park, after which Priestley invited him to a meeting next day with representatives from Armour Institute. Mies accepted.

The Armour people had lost none of their ardor. For three consecutive days Mies lunched at the Tavern Club, first with John Holabird, then with Dean Henry T. Heald, finally with James D. Cunningham, chairman of the Board of Trustees. On the last day a formal offer of the position as director of the School of Architecture was tendered, and Mies, with only a little reflection, accepted subject to an agreement to be ratified after he had completed his proposal for departmental and curricular changes.[21]

America was rapidly imprinting itself. Now Mies expressed the desire to meet Frank Lloyd Wright in Taliesin, whereupon Holabird instructed Priestley: "*You* phone Wright. I don't want to give the old bastard a chance to badmouth my architecture." Priestley's call to Spring Green, Wisconsin, found Wright at home. "Mr. Wright," said Priestley, "Mr. Mies van der Rohe is in Chicago. He would like to meet you."

"I should think he would," snapped Wright without a moment's hesitation. Then he added, "He's welcome."[22]

Wright's invitation to Mies was as rare a gesture as it was spontaneous. He made a point of detesting European architects and the bigger they were the more he detested them: they were always taking credit for ideas today they had filched from him yesterday. He had already been approached earlier in the 1930s by two of the very biggest of them—by Gropius and Le Corbusier—and had rejected each in their efforts to visit him at Taliesin. He was unconscionably rude both times.[23] With Mies on this occasion, however, and on all later ones until relations between the two men cooled, he was never rude. Now, in fact, he was positively expansive, not just because Mies came as a pilgrim paying his respects to a master—Gropius and Le Corbusier had done so, too, and been insulted for their pains—but because Wright genuinely admired Mies's work. He was specially impressed by the Barcelona Pavilion and the Tugendhat House, the products, he felt, of an individual sensibility, not one of the horde of Bauhaus functionalists he so generously despised. It did not hurt, of course, that Mies's treatment of space was perceptibly indebted to

Wright; still, the latter commented that Mies was the only European who had not only the good sense to follow his lead but the independence to create something original in the process.[24]

From all reports Mies himself was properly awed by what he saw at Taliesin, Wright's own compound, designed and built, progressively, from 1902 to 1925. He walked out upon the terrace which commanded a sweeping view of a rolling Wisconsin landscape, looked down at the swans' pond, across the plain to the little family chapel and exclaimed, "Freiheit! Es ist ein Reich!"[25] (Freedom! This is a kingdom!) He applauded the siting of the buildings while motioning with his hands to acknowledge the interpenetrating masses he had known so well from books and saw now for the first time. And Wright grew quickly attached to Mies, whose natural reserve now and then gave way to a warmth all the more attractive for being so evidently spontaneous. What was to have been an afternoon's visit lasted four days. "Poor Mr. Mies," Wright commiserated, "his white shirt is [now] quite gray!"[26] After Priestley, Goldberg, and Black returned to Chicago Wright summoned a chauffeur and personally conducted Mies through the Johnson Wax Building in Racine, under construction at the time, then back to his hotel in Chicago via the Unity Temple in Oak Park, the Coonley House in Riverside, and the Robie House on the city's South Side.

Mies's debt to Rodgers and Priestley mounted after he returned to New York. It was in their office that he worked on the Resor House through the fall and winter, while at the same time putting together a curriculum and composing an educational rationale for Armour Tech.

140. Mies and Frank Lloyd Wright at Taliesin, 1937

Departure and Flight

The house was just one more project that never came to fruition. The foundation to which Mies was obliged to fit his design straddled a mountain stream tributary to the Snake River.[27] Four wall-like bridge supports had already been built there, with a temporary floor laid across them. The two inner piers were sunk into the water bed and to one of the outer ones a service wing had been attached. Mies's efforts thus consisted largely in incorporating what he found into the house he produced. (Such a willingness to compromise must be evidence enough that he had lowered his defenses against America.) In the earliest stage of design, which ran through March 1938—when he returned to Berlin to settle his affairs prior to emigration—work proceeded to the point of construction drawings and the letting of bids. On 5 April, however, while he was en route back to Germany, he received a wire from Mr. Resor: "I am sorry on account of business conditions I shall not build on my property at Wilson, Wyoming."[28]

The project was nevertheless resumed in November 1938, after Mies had returned to Chicago and taken up his duties at Armour. Negotiations and revisions continued fitfully as late as 1943, when a spring flood washed away the piers, destroying all likelihood that the house as contemplated would ever be built. The lengthy history of the Resor House is better read elsewhere. The most memorable and compelling aspect of the project is the relation of the design of the large living room to Mies's total understanding of space. One cannot resist speculating about his response to the vastness of the American West, to the look of the country there, ruder and tougher than anything he had known in the well-manicured Alps. One wonders, too, how he felt in a place so physically and psychologically free, especially in view of all he had left in Germany. There was certainly no contextual reason for the exoskeletal wall of his recent court houses, not in all this openness, and Mies foreswore it. Neither, however, did he fall back upon his still earlier preference for a restless interaction between enclosed-semienclosed volumes and exterior space—the searching factor, as it might be called.

Instead, the Resor living room is ample, rectangular in plan, with great windows taking up the midsection of its long sides. While Mies's compositional treatment of these panes varies in his sketches, a generous view of the landscape consistently remains their chief motivation. The most prominent feature of the interior is a huge, craggy fireplace whose symmetrical location perpendicular to the long walls and nearer the bedrooms than the service wing, draws attention to a kindred regularity in the steel supporting columns. The room, that is to say, has an axis. Another compositional device also asserts itself: the space is closer to being empty of incident than anything Mies ever designed for a residential living area. Though in his drawings he moved a large freestanding bookcase around it as he formerly had walls, this object functions more as a piece of furniture than as an architecturally space-defining element. The room is thus a geometric box, high, wide, invitingly large, and appropriately rustic in feeling. The architect's will to open up interior space had not at all diminished; the glass walls dissolve the sense of enclosure. Yet spatially the room is nearly static, with very little dynamism or subjectivity of organization in evidence.

141. Model of the Resor House
project, Jackson Hole,
Wyoming, 1938
Collection, Mies van der Rohe
Archive, the Museum of
Modern Art, New York. Special
Purchase Fund

Not only contained but packaged, space rests rather than flows, reflecting a state of being rather than becoming. In this sense the Resor House is kin to other works Mies did in the 1930s, and the fact that he conceived it in America, voluntarily, for a family sympathetic to modern art, leads us to reiterate that his recent inclination toward axiality and stasis had less to do with currying Nazi favor and more with a spirit internationally endemic to the decade.

During his stay of several months in New York, Mies lived at the University Club, courtesy of the Resors, who together with their friends saw to it that an appropriate amount of his leisure time was given over to making the rounds of MoMA society. Rodgers interpreted. On one occasion Mies was invited to Columbia University, which briefly gave thought to offering him the deanship of its architectural school.[29] His poor English militated against that. Days not spent on the Resor design were occupied with the Armour teaching program. All surviving evidence indicates that Mies took this last matter very seriously; moreover, the rationale behind it offered a clue to his thinking during the brief period that separated his German past from his American future.

The rationale, however, was not identical with the program. Mies sent the finished program to Dean Heald on 10 December 1937 in the form of a large vertical diagrammatic outline, carefully rendered by Rodgers and Priestley. On the left were two long vertical columns, one titled "General Theory," including such subheadings as mathematics, natural science, the nature of man, and culture as an obligatory task, the other, "Professional Training," featuring various kinds of drawing, as well as financing, structural design, and even office practice. To the right of these columns were three categories arranged in stacked horizontal rows: "Means," which stood for materials—wood, brick, steel, concrete, and the like; "Purposes," which listed functional types of building, for example, dwellings, commercial buildings, and public buildings plus the ordering of these into communities and regions; and "Planning and Creating," the most diverse classification with the most abstract-sounding subheadings, like dependence upon the epoch, possible principles of order, the obligation to realize the potentialities of organic architecture, and architecture, painting, and sculpture as a "Creative Unity."

Mies regarded the subjects listed under "General Theory" and "Professional Training" as the basics of the curriculum, the courses to be taken first by students who would then move to the study of materials ("Means"), on to function ("Purpose"), and finally to the "higher," more speculative issues of "Planning and Creating."

It is worth noting that Mies's program, a document more rational in its totality than in its somewhat eccentric and unparallel parts, reads like a formalization of his own heterogeneous education, an autobiographical curriculum, as it were. The general theory courses reflected the pre-*Gymnasium* study he experienced ever so briefly in the Aachen Cathedral School. The professional training program echoed the practical disciplines he learned in trade school, on the building sites, and in the offices of his teen years. The means, purposes, and planning and creating sections were a reflection of classical Bauhaus thought with an overlay—witness "dependence upon the epoch"—of the philosophy and history he had taught himself in the 1920s and 1930s.

By 1941 this program had been adapted more nearly to an American academic framework of ordered, sequentially numbered courses, though its autobiographical tenor still echoed in his justification of it: "The curriculum leads naturally from the study of the means with which one builds and the purposes for which one builds into the sphere of architecture as an art." Whatever else this was, it sounded to Americans like the functionalist, rationalist language they associated with the new European architecture, especially when it was held up against the Beaux-Arts–influenced programs of most U.S. architectural schools of the day. Thus it was interpreted as Mies's way of rationalizing an educational view antithetical to the historicism, the pictorialism, the preindustrial romanticism of the Beaux-Arts.

And so it was, in practical effect. Yet at the time he designed his diagrammatic chart he was thinking not at all in functionalist terms. A letter of 31 January 1938, written apparently to the curator of prints and drawings at the Art Institute of Chicago, Carl O. Schniewind, suggests what reasoning did lie behind Mies's program. *Here* is the rationale of his program:

> In contrast to the extraordinary order [*grossartigen Sicherheit*] apparent in [today's] technical and economic realms, the cultural sphere, moved by no necessity and possessed of no genuine tradition, is a chaos of directions, opinions . . .
>
> It should be the natural responsibility of the university to bring clarity to this situation . . . . The countless "masters" of our profession, [all forced to be] significant personalities, can hardly find the time to deepen their own philosophical understandings.
>
> Things by themselves create no order. Order as the definition of the meaning and measure of being is missing today; it must be worked toward, anew.[30]

This was Mies calling down the spirit of Thomas Aquinas, as he endeavored to restore culture and drive back the spectre of Spenglerian civilization. The conformity of intellect and things could save us all not only from the idolatry of *Sachlichkeit* but from the greater danger of the chaos that threatened the West. Either way it was a heroic task, achievable only because of Mies's two unshakable convictions, that there was a central Truth divinable from facts by a central route and that such divination in today's world was nothing less than imperative.

Mies was not at all indifferent to history, the way the advocates of the Beaux-Arts suspected he and other European avant-gardists were. Indeed in one sense he was the most conservative of the van, in another an outright romantic, at least insofar as he looked to a Gothic scholasticist to rescue the twentieth-century arts. The Middle Ages, in his mind secure in Truth and in no need of "personalities," would show the way.

Most of his American admirers of the 1930s, and much later, did not understand this aspect of him at all. They knew he was a superb architect, and that was quite enough for them. That he talked the way foreigners talk, especially Germans, densely and theoretically, was something in which they took no great interest, since it seemed to them irrelevant to the practical art of building. They were more comfortable with him when he talked about technology.

Nevertheless, one cannot help recalling that Mies wrote to Schniewind at a time when Western civilization as a whole was wracked by sociopolitical conflicts apparently too grievous for democracy, as his generation had known it, to resolve. To a greater or lesser degree democracy everywhere gave ground to totalitarianism. Germany represented the aggressive extreme of this, but the U.S. itself collectivized as it sought to resist and defeat Germany, indeed as both nations had earlier strained to lift themselves from the depths of the Depression. Correspondingly Mies saw the danger in cultural terms and correspondingly invoked an authoritarian system of thought in his efforts to subdue it. Surely to a degree this explains the rigid axial symmetry and contained static space of his 1930s work, as Le Corbusier's Ville Radieuse, conceived at the turn of the 1930s, was that architect's way of coping with similar doubts about the ability of democracy to control the growth of the metropolis. In view of such a set of international circumstances, it is little wonder the high hopes of 1920s modernism were shaken to their foundations by the end of the 1930s.

Early in February 1938 Mies made one last trip to Chicago before returning to Germany to conclude his affairs there. He met with Dean Heald and others at Armour to discuss as many aspects as possible of the considerable change his appointment would mean to a school long accustomed to a Beaux-Arts orientation. What kind of budget would result from a new curriculum and a remodeled faculty? Who would be hired, who retained, who not? Should the department stay at the Art Institute, which wants to relocate it in a better part of the museum building, or might it more advantageously move to the Glessner House on Prairie Avenue, H. H. Richardson's sole remaining work in Chicago, now owned by Armour?

On 31 March, directly before his departure on the *Queen Mary*, Mies recommended the addition of three new teachers. All were veterans of the Bauhaus and two had taught there: Walter Peterhans, lately immigrated and living in Brooklyn, and Hilberseimer, still in Berlin, who until then lacked any connection that might have offered him a way to the U.S. Mies's third nominee was young John Barney Rodgers. These names were accepted. Mies and Heald agreed to keep the existing faculty, mindful of departmental morale and the eagerness of several incumbents to be part of a fresh new program led by a major international figure. A move to the Glessner House was ruled out; the old space at the Art Institute would do.

On 2 April, with Mies on his way to Germany, Henry Heald, acting president of Armour following Willard Hotchkiss's resignation, sent him the formal offer of a two-year appointment as professor of architecture and director of the Department of Architecture beginning 1 September at an annual salary of $8000.

According to Rodgers, Mies found one unfinished work awaiting him in Germany: the Verseidag administration building, a project akin to the Reichsbank in its axial symmetry and trapezoidal plan, but drier in temper, less monumental, the most pedestrian design of his most difficult decade, the 1930s. It was abandoned when a shortage of concrete followed feverish Nazi efforts to construct fortifications along the western border.[31]

Little time was left Mies to bring his affairs into order and make the appropriate farewells. All in all and with few moments of relief his four months in Berlin in 1938 added up to a melancholy stay and more perilous than he anticipated. On arrival he found his office as he had left it. Hirche, the sole survivor, was still in charge though he was spending most of his hours at Lilly Reich's studio. Ada had moved to Berlin during 1935, in the trough of the Depression, and for a while she lived in one room before she had enough money for an apartment. Mies was supporting her now, from his own resources, and there was little enough of those. Georgia quit the Wigman troupe in 1936 to become an actress. Marianne provided the happiest moment when she gave birth to Dirk, Mies's first grandchild. Waltraut took her *Abitur* at Birklehof, a school attached to Salem, in the south.

Lilly Reich labored on. During Mies's absence she cared faithfully for all administrative affairs pertaining to his practice. The question why he did not take her or any members of his family to the U.S. arises more easily than it is answered certainly. Might he conceivably come home again? Or would he return to bring some of his family, or Lilly, back to the U.S. with him, for good?

On the other hand, did he have any pressing reason to want them to join him there, ever, given that he had made it so clear for so long that creative freedom was important enough to take unqualified priority over any and all personal bonds?

If any doubts about this lingered in his mind, the Nazis once more made his decision for him. By 1938 intraparty arguments over the allowable degree of tolerance of the modern arts had been resolved in favor of the ultra right. A year earlier the Degenerate Art exhibition in Munich ratified official Nazi hostility toward modernism as a whole. Given Mies's own artistic reputation plus his former associations with Jews and leftists—it is enough to recall names like Perls and Fuchs, or Liebknecht and Hilberseimer, and all they stood for—he was in a more endangered position in 1938 than he had been before he left for the U.S.[32] Soon enough he realized that those friends in America who had warned him about going back to Germany, even for a short time, knew what they were talking about. Shortly before his departure from Berlin in August, he was obliged to pay a visit to the local police station to pick up his emigration visa, the completion of which had

142. Georgia van der Rohe
Hildegard Steinmetz

required his leaving his passport there. But he was afraid to go lest he be detained and his travel plans upset if not voided. His former assistant Karl Otto went in his stead, retrieving the passport with the visa and returning to Am Karlsbad 24. There he found Mies, pale as death, being roughly interrogated by two Gestapo officers who had made an unexpected call and were aggrieved to learn that their host did not have his passport with him to identify himself.

Papers now in hand, he managed to placate the officers, but as soon as they left he decided to change his schedule and get out of Berlin immediately, taking only as much as he could hurriedly stuff into a suitcase. Hirche saw him off at the train station, just one soul more than was present when he arrived in the capital thirty-three years earlier. "Hirche," said Mies, ready at last to put the new Germany behind him, "Hirche, come soon yourself."[33] A figurative full circle was completed when Mies's train arrived half a day later in Aachen. Discarding the German emigration visa, he crossed unobtrusively into Holland and made his way to Rotterdam, where, with what we understand to be the help of unknown friends, he succeeded in booking passage on a steamer for New York.[34]

Revival: Modernism without Utopia, 1938–49

Mies van der Rohe's first American address was the Stevens Hotel (now the Conrad Hilton), an enormous edifice of 2000 rooms, at one time the largest hostelry in the world. It fronted the elegant breadth of Michigan Avenue across from the formal gardens of Grant Park, about half a mile south of the Art Institute. There he lived for about a month after his arrival in Chicago in August 1938. He then moved across Balbo Drive to the Blackstone Hotel, where he remained until he took a proper apartment at 200 E. Pearson Street, in 1941. The fact that he was cloistered in a hotel room for fully three years after coming to the U.S. reinforces our image of him as a man of privacy and fortified loneliness. This did not prevent him from socializing, but just as in Germany, he resisted all intrusions into the deepest recesses of himself. He reduced his household needs and gratifications to the barest essentials, requiring only that they be of high quality. Martinis, Havana cigars, and a few expensive suits led the list.

He received at least one large shipment of belongings prior to the outbreak of World War II, and it was from these that the Art Institute of Chicago assembled an exhibition of his work in 1938 which consisted of blowups of photographs and drawings, plus models of two court houses and the Hubbe House. By far the greater portion of his possessions, however, remained in Germany.

One of the items he must have received early was the Beckmann birthday oil. By 1938 he had developed an interest in painting where none existed before, as we infer from letters written him by the former Berlin dealer Karl Nierendorf, lately immigrated to New York. Nierendorf, who had sold him a Kandinsky painting while Mies was still in Germany, now offered to secure works for him by Paul Klee if Mies would persuade Klee (the two men liked each other despite Klee's resignation from the Bauhaus in 1932) to give Nierendorf exclusive American rights to his work. Even in 1939 the Klees Mies got from Nierendorf were kept under his bed at the Blackstone. On rare occasions when he had visitors, he would carefully remove the paintings like shirts from a drawer and perch them around the room. He never paid serious attention to Chicago as the place where he lived and moved, and his own disavowals of any influence from or even knowledge of Chicago's famed commercial architecture are in keeping with this. When he made his way up the avenue to the Armour classes atop the Art Institute, he would pass Adler and Sullivan's Auditorium Building plus several important works by Daniel Burnham and Holabird and Roche. His first office space in America was in Burnham's robust old Railway Exchange Building at Jackson and Michigan, almost exactly across the street from the Art Institute. According to

Philip Johnson, Mies disliked the "excessive" masonry on the Chicago fronts as a whole and he was especially critical of Louis Sullivan's ornament.

By the time he was ensconced in the Railway Exchange Building, the 1938/39 academic year was already underway and its most memorable evening past. On 18 October 1938 Armour Institute hosted a ceremonial dinner in honor of Mies in the Red Lacquer Room of the Palmer House. Approximately four hundred guests attended, among them the heads of some of the leading architectural schools in the country, plus dozens of ranking architects and dozens more of Chicago's social elite.

Mies himself is reported to have requested that Frank Lloyd Wright be invited to introduce him to the assemblage. Wright did indeed come, despite the fact that many of the professional brotherhood at the banquet cared no more for him than he did for them. His introduction of Mies was preceded by statements made at length by Heald, now the president of Armour, Chairman Cunningham, and several academic dignitaries. When Wright rose at last, bored and irritable, he made some uncourtly allusions to the state of the profession as manifest in its representatives that evening, then took more than a little proprietary credit for Mies. He quotes himself: "Ladies and gentlemen, *I* give you Mies van der Rohe. But for me there would have been no Mies—certainly none here tonight. I admire him as an architect, respect and love him as a man. Armour Institute, *I* give you my Mies van der Rohe. You treat him well and love him as I do. He will reward you."[1] (Henry Heald's version of Wright's parting sentence was "God knows you need him!")

Therewith Wright strode out of the room, followed by a train of his acolytes, even as Mies was taking his place at the dais. The conflicting testimony of witnesses leaves us uncertain whether Wright's walk was a deliberate act of upstaging or, as his colleagues insist, he had a pressing out-of-town engagement which forced his hurried departure. "After the dinner was over," Heald later wrote, "I found him at the bar, where he'd been waiting out the rest of the program."[2]

Mies himself never spoke ill of Wright in recalling the event, which gradually took on mythic aspects only as the disciples of the two men came to detest each other over the next twenty years. Mies delivered his own address that evening in German, not without contretemps, for his interpreter, who had not read the text beforehand, so botched the translation that Rodgers was obliged to replace him.

Having arrived a foreigner in Chicago at the moment that separated an enervating depression from a distracting war, Mies could hardly expect to find architectural commissions waiting for him. For most of his first decade in the U.S., he depended on his academic work at Armour Institute to sustain him; he was a teacher in America well before he was a builder. Even so, it was that very school that gave him his first design opportunity, the master plan for the reconstitution of the entire Armour campus. He began working on it early in 1939. World War II retarded its completion and by mid-1945 Mies had seen only parts of several buildings rise on the grounds of the Armour Institute. Yet the others, the majority at any rate, were destined to follow in the course of the next ten years. With the resumption of American building at the end of the 1940s, a perceptibly new phase of his career began.

In the United States, Mies's life fortunes changed. Following decades of unrealized projects, he succeeded in building most of what he designed after 1938, including all but a few of his most important proposals. Having spent most of the 1930s in a homeless frame of mind, he responded to the freedom and security of his new environment and became a naturalized American citizen in 1944. In turn the United States welcomed him as a great artist at a time when it was especially prepared for the art he had to offer, and it provided all the physical means he needed to pursue his ideational ends. In the last decade of his life he had only one peer among the world's architects— Le Corbusier (Wright died in 1959)—and even Le Corbusier did not match him in the influence he exerted on the world's urban landscape. Mies's sway over post–World War II architecture can be measured on the one hand by the rectilinearization of the skylines of all major international cities and on the other by the force of the rebellion against his principles which rose up after his death in 1969.

Success in the New World, however, was due to more than good fortune and a receptive community. He learned from America as surely as it did from him, and he remade his architecture from what he learned, all the while staying his fundamental philosophical course. Mies was forever mindful that the art of building had its origins in materials. As in Germany he had known brick and glass, in America he found steel, on a scale and in quantity he had only dreamed of earlier. Having found it, he used it to bring to concretion his vision of an architecture of structure. Glass only added to this realization. It seemed to Mies, as he made it seem to America, that construction in steel and glass stood most authentically for modern technology. The Americans had a special fondness for technology, believing, especially in view of their spectacular victory in World War II, that they were the people most advanced in it. Thus in their eyes, any artist who elevated it to architecture could only add meaning and merit to American and world culture. Technology for Mies, in turn, was an entity of spiritual as well as physical significance. It was the Zeitgeist manifest. It was *fact*, and the materials of steel and glass, themselves light enough to approach a dematerialized state, could lift fact to the level of essence, thus to Truth in the desired immaterial sense.

Nor did Mies's embrace of structure in America preclude his continued exploration of space. On the contrary, the dematerialization of structure freed him to create a space of supersensible implications. The space that earlier had flowed among walls and columns gave way to the single large emptied-out clear-span area, extending implicitly in all directions and bounded only by columns and glass conceived in a rigorously symmetrical order. That he sought to achieve transcendental goals in architecture while working in a country traditionally pragmatic and materialist in its values constitutes one of the more wondrous marriages of the mind in the arts of the twentieth century.

Mies's formal invitation to redesign the Armour campus might never have come to pass if, in Henry Heald's own words, it had not been for "an act of God."[3] For some time plans had been afoot to merge Armour Institute with Lewis College and to provide the resulting institution with a larger campus derived from the acquisition and clearing of 110 acres of slum land on the South Side. Heald knew how much symbolic adrenalin would be released if such a campus could be planned by a designer of Mies's stature: it would yield the first all-modern college complex in the country.

But there already was another campus design in the works, begun earlier by Alfred Alschuler, a member of the Armour Board of Trustees and a veteran conservative Chicago architect. Heald found little to like in it. Well aware that his board, not to mention his faculty committees, would likely never have volunteered to replace Alschuler with so radical a figure by traditional American standards as the German newly installed in the architecture department, Heald bypassed the bureaucracy and secretly invited Mies to prepare a design of his own. The strategy was to announce Mies's plan only when it was completed, presuming it would be sufficiently impressive to overshadow Alschuler's. Shortly after Mies commenced work on the project, Alschuler died, leaving the way open to a rival he never knew he had.

The school created by the Armour-Lewis merger in 1940 was renamed the Illinois Institute of Technology. Its material means were modest by comparison with Harvard's, and the new campus would have to be realized on a budget far slenderer than the ones Mies had enjoyed at Barcelona or Brno. Nonetheless, with as many as a dozen buildings of substantial size at issue, he would hardly have been granted a commission even remotely like it at Cambridge. Michael van Beuren's prophecy seemed to be proving itself almost to the letter, and Mies, despite his reputation for overspending, proved equal to the challenge. Heald later recalled: "Those of you who think Mies is a man who is hard to work with and inflexible are very much mistaken."[4]

Confronted by the unremitting flatness of IIT's South Side site, as well as the eight-blocks-to-the-mile rhythm of Chicago's constraining rectilinear city plan, Mies laid the campus out on a grid. The unit length was twenty-four feet in both directions, with half of that meant as the modular height of the interiors. The space between as well as within the campus buildings was organized accordingly. This was the first time he ever used such a device as an ordering principle, and in one sense it was a simple concession to practical requirements. Twenty-four feet matched the dimensions of standard American classrooms and laboratories, and modularity made for uniform, thus cheaper, building components which could be organized in a variety of ways. Furthermore, so large a project extending over a period of years implied later parts of the whole to be completed by other designers. More than answering a present economic need, a grid system insured future architectural unity. Mies's concept of generalized building was being put to work as it never had been in Germany.

Originally he proposed a symmetrical layout of the campus in which two superblocks would be created by the elimination of the north-south thoroughfare, Dearborn Street, that longitudinally divided the campus. Each of the two spaces would be dominated by a large building: library and architecture school to the south, administration and

Revival: Modernism without Utopia

student union to the north. After city authorities disallowed the blocking off of Dearborn Street, Mies experimented with dozens of other arrangements, repeatedly shifting the sizes and patterns of buildings. Consistent in all of this effort was the use of the low-rise building form (usually two or three stories) with a flat roof—familiar usages in his architecture though perhaps prompted as well by the geometric tableland of Chicago's South Side. Reminiscent of his designs of the 1920s was the tendency of the buildings, even in the midst of an overall axiality, to slide freely past each other. At ground level, to a moving pedestrian, such a composition produced the shifting sense of blocks appearing and disappearing, not overruling the symmetry but qualifying it, acting as the walls of his houses of the late 1920s had, defining rather than enclosing spaces. The blocks themselves, however, were most often simple parallelepipeds—boxes—which together with his frequent axial arrangements, recalled the static contained spaces of the 1930s. (In the early stages some of these blocks, which stood on stilts, featured externalized auditoriums or staircases that were absorbed within the prismatic masses in the final plan.)

To the untutored eye of the late 1940s and early 1950s his campus buildings had the look of factories—something almost never associated with his European work—while more educated observers came to admire the sophistication and polish with which the detailing in the best passages was carried out. In fact Mies had the experience of the Krefeld Verseidag factory behind him, not to mention his very early work on AEG buildings for Peter Behrens. More important, he must have known of the exceptional quality of some of the German factories of

143. Early preliminary plan of the IIT campus, Chicago, 1939 Collection, Mies van der Rohe Archive, the Museum of Modern Art, New York. Gift of Ludwig Mies van der Rohe

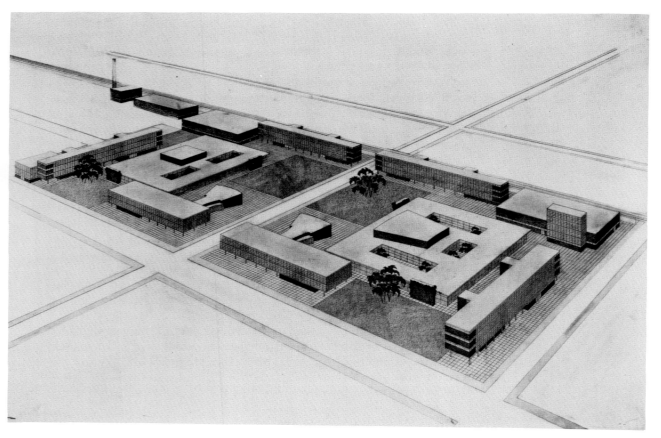

144. Montage showing a later preliminary plan of the IIT campus, 1941

the late 1920s and early 1930s. Theodor Merrill's Königsgrube works in Bochum (1930) had appeared in Johnson and Hitchcock's *International Style*. Also published by 1933 were Fritz Schupp's Zollverein Colliery near Essen (1932) and the boiler plant designed in 1927 by Erich Mendelsohn for the Mosler Publishing Company in Berlin. These three works exemplified a characteristically German way of industrializing the time-honored vernacular of the half-timbered house, a medieval form of skeletal construction. In February 1933 the American journal *Architectural Forum* took note of the huge Zollverein Colliery: "Every structure in the extensive establishment is built upon an iron framework and covered with glazed brick, in Germany, called clinker . . . [This system] promised even with buildings which vary in form and size and purpose throughout the whole complex a general impression of uniformity." That prose might have been written by Mies himself, who must have appreciated how an impersonal architecture of industrial implication could serve as a model for a technological institution of considerable size, variety of purpose (yet budgetary restriction), and potential growth.

Mies's first completed structure, the Minerals and Metal Research Building of 1942–43, is neither a masterpiece nor an exemplar of the IIT building type he perfected later. It is a three-story steel-framed box whose facade consists of a wall of glass rising from an eight-foot-high apron of brick at the base. The framing with brick infill at both ends reflects the interior spatial subdivisions, but the front is less candid and more simply prosaic, considering the fact that the apron covers the framing structure rather than reveals it. Mies seemed to be seeking to adjust, none too easily, to new ground and new ground rules. The Minerals Building is an uncomfortable reminder of how glum the *Sachlichkeit* could be which he had briefly if theoretically espoused in the early 1920s.

Revival: Modernism without Utopia

145. IIT campus
Photo by Joseph J. Lucas, Jr.

It was not the disillusionment of a beaten nation that sobered his architecture now, but rather a wartime economy and the complex pragmatics of the IIT commission. America was anything but defeated, and Mies himself had gained in maturity since writing his tough prose for *G*. By 1945 he had refined his concept of the structure he wanted at IIT, and it is best exemplified by his treatment of the outer building wall.

The Alumni Memorial Hall, completed in 1946, had much of the look of a Merrill-Schupp box built on a steel frame with brick and glass infill. Mies's fireproofed structural steel frame, however, was en-

Revival: Modernism without Utopia

146. IIT campus
Photo by Joseph J. Lucas, Jr.

147. IIT campus
Photo by Joseph J. Lucas, Jr.

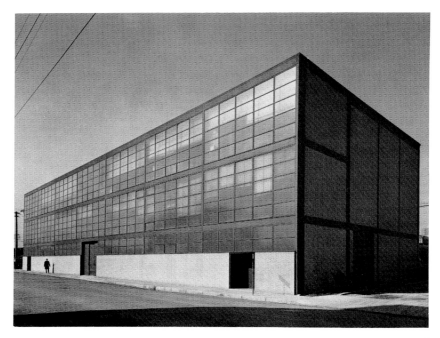

closed by a skin of welded steel members with infill of buff-colored
brick panels and plate glass windows set in aluminum sashes. The
vertical rhythm of the elevation concluded emphatically at each end
of the building in a complex serrated corner.

Mies's treatment of this last element was his way of distinguishing
between the primary structure of the building and the secondary
structure of the skin. The former consisted of wide-flange columns
encased in fireproofing concrete and covered with steel plates, the
latter, of I-beams welded to the steel plates. Each of these components and their connections were *expressively* exposed at the corners,
while a negative reveal between I-beam and brick infill avoided a possibly untrue adjacency between the edges of two materials.

That is to say, the real structure of Alumni Memorial Hall, though
suppressed, is expressed: what one knows is there is not what one
sees, but is made evident by what one sees. Mies's reasoning is tor-
tuous, but ever so much his own: to demonstrate that the supporting
steel frame is the basis, or essence, of the building, it is indicated,
rather than shown, externally; to acknowledge that what shows, moreover, is not fact but symbol of fact, the columnar covering plate and
the skin I-beam stop short of the earth.

There are obviously simpler ways to design and even to reveal structure, and there is no objective proof that the revelation of structure
is obligatory in architecture. American commercial builders of the 1920s
and 1930s had paid little attention to such expression, regarding massing and ornament as more important architectural concerns. Only when
the reductive doctrine of abstraction, of which Mies was a powerful
proponent, singled out structure as architectural essence did the
expression of it become crucial.

Internationally, however, that very moment was now at hand. In
the mid- to late 1940s a substantial change in the arts of Western

civilization occurred: the restoration of modernism. Eclipsed for well over a decade, modernism shone forth again when conditions hostile to it—the Depression and the rise of totalitarianism—were overcome. This accomplished, two points of view fundamental to modernist thinking were revived: abstraction reascended to the state of favored expressive language, and internationalist sympathies replaced those identified with the nationalisms of the 1930s and 1940s.

There were differences, to be sure. For one thing, the new modernism foresaw no utopian union of art and politics. The economic and political cataclysms of the century had been enough to persuade all but the most inflexible ideologues on both sides of the Atlantic that utopia was not possible in the contemporary world. Moreover, America, the country where the modernist revival most dramatically unfolded, was indifferent to political ideologizing. Both her tradition and her recent military triumph saw to that. If there was an "ideal condition" to which the arts might legitimately aspire in the new modernism, it was an aesthetic condition, not a political one. The Americans in their now-dominant world position were not interested in political lessons from the Europeans, but they were eager to learn about art from the many first-generation European modernists who fled to the U.S. to escape the war. These refugees—one recalls Piet Mondrian, Max Ernst, André Masson, and André Breton, to name but several—were received by their American hosts with hospitality bordering on reverence, though the affirmation was confined to the Europeans' activity as artists, not as emissaries of political thought.

Thereupon a new art developed in America. It initially took its inspiration from certain forms of European painting of the first third of the century, chiefly Parisian surrealism, and it gradually dispensed with all literary content. By the mid-1950s American painters—for example, Pollock, Still, Rothko, Newman—had developed a type of formalist abstraction which pushed the reductivist tradition of early modernist painting to a new extreme point, an accomplishment taken in most quarters to be the sign of a newly vital international avant-garde, most evidently active in the United States.

This set of circumstances was almost ideally suited to Mies, and he to it. He was an abstractionist by nature, with no national sympathies, no political ideology, a perfect Prometheus of the new modernism. Just as naturalism in painting was increasingly understood to be a superficiality, a leftover cosmetic of history that concealed the body and bone of the art, its equivalent in architecture—ornament or composition identified with any historical, that is to say outmoded, period—was regarded as a disguise, an unwelcome concealment of the essence of building, which Mies had insisted, ever since 1922, was structure. He was now in a position to put that old conviction to work. For if the Zeitgeist was technology, then steel and glass structure was necessarily the appropriate form of modern building for the modern city, especially the modern American city. Since this conclusion was arrived at "rationally," there was no room for caprice or for "self-expression" in the building art properly practiced. "Architecture," Mies would declare over and over in America, "is not a cocktail."[5] And even if one sensed the arbitrariness of his way of defining "rationality," it was dif-

149. Corner detail of Alumni Memorial Hall, IIT, 1945

Revival: Modernism without Utopia

ficult to argue the point in the sight of those walls at IIT, which *looked* so incontrovertible in their structural logic, largely because they were given form by so unimpeachable an artistic sensibility.

Mies's belief in a rational order in architecture as a sign of higher truth only deepened in America, and with it the appearance of subjectivity in his design gradually diminished. We have suggested that this rationale had already provided him with a way of prevailing in the face of the events and matter of modern existence. Despite the fact that the postwar world was a more hopeful place than anything he had known in the 1930s, it was a world disabused of the hopes of the 1920s. Hiroshima and Auschwitz left less room even for the abstracted subjectivity and purified romanticism that Mies had expressed in the flowing plan of the Barcelona Pavilion. Atomic energy was a fact. So was corporate capitalism, American style. It was all the more necessary to accommodate material reality and to elevate it to Aquinian order. Thus Mies did not deviate from his faith in the Thomist doctrine of essences, or from his conviction that it was materially manifest in the evolution of earthly form. He strengthened these beliefs in a devoted reading of the morphologist D'Arcy Thompson and the neo-Thomist Jacques Maritain. From the latter's argument against the surrender of reason in the modern world he took special comfort, just as he found congenial points of view promoted at the University of Chicago, where, during the 1940s, President Robert Maynard Hutchins and Mortimer Adler presided over a highly active group of neo-Aristotelian thinkers, many of whom were confessed Thomists.

The effect of this reasoning can be read in the modular regularity of Mies's IIT buildings. Transition, of course, did not take place overnight. An interplay of a freer European space with a more rigid American order—tinctured with the scale of his 1930s concepts—can be observed in his plans for the most ambitious single project of the IIT group in the 1940s: the Library and Administration Building, the design of which was completed in 1944. Several factors conspired to prevent the realization of this structure, not least the steel shortage of the time together with a relatively low priority: buildings more pertinent to the war effort or technology at large were constructed first.

150. Library and Administration Building project, IIT, 1942–43

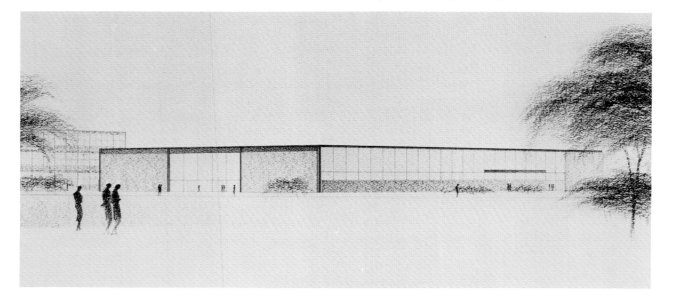

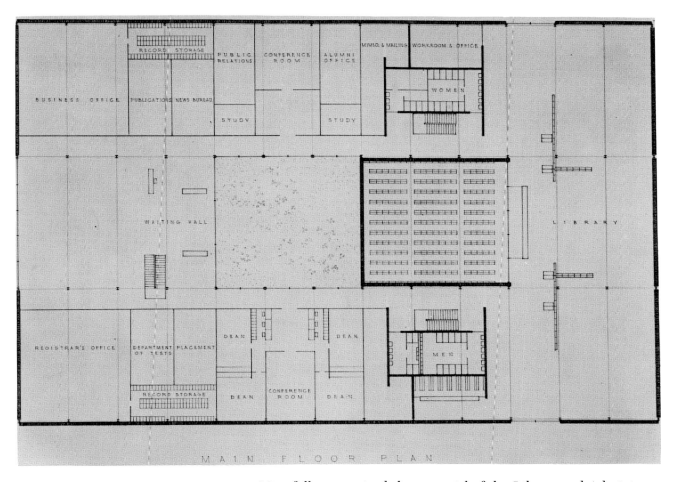

151. Plan of Library, IIT

Mies fully recognized the potential of the Library and Administration Building. Having still never completed any large public work, he was inspired by the dimensions he proposed for this long, low parallelepiped—192 by 312 by 30 feet—to think in monumental terms. He envisioned a lofty one-story elevation, with an interior height of 24 feet, and a plan the structural bays of which measured 24 feet on the long sides of the building, 64 feet on the short sides. This last figure meant compromising his 24-foot campus module, with which 64 feet is only in fractional accord. He also meant to fenestrate the building with the largest panes of glass, 12 by 18 feet, ever used in America up to that time. Meanwhile, instead of a grid plan, he organized the supporting columns in a rectangular system reflective of the short bays on the long side of the building, the long bays on the short side. The result was a layered ranking of space, broken up by an inside court of grass and trees and, most impressively in elevation, by a mezzanine containing the president's office that would have extended partly into the administrative area, hovering over it. Mies made a special point of showing the steel columns and brick panels of the exterior identically on the interior. Moreover, since this could be technically regarded as a one-story building, the fire code permitted his use of unencased steel. This advantage encouraged him to reveal all structural elements, inside and out, with maximal clarity. His concept of essential structure was now uncompromised.

The mezzanine space was no less arresting in turn, representing as it did the one instance in the IIT buildings in which Mies deviated from cubicular regularity. It was a reminder of the subjective spaces of his early Weimar years, though the spectacularly high, wide interior as a whole owed still more to the example of the Brussels Pavilion of 1934. Among his European projects, it was this last work that pointed most directly to his American future.

For some time the future had been germinating on the drawing tables of the IIT ateliers tucked in the attic of the Art Institute. Mies very early established a habit of refining his own ideas through projects assigned to his students. To some extent he had done this with his charges at the German Bauhaus, but in Chicago the process accelerated and grew more varied. It was a method that had little affinity with Beaux-Arts education but much in common, as Mies saw it, with his beloved medieval tradition of masters and apprentices working together and impersonally, toward a common end.

Thus it was that the Library and Administration Building developed out of a master's thesis by Daniel Brenner and the Museum for a Small City from a similar project by George Danforth. Mies oversaw all these activities, pointing the way to each of his students rather than following paths they had plotted. There is no doubt who the master was. Indeed, one reads from student work of the early 1940s that he himself had already begun wrestling earnestly with a problem of space which led at last to the clear span structures of his late great American works.

Even as he busied himself with the Library and Administration Building, he was asked by *Architectural Forum* to produce a project appropriate to the city of the future. Deciding that the design of a "Museum for a Small City," as he called it,[6] would be a fitting response, he drew up a long, low-roofed pavilion with glass walls, flanked by a stone-walled court at one end and the plane of a raised terrace at the other. Freestanding walls, again reminiscent of Germany, were disposed asymmetrically within an interior organized by a grid of col-

152. Perspective of the Museum for a Small City project, 1942

153. Collage of Concert Hall project, 1942

umns. All this was customary enough; his most arresting new device emerged as a way of securing space for an interior auditorium: he removed a number of supporting columns and hung the roof over the auditorium from exposed spanning trusses. These last were a sign of major things to come, but they were not acted upon until Mies had made the most of a photograph that captured his attention about the same time he was at work on the museum.

The photo showed the interior of the Martin Bomber Plant near Baltimore, designed for the war effort by the American Albert Kahn. It was an immense space whose freedom from all interior supports depended on ranks of huge overhead trusses that spanned the entire room. One can imagine easily enough what Mies found to admire in it. It was an exercise in raw structure, not necessarily refined—Kahn was a no-nonsense builder of factories without frills—but clearly indicative of the unique capacity of modern engineering in steel to enclose a stupendous space. Steel technology might fulfill his deepest yearning for an architecture at once monumental yet dematerialized—in his much-quoted phrase *beinahe nichts* ("almost nothing")—robustly structural yet, or thus, spatially most free. In its immensity, moreover, the space was maximally generalized, allowing a variety of specific functions to be acted out within it wherever or for as long as they seemed appropriate. The bomber plant, in short, was the essence of building, a limpid display of the grammar of an expressive language which, as Mies liked to put it, could be assembled into prose or elevated into poetry.

Mies elected to design a serious project based on the photograph. He conceived the installation of a concert hall in the great Kahn factory space. Using his familiar collage-montage technique, he proposed a number of arrangements of wall and ceiling planes, horizontal and vertical, flat and curved, standing and hanging, all meant to define a space within the larger space, where groups of people could attend musical performances. It did not worry him that the openings between the planes presented serious acoustical problems. This was a postu-

Revival: Modernism without Utopia

lation, if practically unfeasible, rich in its theoretical implications: the American equivalent of his 1922 Glass Skyscraper. It can be argued that the Concert Hall was the pivotal work of his career, in the sense that it stood squarely between his German and his American oeuvres, incorporating elements of each equally and separately. The planes, slipping variously into and around space which in turn flowed and curled around them, were the vestiges of his spatial dynamism of the 1920s, while the yawning hall in which all this took place prefigured the vast emptinesses and spatial stasis that characterized his later American works.

Mies's social life during the first year of his American residence was expectedly restricted, a condition due more to his natural reticence than to his limited English. Though his command of the language was meager enough that Rodgers regularly acted as his interpreter in Armour (later IIT) classes, there were German-speaking people in Chicago, not least Hilberseimer and Peterhans, who kept him in contact with the world. And the contact increased. He himself could communicate tolerably well by the summer of 1939, a portion of which he spent at a Pike Lake, Wisconsin, resort at the invitation of William Priestley's friend, the Chicago lawyer E. M. Ashcraft. There Mies alternately worked and relaxed. His assignment was the Armour campus plan, on which he was assisted by Rodgers and the first draftsman he hired in Chicago, George Danforth, with Priestley and Peterhans occasionally drifting by.

There was a woman in the party too. Lilly Reich had made the

154. Erich Mendelsohn, Walter Peterhans, Ludwig Hilberseimer, and Mies, across from Orchestra Hall and Pullman Building, Chicago, about 1940

long trip from Berlin in July and she followed Mies to Wisconsin. For a few weeks in the crisp north woods their little community was Elysian. Work progressed steadily but without haste, professional camaraderie was close, and leisure hours were appropriately free of bourgeois constraints: liquor was limitless, swimming easy in the nude, and evenings passed pleasantly as Ashcraft and Priestley, both trained musicians, offered impromptu jazz concerts. Now and then the great trumpeter Jimmy McPartland, encamped nearby, was Ashcraft's guest. McPartland fascinated and mystified Mies, whose sensitivity to music was inversely proportional to his gift for visual form.

"Why is it," he once asked Danforth, a pianist in his own right, "that you like chazz?"

"Because it is so improvisational," came the reply.

"*Tja*," returned Mies, struggling to uphold the rule of reason in art, "but you must be careful with improvisation, no?"[7]

The days shortened, the shadows lengthened, and the light mood grew dark as the radio daily reported news of the imminence of war in Europe. For Lilly it was the coldest of portents. She wanted to stay with Mies, here, far from the bleak haunts she had left. It is presumed by most of his friends that he did little to persuade her to remain, chiefly because he felt the need to be free of her and her commanding personality. It was a situation akin to that of 1921, when the challenge of post–World War I Berlin prompted him to escape the confinements of family life. Now, faced with a comparably uncertain but no less hopeful new life in America, he would go it alone, unaided but above all unfettered. Besides, it could be rationalized that Lilly had responsibilities back in Germany which quite on their own called for her prompt return. Whatever passed between her and Mies in the waning days of August at Pike Lake, she was gone before the German army invaded Poland on 1 September. She took the train to New York, where she was frustrated yet again as the great North German Lloyd passenger liner *Bremen* slipped away without her one night under cover of darkness, so as to avoid pursuit by the British navy. Tenacious as ever, she managed to get back to Berlin by 22 September, when, faithful as ever, she began a long and dutiful correspondence with Mies. She never saw him again.

Mies met Lora Marx rather by chance at the New Year's Eve party at Charles and Margrette Dornbusch's in Chicago. A willowy beauty recently divorced from the Chicago society architect and art collector Samuel Marx, Lora showed up at the Dornbusch's in the company of one of Mies's German-speaking immigrant friends, the architect Helmut Bartsch, who had asked her earlier if she minded a third in their party. It was Mies himself. As to what followed we have the testimony of Katharine Kuh and Lora herself, both of whom agree that Lora and Mies were drawn to each other suddenly and electrically. "Love at first sight," Lora's summary of it, was not challenged by Kuh's recollection of an "absolutely beautiful" Lora and an unmistakably smitten Mies.[8]

Thus began a relationship that lasted, with brief interruptions, from that night until Mies's death. Lora was the antithesis of Lilly; comely,

155. Mies and Lora Marx at a New Year's Eve party at the home of Charles and Margrette Dornbusch, Chicago, 1940 Private collection

serene, and yielding, not ungifted in her own right as a sculptress but hardly the unassailably accomplished artist that Lilly was. Finally Lora, fourteen years younger than Mies, proved to be the kind of woman he could tolerate having around for a long time. Like Lilly, she maintained a separate residence for the twenty-nine years she was close to him. And she put up with his occasional peccadillos. Unlike Lilly, she played no role in his creativity, as either inspiration or irritant.

Mies and Lora seized the day. It was the 1940s, the most boisterous period of their romance, by consensus of all associated with Mies a decade awash in booze. For a while the excuse was the war and later on, the victory after the war. Mies drank and Lora drank. The students at IIT drank, and the architects and artists, Americans and Europeans, residents and visitors and friends. Once Lora and Mies, with architect Alfred Shaw and his wife Rue, all of them riotously drunk, pooled the ladies' lipsticks and redesigned the face and form of a marble nymph in the lobby of the Blackstone. Hans Richter and refugee art dealer Curt Valentin showed up in Chicago one night and stayed long enough at Lora's for Valentin to fall besotted down a whole flight of steps, nearly killing himself.[9] On yet another occasion Mies and his students and people from his office with all their children drove up

Revival: Modernism without Utopia

to Lake Forest, where one of their number, Peter Roesch, was living as the caretaker of the late Edith Rockefeller McCormick's once magnificent Beaux-Arts estate, Villa Turicum, designed in 1910 by Charles Platt, now a ruin stripped of all its electricity. There they staged a candlelight party that lasted through the night, past dawn, and into the next day.

Despite his modest salary at IIT, Mies, now living in his Pearson Street apartment, kept both cook and butler. Nelli van Doesburg was his houseguest in 1947, when the University of Chicago mounted a retrospective of the work of her husband Theo, dead sixteen years.[10] Max Beckmann dined at Mies's one winter's night in 1948, ending up the evening with Mies, Konrad Wachsmann, and Peterhans in the warmth of a striptease bar on North Clark Street.[11] Richard Neutra appeared in town, and the brothers Naum Gabo and Antoine Pevsner. And always the bottle tilted.

Mies meanwhile assembled a roster of people he disliked, poisonously if privately, to go along with his company of friends. When Moholy-Nagy immigrated to Chicago in 1937, a year before Mies began teaching at Armour Institute, he opened a school of design called the New Bauhaus, which was meant to follow the principles of the old one as Moholy knew them. To Mies this amounted to a rank usurpation of the title "Bauhaus," which had been legally granted him alone, as the last official director of the institution in Germany. Mies never forgave Moholy for this perceived affront, though his animus went deeper and took root earlier, in the 1920s, when Moholy was one of the most outspoken disciples of Mies's ancient rival Gropius.[12]

Mies may have been better off without the name. The Bauhaus, even in America, seemed cursed to a shortened life partly because of the endless animosities among the people who were integral to or just associated with it. Excepting friendships with the designer Konrad Wachsmann, photographers Aaron Siskind and Harry Callahan, and the sculptor-painter Hugo Weber—with occasional attendance at the lecture-appearances of R. Buckminster Fuller—Mies turned a cold shoulder to Moholy and his school even when it was reorganized under the name Institute of Design, and he did not change his mind after Moholy's death in 1946 or following the 1952 incorporation of ID into IIT. Just as Mies had suspected Moholy of professional double-dealing, he was put off by what he saw as the dubious efforts of the latter's successor Serge Chermayeff to insinuate architectural courses (called "shelter design") into an ID curriculum supposedly restricted to interior design.[13] Nor was there anything like long-lasting peace among the bumptious ID staff itself, which broke into open rebellion following changes in administrative personnel and policies rung in by a new director, Jay Doblin, in the mid-1950s. Eventually the school ended up, literally and figuratively, in the basement of Mies's own architecture building, Crown Hall, completed in 1956.

Realizing one day in 1947 that she had become an alcoholic, Lora Marx quit drinking, cold turkey. Mies, his capacity legendary by now, felt no similar need. Fearing that she could not sustain sobriety as long as she was with him, she broke off the relationship. Their separation lasted a year, during which time she took command of her problem.[14] In the interim the Museum of Modern Art staged a full-scale retrospective exhibition of Mies's work which, more than any single event up until that time, brought him to the attention of a wider American art public.

Once again he had Philip Johnson to thank for the favor. In the years since the International Style show, the mercurial Johnson had quit the museum in 1934, taken a brief, freakish fling at radical right-wing politics in behalf of Louisiana's colorful governor Huey Long, returned to the museum and left it again to study architecture at Harvard under Gropius and Marcel Breuer, done a stint in the wartime army, then returned once more to the museum's department of architecture.

The exhibition was propitiously timed, coinciding with the renewal of cultural activity in the postwar period and U.S. ascendancy in the international arts. Johnson spared no pains, as he promised Mies in a letter of 20 December 1946, "to make this the most important exhibition the department has ever held."[15] He secured a generous budget and more display space than the museum had allocated any previous architecture show. For the occasion, furthermore, he was successful in persuading Mies to design the installation, though at the predictable expense of endlessly wheedling and cajoling the master into observing deadlines which the master did not invariably observe.

The exhibition consisted of drawings, photographs, and models of Mies's work ranging from the Kröller House of 1912 (the only entry antedating World War I), through the best-known built and unbuilt designs of the 1920s to projects and buildings-in-progress from the mid-1940s, including the Farnsworth House, the Cantor Drive-In Restaurant of Indianapolis, and more buildings for IIT. Articles of furniture were also on display, together with drawings of a so-called conchoidal chair from the early 1940s, a body-fitting curvilinear object meant to be executed from pressed plastic.

Reaction to the Museum of Modern Art exhibition was decisively affirmative, as everyone devoted to the new modernism in America might have been inclined to predict. Johnson affirmed the special place Mies occupied in his own mind by publishing a monograph accompanying the show that was the most complete summary in any language of Mies's achievements up to that time. It remained the definitive volume on the subject for decades thereafter.*

Writing for *Arts and Architecture*, the rising young star of American design, Charles Eames, paid his respects not only to Mies the architect, as did numerous other critics of the day, but to the uncommon merits of the installation design: "Certainly it is the experience of walking through that space and seeing others move through it that is the high point of the exhibition."[16]

Even the eminence of Taliesin, Frank Lloyd Wright, materialized at the exhibition opening, the very act signifying his own form of homage, even though he did what he could to make himself appear the cynosure of the occasion.

---

*Mies wrote an inscription in Johnson's personal copy of the monograph: "To Philip: It would not be without you; it could not be without me. Mies. September 24, 1947."

156. Conchoidal Chair, early
1940s
Hedrich-Blessing

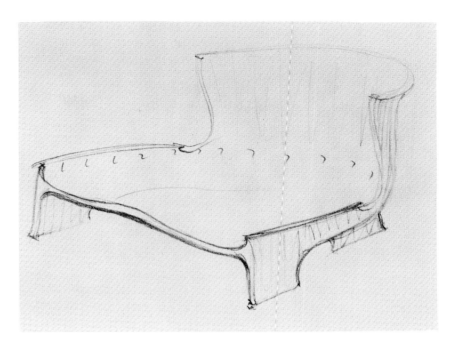

He strode into the gallery late, cape flowing, and quickly and publicly delivered himself of a criticism of Mies which is best related—
together with Mies's response to it—in the exchange of letters that
later passed between the two men.[17]

My dear Mies:

Somebody has told me you were hurt by remarks of mine
when I came to see your New York show . . . But did I tell you
how fine I thought your handling of your materials was?

. . . you know you have frequently said you believe in "doing
next to nothing" [*beinahe nichts*] all down the line. Well, when I
saw the enormous blowups the phrase [*sic*] "Much ado bout 'next
to nothing' " came spontaneously from me.

Then I said the Barcelona Pavilion was your best contribution
to the original "Negation" and you seemed to be still back there
where I was then.

This is probably what hurt (coming from me) and I wish I had
taken you aside to say it to you privately because it does seem to
me that the whole thing called "Modern Architecture" has
bogged down with the architects right there on that line. I
didn't want to classify you with them—but the show struck me
sharply as reactionary in that sense. I am fighting hard against it
myself.

But this note is to say that I wouldn't want to hurt your
feelings—even with the truth. You are the best of them all as an
artist and a man.

You came to see me but once (and that was before you spoke
English) many years ago. You never came since, though often
invited.

So I had no chance to see or say what I said then and say
now.

Revival: Modernism without Utopia

Why don't you come up sometime—unless the break is irreparable—and let's argue.

Sincerely, Frank

And Mies replied:

My dear Frank:

Thank you so much for your letter.

It was an exaggeration if you heard that my feelings were hurt by your remarks at my New York show. If I had heard the crack "Much ado about next-to-nothing" I would have laughed with you. About "Negation"—I feel that you use this word for qualities that I find positive and essential.

It would be a pleasure to see you again sometime in Wisconsin and discuss this subject further.

As ever, Mies

The personalities of the two men are illuminated in these two short pages: Wright warm and aggressive, both in criticism and in fellowship—not to mention vanity; Mies inclined to modesty, distance, and the privacy of his own thoughts. Mies counterpunched only once ("qualities that I find positive and essential"), though that was enough to leave no doubt that he was as certain of his position as Wright of his contrary view.

The friendship surely was genuine; Wright would never have invited anyone else to Taliesin more than twice who did not show up more than once, and Mies would scarcely have bothered to answer, much less make light of, any other critic's reproach.

Yet the signals of eventual separation are evident enough in retrospect. Mies's own tendency toward a harder, leaner, more formally ordered architecture in America was already remarked by Wright, though regretted not at all by Mies. Wright recognized Mies as the best practitioner of modern architecture, but wanted no part of the movement himself, while admitting his own need to struggle "hard against it." Within a few years the two men, like lines crossing on a graph, passed the point where either could hear the other. Silence chilled cordiality at first and later froze civility altogether.

8   America: The Triumph of Steel and Glass, 1949–58

During preparations for the 1947 New York exhibition, Mies was in Manhattan often enough to renew social ties with the museum crowd. He strengthened his friendship with curator and critic James Johnson Sweeney, whom he had met as early as 1933 in Berlin, and he got to know better the sculptress Mary Callery, with whom in the course of the next decade he carried on the kind of light, desultory romantic affair to which he was long accustomed in the old country.[1] Yet the acquaintances he made in Chicago during the same period, the mid to late 1940s, proved immeasurably more important to his career. And among these none was more fruitful than his relationship with a rabbinical scholar turned real estate developer, Herbert Greenwald.

Greenwald it was who commissioned and, more significantly, brought to actual completion, Mies's first large-scale commercial work. He was thus the agent of Mies's escape from the campus into the public world. If the Museum of Modern Art show established Mies's reputation in the U.S. as a designer and theoretician, it was Greenwald who enabled him to build his architecture, in quantity, at long last.

The accomplishment brings Michael van Beuren back to mind. Like Holabird and Heald, Greenwald was the sort of resourceful Chicagoan van Beuren had told Mies about: a man responsive to contemporary talent but no less eager to put it on the market. His rabbinical studies were supplemented by courses at the University of Chicago, where the Great Books program initiated by Hutchins and Adler created its own self-consciously special atmosphere of postwar intellectual adventure. Greenwald was more than a little affected by his experience at the university, so that while he opted for a career in real estate, he became a devoted amateur aesthete as well. It was only a matter of time before he recognized how much cultural and material profit might be realized from a striking coincidence: that new building was badly needed in a country whose domestic economy had been idled by a depression and a war and that the most internationally illustrious artist living within reach of him in Chicago was an architect.

Mies met Greenwald in 1946. The former was sixty, the latter twenty-nine. In the thirteen years that passed before Greenwald perished in an airplane crash, he and Mies captured the attention of the worlds of business and architecture alike with a series of buildings that revolutionized both realms. The Weimar Republic's most elitist designer proved to be the most potent public architect of the American postwar period.

If in its early stages Mies's first joint effort with Greenwald was nothing less than prophetic, in its final form it turned out to be little better than mediocre. The 22-story Promontory Apartments building,

157. Promontory Apartments, Chicago, 1946–49
Hedrich-Blessing

conceived initially with a steel-and-glass curtain wall, had to be built in reinforced concrete due to the persistence of the wartime steel shortage. Completed in 1949 on Chicago's South Lake Shore Drive, Promontory Apartments was altogether modern in its rectilinear profile and Miesian enough in the composition of its facade—windows running above brick panels set slightly behind supporting columns— but nothing else about it was of more than middling merit.

The second Mies-Greenwald collaboration proved to be a qualitatively different matter. The twin apartment buildings erected between 1949 and 1951 at 860–880 Lake Shore Drive belong among the several most influential designs for high-rise structures of the twentieth century. They were surely the most important conceived after the Art Deco skyscrapers that flourished in America at the turn of the 1930s. Slender, flat-topped 26-story towers whose surfaces were almost all glass, they affected for a quarter of a century the anatomy of most of the world's skyscrapers. Even at this writing, in the mid-1980s, with the rebellion against Mies and modernism a fact of history, the average tall urban building still harks back in some measure to the geometry of his Lake Shore Drive apartments.

Their immediate antecedent was the alternate, unbuilt version of the Promontory Apartments. At 860–880 Mies constructed each building on a steel skeleton which rose from a 3-by-5, 21-foot-square bay plan. His main objective was to reveal the structural cage as clearly and as forcefully as possible. The supporting columns and the spandrels provide the chief rhythm of the facade. The area enclosed by columns and spandrels and divided by mullions is given over to glass,

158. Perspective of Promontory Apartments as planned with steel facade

159. Herbert Greenwald and Mies, about 1955

yielding four aluminum-framed floor-to-ceiling windows in each bay. The windows, higher than they are wide, together with the mullions, accentuate the vertical flight of the building. Since columns, spandrels, and windows are in the same plane, Mies elected to relieve the resultant flatness of facade surface by welding I-beams onto the mullions and the columns. The ground floor area of each tower is even with grade, walled with glass—clear for the lobby and opaque for the service area—and set back behind the supporting columns with the effect that an arcaded walkway surrounds the base. The Adam Building project of 1928 comes to mind. Like the buildings at IIT, each tower of 860–880 is a compact mass, symmetrical unto itself, but related to the other in faint recollection of the informal geometry of de Stijl. Eight sixty, its short side facing east, is set forward and eastward of 880, which faces north. A steel-framed one-story-high canopy runs from the south face of 880 to the north face of 860. The form of this connecting element is repeated in the canopies that project over the entrances to both buildings.

With the completion of these two apartment towers Mies took a long step in adjusting his architecture to American conditions without compromising the philosophical basis of it. Several of his old dreams were fulfilled: for one, a tall building, the form of which derived from the structure—a derivation he had never carried out in detail before, even on paper; for another, a work whose reduction to structural essence expressed the aspiration to universality he had associated with the modern sensibility. The 860–880 towers were, moreover, consonant with the *Zeitgeist* of technology which he had more and more in his thirteen years in America come to identify with steel and glass.

And he refined his own iconography. The attached I-beam had the practical advantage of strengthening the mullions, thus stiffening each bay frame, but Mies himself said he employed it primarily because the building without it "did not look right."[2] Its purpose, then, like the famous IIT corner, was more aesthetic than functional, and his continued reliance on it for the remainder of his career signified that it had become a prime symbol for the transcendence of technology into architecture, prose into poetry. The I-beam, that is to say, took on decorative significance. Those Americans who saw Mies as a rational functionalist in the tradition of *Sachlichkeit* were put off by his application of this device not just to the mullions of 860–880 but to the columns, where it was apparently useless. Despite this and other occasional surrenders to subjectivity, his admirers doggedly insisted that he was the purest of rationalists. It must be added that in his own yearning to be rational—not to mention magisterial—he did little to correct this public impression. Very likely because in the U.S. he was a teacher, not just a practicing architect, and because this was pragmatic America, not philosophy-minded Germany, he talked increasingly about objectivity and reason after 1940 and less about spirit. Yet everything we said earlier (see pp. 172–73) about his commitment to spirit applies as much to his work in America as to that in Germany, whether the work grew drier in America or not. For we affirmed that a major element of "spirit" for Mies was aesthetic, and it is art, not reason, that most distinguishes 860–880, generations after it was built,

America: The Triumph of Steel and Glass

from the depressing multitude of buildings by other architects who sought to emulate what they presumed to be its ineluctable logic. The excellence of 860–880 lies in the sensitive relationships of width to height in the windows, spandrel to column and bay to facade, not to mention the powerful thrust and careful detailing of the connecting canopy and the secure placement of one building mass relative to the other.*

Functionally speaking, in fact, alterations were imposed on Mies's first plans before the buildings were approved by Greenwald and his financial partners. Budgetary restrictions kept Mies from installing the central air-conditioning he had recommended, and his open plan in the apartments was changed to a more cubicular arrangement in consideration of the traditional preference of closing off rooms for privacy.

*Mies also insured a uniform look to the exterior surface of the building by insisting on identical, off-white draperies in all the apartments. These hangings showed to the outside. Behind them draperies of the tenants' own choosing, visible from within but not from without, could be installed.

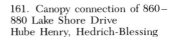

161. Canopy connection of 860–880 Lake Shore Drive
Hube Henry, Hedrich-Blessing

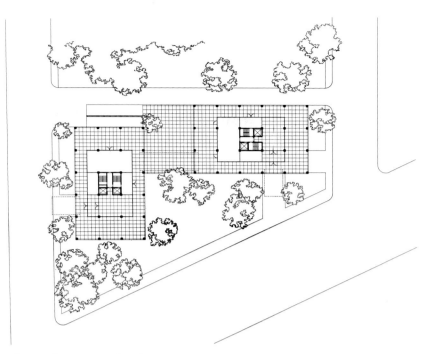

These changes made, however, Greenwald studied the cost and found
it good: $10.38 per square foot, a figure lower than that of most com-
parable residential complexes of the day. In addition to the advantage
of these numbers, he could point to the signature of Mies van der
Rohe.

Thirty-seven years had passed since Bruno Taut's epochal experiment in glass at the Cologne Werkbund exhibitions, and thirty since
Mies's own Honeycomb. Notice should be taken of other precedents
for 860–880, especially the efforts at modernizing the skyscraper which
had occurred in America during the 1920s, 1930s, and 1940s; for example, Raymond Hood's McGraw-Hill Building of 1929 in New York,
Howe and Lescaze's Philadelphia Savings Fund Society Building of
1926–32, and postwar examples in slab form, most notably the United
Nations Secretariat of 1947–50 in New York, supervised by Harrison
and Abramovitz. These various works undoubtedly paved the way for
860–880, just as Mies's 1947 exhibition at the Museum of Modern
Art drew greater attention to him than to anyone else as the central
figure of international technological architecture.

For all of that, however, the twin towers on Lake Shore Drive were
the purest expression of the vitreous high-rise yet achieved. In 1952
Gordon Bunshaft of Skidmore, Owings, and Merrill offered the first
major material acknowledgment of Mies's accomplishment by putting
up the all-glass Lever House on New York's Park Avenue, thus demonstrating that the 860–880 solution was applicable to the design of
offices as well as apartments.

Mies's own first office building, the lordly Seagram, was still half
a decade away, but he used that intervening time to carry out both
variations and refinements on the theme of the tall building conceived
as a glass box. His relationship with Greenwald became ever more

163. Facade of Commonwealth
Apartments, Chicago, 1953–56
Bill Engdahl, Hedrich-Blessing

hopeful as the critics responded ever more affirmatively to 860–880; thus he increased both his staff and his office space in 1952 when he moved to Holabird and Roche's Champlain Building at 37 S. Wabash. A year later he had begun work on the design of two more large apartment groups in Chicago: the two towers of 900 Esplanade, meant for a site immediately north of 860–880, and the Commonwealth Promenade complex of four separate structures, scheduled to be erected two-and-one-half miles north, on Diversey Parkway at Lincoln Park. The latter project was interrupted by Greenwald's death in 1959, after only the southern pair of buildings were completed in 1956. Their counterparts to the north were never built. Thus, Commonwealth and Esplanade ended up each with one long slab set ajog a shorter one, though at Esplanade the relationship of the masses was perpendicular, at Commonwealth, parallel.

The similarities of the two groups were more emphatic, especially visually, than their differences. The former included several features taken from 860–880 which Mies evidently liked well enough to make constants in almost all his later high-rise buildings. The basic form of each individual structure was the flat-faced, flat-roofed reductivist prism, with all joints and corners rectangular, all windows vertical and I-beams welded to all external mullions. The ground floor was set back at grade from the columns, a treatment that not only underscored the supportive character of the columns but created an openness at bottom which, together with the sliding compositional arrangement of the paired building masses, widened or narrowed as one walked through it.

The principal differences between 860–880 and the two later groups were more subtle than the kinships of all three, but hardly of less consequence. In order to reduce overall costs, both Commonwealth and Esplanade were built with reinforced concrete columns at the lower stories and steel columns in the upper stories. Each was covered in a prefabricated aluminum skin frame which implied a significantly different treatment of the wall, also prompted by practical considerations. By hanging the glass skin in front of the columns, Mies protected the entire building from temperature fluctuations (and consequent expansion and contraction) which were more pronounced at 860–880, where columns and girder cover plates were exposed. He also secured a space between the concrete columns and the skin mullions into which he installed risers for the heating and air-conditioning systems.

This was the curtain wall adumbrated in Promontory and thereafter employed by Mies in virtually all his tall buildings, so steadily indeed that it became the most identifiable mark of his mature American architecture. Yet whatever his motives in using it, they had the effect of concealing rather than revealing structure, thus of overriding one of his presumably most sacred principles. Peter Carter writes that Mies himself called the curtain wall of Commonwealth-Esplanade "a more technological solution"[3] than the exposed frames of 860–880, though Carter leaves the matter at that, with no explanation of what was meant by "more technological." If Mies was alluding to the practical advantages cited in the previous paragraph, he gained them only at the expense of rationalizing them, hardly the first time he did such a thing.

America: The Triumph of Steel and Glass

The observation is offered less to suggest that he was inconsistent in his principles and more to affirm that he was an artist before he was an engineer, an architect—or a philosopher. In his best high-rise buildings the curtain wall has an elegantly structural *look* about it, even if it is not structural, just as Mies invariably *sounded* logically consistent even if he wasn't always in fact. As with structure, so with materials. We have acknowledged his surpassing sensitivity to them. We have not, however, insisted that he used them technically to the best of their capacities. The clear glass at 860–880 is beautiful, but on account of its single thickness, it offers relatively little resistance to shifts of heat and cold. The walkways at the base of those two towers are laid with travertine, a stone subtle in its richness but so porous that accumulated water freezes in its crevices during the harsh Chicago winters, causing more than a little cracking.

Yet Mies was not the only great architect with such habits. The rapid deterioration of the "natural" wood in Frank Lloyd Wright's houses comes to mind, likewise that of the stucco in Le Corbusier's. *Magister dixit.* The master speaks: it is enough for faith, and was so in the 1950s as well, when Mies's steel and glass minimalism arrested the attention of both the aesthetes and the corporation executives. Responses among the latter ranged from simple fiscal satisfaction in Mies's remarkably low American budgets to a form of nationalistic idealism that saw a connection between America's new economic world hegemony, fine and clean, and modern architecture's formal regularity and abstract purity. As for the aesthetes, the glass experience was nearly as thrilling as Bruno Taut had predicted in 1919. Recalling her first visit to 860–880 in 1954, Lilly von Schnitzler said: "It was a glorious starry night. I couldn't sleep, for I had the feeling the stars would fall on my head. I was between heaven and earth."[4] And composer John Cage, also from the upper stories of 860–880 but with a storm breaking over the lake: "Wasn't it splendid of Mies to invent the lightning?"[5]

The single sustained correspondence we find in Mies's files passed between himself and Lilly Reich between July 1939 and June 1940.[6] Thereafter it stops completely, due to the interruption of the mail service on which they had relied. All his letters to her are apparently lost; we know of them only from hers to him, which are nevertheless enough to illuminate more than any other source his purely personal relationship with her, his family, and friends. Reich wrote Mies as she did everything else with and for him—thoroughly and solicitously. Her affection for him is obvious from the exhaustiveness and the constancy with which she cares for his legal affairs and reports on the lives of Ada, Georgia, Marianne, Waltraut, Ewald, and various old colleagues. If the daughters still disliked her, no sign of it appears in her narrative. Her tone is usually level, one might say studiously *sachlich*, yet now and then she gives way to the pain of the war and her hopeless distance from Mies. Ada, she says, is persistently sickly and Waltraut suffers from illnesses together with apparently immature personal relationships that threaten her studies. Marianne and Georgia, both older, are steadier and more purposeful. The problems pertaining to Mies's patents seem endless. And what of his own health? Reich worries over what he has told her of his old leg injury, sustained in a 1920s skiing accident. Please see a doctor, she urges.

The most surprising thing about Mies's own letters is that he sent at least 22 of them to Reich in less than a year—a remarkably faithful correspondence in view of the fact that Marianne once recalled that "I got no more than three or four letters from him in my entire life."[7] He was no less dutiful in sending food packages to Reich and all the family as well as friends. (He continued to do this after the war as well.) For all of that Reich complains gently when he does not write, and in a letter of 12 June 1940, which she supposes will be her last to him, she makes a rare reference to the fact that she has lost him:

> I am powerfully reminded of the last days and hours in Chicago. I fear my instincts did not deceive me, despite the fact that I wished nothing more, both then and now, than to be proven wrong. I am sad that I have received only the slightest word from you in the last weeks, and that, pertaining solely to business affairs. Perhaps you have no time, perhaps you have sent more letters than I know. That the mail connections stop now makes it all the harder to bear.
>
> I suspect we have more to worry about with you. I will hear nothing from you, know nothing about you. Will you try to find a way to be in touch? I am happy that you have friends now, and it comforts me somewhat that I was once with you over there. How helpless we are all delivered up![8]

Reich's "instincts" were right, of course. Mies had already made his decision before she left the U.S. It was too much to ask of him that he compromise his freedom and his art, for her satisfaction or anyone's, including his own. Loneliness was the price of the quest. "I don't belong to anyone," he once told Lora Marx, "who cannot live alone."[9]

From sources other than Reich we learn that Ada spent most of the war in Berlin. There, in the worst of times, the best of her sorrow-laden spirit expressed itself. She concealed several Jewish fugitives in her small apartment in the Bayerischestrasse, most notably a Doctor Levy and his wife, who tried—in vain, as it turned out—to get from Latvia to a haven in Switzerland. In 1942 the Allied forces stepped up their air raids in Berlin and Ada managed to remove her possessions from her apartment only days before it was destroyed by bombs. That same year Georgia, already a rising young actress in the local Regensburg troupe, married the director of the *Stadttheater* there, Fritz Herterich. They had a child, Frank, in November 1943 by which time Ada, having lived for a time with friends in Berlin, joined the Herterichs in Regensburg.

Marianne, together with her seven-year-old son Dirk and two younger daughters, Ulrike, six, and Karin, five, was forced to flee Rathenow early in 1945, when an air attack leveled the community. Several months later, with the war ended and the Third Reich in nearly total ruins, they were in Halle, which later became part of the Russian occupation zone. A succession of anxious moves followed during the late 1940s, in the course of which Wolfgang Lohan, having been freed from prisoner-of-war camp, succeeded at last in bringing his family west to Salem, where he was installed in a teaching position. By 1951 they were settled in nearby Freiburg, in the Black Forest. Waltraut meanwhile matriculated at the University of Munich and received a doctorate in art history in 1945.

For Germany as a whole the late 1940s were a desperate time. The arts did not revive as they had after World War I, either in actual or in visionary form. The country was a physical and spiritual wasteland, quite at the mercy of its conquerors, who quarreled among themselves more, and more portentously, than in 1919. For a time Marianne helped feed her family by making costumed dolls which she exchanged for American cigarettes. Georgia worked for Amerika Haus and the public relations office of the U.S. military government, shuttling between Munich and Regensburg. Lilly, back in Berlin after spending the last months of the war in Saxony, wrote Mies, asking him to send anything that might help her reequip her atelier—pencils, paper, ink, straightedges, the most primitive architectural tools.

Toward the end of 1948 Georgia and Waltraut sailed for America, making their way to Chicago, where they encamped in Mies's apartment on Pearson Street. After eight months of study at the Goodman School of Drama, Georgia returned to Munich, where Ada joined her yet again. The latter's condition steadily worsened and in 1951 her troubled passage through the world came to an end in a Regensburg hospital, where she succumbed to cancer. Waltraut elected to remain in Chicago for good, living with Mies and working in the library of the Art Institute of Chicago until her own death in 1959 of the same sickness that took her mother. Marianne also made a trip to the U.S., in 1950, spending four months with Mies and Waltraut. She returned to Chicago on several later occasions, ministering to Waltraut in 1959 and living from 1963 to 1975 by herself, following her divorce from Wolfgang Lohan.

Mies, now profoundly set in his ways, put up with these various filial intrusions, but never gladly. Lora Marx, who continued to keep intimate company with him, reports that friction was frequent between father and daughters, especially when more than one of the women shared the apartment with him. His abode was comfortable, not ample. Consisting of a living room, a dining room, a kitchen, and two bedrooms, it was ideal for a bachelor or a couple, less than that for two or three professional people who slept apart, especially when more than one of them had a study and one of them was accustomed to, indeed dependent on, his privacy and solitude. One can hardly wonder that Mies never accepted Greenwald's offer of a comparably sized apartment in 860–880. He shied from the prospect of riding the elevator with tenants who might have subjected him either to compliments for designing the building they shared with him or to complaints for failing to design it to their satisfaction. He preferred the old Renaissance-revival palazzo he lived in, a building discreetly handsome enough to suit his position, anonymous enough for his temperament.

Psychologically, Mies was a nautilus; he would emerge at will to survey the world and enjoy his companions, then withdraw from it and them, similarly as and when he chose. Yet the simile must be qualified: he was not so much lacking in long-standing affection as he was in the ability, even the will, to express it. Poor Waltraut worshipped him and devoted herself endlessly to him. He was inclined to let her, with little display of love in return and less belief that it was called for. Yet he was deeply proud of her intellectual accomplishment; it was something he had wanted for himself and would never attain. He clothed her corpse in his own academic robes.[10]

He could not help himself. When he returned to Europe for the first time after the war, in 1953, he visited the Lohans in Freiburg. Nineteenth-century German that he was and father of three girls but no boys, he was eager to see fifteen-year-old Dirk, who in turn anticipated the meeting with his grandsire in a state of absolutely tongue-tied awe. It was decided that Mies would take Dirk and Ulrike and Karin for an afternoon drive through the Black Forest. Yet the old man found nothing to chat about with the children, nor could they break the silence themselves. "It was a bad time for all of them," Marianne recalls, adding that a few days later she took a sojourn with Mies, just the two of them, father and daughter, in the resort village of Feldafing in Bavaria.[11] He took a book with him, and Marianne reports that he read it not once but twice, conversing with her barely at all, not even over meals. One day he said quite suddenly, "Do we have anything at the cleaner's?"

"Yes," replied Marianne.

"We must get it quickly. See to it that I have a ticket to Chicago. I must get back to work."

"But what of your trip to Berlin? They are waiting for you, all your old students, to welcome you!"

"I cannot go. I have to get back to work."

Marianne interpreted her father's behavior as an overpowering self-absorption whose effect was more than a little hurtful to her. It was just as surely another manifestation of Mies's singular will, a faculty that expressed itself in matters as small as silence at dinner or as great as his efforts to superimpose an idealizing order on the whole clamorous variety of architectural directions in the modern world. In Lilly Reich's letters of 1940 to Mies she had commiserated with him over his lonely isolation in a foreign land. Perhaps in his own correspondence he confessed suffering such a condition. Or perhaps not. Whatever inner pains Mies endured he habitually sublimated in work or the most withdrawn reflection. And the work waiting for him when he returned from Feldafing in 1952 was quite enough to call for a will, so much the better if it were monumental.

During the period when his family and friends were struggling to survive Germany's total military defeat, Mies was adjusting to changing conditions of a benignly different sort in America. The number of architectural students at IIT had dropped to about fifty by war's end, but the return of the armed forces promised a jump in enrollment within a short time. Mies's classes were shifted in 1945 from the Art Institute to a pair of spaces, one at 37 S. Wabash, where he kept his own offices, and another at 18 S. Michigan Avenue, a building by Holabird and Roche with a facade by Louis Sullivan. Two years later the department moved again, taking over most of Alumni Memorial Hall, on the IIT campus.

Mies initially increased his war-depleted faculty by appointing the landscape architect Alfred Caldwell in 1945 and welcoming Danforth back from service in 1946. By the early 1950s, Daniel Brenner, Jacques Brownson, William Dunlap, and Reginald Malcolmson were among his junior teaching colleagues, with Hilberseimer and Peterhans retaining their professorial posts. His office at 37 S. Wabash meanwhile also grew, with assistants Edward Olencki and Edward Duckett joined in 1945 by Joseph Fujikawa and John Weese. A year later Myron Goldsmith hired on. The office business manager was Felix Bonnet, a loyal but fussy little Frenchman who complained constantly, if justifiably, about the noise and dust kicked up by a model-making shop—an indispensable tool in Mies's design process—that had been located in the open passage between Bonnet's desk and the drafting room. A two-year spell in 1946 and 1947 during which the office had little work coming in, ended with Greenwald's commission of the Promontory Apartments. Thereafter labor was steady and unremitting, though by the early 1950s, when Mies entered the most productive phase of his American career, his staff never exceeded ten. It was at about this time that he made his abrupt return from Feldafing to Chicago.

Mies had more on his mind than building, though there was enough of that waiting for him. A year earlier, in 1951, he had had a grave falling out with a client, and it had not cleared up in the meantime. Nor would it thenceforward. By spring of 1953 the suit he lodged against Edith Farnsworth and her subsequent countersuit against him had led to a hostile courtroom confrontation and a lengthy, enervating litigation. Client and architect sought without mercy to wound each other, and both succeeded. Mies won the battle, at great expense of spirit, while Farnsworth, no less formidable a human being than her adversary, deserved better than her eventual humiliation, regardless of the merits or the demerits of her case.

Technically at issue was the question of who owed what to whom for the unexpectedly high cost of the house Mies designed and built for Farnsworth between 1946 and 1951. The real struggle, however, was over bigger stakes. It was a clash of two personalities of immense force and authority. The subject of their dispute, the house itself, was no less arresting as a monument in the history of modern architecture.

Farnsworth, who came from a socially prominent Chicago family, met Mies late in 1945 at the home of a mutual friend. Early in her life she had aspired to the violin, which she studied for a time with Mario Corti in Italy. She later decided she was not gifted enough for the instrument. Following graduation from Northwestern University Medical School she set up practice in Chicago and eventually gained a national reputation as a nephrologist. Her ambition in middle age to build a weekend country house for herself prompted her to ask the Museum of Modern Art to recommend an architect. The names of Le Corbusier, Wright, and Mies were advanced, and she settled on Mies, very likely because he was the most accessible of the three. That proximity became more than geographic and her relationship with him something other than purely professional. "She was mesmerized by him," her sister Marian Carpenter recalls, "and she probably had an affair with him."[12] Most witnesses to the Mies-Farnsworth friendship agree that it was a romance of some sort for a time, yet proof of the extent of it is lacking. When Mies himself later contended, rather ungallantly, that "the lady expected the architect to go along with the house," he was already at swords' points with her.[13] Most literate of women, she later had a few words of her own for him: "Perhaps as a man he is not the clairvoyant primitive that I thought he was, but simply colder and more cruel than anybody I have ever known. Perhaps it was never a friend and a collaborator, so to speak, that he wanted, but a dupe and a victim."[14]

Obviously she felt differently when she asked Mies to build the house. The two of them got on at once and famously, and his germinal idea for the design, which he produced with exceptional dispatch early in 1946, suggests that he recognized the commission was as nearly ideal as any he could have hoped for. Intended as a rural retreat for a single woman, it was to be built on a 9.6 acre tract, isolated in woods bordering the north bank of the Fox River near Plano, Illinois, 47 miles west of Chicago. As such it imposed a minimum of functional constraints upon the architect.

If Mies rapidly arrived at his concept of the house, he dawdled thereafter. He and Farnsworth enjoyed each other's society at considerable leisure. They both agreed on his design, but neither appeared in any special hurry to get it built. They regularly drove out to the site from Chicago, picnicked on the riverbank and drove back again, seeing each other frequently enough on other occasions in the city. Fully two years after the model of the house was shown in the 1947 Museum of Modern Art exhibition, the concrete footings were prepared. Construction began in earnest in September 1949 and was completed in 1951.

The house was unlike any conceived before it.[15] It was a totally glassed-in rectangular box, consisting of roof slab and floor slab—the latter suspended five feet above the open ground, partly so as to ride above the level of the river's occasional floods. Both roof and floor planes were supported by eight wide-flange columns, four of them welded to the fascias of each of the long sides. The spaces between the planes and columns—the walls, that is—were given over completely to single panes of one-quarter-inch-thick glass. The plan measured 28 by 77 feet. The long walls faced north to a gentle grassy rise, south to the wooded riverbank. A patio as wide as the house extended the length of one bay from the west end.

Access from ground level was gained by a low stair that rose to the long side of a rectangular terrace nearly as large in plan as the house. This lay parallel to the house while sliding somewhat west of it and was similarly suspended above the ground. Another low stair ascended from terrace to patio, where a 90-degree turn was required for entry into the sole portal of the house, located in the middle of the west wall.

The interior was a single space, one room, whose major subdivision was provided by a freestanding, longitudinal, asymmetrically placed

core containing kitchen to the north, bathrooms to east and west—
separated by a utility space—and fireplace to the south. A freestanding cabinet-closet close to the southeast corner and parallel to the east
wall bordered the sleeping area without enclosing it. The "living room"
area, which spread before the fireplace with a view of the river, was
equally suggested rather than defined. The roof and floor slab were
cantilevered at both ends, so that the vitreous corners of the room
were totally transparent. There was no air-conditioning. Cross ventilation could be encouraged by opening the portal and two hopper windows, the latter located at the base of the east wall at the other end
of the house.

The floor, whose surface was laid out in a geometric grid, was deep
enough to accommodate a coil system for heating as well as the pipes
that served the kitchens, bathrooms, and utility space. An element
extending upward from the core carried exhausts from the kitchen.
The roof dipped slightly inward and downward from its perimeter to
permit drainage, which, together with all pipes and utility lines, descended into a stack, the only connection—other than the columns—
between the house and the ground.

The minimalism of all aspects of Mies's design can be inferred from
this description. Similarly, the treatment of structure and space reflected his changed attitudes toward both in his American years. What
remained of Europe was chiefly the asymmetry, most noticeable in
the sliding terrace and the placement of the core, and Mies's use of
materials. He employed Roman travertine for all deck and floor areas.
The primavera core was specially constructed by a German immigrant
craftsman, Karl Freund. The steel frame, once completed, was sand-
blasted to guarantee the smoothest of surfaces, then painted white.
Mies personally supervised the selection of the travertine slabs and
demanded uncommonly fine tolerances in the joining of all parts.

165. Plan of the Farnsworth
House

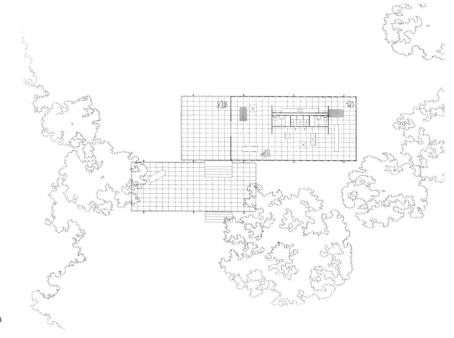

166. Interior of the Farnsworth
House
Bill Hedrich, Hedrich-Blessing

Thus, while the most evident components of the house—sheets of plate glass and lengths of wide-flange steel—were drawn from the inventory of modern technology, they were brought to completion by methods more suggestive of the crafts. This was quintessential Mies: matter accepted then transformed, temporal fact elevated to the level of ageless truth. The Farnsworth House is unmistakably "modern" in its abstracted geometry, yet it is history that Mies abstracted as surely as he did structure. The building has reminded some observers of an eighteenth-century country pavilion, others of a Shinto shrine. The white paint, not to mention the sandblasting that preceded it, denies the steel its rugged industrial origins while converting the supporting piers into something more akin to the classical column. The wide flange, that is, is made over into the sign of an architectural order, equivalent to the Doric or Ionic though expressive of Mies's "epoch." The empty space beneath the house is a volumetric inversion of Schinkel's podium.

Certainly the house is more nearly a temple than a dwelling, and it rewards aesthetic contemplation before it fulfills domestic necessity. Mies's technology, in fact, often proved unequal to it in a strictly material sense. In cold weather the great glass panes tended to accumulate an overabundance of condensation, due to an imbalance in the heating system. In summer, despite the protection afforded by a glorious black sugar maple tree just outside the south wall, the sun turned the interior into a cooker. The cross ventilation availed little and the draperies which could be drawn along the walls were hardly more effective in reducing interior heat. Mies rejected the idea of a screen covering for the door, and it was only his painful experience with the river valley mosquitoes that caused him to yield to Farnsworth's demand for a track on the ceiling of the patio from which screens could be hung, thus permitting comfortable outdoor sitting. Peter Palumbo, the London real estate developer who purchased the house from Farnsworth in 1962, and who confesses to a reverence for Mies's architecture, has accepted the master's will: he removed the screens and, during hot summer days, leaves the door and windows open, putting up uncomplainingly with the insect life that finds its way into the house. (Nonetheless, he keeps a large floor fan at work in each corner of the interior.) Similarly, he has followed Mies's instructions not to hang pictures on the exquisitely finished surfaces of the primavera core. Instead the art he keeps around him is sculpture.[16]

Palumbo is the ideal owner of this house. He is wealthy enough to maintain it with the infinite and eternal care it requires, and he lives in it for only short periods during any given year. Thus he finds it easier to do what anyone must who chooses to *reside* there: he derives sufficient spiritual sustenance from the reductivist beauty of the place to endure its creature discomforts.

That beauty in any case is immensely persuasive. The chaste geometry of the house and the impeccable proportions of its parts are expressive of a human presence held in counterpoise with the woody natural surround. From within and seen in 360 degrees through the transparent walls, nature, especially in the changes of light and the seasons, becomes a pervasive and integral part of the experience of any and all time spent there. The Farnsworth House is a classical design with romantic implications, a work of art that architecturally mediates between man and nature. In that sense it invokes again the spirit of Schinkel.

Yet Mies was content to dismiss the open plan of his European residences and their asymmetrical anatomies that reached out freely into space. The rigor of the rectangle axially oriented and the contained unitary interior volume make for a still, not a flowing space. The dweller feels little impulse to move inquiringly about within but rather prefers to sit and look. Nature may change; the house rests in its geometric certitude. In none of Mies's buildings did he come closer to the dematerialization of architecture leading to the expression of a fixed and supersensible order. The Farnsworth House is to his American career what the Barcelona Pavilion was to his European period: the apotheosis of a worldview, now changed from the conditionality of his early years to the objective finality for which he strove, no less than religiously hence with implacable urgency, as he grew older.

167. Farnsworth House, with Peter Palumbo on the terrace Karant and Associates

One can begin to appreciate, then, how the house finally drove a wedge between Mies and Edith. The closer it came to completion and the more he saw it realize his transcendent ends, the less the relationship with the client meant to him. She in turn, for whom the house symbolized her union with him rather than his with God, grew disaffected. Costs rose. The original budget of $40,000 climbed 50% by the start of construction. Mies accounted for this by his need for only the best materials and craftsmanship, not to mention the effect of the inflation attendant to the Korean war. Edith read the whole matter differently. For one thing, it was her money, not his, and his seeming indifference to expense only increased her worry over it. A disagreement also developed over the interior decor. Mies wanted Edith to use furniture of his own design and draperies of his selection. She resisted on both counts.

Yet these quarrels over taste and finances, serious though they were, were not enough to account for the depth of the spiritual rupture that ensued. For someone who had spent so many happy hours with Mies between 1946 and 1949 and who had a fairly sound idea of what kind of building he had prepared, Farnsworth could not have been seized by such a rage as she later felt without perceiving that Mies had hurt her personally, not just disappointed her professionally. Alfred Caldwell recalls an occasion at the building site when Mies, standing some yards from the house, asked Edith to "walk up to the terrace level, so that I can have a look at you." Flattered, Edith obliged. "Good. I just wanted to check scale," said Mies, turning away and leaving the poor woman altogether deflated.[17]

Edith was no beauty. Six feet tall, ungainly of carriage, and, as witnesses agreed, rather equine in features, she was sensitive about her physical person and may very well have compensated for it by cultivating her considerable mental powers. Doubtless it was these that attracted Mies to her in the first place and in turn persuaded her that he was a great talent in his own right. We do not know the intimate details of the Mies-Farnsworth breakup, only those by which it was rationalized later in court. The proceedings that unfolded in a steamy little courtroom in Yorkville, Illinois, during the spring and summer of 1953 were tedious and taxing to all parties. Mies claimed Farnsworth owed him $28,173 which he had already expended on the house. Edith answered this with a $33,872 counterdemand of her own, arguing that *she* had spent that much more than the original stipulated costs. Moreover, she accused Mies and his staff, led by Myron Goldsmith, of all-around incompetence. "You should have heard him," she quoted her lawyer Randolph Bohrer, describing Mies's testimony on a day she was absent from court. "You can't imagine what an exhibition of ignorance he put on! He didn't know anything about steel, its properties or its standard dimensions. Nor about construction or high school physics or just plain common sense. All he knows is that guff about his concept and in the Kendall County Courthouse that doesn't go down. I tell you, we had him sweating blood—he was heard to say afterwards that he would never start another law suit."[18]

Edith, however, who lost the case (Mies was awarded a $14,000 settlement), took no less a beating. After the litigation had ended and

168. Edith Farnsworth, about 1973
Private collection

America: The Triumph of Steel and Glass

the architectural journals had added their judgments to those of the law, she wrote bitterly:

> The big glossy reviews polished up their terms and phrases with such patience that the simpler minds that came to have a look expected to find the glass box light enough to stay afloat in air or water, moored to its columns and enclosing its mystic space. So "culture spreads by proclamation," and one got the impression that if the house had had the form of a banana rampant instead of a rectangle couchant, the proclamation would have been just as imperative . . . The alienation which I feel today must have had its beginnings on that shady river bank all too soon abandoned by the herons which flew away to seek their lost seclusion farther upstream.[19]

Indeed the majority of the professional critics were deeply moved by Mies's design, and they responded to it with a flow of superlatives. There were, however, exceptions, the most spectacular of which appeared in the April 1953 issue of the popular and influential magazine *House Beautiful*. The dominant article by Elizabeth Gordon, "The Threat to the Next America," extended the argument against the Farnsworth House beyond its owner's objections and into a broadside attack on the International Style in general and the Bauhaus in particular. Gordon associated Le Corbusier with the former, Gropius with the latter, and Mies with both. She found Mies's architecture "cold" and "barren," his furniture, by inference, "sterile," "thin," and "uncomfortable." The title of her piece suggested, too, that European-inspired modernism had already succeeded well enough in the U.S. by 1953 to elicit the sort of protest couched in nationalist terms that Schultze-Naumburg had lodged against the New Architecture in Germany during the 1920s and 1930s. The consequences, quite obviously, were very different: America never suffered so complete and pernicious a right-wing ascendancy as Germany eventually did. Nevertheless, Gordon's sentiments found an echo in the words of Frank Lloyd Wright, who effectively brought his friendship with Mies to an end: "These Bauhaus architects [with whom Wright now identified Mies] ran from political totalitarianism in Germany to what is now made by specious promotion to seem their own totalitarianism in art here in America . . . Why do I distrust and defy such 'internationalism' as I do communism? Because both must by their nature do this very leveling in the name of civilization."[20]

Typically, Mies neither answered Wright nor ever communicated with him again. It did not matter, so long as the house was built.

Moreover, the technical elements and conceptual implications of Mies's design for Edith Farnsworth led directly or indirectly to most of the important works of his remaining years. Though it was the only private residence of any consequence that he erected in America, it inspired one project for a house which on paper was at least as challenging and would have been, if built, probably just as problematical a living space.

The 50 by 50 House of 1950–51 was also a clear-span structure consisting of a single glazed volume that enclosed a core of kitchen,

169. 50 by 50 House project,
1950–51
Hedrich-Blessing

two bathrooms, utility room, and fireplace. Though square in plan and set at ground level, it featured, as did the Farnsworth House, an off-center placement of the core as well as a patio that grew asymmetrically away from one corner, albeit with no change in level. On the other hand, the house was meant to accommodate a family, and it was even more structurally distilled than the Fox River house. The eight columns of the latter were here reduced to four, with one located exactly in the middle of each wall. The absence of piers not only at the corners but even near them amplified the dweller's sense of a structural immateriality and a spatial infinitude beyond the glass

170. Plan of the 50 by 50
House

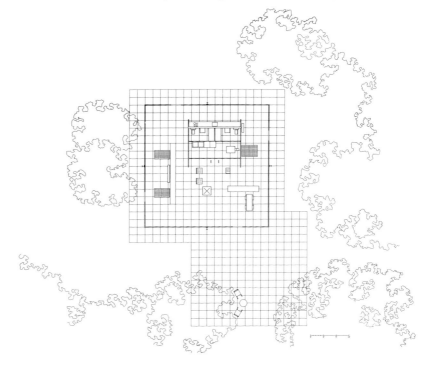

America: The Triumph of Steel and Glass

walls. In order to assure the strength of so exceptional a system, with its cantilevered corners and minimized piers, Mies designed a rigid two-way stressed roof of welded steel.

Having for the most part resisted the idea of mass housing during his German years, he now embraced it. The 50 by 50 House was intended to be a prototype that could be made forty, fifty, or sixty feet square. "Since there seems to be a real need for such homes," he explained, in words with a remarkably American ring, "we have attempted to solve the problem by developing a steel skeleton and a core that could be used for all houses." Then, sounding far more like the old Mies of universalist yearning, he added, "The interior is left open for flexibility."[21]

It is too much to believe that American families with children would have accepted the lack of privacy which Mies's generalized, uncubicled interior implied. Still the Weimar free spirit and forever the solitary bachelor, he tried to argue that curtains provided privacy better than doors did. Besides, he maintained, the cabinet partitions, which also acted as separating elements, could be moved around, allowing the size, shape and placement of sleeping and living areas to be changed at will.

Not surprisingly, Mies did not persist past the early 1950s with the design of private houses. If the concept of universal space must prevail, and for Mies of the American years it indubitably must, it would have to be given some form more practically acceptable. The solution, logical and simple as always, was the institutional rather than the private building.

Thus, in the first half of the decade of the 1950s, when Mies was already in his middle and late sixties, he produced three designs for large public works which advanced clear-span structure to its utmost in both technique and expression. Their size worked only to their advantage, since it forced Mies to his most inventive use of structure, in turn enabling him to achieve the most nearly consummate objectification of his concept of architectural space.

We have affirmed that that concept took on different form in America from what he had most often employed in Germany. Yet space was still, as it always had been, the expressive end of nearly all his most serious efforts, with structure functioning more often than not as the means to it. Nor is there better proof of his deepening preoccupation with space in the 1950s than the design of Crown Hall, the School of Architecture at IIT and the single building he most prized on the campus. For in both its measurements and placement it deviated markedly from the 12 by 24 foot modular layout of the grounds which he had formulated at the turn of the 1940s.

Crown Hall is one enormous glass-enclosed rectangular room, 120 by 220 feet in plan and 18 feet in height.[22] The most striking feature of the building both conceptually and visually is the system by which its interior is kept free of supporting members. Four pairs of wide flange columns 60 feet apart on center rise along the two long sides of the rectangle to connect with plate girders that cross between them. The roof is suspended from the underside of these girders and cantilevered 20 feet in the long direction from the outermost of them.

Since these great steel bents are exposed to view from the exterior, their structural function is unmistakable, more readable even to the uneducated eye than Mies's treatment of the primary and secondary structural frames in Alumni Memorial Hall and most of his other IIT buildings. When Crown Hall was completed in 1956, following six years of preliminary labor, it was the most dramatically candid example among all his built works of his reliance on clear structure for the genesis of expressive form.

The floor slab was raised 6 feet above the ground so as to provide light and ventilation to the workshops and lecture rooms of the Institute of Design, a floor below. The building is approached up a low stair that leads first to a suspended platform, then to another stair and finally to the entry, located in the long south wall. This much of the description suggests derivation from the Farnsworth House. Otherwise, however, since Crown Hall is an institutional building in an urban context, Mies imposed a rigorously neutral symmetry upon it. The axis is lateral and perceptible from within: two staircases evenly flank a central exhibition space that leads past two nonstructural service shafts to a small group of offices only partially concealed behind free-standing partitions. A smaller entrance on the north wall completes the axial flow.

Crown Hall was the largest interior space Mies had ever realized, and while he rationalized it as he always had, namely, that it was by its very generality forever adaptable to changing specific purposes, he had another end in mind as well. The building was a materialization in modern form of the medieval *Bauhütte*, the shelter where master

171. Crown Hall, IIT,
1950–56
Bill Engdahl, Hedrich-Blessing

America: The Triumph of Steel and Glass

builder, foremen, workmen and apprentices met, planned, taught, and learned, in concert.

Such a place was, for Mies, the perfect setting for a school of *Baukunst*—literally "building art," a word free of the more aestheticized connotation of "architecture." As a shared space, it implied shared goals and methods held in common by its users, *shared values*. The "chaos of directions" of the modern world which he lamented in his 1937 letter to Carl O. Schniewind might here be put to order by the formative, clarifying mind communally and impersonally striving to elevate fact into truth. Crown Hall was "the clearest structure we have done, the best to express our philosophy," as Mies himself put it in his familiar, quasi-papal first person plural.[23] It mattered not that practical inconveniences attended its use, that noise, for example, from one class or project might interfere with the concentration of another a few feet away. These distractions in Mies's mind were of no more importance than the cold that doubtless chilled the *Bauhütte* during the winters of the Gothic Age. For a warmth of the spirit would more than dispel it. Crown Hall was what the Bauhaus could have been if Mies had had his way with it: a school with a curriculum unadulterated by what he saw as the frivolous experimentation for experimentation's sake that Gropius had indulged Moholy-Nagy to encourage at Dessau. In Mies's eyes Moholy had wrongfully and wrongheadedly revived that sort of thing at the Institute of Design—a facility now consigned, by Mies, in his own meting out of poetic justice, to the lower regions of IIT.

And so Mies surrounded himself with his acolytes, who came to love Crown Hall as he did and accepted life and learning conditioned by the paradox of spatial freedom and intellectual constraint for which the great room stood. Like a Gothic cathedral, its splendid openness did not stop at its physical boundaries but, through the medium of glass, extended outward in all directions to the world even as the same vitreous walls, marshalled by Mies's geometry and his own exceptional eye, insured a precise, protected, and unassailable order within. As space became both institutionalized and monumentalized at Crown Hall, it commenced to lose the romantic implications which the interflow of architectural space and natural environment had lent it as recently as the Farnsworth and 50 by 50 houses. When Mies relinquished residential design in the early 50s, he became totally committed to the urban context, not, however, as later postmodernists would, seeking to adjust their styles and moods to the styles and moods they found in a given city place. Style and mood were anathema to Mies. The city was the fact that required transformation by a superior order, not "adjustment" to an already prevailing clamor of expressive caprice. Thus he was both impressed and baffled by the free plasticity of Le Corbusier's revolutionary Ronchamp chapel of 1955, completed somewhat before Crown Hall was opened. "You have to expect of Corbusier, who is a great artist," said Mies, "that he makes a piece of art. [But] I don't think [it] is possible . . . that you should attempt to build this chapel . . . on Fifth Avenue."[24]

In the 1950s Mies narrowed his vision and became more devoted to formal organization again, rather as he was when he designed the Perls House. The symmetrical plan and elevation of Crown Hall together with the regular march of its columns and mullions recalled Schinkel's Altes Museum. Mies, as it were, dismissed from his mind Schinkel's romantic villas along the Havel near Potsdam and remembered only what the old Prussian had put up in the heart of Berlin. While there was no room at Crown Hall for the spacious plaza by which Schinkel had connected his museum to the Brandenburg Gate–Alexanderplatz concourse, Mies would retain the idea for future reference. Meanwhile, between the concept and the completion of Crown Hall he produced two other major works, never built, in which he demonstrated how powerful an impact the column-free structure might make on an urban setting.

Invited to participate in a competition for a National Theater in Mannheim that would house two auditoriums of different sizes, plus auxiliary spaces, Mies designed a building far larger than Crown Hall: a two-story structure 262 by 524 feet in plan with an upper or main floor 39 feet high and a recessed ground floor 13 feet high.[25] His project, which dates from 1952–53, is unique among his clear-span works in that he filled it full of things rather than left it free of them, or, as he put it himself in reverse terms: "I came to the conclusion that the best way to enclose this complicated spatial organism was to cover it with a huge column-free hall of steel and colored glass . . . [that is,] to place the whole theater organism inside such a hall."[26]

The structure of the hall followed conceptually from Crown Hall at least insofar as the roof was hung from lateral overhead spans resting on wide-flange columns welded to floor and roof slabs. At Mannheim seven such piers carried not plate girders but 26-foot-deep trusses, spaced 70 feet on center, with 26-foot cantilevers at both ends. Thus Mies returned to the overhead truss he had proposed first in the 1942 project for a Museum for a Small City and treated more dramatically

173. Mannheim National Theater project, 1952–53 Bill Hedrich, Hedrich-Blessing

in his 1942 project for the Cantor Drive-In Restaurant in Indianapolis. The structure of Mannheim is traceable to these sources, while its space looks back to his Concert Hall of 1942 and the Albert Kahn bomber plant that inspired it.

All discernible antecedents, however, were both unified and refined to produce the very "organism" Mies called it. The exterior of the theater consistently projected the generalizing aspect he sought so strenuously throughout his American years. That he meant to evolve an objectively definable grammar of architecture applicable to a wide variety of modern purposes is apparent from his use of the overhead truss not only earlier than Mannheim—in the museum and the restaurant—but later, in a preliminary scheme for a bank building in Des Moines. In further service to his long-expressed objectives, the great trusses at Mannheim, each nearly three stories deep, were derived from such characteristic employments of modern technology as bridge structures. Externally, then, "structure" and "technology" clearly radiate from every view of the theater, while again consonant with Mies's insistence on the distinction between technology and architecture, *these* trusses are perceptibly more graceful in form than standard bridge trusses. Just as the industrial wide flange had been polished well past an industrial look at the Farnsworth House, all devices at Mannheim suggest art consciously taken beyond technique. Mies was aware of his ancient debt to craft as well: from beneath the immense prismatic mass two walls of marble clamp the sides of the recessed ground floor—Tinian marble at that, meant to be as rich as anything at Barcelona.

The interior of the hall was equally receptive to Mies's pains. Entry to the larger, 1300-seat theater was made axially through one of the short sides. Twin staircases symmetrically placed led upward from the ground level to the auditorium, which was majestically cantilevered into the open space of the 55-foot-high foyer, "to combine," again in Mies's words, "both the upper and lower stories into an imposing and festive hall."[27] The opposite end of the building was given over to the smaller, 500-seat theater, which was narrow enough to allow for flank-

174. Convention Hall project,
Chicago, 1953–54
Hedrich-Blessing

ing scenery, workshop and storage areas. Between the two auditoriums
were their respective stages, with accompanying service, storage, and
dressing room areas, while a promenade as lofty as the foyers girded
the whole inner mass. Of all Mies's clear-span structures, the Mannheim National Theater was the most convincing demonstration that a
unitary space could accommodate diversification as well as provide
flexibility.

A different set of superlatives applies to a design Mies began even
before he finished the Mannheim assignment. The South Side Planning Board of Chicago had earlier asked him to design a convention
hall for a site between the Loop and the IIT campus. The board was
not empowered to make such a commission formal; it hoped only to
publicize its proposal, thus to persuade the city government eventually
to accept it or to act upon the idea behind it.

Certainly Chicago needed a new facility to accommodate the
hundreds of various conventions, expositions, entertainment and political events it hosted annually. Such a building would have to be large
and versatile, and easy to reach from the hotels downtown. The proposed site seemed ideal. A motley district of commercial and industrial
building plus scattered and mostly tatterdemalion housing, it was perceived as the sort of neighborhood that ought to be regenerated by
the zealous urban renewal spirit of the 1950s. Once cleared, it would
present few contextual obstacles to its designer, who himself should
be committed to modernizing the cityscape and possessed of a stature
equal to Chicago's historical architectural heritage. Mies was eminently suitable on all counts, while from his own point of view the
project, rather like the Barcelona Pavilion, the Tugendhat House, and
the Farnsworth House, amounted to an opportunity little short of
heaven-sent.

Working with a trio of IIT graduate students, Yujiro Miwa, Henry
Kanazawa, and Pao-Chi Chang, and his favorite structural engineer
Frank Kornacker, Mies produced his single most monumental clear-
span structure, by far the largest space he had ever designed, ampler

indeed than that of any exposition hall in the world at the time.[28] It was a gargantuan volume 720 feet square in plan, covering over 500,000 square feet in floor area, with an interior height of 85 feet. In order to keep the space free of columns, he conceived a roof structure, also without precedent, that was made up of 30-foot-deep two-directional steel trusses on 30-foot centers, each truss consisting of 14-inch wide flange sections. The roof was supported along its perimeter by 36 trusses 60 feet deep, six to a side, spanning 120 feet between column supports and cantilevered 60 feet at the corners. The building rose to a height of 110 feet above grade. A skin of infill panels set between the exposed structural members enclosed the whole, assuring an identical surface in both the interior and exterior. Access could be gained on any side, through a recessed wall at ground level. The floor within was depressed ten feet so that the whole space was visible to the visitor upon entering. Moreover, since the floor rested on the earth, with no basement, objects and internal structures of virtually any weight could safely be placed on it. Surrounding the vast arena were eighteen tiers of 17,000 permanent seats. Temporary seating increased the capacity to 50,000.

In the course of planning, numerous solutions to specific problems were considered—variations in the dimensions and weight of the roof trusses, in the treatment of the expression of the diagonal bracings, in the material of the skin (marble in one scheme, aluminum in different textures in another). What remained constant, however, was the stupendous cubic anatomy of clear structure and overpowering space.

Mies's practical rationale was also consistent with what it had al-

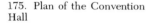

175. Plan of the Convention Hall

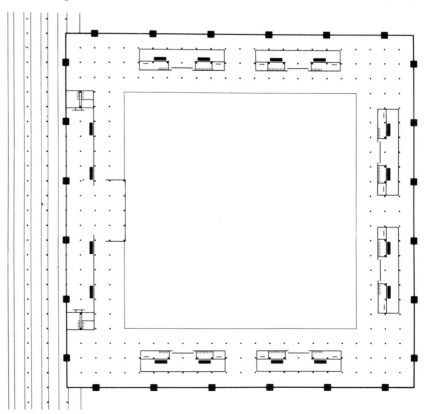

America: The Triumph of Steel and Glass

ways been: such a volume, precisely because it was undifferentiated, could accommodate any and all activities appropriate to it, ranging from national political conventions to trade fairs and sporting contests. The integrity of individual events could be guaranteed by the free-standing partitions that had always been Mies's favored device for assuring the versatility of universal space.

This very reasoning must lead us to infer once again that space was the end of his efforts here, structure the means. To be sure, the means in this case were spectacular. Of all the projects Mies had done in his sixty-eight years and all he would do in the fifteen years still remaining to him, none was so adventurous in its method or so bold in its expression of construction as the Convention Hall. From within, the soaring roof must have evoked awe all by itself, while the clarity of its passage to the supporting trusses and columns was only more compelling. From without, the structure was no less grandly readable, its identity with the architecture reaffirmed. Mies's ability to produce high art by what appeared the most uncompromisingly rational of means was never so manifest.

At the same time, the motive for a colossal exercise of structure was the production of a colossal experience of space, which would not only provide for manifold interior functions but, just as important, provoke the realization that the physical medium had been seized, defined, and made intellectually manageable at a titanic scale. Surely this building was Mies's most grandiose endeavor. By comparison, an earlier monumental project like the Reichsbank seemed almost sluggish and earthbound. The objective order with which he sought to

176. Collage showing interior of the Convention Hall with a crowd
Courtesy of the estate of Mies van der Rohe

America: The Triumph of Steel and Glass

177. Mies studying model of Convention Hall

imbue his public designs of the 1930s took flight, as it were, in the clear-span structures of the 1940s and 1950s, and in the Convention Hall Mies pursued it more remorselessly than in any other of his works. Not only did he exchange the rectangle for a more universally simplified form, the square, he subjected all surrounding elements, not just some, to the rigor of axial geometry. The asymmetrical recollections of de Stijl that were still detectable in the relationship of the mass of 860 to that of 880, of the terrace to the Farnsworth House or the patio to the 50 by 50 House: all these informalities were expunged in the Convention Hall. The parking lot, somewhat reminiscent of the plaza in front of Schinkel's Altes Museum, extended axially south of the building mass. At its edges, ranged in evenest order, were the outbuildings meant to house the restaurants, utilities and other secondary necessities which he externalized so as to honor the primary necessity of uncluttered form and space in the hall proper. This regularization of plan was partly a consequence of the evolution of his thinking from Germany to America, but it was also a factor of the Convention Hall project itself. Not only the largest space he ever designed, it was by nature the most public and impersonal, and, on account of its versatility, the most generalized.

With the completion of the design of it, Mies's reputation as the great rationalist of modern architecture was powerfully enhanced. Yet emerging from the very scope and heroic logic of the work was a major paradox. For there was, in fact, no pressing practical reason for the absolutely clear span he proposed. Mies could have placed a columnar grid within the hall, spacing it widely enough to gain the flexibility he so prized. And he would have lowered costs in the process, while requiring less expense in sheer engineering ingenuity. His own former student and associate Gene Summers, working for C. F. Murphy and Associates, designed and built such a hall in 1971 in Chicago.[29] The 150-foot spans between the columns that supported its huge roof made it as sensible a structure as it was rational.

Mies knew full well he could have offered a similar solution in the case of his own Convention Hall, just as he knew he could have put enclosing walls in Edith Farnsworth's house or in Crown Hall. What kept him from doing so was not so much the force of reason and logic as the counterforce of passion and will created by the extension of reason and logic. So certain that the truth of his architecture was rooted in unimpeachable rationality, he carried rationality to its irrational extreme. Very likely in no other way could he have produced so daring and glorious a space.

This is another way of reaffirming that he was an artist before all else. Publicly he did not associate himself with art as such, but instead sought to characterize the source of his professional endeavor as necessity rather than willful choice. "There are certain rules," he said, "and if you look through history—all the great epochs, they were certainly able to do anything, but they restricted themselves to a very clear principle, and that is the only way you can make important architecture."[30] Such a statement from a major figure of the modern architectural revolution sounds curiously unmodern and unrevolutionary, and in 1951 he admitted as much: "I am not a reformer. I don't want to change the world, I want to express it. That's all I want."[31] Mies, then, became a system builder in an age suspicious of systems, and part of his genius consisted in his ability to reconcile two such implicitly opposing positions. He made *his* rules seem not so much a framework of authoritarianism as a method of seeking and finding a noble lost truth. It was his will, the hardness and finality of it, that persuaded the architecture world of the 1950s that he was a man of reason, not simply an autocrat, and therefore that he need not, even should not, be contradicted. Yet without the simple excellence of his formative capabilities—his *art*—even his will and the charisma that radiated from it would not have been enough to win the nearly universal acclaim that came to him. At the height of his American popularity it became conventional wisdom to acknowledge that Mies's architecture, because it was reasonable and systematic, was the most teachable of architectures. Indeed it was not at all, and may have been among the least teachable. The acres of stillborn design in the Miesian manner that transformed the American cityscape in the 1950s and 1960s are a palpable indication of this. It is the majestic form given to what seems irresistibly logical in his Convention Hall, not the logic per se, that forces us to grope for appropriately affirmative adjectives.

And Mies for all his narrowness of purpose and sameness of means, created a remarkably diversified body of work out of this purpose and these means. He proved it in his 1951 design for the Arts Club of Chicago, the only public interior he realized in a building not of his making. There he managed a graceful union of the club's assortedly traditional furniture and his own clean, understated spaces, adding to this a foyer dominated by an exceptionally handsome staircase. Thus, too, in producing his most axially formal skyscraper, he tempered its stern regularity with a freedom of massing that could have been conceived only by an artist sufficiently in command of his system not to be enslaved by its "rules."

During the early 1950s New York City was nearing the crest of its biggest building boom since the 1920s. Two decades of idleness caused by depression and war had resulted in a massive need for modernized office space, a pressure which only increased in the prosperous atmosphere of the 1950s. A tropical growth of skyscrapers spread over Manhattan, invading even the once exclusively residential precincts of Park Avenue. Most of these buildings were done either in the traditional New York ziggurat form or in variations of the slab that became popular following the favorable response to Skidmore, Owings and Merrill's Lever House of 1952. Few of the new works approached the Mies-inspired precision of Lever House. The majority were meretricious recipe pieces thrown up with a view to quick profit and little else.

In 1954 the Joseph E. Seagram and Sons Corporation announced plans for an office building of its own, to be completed on a Park Avenue site by 1958, in celebration of the company's one hundredth anniversary. The singularity of the occasion prompted Seagram president Samuel Bronfman to look for a design that would be a substantial cut in sophistication above the clotted heap of steel and glass already rising on Park Avenue, and he awarded the commission to Luckman and Pereira, a California firm whose promise, by consensus, seemed already warranted by a postwar record of success in the production of commercial buildings.

Reading of the commission from the distance of her home in Paris, Phyllis Bronfman Lambert took an emphatically dim view of it. The fact that she was the daughter of the chief executive officer of Seagram's gave some force to her judgments in the matter, but they would seem to have rested on limited professional experience in the arts. She nevertheless took it upon herself to fly back to New York, where she remonstrated with her father over his choice of a "very mediocre building." In fact Bronfman was moved by her argument, in which she strenuously reminded him of his declared intention to erect a significant, not simply an adequate, building. She was put in charge of further research leading to the final choice of an architect.

Lambert took her responsibilities as seriously as she did Seagram's commitment to quality. She called upon Philip Johnson, now rein-

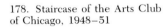
178. Staircase of the Arts Club of Chicago, 1948–51

America: The Triumph of Steel and Glass

stalled as director of the Department of Architecture at the Museum of Modern Art. With his help and that of advisers he recommended she made a detailed study of the work of the leading international modernists of the day, including Gropius and Breuer, Harrison and Abramovitz, Howe and Lescaze, Eero Saarinen, Louis Kahn, Minoru Yamasaki, I. M. Pei, Frank Lloyd Wright, Le Corbusier, and Mies.[32] It appears that the last three of these most arrested her attention, and by November 1954 she had made her choice among them:

> [Wright's] is not the statement that is needed now. America has grown up a bit and [he] has expressed what it was when its energies were unharnessed . . . . One is fascinated by [Le Corbusier's] spaces, his sculptural forms, but are not people likely to be blinded by these and skip over the surface only? Mies forces you in. You have to go deeper. You might think this austere strength, this ugly beauty, is terribly severe. It is, and yet all the more beauty in it.
>
> The younger men, the second generation, are talking in terms of Mies or denying him. They talk of new forms in articulating the skin or facade to get a play of light and shadow. But Mies has said, "Form is not the aim of our work, but only the result."[33]

Mies, then, seemed to Lambert the pivotal figure in the argument if not the inescapable candidate for the assignment. In November he signed a contract with Seagram's and directly invited Kahn and Jacobs, an old New York firm, to serve as associate architects. He also asked Johnson himself to assist him. This last selection seemed eminently sensible at the time, since no American had been more dedicated to Mies than Johnson or for a longer time or with greater effectiveness in bringing Mies to the attention of the world. Johnson was by now a professional architect in his own right, happily in the Miesian manner. What Mies could not foresee was that this commitment would change before work on Seagram's ended. Johnson would grow restive in his discipleship and begin to cast it off, to the permanent detriment of his relationship with the master. But for now, the autumn of 1954, he was prepared to accept Mies's bid, and labor commenced on a project which developed finally into the most important tall building of the post–World War II period.

It could not have attained so high a rank without the generosity of the Seagram Company, which granted Mies not only a lavish budget (the final cost of the building was calculated at $45 million) but a freedom of decision enjoyed by no other skyscraper designer of the day. Mies responded with the full creative force he always brought to bear when a client treated him openhandedly. He gave back to Seagram's a work animated far less by license than by a thoughtful, even strikingly inventive, response to problems intrinsic to the building itself and to its surroundings.

This last consideration—the setting of the structure—deserves special acknowledgment, since Mies, like other modernist masters of the 1920s, had a reputation for designing architectural objects as self-referential bodies independent of (i.e., supposedly superior to) the

context in which they found themselves. To some of his projects, like
the Reichsbank and his early Berlin proposals for skyscrapers, this
criticism may be justifiably applied. It is decidedly not true of the
Seagram Building.

There was the site, to begin with: Seagram had purchased the land
along the east side of Park Avenue between 52d and 53d streets. The
old Montana apartments that had stood there since 1914 were scheduled to be razed. From the beginning it was understood that Mies
would replace them with a tall building. New York zoning laws forbade
any structure to rise from the sidewalk without progressive setbacks
above a certain height—hence the standard ziggurat form—with the
tower portion of any such building not to cover more than 25 percent
of the plot. Given the Seagram site, this would have meant a tower
with only 8000 square feet gross per floor—an unworkable space.

The company then decided to demolish several other, smaller buildings which it owned on 52d and 53d streets, immediately adjacent to
the purchased land. This gave more ground area to Mies, who by then
was devoting most of his time to a study of the neighborhood. In December, Lambert wrote:

> I can't wait to see what Mies comes up with for this
> building—he has a cardboard model made of Park Avenue
> between 46th and 57th streets with all the buildings on the
> Avenue and some going in the blocks and then he has a number
> of towers for different solutions that he places in the empty place
> of the old 375 [the Park Avenue address] and this model is up on
> a high table so that when sitting in a chair his eye is just level
> with the table top which equals the street—and for hours on
> end he peers down his Park Avenue trying out the different
> towers.[34]

America: The Triumph of Steel and Glass

180. Seagram Building, New
York, 1954–58

Mies's devotion to simplicity of form quite ruled out any use of the ziggurat, or "wedding cake," model for his building. He also discarded two other concepts: a square tower and a slab set like Lever House at right angles to the avenue. He settled finally on a lofty rectangular tower of 3-by-5 bay ratio, to be placed parallel to the street with its long front recessed ninety feet from Park Avenue, its side elevations thirty feet from the side streets.

Such a concept insured a simplified mass at the expense of a loss in the amount of rentable floor area permissible by code. This was the first evidence that architectural gain had taken priority over economic return, though Seagram's was not without a fiscal rationalization of its decision. The building was expected to sell itself on the basis of the elegance of its spaces and their material appointments, not to mention the overall excellence and uniqueness of its design; thus higher rents plus later rental reassessments would yield an eventual margin of profit.

To the citizen's eye the most immediate result of this strategy was the creation of a spacious plaza in front of the building. At the time it was designed, there was no comparable open urban space anywhere in the grid of midtown New York, with the exception of the Rockefeller Center mall. Mies recognized that the existing density of buildings along Park Avenue made it nearly impossible to see any one of them except by crossing the street. A plaza provided a welcome moment of spatial relief in a nearly rhythmless architectural cliff, while enhancing the very sensation by which the pedestrian perceived the building. Lambert summed it up: "you don't know what is there and then you come upon IT—with a magnificent plaza and the building not zooming up in front of your nose so that you can't see it."[35]

Another advantage was evident in the flow of the plaza into the surrounding neighborhood. Directly across the avenue from the Seagram site stood a gruff old neo-Florentine palazzo, the Racquet and Tennis Club, built in 1918 by McKim, Mead, and White. If, in opening up his plaza Mies relieved the deadening general thickness of commercial building all around it, his composition established a specific dialogue between Seagram's and the Racquet Club that elevated the quality of both. The Racquet Club was solid masonry, the Seagram Building, glass. The former was four stories high and built up to the edge of its sidewalk; the latter, at thirty-nine stories, stood back from the eastern apron of the thoroughfare. Both structures were symmetrical and shared a common axis. Thus, in similarities of planning organization and contrasts of mass, volume, height, and spatial displacement, the relationship between the two huge forms produced one of the most arresting block environments in the city.

Once the viewer turned away from the avenue and faced the Seagram Building itself, he noted a further close harmony between the tower and its immediate space envelope. Since 52d and 53d streets sloped downward to the east, Mies elevated the plaza on a low podium to which frontal access was gained by three steps. The expanse of pink granite, 90 feet deep, 150 feet wide, was free of all incident except a flagpole—the sole concession to asymmetry—and, at the left and right edges of the space, two symmetrical pools. Each basin was bordered at its outer margin by a long banquette of Tinian marble which, together with the podium, created a subtle sense of isolation from the surrounding traffic even as the vast openness united the plaza with the building masses around it.

The Seagram tower reared up beyond, a great prismatic shaft whose 516-foot height was dramatized not only by the boldness with which it ascended from its serene horizontal base but by a curtain wall whose accents were almost, but not quite, unrelievedly vertical. Six columns

181. Entrance to the Seagram Building with canopy in the foreground
Esto Photographics, Inc.

America: The Triumph of Steel and Glass

separated 28 feet on center rose from the granite to the height of a 24-foot ground story, then gave way to a curtain wall set in front of the structure in the manner Mies had employed in the Esplanade and Commonwealth apartments in Chicago. The horizontality of the spandrels was dominated by the verticality of the mullions, which were made more pronounced by the now familiar three-dimensional effect of attached I-beams. Spandrels and structural columns, the latter recessed but visible, kept the vertical thrust from growing monotonous, while color effected a unity among all contrasting forces on the building surface. Mies used a pink gray glass for the curtain, binding up the facade with that most patrician of building metals, bronze. Thus the whole volume shone with the warm, tranquil, matte finish of old coins, and as time passed it grew only more certainly and solidly aristocratic.

This much would have been visible to anyone standing in the plaza, where he might have realized that here at last Mies had returned to the example of the plaza Schinkel had designed as the approach to the comparably bluff, serenely regular facade of the Altes Museum. Moving to right or left, however, the viewer at Seagram's would have noticed, beyond a stand of ginkgo trees flanking the short sides of the tower, an extraordinary rear extension. Mies had attached to the tower a one-bay-deep "spine" which rose the full thirty-nine stories, while adding to the face of it a three-bay-deep, ten-story-high "bustle" and flanking the latter with a pair of three-bay-deep, four-story-high wings. Between each of the wings and the tower a space the depth of the spine was turned into a side entrance. The external effect of this whole eastern addition was remarkable not only for the union of the axiality typical of his American phase with a free massing reminiscent of the constructivist form he had employed in the 1920s. To more practical purpose, it added square footage without sacrificing the integrity of the tower or defying the building code. Thus Seagram's loss of office space, while not compensated totally, was nonetheless significantly reduced. Mies had produced a New York–type compartmentalized building that did not look like anything but his own.

A further gain derived from the rear massing. In order to enhance the image of a luxury building, the Seagram program had called for a large public space on the ground floor. Mies's solution allowed for one room in each of the opposing wings, a bar to the south, a restaurant to the north. By thickening the transfer girders that spanned the wings and eliminating a column in each room, he achieved a pair of spaces whose three monumental dimensions (55 by 55 by 24 feet) could otherwise not have been managed within the governing grid of a standard office building.

This was not his only atypical treatment of space at Seagram's. While the entry to the building was conventional in one Miesian sense, in another it was not, and in the passage to which it led, less still. He placed the foyer characteristically at ground level so that the visitor on passing through one of the three portals found himself separated from the outdoors only by glass. Thus the space of the plaza implicitly flowed into the space of the building. At the same time the very axiality of the plan, underscored by the centrally hung entrance canopy, lent a psychic formality to the act of entry, as if the building were a

classical edifice. This perception was reinforced by the four monumental banks of elevators, regularly spaced and parallel to the axis
which led between the second and third of them to the staircase at
the rear of the tower. These stairs led to a landing from which a pair
of low passages emptied with dramatic suddenness into the immensity
of the bar-restaurant spaces to the south and north. All walls in the
foyer were dressed in travertine, the ceilings finished in gray glass
mosaic, the floors laid in granite.

The Seagram tower, then, together with its plaza, was the most
nearly classical structure Mies erected in America; indeed its traffic
patterns were remarkably akin to the manner of the Beaux-Arts. Even
the Convention Hall, whose symmetry was simpler and clearer, was
also more patently modern in the force of its structural candor. In
Seagram's Mies seemed willing to make whatever concessions would
guarantee the purity of his tower and the classically timeless quality
it evoked. Gene Summers, his chief assistant at Seagram's, reports that
a need for an elevator area sufficient to a thirty-nine story height persuaded him to break the grid in the foyer and move the elevator banks
forward half a bay.[36] Philip Johnson marveled—given Mies's reputation for consistency and clarity—at both the thickening and the con-

America: The Triumph of Steel and Glass

cealment of the transfer girders in the wings.[37] Moreover, in order to brace the lofty but slender profile of the building against wind force, shear walls were installed in the north and south faces of the spine. These two elements, though constructed of concrete, were clad in Tinian marble then covered, yet again cosmetically, with a network of mullions and spandrels that imitated the treatment of all other walls. These devices were hardly true to Mies's purported devotion to logic and clarity, while in some of the detailing he exercised all the care for which he was noted: Johnson recalls the infinite pains Mies took in designing a lip for the flange of the I-beam so that the flange would not appear insubstantial in profile. There is little doubt that Mies spent more personal effort on Seagram's than on any other building of his American career. He not only took a New York office with Johnson but established New York residence in a suite at the Barclay Hotel. Nevertheless, the work he did in both settings amounted, typically, to endless hours of immobilized reflection.

In short, Mies at Seagram was his own stern and sovereign self,

183. Plan of the Seagram Building

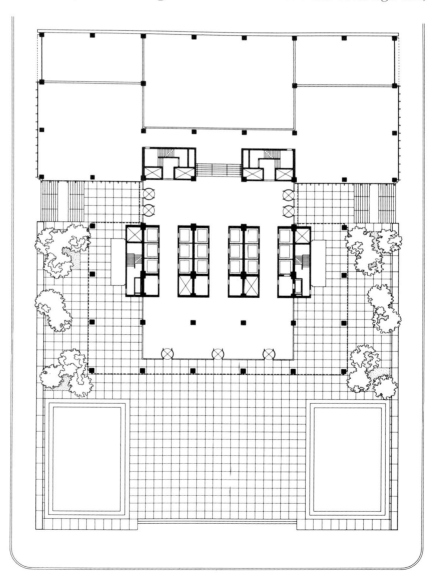

capable on some occasions of pursuing his precepts with religious fidelity, on others of essaying ideas quite foreign to the image the world had of him. Among the latter were two curious maquettes in silver foil which he designed in an effort to find a solution to the eventually abandoned notion of sculpture in the plaza. These sketches were provisional; Mies had no serious intention of carrying them out. Still, their striking resemblance to the scraggly, organic sculptural style of the abstract expressionism–dominated 1950s gives them a place in his personal catalog at least as odd as that of the conchoidal chairs, demonstrating again that he was among all Miesians least bound by Miesianism.

Even his pride conflicted—at least for a time—with his dedication to the very project on which he had spent the best of his creative energies. Construction had already begun on the Seagram Building when he received a letter from the New York Department of Education reminding him that he did not have a license to practice architecture in the state of New York and would not be granted one

184. Model of the Seagram Building with Mies's sculpture Photo courtesy of the Museum of Modern Art, New York

America: The Triumph of Steel and Glass

until he passed an examination after showing proof of the equivalent of a high school education.

On hearing this Mies stopped everything he was doing and mounted a great, silent fury. According to Summers, he lost little time in leaving his Barclay suite and the office he shared with Johnson. He returned to Chicago. Weeks passed during which there was little communication between him and Johnson, whom he had instructed simply to stay on the job.[38] He remained indifferent to all efforts by people of influence to intercede in his behalf. Summers meanwhile wrote to the cathedral school in Aachen, which furnished him with Mies's records. This simple step proved to be all that was needed to persuade the New York Board of Registration to waive the examination and issue Mies his license, though nothing else or less would have been sufficient in his eyes.

If, then, at the age of seventy he was rich enough in years as well as in laurels to indulge his pride, he could do the same, for the same reasons, with his impulses, especially at the level of personal relationships. He was far more patient, for example, with his client Bronfman than he was mindful of the feelings of his associate Johnson. When Bronfman, studying the model of the Seagram Building, inquired irritably why "the columns showed," Mies politely invited him to lean over so that he could see "how nice it is to look at the columns through the lighted lobby."[39] Mies made a special trip to Bronfman's home in Tarrytown, where he argued, ever so gently, Lambert reports, against a proposal to extend the building forward into the plaza in order to provide space for a local bank.[40]

Johnson was treated with less deference. During the Seagram period he was already beginning in his own commissions to abandon the Miesian structural credo in favor of a sleekly sculpted, streamlined neoclassicism. Mies despised it, though he was even more offended by what he perceived to be an act of defection.

One evening Johnson invited Mies to his compound in Connecticut, where the two men spent several bibulous hours in the famous glass house the younger of them had designed and built for himself in 1949.[41] Completed earlier than the Farnsworth House but clearly indebted to it in concept, the Johnson House was a rectangular transparent box containing a single room. Unlike Farnsworth it was axially self-contained, with its supporting columns located at the corners and entrances in the centers of all four sides. It sat on a low brick-covered base connected to the ground. The space within was defined asymmetrically by freestanding cabinets plus a cylindrical bathroom core, an arrangement which Johnson said was inspired by a painting by Kazimir Malevich.[42] Mies disdained the house not simply because it was an imitation but because he considered it poorly detailed as well.*

The evening grew late and liquor-logged and the subject got round to Berlage. Johnson said he could hardly fathom what Mies liked about

---

*Personal conversation with Johnson, March 1985. The aphorism, "God is in the details," has been endlessly attributed to Mies, though I have found no one who ever heard him say it. In *Meaning in the Visual Arts* (New York, 1955, p. 5), Erwin Panofsky quotes Flaubert: "Le bon Dieu est dans le détail." Mies may have read Panofsky—or even Flaubert—but there is no proof of that either.

185. Philip Johnson, Glass
House, New Canaan,
Connecticut, 1949

the Amsterdam Stock Exchange. Still less could he see Mies in it.
Thereupon, Mies exploded in anger and, without bothering to answer
Johnson, got up to leave. "It made no sense!" Johnson later recalled.
"Obviously, millions of things were boiling around in his drunken brain,
but he never returned to the house."[43] Mies was put up for the night
at the home of a friend nearby.

The rift never healed. Dirk Lohan, in his 1968 Chicago interview,
asked Mies about Johnson as he knew him during the early 1930s,
when the two men first met.

LOHAN: "Was he an art historian or an architect?"

MIES: "Neither. Nothing at all. He had only studied at Harvard
and later struck up a connection with the Museum of Modern Art. So
now and then he would call himself an historian, if he wanted to emphasize a point."

Several sentences later Lohan asked again, "Why did he study with
Gropius and not here in Chicago?"

His voice heavy with sarcasm, as if he were remembering an assortment of past grievances, Mies responded: "Harvard is a very special school, isn't it, where only fine people go? (They just went on
strike, didn't they, the fine people!) [Mies referred to one of the student uprisings of the late 1960s.] Well, he [Johnson] was earlier at

Harvard, as a poor student. Gropius, after all, was not *so* bad that Philip would want to give up his alma mater!"

LOHAN: "I only meant that he had been with you so often in Berlin."

MIES: "He did come around here [Chicago] from time to time. He would snoop through all the details and copy them. The mistakes he made in the details occurred because he hadn't worked them through, but just sniffed around them."[44]

In sum, Mies's late opinion of his former associate was harsh and overwrought, even though he was hardly the kind of man ever to modify it. In fact, the quality of Johnson's contribution to the Seagram Building was equal to the role he played in it. He was responsible for many of the best interior appointments, most notably the Four Seasons bar and restaurant, both of which featured Mies's furniture. The decor of the restaurant, including Marie Nichols's elegant metallic draperies and Johnson's own installation of a central pool, constituted a masterly completion of a noble space. Johnson also designed the elevators and the glass-roofed canopies leading to the side entrances. He secured the Richard Lippold sculpture for the bar as well as the Picasso tapestry for the landing that issued into the restaurant and bar. For the sake of Mies's architecture it is well that a man of Johnson's talents assisted him at Seagram's. For the good of Johnson's career, it was no less fitting that he departed the shadow of the master when he did.

Recessional, 1958–69

By 1958 the arthritis that grew apparently out of Mies's old skiing accident had hobbled him to the extent that he could not attend the ceremonies marking the opening of the Seagram Building. For the last decade of his life he was confined to a wheelchair; only with herculean effort was he able to hoist himself up on crutches and move about, painfully, ponderously. During those very years, however, his economic fortunes rose as his physical condition deteriorated. Seagram's made him, for the first time in his life, a man of means by virtue of his architecture, not of someone else's wealth. Even as he worked on the great skyscraper, his office was busy with several dozen other commissions and was obliged to turn away more.

Procedure in the office reflected these changes. Mies was never comfortable with a large staff, but in the mid to late 1950s his collaboration with Greenwald grew so successful that there was no alternative to increasing the size of his atelier space and the number of his assistants. Having moved in 1952 to quarters in a Chicago loft building at 230 E. Ohio Sreet, he took over an entire floor of the same structure in 1959. His staff ballooned to thirty-five. He made a studious point of hiring IIT graduates, and he saw to it that all the design work on any given project was done by himself or his own people. Associate architects were taken on only for drafting or technical assistance. He depended uncommonly on the use of models in the design process, a practice which not only distinguished him from most other American architects of the time but reflected his youthful experience with actual buildings on the construction sites of Aachen—as distinct from the Beaux-Arts form that emerged from drawing board postulations.

Among his original post–World War II staff, Joseph Fujikawa was put in charge of the Greenwald projects following the completion of the 860–880 Lake Shore Drive Apartments. As early as the late 1940s Edward Duckett, the director of the model shop, had begun transforming Mies's furniture of the Weimar period into stainless steel, thus facilitating mass production of it at high-quality levels in America, first by Gerry Griffith of Chicago, later by the Knoll Company of Pennsylvania. William Dunlap, who left the office to join Skidmore, Owings, and Merrill, worked effectively to turn that firm into the most powerful, and most Mies-influenced, large office in the United States. George Danforth and Daniel Brenner became Mies's faculty colleagues at IIT and, with Deever Rockwell, opened their own practice in Chicago in 1961. Two of Mies's earliest students, Jacques Brownson, who had worked on 860–880, and Myron Goldsmith, centrally involved in the Farnsworth and 50 by 50 houses, also taught at IIT, even after leaving the Mies office in the early 1950s to gain international reputations as architects in their own right. Both, in fact, were key figures in the ascendancy of a collective Miesian architecture that came to be known in the 1960s as the Second Chicago School (the first associated with the revolutionary commercial work of the Louis Sullivan–Daniel Burnham–John Root generation of the 1880s and 1890s): Goldsmith at Skidmore, Owings, and Merrill, Brownson at C. F. Murphy Associates.

Mies relied heavily during the 1950s on several people not formally employed by his office, including structural engineer Frank Kornacker and IIT professor Alfred Caldwell, an accomplished landscape architect. Hilberseimer remained his closest personal ally at IIT, a consultant in all academic and professional matters, especially those pertaining to urban planning studies.

Gene Summers meanwhile emerged in the late 1950s as Mies's most trusted office lieutenant. Partly his elevation was the reflection of an exceptional designing talent; like Brownson and Goldsmith, Summers later contributed several major works to the Second Chicago School when he worked for C. F. Murphy Associates. Before he left Mies, however, he imposed upon the office a methodical administrative discipline which Mies himself was too much the European *Künstler* ever to have bothered with and which had not seemed necessary in the old days, when the staff was manageably small and Felix Bonnet's quixotic ways were equal to its business needs.

Even before the completion of Seagram's, Mies began to relax his personal commitment to the other high-rise projects coming out of his office; a form universally applicable to the tall building had been found, after all, and true to his conviction that new architectures are not invented weekly, he was content to leave the Greenwald assignments more and more to Fujikawa. Greenwald's death in any case had the effect of slowing work on projects of his sponsorship. Gradually as the 1950s turned into the 1960s, Mies's energies gave way to advancing age and physical disability; thus he concentrated on his most challenging commissions, chief among them the Lafayette Park residential project in Detroit and pavilions for the Museum of Fine Arts in Houston, the Bacardi Company in Cuba, and the National Gallery in Berlin. More often than not Summers was his right arm in these endeavors, a role which only increased the young Texan's authority within the office. He exercised it with a will as well as a fierce and unsentimental efficiency that brought a businesslike steadiness to the affairs of the office even if it did not earn him the affection of all the people who worked there.[1] As matters developed, his own age group, which included Y. C. Wong, Ogden Hannaford, Arthur Takeuchi, Louis Rocah, and David Haid, all of them employed by Mies between 1950 and 1953, was the last of the IIT alumni to assume positions of responsibility in the master's atelier.[2]

Mies in fact formally retired from IIT in 1958, at age seventy-two, though some of the officers of the school administration would informally have argued that he stopped teaching, to all intents and purposes, rather earlier. Certainly the growth of his own practice during the 1950s together with its increasing geographic range and the rapid

spread of his global renown had diverted him from his academic duties at the South Side campus. Between his Promontory Apartments of 1949, the first building he put up in Chicago apart from IIT, and the opening of Seagram's in 1958, the Mies office was occupied with over one hundred separate design commissions on three continents. Among these were most of the twenty-two buildings he finally realized at IIT, several of which, like the 1952 Chapel and the 1953 Commons, as well as Crown Hall, belong to his most memorable contributions to the master plan on which he began work in 1939.

Nevertheless, the IIT administration chafed under what they perceived as Mies's distracted attention to the completion of that plan. Whatever the merits of their case, there is no doubt that Henry Heald's successor, President John Rettaliata, had less appreciation than Heald of the presence of an internationally eminent architect in his midst, and still less patience with the unconventional working habits of that man. In 1958, shortly after Mies's retirement, IIT relieved him of the campus commission, turning it over to Skidmore, Owings, and Merrill, the very firm that had most profited from the examples Mies had offered the American architectural world.

Given the slow decline of his strength, which he had now to husband carefully in order to see several other precious commissions through, the question arises whether Mies would really have added much of significance to the campus had he kept control of it. Notwithstanding that speculation, it is certain that he felt rebuffed and humiliated by the administration, which had rendered a decision he felt was his own to make, even more so since Rettaliata had not been party to the conception of the campus plan in the first place.

An indignant reaction to the school's shift from Mies to Skidmore was expressed nationwide in the profession. The Skidmore people themselves were uneasy in their inheritance. Gordon Bunshaft, designer of Lever House, wrote Mies from New York, offering to put him in charge of the Skidmore commission at IIT. "Thinking over the whole problem of IIT," Mies answered Bunshaft, "I feel it would be a mistake to accept your friendly proposal. The campus is an idea which should be finished as planned. If this will not be done, I have to accept its torso."[3]

Mies's fatalism insured that Rettaliata would have his way. Dunlap, representing Skidmore, Owings, and Merrill, later organized a dinner at the Chicago Athletic Club in an effort to honor Mies, in retrospect, as it were. He was rewarded for his efforts with a fracas initiated by Hilberseimer, who, suspecting that the event was merely the enactment of a pious hypocrisy, at one point accused the newly designated architects of just that motive and blurted out, "The trouble is that Mies is a gentleman. You, and you, and you, are not!"[4]

The evening broke up on a sour note. Caldwell promptly tendered his resignation, but Caldwell was an impulsive man with a history of resigning his job at the perception of the smallest slight, then returning to it. His gesture affected nothing. The IIT decision stood firm. Skidmore was already at work on several new campus buildings.

Thus ended Mies's career at IIT, though a double postscript remains to be added to it. The first Skidmore buildings to go up following the firm's assumption of the campus plan were obviously based on the model of Crown Hall and just as manifestly clumsy in their misunderstanding of it. Each of two large pavilions, Grover Hermann Hall and the John Crerar Library, was dominated by overhead plate girders prominently crossing its short dimension, but these spanning devices were patently unintegrated with the piers supporting them.

No less worthy of reflection after the fact were the reverence and affection Mies's faculty showed him at the time of his loss of the IIT commission. The two attitudes require differentiation. Most architectural geniuses have had their legions of star-struck followers whose admiration all too often hardened into a dogma from which the geniuses themselves felt greater liberty to depart. So it was with Mies and his believers, not only at the Bauhaus but at IIT, and the record should show that in his own quietly narcissistic way he permitted it.

But his form of narcissism, like his architecture, was so publicly restrained that it appeared to those around him not as self-love but as the modesty of a seeker after impersonal verity who was distinguished only in his discovery of it. He did not need to display himself; to celebrate the truth seemed enough. In any case he was indeed, as Hilberseimer passionately insisted, a gentleman, a natural spiritual aristocrat who, when in the company of those with whom he felt comfortable, was altogether easy at first to respect, later to venerate, at last to cherish.

At the beginning of a typical evening affair in the home of a colleague or friend, he would make his laborious entry. All talk ceased, all heads took note, as if Wotan, crippled but magnificent, had just materialized. Mies would establish his ample girth in a chair, volunteering little of himself. He looked bigger than he was, his head massive, with thinning white hair and heavy jowls, his face deeply lined, like unpolished granite. His countenance was neither lively nor impassive, but he would commence to smile, at first shyly, then more

187. Mies and Harry Weese at the Graham Foundation, 1962(?) Courtesy of Dirk Lohan

broadly as the spirituous lubrication he first came to prize as an apprentice in Aachen eased his emergence from the shell he kept by second nature around himself. Then as the faithful collected, sometimes literally at his feet, he would grow expansive, now and then even garrulous. He would light a huge cigar which he brandished like a baton, accentuating the cadence of his remarks. His voice was mahogany, his speech deliberate but steady, his thought simple and unaffectedly clear as the buildings he made. The more he drank and the later it got the more he warmed to the occasion. Reminiscences flowed, anecdotes and aphorisms; it became increasingly difficult for anyone in his presence not to be moved and even charmed by what seemed so incontestably great and modest a human being. The judgment was all the more pronounced in view of the knowledge that Mies was customarily so unapproachable, so capable at times of cold rage. It is little wonder no one knew his personal life very well at all or challenged him in matters of principle. "Do you ask God," Philip Johnson once remarked, "where He got the Commandments?"[5]

Such an image of Mies was not shared by all who met him, though there was nothing really inconsistent in his behavior. If he found himself in the company of people with whom he had nothing in common, he would withdraw to one of his nautilus chambers, stolid to the point of rude indifference. "A terrible snob," was the assessment of Harold Joachim, the curator of prints and drawings at the Art Institute of Chicago.[6] "I found him indigestible," recalled Edith Farnsworth's sister Marian Carpenter. "My husband called him a big German lump. He didn't talk or respond. Nothing but silence. They told us he didn't talk unless he was pumped full of liquor. Evidently we didn't pump him enough."[7]

Mies in his old age was made lonelier by his immobility and was thus inclined now and then to welcome occasions when comrades, especially those fluent in German, like Konrad Wachsmann and Hugo Weber, stopped by Pearson Street. Conversation would often go on nearly until dawn. It seemed somehow appropriate that he was a nocturnal animal who retired late because, as he once told Lora Marx, "I have to wait until the music dies down."[8] He would rise shortly before noon, appear at the office seldom earlier than the close of the lunch period, read his mail, study current projects with unhurried concentration, and discuss them in like manner with his staff, then return to his apartment at the end of the afternoon. Dinner would follow, often with Summers or with Lora Marx.

Lora loved him unqualifiedly. She asked little of him, which was the best way to keep him as close as Mies was likely to be with anyone. Indeed he could be tender in his regard for her and, significantly, capable even of small talk. She kept a record of his offhand remarks, treasuring his attentions and savoring his special way with a second language. Once, when she was bending over to fasten her boots, he said, "You look nice even from the top. God must have pleasure to look at you." On the occasion of a storm that stirred up the surface of Lake Michigan, he exclaimed, "Windcaps! How sharp they go ahead!"

"———— was very excited," Mies reported to Lora after a phone conversation. "You could hear his brain clobbering. So metallic—like a typewriter."

"It isn't raining, it's mizzling."

"I enjoy my salad, like a cow in the Alps."

"Tomorrow night at this time I will be in Mexico, drinking kweela."[9]

Lora and Mies had their own circle of friends apart from the IIT group. Together they saw a good deal of Alfred and Rue Shaw, the former an architect whose companionship—though hardly his work—Mies enjoyed, the latter the president of the Arts Club of Chicago, who commissioned the aforementioned interior space which Mies designed without fee at the turn of the 1950s. No one, not even Philip Johnson, wrote more engaging letters to Mies than Lora's ex-husband Samuel Marx, a society architect whose houses commanded little more of Mies's respect than Shaw's buildings, but whose invitations to Mies were unfailingly winning:

> For me at least, my annual party is becoming more important as the years go by, and my greatest fear is that for some reason or other you may not be able to foregather in the grass circle back of my house—1140 Sheridan Road, Glencoe—on Monday, August 27th, around 5:00 o'clock.
>
> Incidently, my three next greatest fears of 1956 are:
> (1) That Nashua is sterile
> (2) That Grace Kelly Rainier is sterile*
>   and
> (3) That Margaret Truman isn't.
> Horizontal transportation will be provided. Please try and come.
> (Sam)
> *Since dictating it, this fear has been removed.[10]

Despite his physical handicap Mies traveled widely and often during the 1950s, mostly on professional assignments, occasionally on vacation trips, in America and abroad. A 1957 swing through the north-

188. Ewald Mies and Mies at
Miesville, Wisconsin, 1957
Private collection

ern Mississippi River country, taken with Lora, Waltraut, and his visiting brother, eighty-year-old Ewald, was notable chiefly for their discovery of a Wisconsin hamlet called Miesville, which proved to be named after no one at all related to the family tree. In the spring and summer of 1959 Lora joined Mies on his second postwar trip to Europe, which included his first visit to Greece. In Athens he paid the Parthenon his highest compliment by rising exceptionally early one day so that he could give it, together with the Acropolis, the time one might expect him to have needed for the task. He studied the sacred shrines for what seemed to Lora an age, then returned to his hotel to ponder them for several more days from the balcony of their room. Delphi and Epidaurus followed. Fifty-two years earlier, on his *italienische Reise* with Joseph Popp, he had been disturbed by the unrelenting Mediterranean light; now, in mellower years, the same atmosphere seemed to him benign. With the help of Schinkel and Behrens, Greece had become one of the "great epochs" so crucial to Mies's worldview, and the golden light of the south seemed to him a condition germinal to the glorious form Greek architecture took. A Gothic cathedral, he told Lora—however much he loved it—would "look like an old spiderweb here."[11]

He was evidently less enthralled by the rococo extravagance of the Wieskirche near Munich, which he would not have seen at all if Lora had not insisted that he get out of the car and come inside for a look. "Did you like it?" she asked, enthusiastically. "I liked the light," he replied, unenthusiastically.[12]

Mies's official purpose on the 1959 trip was to accept the Gold

189. Waltraut Mies van der
Rohe and Mies, Chicago, 1955
Private collection

Medal of the Royal Institute of British Architects in London and membership in the Académie d'Architecture in Paris, two of the awards
bestowed upon him in abundance during his most fecund American
decade. Three years before he had been elected a fellow of the American Academy of Arts and Sciences and in 1957 West Germany made
him an honorary senator in that country's Academy of Arts. Honorary
doctorates in 1950 from the technical institutes of both Karlsruhe and
Braunschweig were followed in 1956 by a comparable degree from
North Carolina State University. With the 1960s his honorifics built
to a near cascade, though one more awaited him on this trip. Returning to Aachen for the first time since his panicky escape in 1938, he
was invited to sign the city's golden book at the same time a boulevard
was formally named after him. "Next to Charlemagne," exulted a German newspaper, Mies "is very likely Aachen's proudest son."[13] A re-

Recessional

191. Mies at Epidaurus, 1959
Courtesy of A. James Speyer

192. Mies at the Acropolis
looking toward the Erechtheum,
Athens, 1959
Private collection

union with Ewald and his sisters Maria and Elise, described by Lora
as a warm and touching moment, rounded out the journey.

Not all of 1959 was so halcyon. The deaths of Greenwald and Waltraut stole from Mies two of the people he cared for most. At the
time his career was at its zenith, but the twin losses, each in its way,
signaled the onset of his last mortal decade. Waltraut's surrender to
cancer prefigured his own, ten years hence. Greenwald's passing turned
him to the full-scale commitment of what strength was left him to the
final major works of his life.

When Herbert Greenwald's plane went down in Flushing Bay on
its approach to New York's La Guardia Airport in February 1959, Lafayette Park in Detroit was still incomplete. It was in fact never finished in the form Mies and Greenwald had meant it to take in their
original 1955–56 scheme. Clearly this was a misfortune in one sense,
since the project was a large-scale urban housing development which
came closer than anything Mies ever designed to a realization of his
ideas of modern architecture in service of modern American city liv-

193. Mies and Lora Marx at
Nafplion, 1959
Courtesy of A. James Speyer

194. Mies's sister Maria and
Marianne Lohan, 1962
Private collection

ing. In another sense it can be argued that he finished enough of it
to prove his purpose, but that the purpose itself was open to serious
question.

In basic concept Lafayette Park was an example of the hopeful but
largely futile programs for urban planning in the 1950s. These ideals
rested on the assumption that the chaotic and delapidated neighborhoods festering in so many parts of the contemporary inner city could
be made whole and optimally functional by being demolished, then
replaced with residential parks. On airy, sunlit meadows apartment
buildings, town houses, schools, and community centers would rise,
free not only of the overcrowding of tenement-lined streets but of vehicular traffic, which would be consigned to thoroughfares encircling
the parklands or to entrance routes at lower levels.

This was Ludwig Hilberseimer's plan for the new city as it materialized in Lafayette Park, the single instance in which he and Mies
collaborated formally on a major design effort. Hilberseimer in turn
owed much of his dream to Le Corbusier, whose city planning ideas
of the 1920s developed in part out of the same post–World War I
revolutionary mood that produced European modernist architecture
as a whole.

Despite the vision of a new metropolis as the setting for a new
architecture, urban renewal failed in America during the 1960s largely
because of the inability of private enterprise to work in concert with
public purpose: the interests of private developers too often ran con-

trary to the aspirations of social planners, who in any case possessed insufficient political power to override the developers.

However, the Corbusian residential parks, even where realized, often had the effect of destroying the neighborhoods along with the neighborhood slums. The sense of intermingling community that was a natural consequence of well-trafficked streets was lost in the windy greenswards, which in too many cases put people at unmanageable distances from services as well as from each other. The problem grew critical in low-income housing projects which turned into nocturnal no-man's-lands. More and more urban renewal became identified with housing for the poor, since people of means could and did choose to live in urban environments more accommodative to freedom of movement and choice among amenities.

Lafayette Park was neither poor man's nor rich man's housing, though a variety of factors kept it from reaching the goals Mies and Hilberseimer set for it. Located half a mile from downtown Detroit, it was meant to appeal to middle-class people, most of them career professionals who wanted to stay in the city rather than flee to the suburbs. The complex as Mies designed it consisted of three building types. Low-rise row houses one story high looked out onto individual yards enclosed by brick walls, formally and economically scaled-down versions of Mies's court houses of the 1930s. Two-story houses, their steel and aluminum framed fronts amply glazed, were also set in rows. Dominating the 78-acre land parcel were three 21-story apartment towers, the last two of them finished as late as 1963. The three types were originally arranged in a more formal order than the buildings at

195. Ewald Mies and Mies at the Schlosshotel Guelpen, The Netherlands, 1961
Private collection

Recessional

196. Model of the Lafayette
Park Housing Project, Detroit,
1955–56
Bill Engdahl, Hedrich-Blessing

197. Residential tower and row
house of Lafayette Park
Balthazar Korab, Ltd.

IIT, but Mies's characteristic device of situating them ajog of each other in final form created a smoothly dynamic spatial flow throughout the whole tract. A system of closed streets prevented through traffic while insuring accessibility to each building by auto. Although the Mies-Hilberseimer plan was stopped short of its completion, it was one of the handsomer endeavors of its kind erected during the 1950s. Greenwald's death, however, intervened and the socioeconomic problems he might have addressed at least at the level of a single project, if not of a whole city, became insuperable. Lafayette Park was eventually taken over by other developers, other architects. Mies's later exercises in city planning proved more successful when he confined them to downtown superblocks whose purpose was more commercial and governmental than residential.

These last were commissioned and executed mostly during his final decade, and while he was intimately involved in the design of only one of them—the Toronto Dominion Centre—they were individually and together the summary products of the process by which he arrived at the building types he regarded as most appropriate to the modern cityscape. Evidence of this may be discerned principally from the fact that the Dominion Centre, done between 1963 and 1969, the Chicago Federal Center of 1959–64, and Montreal's Westmount Square of 1965–68—his three major later essays in superblock design—differed markedly in function yet yielded strikingly similar solutions.

To Mies this represented architectural virtue. By the turn of the 1960s, his American work had resolved itself into two basic forms, the prismatic tower and the pavilion of unitary space. His critics saw this approach to building as both reductivist and repetitious, one of the signs of a gathering crisis in post–World War II modernism. Next to it his European work seemed fresh and free, if now lamentably lost. In his own eyes and those of his co-workers, modernism was not the issue; to them Mies's architecture was a concretization of logic that marshalled chaos into order, thus offering a solution to the problem Mies expressed so earnestly in his 1938 letter to Carl O. Schniewind (see p. 214). To the very end of his life, he remained true to his understanding of the Spenglerian-Aquinian argument, namely, that culture depended on an overarching truth gaining command of fact in the act of recognizing it.

In Chicago, Toronto, and Montreal, Mies put his will to work in fulfillment of this view. The Federal Center required a post office, courtrooms, and offices. In Toronto the Dominion Centre called for offices, a bank, and a variety of urban amenities—restaurants, shops, a theater—to be made available to the public who used the buildings and the immediate neighborhood. The needs in Montreal were similar to those in Toronto, except that provisions for housing were added to the functional package.

In each instance Mies proposed asymmetrical groupings of towers and pavilions separated by plazas. The informality of these plans was an echo, however faint, of the composition he had learned from de Stijl and never fully unlearned. Each individual building, on the other hand, was axial. The superblock thus became the monumentally up-scaled equivalent of his 1920s interior spaces, with buildings func-

tioning as freestanding walls and space flowing freely through the plazas around them.

In Chicago, by implanting two-story courtrooms in the upper floors of a 30-story tower, he preserved the prismatic austerity of the structure and granted the post office its own one-story pavilion space. Similarly, in Toronto, he avoided the solution preferred by other architects of the day—namely, creating a large space for the bank at the base of a single building and tapering the profile upward—by giving the offices their own towers and the bank its sovereign one-story clear-span structure. The shops and restaurants were strung along underground corridors, none of them showing externally. In Montreal the apartments and offices occupied rectilinearly identical towers.

In short, the three projects were demonstrations anew of the tension Mies many times, especially in America, permitted between clarity of expression and generality of form. His own unerring sensitivity to space, proportions and materials went a long way toward resolving a potential conflict of objectives. The bank in Toronto is a splendidly free, impeccably appointed, altogether inviting interior. The grouping of the two tall buildings in the Federal Center relative to the low post office is not only intrinsically persuasive, but quite at home amid the typical Chicago massing of the rectangular buildings immediately around it.

There was a paradox to all this, signifying the triumph of modernism and its failure. For by the 1960s the look of the American city had indeed been greatly altered by the dominant presence of buildings erected in the modern "manner"—lean, unornamented, steel-and-glass structures obviously indebted to the example of Mies's generation and himself in particular. Yet this development had apparently not produced a unified landscape. The chaos was still there, and it became increasingly evident that it could not be swept away by architects alone. Most designers were not as good as Mies anyway, though he came under fire himself for having produced the identical building type over and over again. Monotony was not unity. Nor, perhaps, was "chaos" quite the deleterious phenomenon it had been presumed to be.

The message of Robert Venturi's book *Complexity and Contradiction in Architecture* was that the title implied affirmative qualities. "Orthodox modernism," Venturi maintained, had taught simplistic lessons that deprived the city—whatever its ills—of the richness of variety, the vitality of change, the deeper meaning which ambiguity in form and ornamentation could confer on the art of architecture; little wonder that even when modernism had the landscape to itself the landscape looked pinched and cold. "Less is a bore," protested Venturi, mocking the Miesian credo.[14]

Thus the 1960s brought forth a new retreat from modernism, prompted not by external threats from regressive totalitarian regimes as in the 1930s, but by a perception throughout the profession not only that the modern world was too complex and too enveloped in flux to be controlled by any institution or philosophy, including that of the avant-garde, but that such control was of dubious value anyway. Not insignificantly, these changes occurred during a period in Western civilization when hierarchies of power and authority everywhere grew

blurred and uncertain. In the political sphere, the inability of great
nations to impose their will on lesser ones, as they previously had,
was dramatized by the Viet Nam war and the emergence of the Third
World. In the visual arts, Pop Art threw into question the very image
of serious high art. In architecture, accommodation replaced revolution as the watchword of a disabused generation, and the mood of
heroic aspiration of early modernism was transformed, by an act of
psychic self-defense, into irony.

If Mies understood irony, he surely had no sense for it. He had
been born in a time when idealist thought was a natural part of the
spiritual patrimony of all western Europeans, and even the worst cultural shocks of his productive lifetime, including two world wars, did
nothing to weaken his presupposition of hope and everything to temper it, so to speak, in the fires of adversity. Occidental reason for him
had been the instrument of this idealism; it had led him to appreciate
the importance of morphology in the evolution of natural form, and
to seek a morphological equivalent in the making of art. The goal of
such a process must lead inevitably to generality; for Mies there was
no alternative, no room for other, "lesser" arguments, including Venturi's circuitous subtleties. He never turned back. During the very
years when he oversaw the distillation of architectural structure in
the universal tower he pursued the universalization of architectural
space in the clear-span pavilion.

In a 1968 documentary film produced by his daughter Georgia van
der Rohe, Mies, aged eighty-two, was asked what he most wanted to
build that he had not yet built. "A cathedral," he replied.[15] It was too
late for any such thing, both in his own lifetime and that of the West,
yet the most important works of his last years were great single spaces,

the last of them coming as close as Mies could to the expression of the spiritual dimension implicit in his answer to the interviewer's question. Clearly he was disappointed never to have seen his single most stupendous space, the Convention Hall, come to pass. But, as we shall see, there were other commissions that followed, leading to a late building, the Berlin National Gallery, which, partly on account of its formal character and partly because it was a house of art and thus the secular counterpart of a sacred space, may be interpreted as the climactic endeavor of his life.

The first museum Mies built (the Museum for a Small City of 1942 having been a project only) was the Cullinan Wing of the Museum of Fine Arts in Houston, its design dating from 1954. This work was less a prefiguration of things to come than an amalgam of earlier ideas. Mies was required to build an addition to the existing museum, a building which consisted of a rectangular Beaux-Arts pavilion to which two splayed wings had been attached. In plan it must have recalled the trapezoidal layouts of his 1933 Reichsbank and 1937 Verseidag Administration Building. Appropriately, he filled in the area between the two wings with a single space whose facade opposite the main building was a gently curved glazed wall that decidedly recollected similar usages in the Reichsbank and the Verseidag Building. He spanned this space with plate girders, as he had in Crown Hall, then painted them white, as he did the piers and mullions along the outer wall. While the color was a concession to the classical character of the main building, he later, between 1965 and 1968, designed the still larger Brown Wing, dissolving the Cullinan wall, extending the whole structure still farther outward in the direction of the wide corners of the trapezoid, and painting the structural members his more familiar black. Once again he crowned the roof with plate girders, although, since the Brown Wing was supported by a grid of columns, the freest space within the museum remained the central area, the remnant, that is, of the Cullinan Wing. There Mies proposed exhibiting works by placing sculpture informally among paintings that were hung on panels suspended by wires from the ceiling. The panels defined the space as

200. "Six Master Paintings, Two Glasses, One Sculpture," installation by Mies of exhibition, Cullinan Hall, 20 March–15 April 1963

freestanding walls might have, but their levitation only increased a pervasive sense of weightlessness.

Mies never made formal response to the criticism that his architecture was repetitious. He had in effect done so long since, by arguing that solutions are better developed than invented and that the best idea is one basic enough to permit not only its application to a variety of functions but its refinement in the course of logical development. Such reasoning would derive the excellence of Seagram's from the Promontory and 860–880 types and the space and structure of the Convention Hall from the 50 by 50 House. Mies obviously made room for invention, but within a system; indeed refinement and invention were part of a continuum, with one not always or necessarily distinguishable from the other.

The Bacardi Office Building project in Cuba was traceable in virtually every detail to previous ideas, yet in final form it remains one of Mies's most demonstrably inventive building types. Its history also suggests that he could adapt himself, that is to say his system, to specific conditions as readily as he could rationalize them away.

The commission was awarded Mies in 1957 by the president of Bacardi Rum, José M. Bosch, who had been greatly impressed by Crown Hall on a previous visit to IIT. "My ideal office," Bosch wrote Mies, "is one where there are no partitions, where everybody, both officers and employees, see each other."[16] Mies could not have asked for a more supportive endorsement of his own views, and by the time he and Summers arrived in Havana on their way to the Santiago building site, Mies had in mind designing a building for Bacardi that would be based on the Crown Hall model.

According to a letter written by Summers to his son, this notion grew less secure on the first night in Cuba, when Mies observed how badly the iron railing of his Havana hotel balcony had suffered rust deterioration "in that wonderful salt-laden sea air." On the following day, confronted with another local climatic condition, the withering Caribbean sunlight, Mies "realized that this was definitely not Chicago where the light and warmth of the sun is welcome within a building most of the year."[17] Crown Hall, its glass flush with the edge of a roof suspended by steel, was clearly unacceptable as a point of departure.

Summers went on to report another observation Mies made on his return to Havana and the same hotel. Relaxing in the garden court surrounded on three sides by a veranda supported by wooden columns, Mies noted that

> the enclosing wall of the hotel lobby was . . . fifteen feet [in] from the columns . . . It was a nice proportion, a nice space, and it shaded the building wall. Mies leaned forward in his chair, in a very characteristic way, and said, "What if we reverse it? Let's put a walk under the roof [of the Bacardi building] on the outside of the glass line." With that he asked me to make a sketch, which I promptly did on the back of the cocktail napkin—it was a large square roof supported by columns only on the exterior edge, with column centers at about ten feet and with

201. Model of the Bacardi
Office Building project,
Santiago, Cuba 1957–58

the glass line back 30 feet from the roof line. I passed the sketch
to Mies and he quietly looked, while puffing on his Monte Cristo
cigar—he said, "No, it looks like a consulate—one that Gropius
would do—there are too many columns—take some out." Back
to the cocktail napkin. This time with only two columns on each
side, Mies said, "That's it—let me have your pen . . ."[18]

The Bacardi Building was thus drawn up as a single large space 130
feet square and 18 feet high, its flat roof extending some 20 feet outward from its glass walls. Eight pin-joint columns, two on each side,
supported the roof at its edges. The principal structural material was
concrete, not steel.

This much reflected the "inventive" part of the design—Mies's way,
that is, of responding to the specific conditions in Santiago. The rest
of the building, however, depended on structural, spatial, historical,
and philosophical precedents. The roof was a post-tensioned monolithic concrete structure made up chiefly of interior beams spanning
both directions and built with increasing thickness toward the center.
Edge beams and a top slab completed it. Antecedents for such devices
could be found in the Convention Hall and, earlier still, in the 50 by
50 House. The latter could likewise be regarded as one of the sources
of the supporting columns. The glass wall set back from the roof edge
was customary in the expression of the ground floor in most Miesian
towers. The single vast room, closest to Mies's heart and to José Bosch's,
was symmetrical in plan, thus typical of Mies's American years, but
it was subdivided by two freestanding marble walls and a hardwood-
panelled mechanical stack laid out in informal composition, a clear
reminder of his European habits. The whole building, partially enclosed by screening brick walls reminiscent of the Barcelona Pavilion,
was set on a podium that was as classical in concept as anything Schinkel ever did, even as it served as the enclosure of a basement given
over to ancillary services. Access, however, was unclassical, requiring
the visitor to ascend an unaxial staircase first to a lower podium, then

to make a right-hand 90-degree turn to rise, axially, to the main podium. Seen from podium level, the low-lying volume was strikingly transparent and implicitly weightless, while the roof and columns in their concrete form were more perceptibly solid and substantial than most of Mies's previous efforts. Bacardi was, in short, a compact lesson in its designer's uncommon ability to be true to a philosophy of architecture while writing variations on it and paying homage consistently to antecedents in his own work and that of others.

The project was abandoned when Fidel Castro assumed power in Cuba, but since it had evolved as the refinement of previous Miesian ideas, it qualified in its own right as a model for later ones. In simplest terms, the Berlin National Gallery is Bacardi in steel, though Mies took the intermediate step of designing a museum in much the same form which preceded Berlin.

It was the one building commission of his American career in which family connections directly played a part. In 1959 his grandson Dirk Lohan, already an architecture student at the *Technische Hochschule* in Munich, married Heidemarie Schaefer, daughter of Georg Schaefer, a wealthy industrialist from Bavaria who owned the most important private collection of nineteenth-century German art in the world. Schaefer kept his possessions in a castle near Schweinfurt, but he nursed ambitions to build a repository in the city where the work could be put on permanent public display. Museum and collection would be donated to Schweinfurt.

Young Lohan persuaded his father-in-law to offer the commission to Mies, who saw in it the opportunity not only to build the kind of sovereign space he always believed best for the exhibition of art, but to give it the form of the Bacardi building, scaled down but constructed in his beloved steel. The Cullinan and Brown wings in Houston had, after all, been additions only; the Schaefer Museum would be a structure unto itself, a resurrection, moreover, of a design Mies had come to care for greatly.

Indeed, his very regard for the Bacardi form proved ironically to be one of the factors that prevented the Schaefer Museum from being realized. Well along in the planning process, Mies was approached by

202. Collage showing the interior of the Bacardi Office Building
Collection, Mies van der Rohe Archive, the Museum of Modern Art, New York. Gift of Ludwig Mies van der Rohe

203. Model of the Schaefer
Museum project, Schweinfurt,
1960–63
Hube Henry, Hedrich-Blessing

the city of Berlin with the offer of another, more ambitious museum commission. This one would accommodate the formidable Prussian state collection of nineteenth- and twentieth-century art, one of the finest ensembles of its kind anywhere, much of it in storage since World War II. The prospect of erecting so important a building as part of an entire municipal cultural center in the city of his creatively formative years appealed powerfully to Mies. Here, he recognized, conditions were ideal for a Bacardian structure to be transformed into a Miesian museum space. His determination to achieve this deepened, commitments to Schaefer notwithstanding. The matter was resolved when Schaefer decided that he was less than enthusiastic about putting his nineteenth-century holdings in a modern steel building, and the city of Schweinfurt, doubtful that it could carry the costs of maintaining the museum, saw a chance to wash its hands of the whole matter. Architect, client, and city government agreed to end negotiations, all parties feeling relieved in the process. Mies was free to begin work on the building that took up the most devoted efforts of his declining years.

Mies's work on the Berlin National Gallery was slowed in its early stages by a flareup of his arthritis so painful that he was hospitalized for a period of weeks and forced to absent himself from his office for nearly a year in 1962 and 1963. During 1962 Dirk Lohan, newly graduated from Munich, moved to Chicago, where he joined Mies's staff and gradually rose to a central place in Mies's personal and professional life. However much sway Gene Summers had with the old man and however close Lora Marx was to Mies, neither could finally match Lohan in two crucial respects: Lohan was family, and he spoke German. He was not Mies's only grandson; Georgia had two boys, Frank, born in 1943, and Mark, born in 1957. But Lohan's adopted profession was the same as his and in the isolation of his later years Mies could not help appreciating the attentions of a cultivated young European—a *Landsmann*, no less—who increasingly took on the surrogate identity of the *Stammhalter* Mies had never himself begotten. Lohan in turn, recalling the awe in which he held Mies when the two met, wordlessly and uneasily, in 1953, was now old enough to talk to his grandfather and to be rationally aware of the roots of his lifelong respect for him.

The respect deepened into affection, on both sides. The combination of Mies's singular abilities and introverted unworldliness had long made him attractive to those who wanted to care for him while nourishing themselves in his light. He was quite prepared to accept such care, but only up to a point which Ada and Lilly, to name but two, had earlier exceeded. Thus Mies found it easy to feel warmth for his alert young grandson while suffering not at all from the threat of strangulating love.

Gradually and unavoidably a quiet rivalry developed between Lohan and Summers, the latter secure in his experience and Mies's professional trust, but at a growing disadvantage on the personal level. Blood won out. Summers, who had already begun quite reasonably to wonder what would become of the office once Mies was dead, now saw hopes fade that the gauntlet would pass to him. As work on the National Gallery progressed, his role as Mies's most trusted assistant was slowly taken over by Lohan.

Summers accepted the situation reluctantly but with typically cool resolve. "We were at a good and firm point in office fortunes," he recalled. "Various projects were in hand and underway. So I said to Mies one day that I wanted to leave."

"I wish you'd stay a few more years," replied Mies.

"But then I might have to stay longer."

"Well," said Mies, his thoughts returning to his last hours with Peter Behrens in 1912, "I appreciate that. I had to make a similar decision once. When do you want to go?"

"In two weeks."[19]

It was 1965. Summers resigned, set up his own office about a block from Mies's and hired an assistant, a young German immigrant named Helmut Jahn, fresh out of IIT. The two men worked on a number of projects together before Summers joined C. F. Murphy & Associates, where in 1967 he was assigned the design of a new convention hall in Chicago to replace one destroyed by fire earlier in the year. The latter structure had been the object of heated civic controversy, less because of its palpable architectural inferiority to Mies's own unbuilt design and more because it took up a substantial portion of Chicago's traditionally open lakefront land.

Still, the city was determined to erect the new hall on the same spot. Summers took on the commission, insisting first, however, that Mies be made his partner and put in charge of the design. He personally carried this proposition to his former chief.

Mies shook his old head. "If it were the Parthenon, I wouldn't do it," he said firmly, mindful not only of the ongoing quarrel over the building site but of his own limited energies. He was eighty-one, in no mood to undertake a project as complex as it was discordant. The Berlin Gallery was swan song enough.

True to his makeup, Mies made no voluntary effort to see Summers after their professional parting. No less characteristically, he asked Lora Marx in 1969 to drive him past Summer's enormous hall, now at last under construction. "It is a good building," he said simply, closing another chapter in his life with a minimum of sentiment.[20]

The National Gallery stands within several hundred yards of the location of Mies's old abode, which had been taken down by the Nazis to make room for Albert Speer's colossal but unrealized North-South Axis concourse.[21] Whether Mies ever made his way back to the Am Karlsbad 24 site is not recorded, but there can be no doubt that his return to Berlin by itself was a profound and symbolically far-reaching emotional experience. It stood for infinitely more than his reunion with Aachen. Berlin it was that shaped his art, his thought, his life at the flood, and it is not out of place to suggest that he returned the favor, giving form to the great city's own vision of architecture in the twentieth century—even if he left no significant modern buildings there to prove it.

Now, however, the opportunity to do just that had presented itself in the form of a commission for a museum on the Kemperplatz that would serve as a treasury of the paintings and sculptures—the trophies, as it were—of his own time, the "epoch" he had contemplated so intensely, so long. He had completed an odyssey of sorts near the end of his mortal days, and it can hardly be an accident that he gave his building a form analogous to that of a classical temple, columned, axially symmetrical, set upon a podium. To be sure, it was the Bacardi Building done over rather than invented, but fitting both to this extraordinary occasion and to the expression thereof. The occasion was a valedictory, delivered on his native soil, the expression, the noblest clear-span space he was likely ever to see built.

204. National Gallery, Berlin, 1962–67
David L. Hirsch

205. Main hall of the National
Gallery
David L. Hirsch

Mies's determination to carry the project through on his own terms
was indomitable. Even as he lay in he hospital in 1963 he exercised
the closest control over the design as it took detailed form in his office, and he ordered a 1:10 section of column built in his model shop.
Once returned to work he studied and refined it over a period of
months, with all the laborious dedication of his younger, stronger years.
He undertook the physically exhausting trip to Berlin several times in
the course of planning and at the ground-breaking ceremony in 1965
insisted on lifting his weakened body out of his wheelchair and onto
his crutches as he struck a stone tablet with a hammer and affirmed
his hope that the building would serve as the "appropriate frame of a
noble endeavor."[22]

In fact the frame became the endeavor, the museum its own most
important exhibition piece. Above all Mies wanted to carry out on a
more monumental scale the unitary space and surrounding structure
that he had conceived for Bacardi. The great room would house temporary exhibitions while the permanent collection together with ad-

ministrative offices and auxiliary services would be lodged in the podium, where they would not violate the integrity of the temple above.

Once completed, the hall, walled totally in glass, measured 166 feet square, with a 26-foot height, comprising an area of 27,000 square feet. The 213-foot-square roof, the first rigid plate ever executed, was constructed in the form of an orthogonal grid of web girders 6 feet deep separated at 12-foot intervals. The grid was covered by a continuous compression plate reinforced with steel ribs on its underside to prevent buckling. The camber in the center of the plate counteracted deflection; cambers at the four corners insured a flat appearance. Eight flanged cruciform steel columns painted black, two to a side, tapered gently upward to pin-joint connections that met the roof at its edges.

Access to the 346-by-362-foot granite-paved podium was gained mainly via a broad axial staircase to the east, though Mies elsewhere broke with classical precedent by inserting secondary stairs at the northwest and southeast corners of the platform. The glass box, however, was the most austerely symmetrical large interior he had designed since the Convention Hall. The absoluteness of the square plan, echoed structurally in the square coffers of the roof grid overhead, was underscored spatially by the immense interior expanse—broken only by matched pairs of marble-sheathed mechanical stacks, hardwood-panelled cores, and staircases leading below—and the implicit infinitude of movement in all directions beyond the transparent walls. To achieve so ineffable an architectural effect Mies was content to leave most of the downstairs galleries to the mercy of a pedestrian arrangement of spaces, most of them artificially illuminated.

The temple itself, not so flexible a space as inflexible, has remained by consensus an inhospitable arena in which to display any but the largest objects. In the inaugural exhibition, Piet Mondrian's paintings

Recessional

were hung, according to the Cullinan model, on large white panels suspended from the ceiling. In ensemble the panels themselves were an impressive study in weightlessness, but the paintings they bore seemed drowned in the ocean of surrounding space. And now the aged Mies barely bothered to rationalize his solution in the familiar terms of universality of function. "It is such a huge hall," he declared, "that of course it means great difficulties for the exhibiting of art. I am fully aware of that. But it has such potential that I simply cannot take those difficulties into account."[23]

He was no less singleminded in his attention to the structure. The exactitude of the detailing of a single column—the degree of its taper, the ratio of its width to the width of the flanges, the delicate curve that connected the flanges at the peak of the column—would be evidence enough of that. But witnesses remain enthralled by their memory of Mies's own appearance at the building site in 1967 when the vast roof grid, having been constructed in sections on the spot, was raised as a single piece by eight hydraulic jacks placed at the points along the perimeter of the roof structure which would be finally supported by the columns.

At 9 A.M. on 5 April, Mies appeared at the site. He had been driven there in a white Mercedes sedan from which he gravely watched the entire operation. It required nine hours and proceeded faultlessly. The jacks were so precisely synchronized that the differences in elevation of the 1250-ton roof as it rose never exceeded two millimeters. At a certain point the great plate was lifted high enough off the ground that the columns could be secured to their foundations and the roof lowered onto their pin-joint connections.

Like a venerable owl Mies observed it all, and that is all he did. If he had spent his life resisting distraction—moral, political, romantic, even conversational—he was never more concentrated in his attentions to the completion of his art than on that chilly spring morning of his eighty-second year. Even the champagne reception in honor of the occasion—of himself, that is—left him in a state of bored irritability, to which he gave voice when finally called upon to deliver a statement to the company formally assembled there. It was pure Mies,

208. Raising the roof of the National Gallery, April 1967
Photo by Dirk Lohan

209. Mies at the raising of the National Gallery's roof
Courtesy of Reinhard Friedrich

compact, disdainful of ceremony, respectful of labor, and flavored with the accents of his youth on the Rhine:

> Es hat ja jeheissen, jeder sollte nur fünf Minuten sprechen. Wat da jeschwindelt wurde! Ich will hier nur den Stahlfritzen danken, und den Betonleuten. Und als das jrosse Dach sich lautlos hob, da hab' ich jestaunt!![24] [It was agreed that nobody would speak more than five minutes. What humbug that was! I

210. Henry Moore and Mies at the Berlin National Gallery, 1967

want to thank the blokes who worked the steel, and the ones who did the concrete. And when the great roof raised itself up without a sound, I was amazed!

This was Mies's last visit to the museum. He was too incapacitated to return to Berlin for the official dedication in September 1968. Yet his presence in the city was now established permanently, in the form he valued most, that of clear and structured architecture which, moreover, flowed outward from the Kemperplatz in both space and time. Even if his massive black vitrine had grown directly out of a white one meant for the Caribbean sunlight—and more indirectly out of the jewel-like 50 by 50 House—its relationship with the legacy of Karl Friedrich Schinkel seemed no less apparent. The Altes Museum stood nearby, secure on its own podium, wrapped in its columns and its own classical air, and even though its location behind the Wall in East Berlin left it separated from the National Gallery by an ideological gulf far greater than a few actual city blocks, Mies's design had created an immaterial but unbreakable connection with a tradition and a mas-

211. Mies in conversation with Stephan Waetzoldt, with Dirk Lohan in the background, Berlin, 1967
Courtesy of Reinhard Friedrich

ter he learned to revere sixty years before. A more immediate, if grimmer, nexus was likewise manifest on the day of the dedication at a spot along the Landwehr Canal, a few hundred feet from the museum. There the bodies of the slain Karl Liebknecht and Rosa Luxemburg had been found in 1919, and now, in the revolutionary days of the later 1960s, the students were clamoring for the construction of another wall—the reconstruction, that is, of Mies's 1926 monument to the fallen radical leaders.

It was too late for Mies to respond to what seemed to be yet another distraction. The weariness was on him by now, and the satisfaction deep enough in any case that the "noble endeavor" had been served. The century's most famous advocate of impersonal architecture had had his own personal way in the end.

Mies spent his declining years quite as might have been anticipated from the habits of his robust ones. The solitariness deepened, and he did less of nearly everything that taxed him or seemed irrelevant to his life's purposes. On those few occasions in the 1960s when he was faced with an assignment he found genuinely challenging, like the Berlin National Gallery, he could still bring to bear upon it the almost unnatural concentration that had always distinguished his creative faculties. Otherwise, he left to his subordinates most of the numerous commissions that came into his office. Legions of students and fellow architects from all over the world sought audiences with him, and these he granted frequently, but he both knew and carefully observed the difference between important and unimportant supplicants. He could ignore scores of letters which pleaded, sometimes eloquently, for this or that favor, but he was usually prompt to accept institutional honors and awards, and the greater the honor, the prompter his acceptance. His early yearning for higher things did not abandon him late. Seven honorary doctorates were bestowed upon him during the 1960s, plus an equal number of memberships in professional societies and gold medals from the American Institute of Architects, the Architectural League of New York, the National Institute of Arts and Letters, the Institute of German Architects and the Chicago chapter of the American Institute of Architects. His most prized awards were the highest civilian peacetime decorations of the two countries in which he had resided: the Knight Commander's Cross of the German Order of Merit and the Presidential Medal of Freedom of the United States. Notification of the latter came from John F. Kennedy four months before

212. Mies receiving Medal of Freedom from
President Lyndon B. Johnson,
Washington, D.C.,
December 1963
World Wide Photos

his assassination in November 1963; the medal was personally presented to Mies by Lyndon B. Johnson a few weeks after he took office.[25] Properly fascinated by and quite taken with the Kennedy mystique, Mies was one of the architects considered for the design of the Kennedy Library in 1964, the one major commission of his last years that he wanted and did not get.

Mies in his seventies and eighties was financially comfortable, but he continued to have little use for any but a few material pleasures. Liquor and cigars were less a luxury than a staple. His apartment was furnished simply, neither richly nor scrupulously; what he did for the Tugendhats was hardly necessary for himself. Before his eyesight failed, he and Lora occasionally took in a movie, far less often a concert or recital—and then usually by the singer he most admired, Marian Anderson—and never the theater. He was content to own a demonstration model automobile, a pale yellow Oldsmobile. He could not drive it; Lora did. His interest in the acquisition of art was mostly a development of his American years, though he could never have been regarded as a studious collector. When he left Germany, he owned two paintings, by Beckmann and Kandinsky. Once in the U.S., he obtained several works by old friends Klee and Kurt Schwitters, as well as an oil by Picasso, a collage by Georges Braque, and as many as ninety etchings and lithographs by Edvard Munch. Despite his early contact with the constructivists and Theo van Doesburg, he never owned a piece of geometric abstraction. When asked why, he said, "You don't have to have everything," a reply which explained nothing.[26] He bought as the spirit or the occasion moved him, and apparently neither ever prompted him to purchase art that looked at all like his architecture.

At home his life in the 1960s was simple, quiet, even monastic. He was never without access to companionship, as the visits of intimates guaranteed, but except for vacations and the most necessary business trips he was confined to his abode by his arthritis and the fundamental introversion that both led and drove him further into the recesses of his mind. He could sit literally for hours, not only by himself but in the company of others, rapt in immobilized silence and thought. In the early 1960s he dined often with Lora and Gene Summers, and he saw a good deal of Phyllis Lambert as well, who, having become an architecture student at IIT in the late 1950s, took her own apartment at 860 Lake Shore Drive, a few blocks from Mies's place. In the latter half of the 1960s Dirk Lohan was in constant attention, and only a little less so Marianne.

But always these visitors departed at the end of an evening, leaving Mies to himself and his reflections. He read as he always had, and much the same philosophical fare, though his earlier preoccupation with morphological subjects shifted—logically, one would like to infer—toward an interest in physics and cosmology. He labored earnestly at this, poring over the same texts in German and English by Werner Heisenberg and Erwin Schrödinger and sometimes finding himself unable to understand what he had read. Typically, he would go back to it again and again, insisting to Lora that it was imperative he learn the deeper truth he knew was there. "Sometimes late at night when I am tired," he once said, "I am overcome with a desire to do

213. Mies in his apartment with
painting by Paul Klee and
sculpture by Pablo Picasso

214. Four generations: Mies with Marianne Lohan, Dirk Lohan, and Dirk's children, Caroline and Lars, mid-1960s Photo by Dirk Lohan

something just because I like to. Then I know it is too late; I've been working too long. You don't do a thing because you like to do it, but because it is right."[27] This was the monk in old Mies speaking, who seemed possessed in his last years of a search that went beyond reason to religion. This he pressed with all the dedication he had given to his researches in the late 1920s and early 1930s. Then he had been impelled by the failing light of the Weimar Republic, now simply by the shortness of his own time.

As ever, he would seek in his own way. It is certain he was indifferent to the formal church, and while he was no friend of psychoanalysis either, the one book he read by Sigmund Freud was an attack on religion itself, *The Future of an Illusion*.[28] He appears to have been

215. Mies revisiting IIT, surrounded by students and colleagues, mid-1960s Courtesy of Dirk Lohan

Recessional

216. Mies revisiting IIT,
surrounded by students and
colleagues, mid-1960s
Courtesy of Dirk Lohan

looking for the confirmation of a higher system in the theoretical postulates of science, thus his further reading in Julian Huxley, Karl von
Weizsäcker, and Arthur Eddington. Yet he went on studying theology
as well, adding to his library texts by his old Roman Catholic friend
Romano Guardini.[29] The autodidactic manner of his quest and the privacy with which he conducted it were already evident from the attention he paid during the 1950s to the writings of Rudolf Schwarz,
an architect who was among the leaders in the modernization of church
building that began in Germany prior to Hitler and continued after
World War II. There is little about Schwarz's designs that would seem
attractive to Mies in a strictly architectural sense, but the former, a
Rhinelander who in 1930 built a church in Aachen which Mies must
have known, wrote about church architecture with the same belief in
the necessary consonance of spirit and form that Mies made the cor-
nerstone of his own thinking. One of the few pieces of prose that Mies
wrote in America with publication consciously in mind, was the foreword to the English translation of Schwarz's book, *The Church
Incarnate.*[30]

We are led to wonder, then, whether Mies's expressed desire to
build a cathedral (see p. 299) was more than an idle fancy. Yet there
is little else to do but wonder, since he designed only one ecclesiastical work—the IIT Chapel—and gave us no further clues into his ambitions in this respect, not so much as a remark or a drawing. If there
was an underlying logic to his behavior, it was that his ambition to
give form to the epoch was qualified by a fatalist turn of mind that
became more deeply ingrained with the years. He would not go to

the mountain, but if it came to him he would respond, on his own terms. Nobody ever asked him to design a church.

Commercial buildings were forever another matter. In 1962 Peter Palumbo paid a visit to Chicago, carrying with him the offer of a commission to design a high-budget office tower on a piece of land the wealthy Palumbo family controlled in the heart of the City of London. Mies accepted the charge, even though he knew any work he conceived would not be built until 1986—after his death, surely—because of a lengthy leasehold on the site that would not be retired until that time. Yet he was driven by the singular opportunity to place a building in a great city where none of his works had ever stood.

And so he flew to London in 1964, to survey the site. It lay across from George Dance the Elder's Mansion House of 1739, with the 1936 Midland Bank of Edwin Lutyens and the 1672 Church of St. Stephen Walbrook of Christopher Wren and John Vanbrugh close by. The environment was more freighted with history and historical styles than anything Mies would have encountered in downtown Chicago or New York. "He was very careful," Palumbo reports, "and looked at the site from every conceivable angle, sight lines, buildings around it; he took very careful notes."[31]

Yet the solution he gave Palumbo, in 1967, was a typical Miesian curtain wall prism, meant to be clad in bronze but otherwise mostly indistinguishable from the glass boxes put up by the Mies office on dozens of sites in America. Its merits were also typical: an immaculateness of proportion and a precision of detail that drew more attention to the structure as a discrete form than to the role it might play

217. Mies reading *Bauen seit 1900 in Berlin*, by Rave and Knöfel, 1967
Photo by Dirk Lohan

218. Model of Mansion House Square project, London, 1967 Photo by John Donat

in its obviously premodern neighborhood. Yet by the 1980s a revived respect for historical styles and a concern for preserving the environmental "context" had prompted a majority of critics to see Mies's Mansion House Square project as a piece of architecture past its time and neglectful of its place. In May 1985 Britain's Environment Minister Patrick Jenkin rejected Palumbo's petition to build it.

With his long and debilitating illness of 1962–63, the fact of Mies's mortality intruded itself on the people close to him. Like Summers earlier, Lohan, who became Mies's most intimate professional associate in the mid-1960s, questioned the old man repeatedly about the ultimate fate of his office. At first Mies was predictably indifferent to the matter, regarding it as precisely the sort of tedious worldly business he had always shied from, especially if there were a Reich or a Summers or a Lohan around to tend to it for him. And Lohan finally did, working out an agreement in 1969 by which Mies established a partnership with him, Joseph Fujikawa, and Bruno Conterato. Following Mies's death that same year, the Office of Mies van der Rohe continued the practice until 1975, when its name was formally changed to FCL Associates. In 1982, Fujikawa and Gerald Johnson separated from the firm to become Fujikawa Johnson Associates, Inc.

The Europeans meanwhile had busied themselves with another aspect of the preservation of one of the twentieth century's foremost architectural heritages. Prior to the end of World War II the contents of Mies's atelier which he had been forced to leave behind in Berlin were packed into wooden storage cases by Lilly Reich and a former Bauhaus student, Eduard Ludwig, and shipped off to the Mühlhausen home of Ludwig's parents in Thuringia, a province later incorporated in the German Democratic Republic. There the crates reposed through the 1940s and the 1950s, while Ludwig remained in dutiful correspondence with Mies. In 1959, an effort to recover them and return them to Mies made major headway when Hans Maria Wingler of the Bauhaus Archive in West Germany obtained East German permission to visit Mühlhausen, under the pretext of carrying on research in medieval sculpture.[32] Wingler made his way to the Ludwig home, where he surreptitiously opened and examined the five boxes he found there. He reported their contents to Mies: principally drawings, photographs, correspondence, job files, competition papers, copies of periodicals, Bauhaus documents.

The value of this material, which comprised the larger portion of the personal and professional effects Mies had accumulated during his German career, was obvious. Lengthy and delicate negotiations followed between representatives of the mutually unfriendly West German and East German states. Four years passed, during which the faithful Eduard Ludwig lost his life in a traffic accident in 1960. From Chicago Dirk Lohan continued to press for a return of Mies's property. Late in 1963, the general secretary of the Academy of Arts in West Berlin, Freiherr von Buttlar, and his directorial counterpart at the German Academy of Arts in East Berlin, Otto Nagel, effected a transfer of the crates to West Berlin, though the East Germans insisted on retaining all files pertaining to the Dessau Bauhaus. Finally, in December, the treasure arrived in Chicago, where Mies, to the exasperation of his staff, let it sit for weeks before opening it up.[33]

The contents were at last duly and formally examined, in fact shortly after Mies and the Museum of Modern Art had begun conversing about his possible donation of drawings he had loaned for the 1947 New York exhibition. In the course of these and subsequent talks Mies, who did not care to see his work edited in any way, let it be known that he would give the museum more, not fewer, of his professional possessions, including most of the Mühlhausen material and his American files.[34] The result was the official establishment in 1968 of the Mies van der Rohe Archive, a division of the museum's Department of Architecture and Design. This cache contains over 20,000 items, most notably drawings, job correspondence and papers pertaining to building assignments. In his will Mies bequeathed 22,000 other documents, chiefly personal and professional letters unrelated to specific buildings, to the Library of Congress.

Mies recovery from his acute attack of arthritis in 1963 was shortlived. Mobility never returned but the pain did, so strongly in 1965 that he confided to Lora his inability to think concentratedly. "The worst thing about pain," he told her, "is that it is boring."[35] Since his discomfort was made worse by the tautness of the musculature around his waist, his doctors decided on a surgical procedure in which they notched some of his muscles laterally, lengthening them, thus relaxing them and bringing him the first pronounced relief from pain that he had felt in years. Clearly he would never walk unassisted again, but he was able to resume a moderate work schedule.

Le Corbusier died in the same year, suffering a heart attack while swimming in the Mediterranean. Wright had passed on in 1959. Only Gropius and Mies remained of the great generation of European modernists born in the 1880s. The debt of the years was mounting up, demanding ever more urgently to be paid. In the 1960s Mies developed divergent strabismus, a condition known as wall-eye. It left him incapable of focusing his gaze for long on the printed page. Eventually he relied on Lora to read to him, which she did as diligently as he would otherwise have done himself. His intimacy with her, and hers with him, deepened, and one evening she laid her book aside and addressed him, gently. "Tell me," she said, "why you never married me."

Mies heaved a great sigh. "I think I was a fool. I was afraid I would lose my freedom. I wouldn't have. It was a senseless worry." He paused. Then he asked her, "Shall we do it now?"

"No," she replied, knowing him better at the time than he knew himself. "It is rather too late for that; it would only spoil things. I guess I just wanted to know."[36]

Lora was content with the responsibility she had set for herself, which was to help him approach his death with as much ease as she could arrange.

The first symptoms of cancer of the esophagus appeared sometime in 1966, shortly after a shower of congratulatory messages descended upon him on the occasion of his eightieth birthday. Surgery was out of the question; for this condition his age precluded it. Radiation treatment reduced the size of the obstruction and gave him back a measure of comfort, but the odds remained high against full recovery. In 1968, Lora remembers, she and Mies took one "last lovely trip" of several weeks to Santa Barbara, from which Mies returned looking tan and fit. For about a year in 1968 and 1969 his physician, George Allen, kept him functioning by regularly dilating his esophagus, an unpleasant business which Mies endured with much the same stoicism that marked all his encounters with physical disability.[37]

He died in the summer of 1969, just weeks after Gropius. One evening at dinner, Lora noticed that Mies had a slight cold and was looking pale. She decided to spend the night, close to him, at his apartment. Next morning she found him in bed, trembling, gasping for breath, his fists clenched tightly under his chin. An ambulance was summoned and he was taken to Wesley Memorial Hospital.

Georgia flew in from New York. Marianne was already in Chicago. What appeared at first to have been a heart attack proved to be pneumonia. For two weeks Mies drifted in and out of consciousness. Marianne recalls the last several days:

> Every few hours the crisis, then the means taken against it—
> to lower the fever and all that. They turned him constantly,
> to keep him from becoming sore. Every hour they took his

blood pressure, and all kinds of other tests. With charts. And instruments. Once I came to his room but couldn't get in because there were three doctors with him. He had lapsed into a coma.

They were busily discussing the case among themselves, and I was growing more and more furious. I waited until they came out of the room. Then I said, "I'm angry with you! Can't you give a man time to die? He is eighty-three years old. He has had a full, rich life. He is terminally ill—you know that—and now he has a pneumonia which could take him quickly and mercifully. And all you do is fuss around with your tests and charts!"

"We only want to help him."

"You could help him more if you gave him the time to come to his own peace."

A heart specialist now reported in, and Marianne turned her ire upon him. He retreated. "We'll go easy on the tests," he promised.

Two days passed. On 19 August Mies grew ashen and inert, his breathing perceptibly shallower. Again it was Marianne who was with him at the time. A nurse came by, who, observing what had happened, prepared to call a doctor. "No," Marianne objected, "let nature take its course." Over the nurse's protests she blocked the door.[38]

Now came Georgia, who immediately phoned Lora and Dirk. Lora sped to the hospital. Dirk could not be located. Within a half hour Mies's breathing stopped.

The daughters closed their father's eyes and Georgia, taking a bunch of yellow roses from a vase nearby, placed them in his hands. Marianne had done the same with Ada seventeen years before.

Lora arrived shortly after Mies died. The family entrusted her with the funeral arrangements, which she limited to a brief service in the chapel at Graceland Cemetery. Georgia, Marianne, Lora, Heidemarie, Dirk, and Mies's cook Caroline Regis were in attendance. Dirk spoke briefly and the organist offered Bach's *O Haupt voll Blut und Wunden*.[39] Mies was cremated, his ashes buried in a plot within sight of the graves of Daniel Burnham and Louis Sullivan.

Two months later the rest of the world had its opportunity for a last gesture of remembrance. On 25 October 1969, a group of friends, colleagues, students, and admirers assembled in Crown Hall to hear more Bach issue from the cello of Janos Starker, and the following words, excerpted from the encomium delivered by Mies's old chum James Johnson Sweeney:

It is characteristic of the depth, complexity, and subtlety of Mies's view of architecture that the man whose epicurean taste would wish to combine Roman travertine, Tinian marble, gray transparent glass, onyx, and chromium-plated steel columns in his Barcelona pavilion and walls of striped black and pale brown Macassar ebony and tawny, gold-and-white onyx in his Tugendhat House could also declare with warmth and sincerity: "Where can we find greater structural clarity than in the wooden buildings of old? Where can we find such unity of material, construction, and form? What feeling for material and what power of expression there is in these buildings! What warmth and beauty they have! They seem to be the echoes of old songs!" This from the Mies we associate with the statement that concrete, steel, and glass are the materials of our time and from these materials the forms of our epoch should evolve! But for Mies everything depended on "how we use a material, not on the material itself—each material," as he said, "is only what we make it." And Mies, in no matter what material he employed, as the bequest of buildings he has left Chicago bears witness, was essentially a builder. He never forgot his early lessons from his master-mason father. "I learned about stone from him." And I recall how pleased he was to recount the fact that as a young man—barely more than a boy—he had qualified as a journeyman bricklayer. "Now a brick," as he would say, "That is really something! How sensible is this small, handy shape, so useful for every purpose! What logic in its bonding, pattern, and texture! What richness in the simplest wall surface! But what discipline this material imposes!" On this homely basis Mies established an unparalleled expression of new materials and engineering techniques: "a form for an epoch." Discipline, order, form: this was the progress he saw underlying the statement from Saint Augustine he was so fond of quoting. This, for him, in architecture, was Truth. Beauty was its splendor.[40]

No one had a better right to speak in behalf of Mies than Sweeney, whose eloquence was inspired not only by personal friendship but by a secure knowledge of the arts of the first two-thirds of the twentieth century. Still, his remarks eulogized an outlook as much as they did the man who shaped it. Even as Mies died quietly in his bed, a storm was breaking over his head. For a second time in the span of his lifetime modernism was in retreat, called into question by a generation of architects and critics too young to remember the issues of the 1920s at first hand, but old enough to believe that the values the European pioneers fashioned of those issues had either run their course or simply proved illusory. During the 1960s the modern movement, having made common cause with capitalist enterprise, seemed motivated less by a sense of mission and more by a reliance on a formula certified by corporate success. The failure of urban renewal, the flight of the population from the inner city, coincident with the crowding of both downtown and suburban belts with heaps of undifferentiated high-rise boxes: all this seemed proof that the bureaucrat's prospectus and the real estate developer's budget sheet had replaced the architect's manifesto as the guiding principle of modern planning and design.

Even at the level of theory, as distinct from the everyday look of things, disenchantment reared up. Many observers felt forced to the conclusion that the search for a binding, logically developed grammar of architectural form had produced less purity of expression, only more sterility. In its exertions to cast off the burden of historical "style" by cleaving to a doctrine of reductivist abstraction, modern architecture appeared to have lost its capacity to convey content and meaning through ornament, figurative symbol, or kindred allusion to the uses of tra-

219. Mies memorial service at IIT, 1968. In foreground, left to right, Dirk Lohan, James Johnson Sweeney, Lora Marx, Marianne Lohan, Laura Sweeney, Phyllis Lambert, Philip Johnson.
Courtesy of Illinois Institute of Technology

dition. The designer's opportunity, not to say obligation, to enhance an environment by adapting his work to it, thus drawing richness from it, seemed to have been sacrificed to the false ideal of an architecture unto itself, disdainful of its environment, thus all too often hermetically sealed off from it.

Not all of these grievances could be nailed to Mies's door. Yet the very influence he had exerted on the look of contemporary cities together with his austere philosophy of architecture made him a focal figure, indeed the prime target, of the argument. To a majority of the new critics his work represented the most uncompromising form of orthodox modernism. He was the century's arch-abstractionist, to whose IIT Chapel it had been necessary to affix the label "Chapel," since nothing in that building's generalized form suggested anything so specific as a religious sanctuary. He was the period's most determinedly impersonal rationalist, an authoritarian who had abjured his own late evening impulses "to do something just because I like to," in favor of the formal declaration that "architecture is not a cocktail." In a world where time was compressed into precipitous change and space encompassed the sprawl of Dallas as well as the grid of downtown Chicago, Mies's deductive manner of drawing buildings out of fixed concepts rather than from particular needs seemed impossibly outmoded. Universals appeared inappropriate, at the very least, to an aging century that had already given up too much of its blood to ideology.

We have pictured Mies here as a designer of uncommon sensibility and a thinker whose tendency to profound introspection was fortified by a monumental will. The satisfaction he derived early on from the craftsmanly construction of buildings was transformed by the cultural and technological ambitions of Wilhelmine Germany into the decision to become an architect. Soon enough he associated that calling with art and the lofty spiritual condition European thinking of the time typically attributed to art. Yet his maturing worldview, affected by the catastrophe of World War I and the grim landscape left in its wake, persuaded him of the idleness of art left to its own desserts and the narrowed options of all serious creative activity in the late Faustian age. Art, which is to say architecture, must therefore be made rationally, since the period gave force only to that expression which was rational. This stern perception led him finally to an inspiriting belief that creative endeavor could nevertheless be exalted by being mortified, passed, as it were, through the eye of a metaphysical needle, to a higher system of truth divinable from the tenets of idealist philosophy. We have acknowledged that Mies was formally untrained in philosophy. What he finally learned of it, through painful self-education, was based on his modest but firmly rooted early training in a Roman Catholic elementary school. That was enough to direct him to such thinkers as Plato, Saint Augustine, Kant, and above all to Saint Thomas Aquinas, who accommodated and accounted for the facts of the world as reflection of a supersensible system.

To understand that system, then, and to devote his own formative abilities to it—thus to bring a measure of order to the later Faustian chaos—became a quest requiring the most concentrated mental discipline. All else was assigned a secondary priority, and the older Mies grew the more distance he put between the quest and worldly irrelevances. It is enough to remember his indifference to his family and his disregard of political realities in Nazi Germany, not to mention his protracted lassitude in the face of the open hostility the Nazis eventually showed him. The effort to distill architecture to general forms and universal spaces was influenced by more than either the reductivist aesthetic of early modernism or his own endless study of natural and cosmic morphology. It had religious implications too: the building became a modern equivalent of the major material instrumentality of Saint Thomas's time, the Gothic cathedral—a skin made as (spiritually) transparent as possible though substantial enough to *be* an architecture, thus to enclose space while transfiguring it, to make space a mystical entity, the immaterial manifestation of the higher truth.

In the final analysis and at the end of his life Mies was the century's supreme architect of the one-room building. His concept of it had begun in the open plan of the 1920s with its dynamically flowing spaces and ended in the equilibrated symmetry and still vastness of his squared clear-span halls of the 1950s and 1960s. To achieve these compelling interiors of his later years, enclosing structures of unimpeachable integrity were required, but their rational composition was carried at last to nonrational ends: reason ascended to the mystic.

Thus even if he had lived, he would have been no more receptive to the eclectic tastes of the post-Miesians than they were to his own narrowly focused asceticism. He died at the right moment, living long enough to finish the Berlin National Gallery but not so long that he would have had to endure a period filled with more unsettling doubts than those which he had struggled so heroically to overcome. In life his personal taciturnity, like the very elementalism of his work, generated a charisma finally as arresting to his critics as to his champions. Death, which made him ultimately unapproachable and unaccountable, only added to his mythic stature.

That rationality could lead to so elevated a form of aesthetic mysticism, especially in a century more predisposed to rational than to mystical explanations of reality, is as remarkable a fact as any about Mies van der Rohe. Ironically, it suggests that his critics were justified in their contention that no one philosophy has been enough to account for modern experience. There is surely no certainty that the epoch is identical with Spengler's late Faustian age or that Thomistic essences overarch all fact. Answers elude us as they did Mies.

Thus his place in history is assured not so much by the infallibility of his thinking as by the subtlety and refinement of his art. Even so, that art was dependent on the concentrated mental rigor to which he forever subjected it. Less than ever could architecture after Mies escape the implications of discipline, logic, and method as driving forces in the profession, hearkening to them or fleeing from them, but in either case only with conscious forethought. If he did not divine the epoch, he left his personal stamp on it, this most impersonal of artists; for years it would have to deal with him as surely as he strove heroically to deal with it. Pluralistic as world architecture is near the end of the twentieth century, it is made more so, paradoxically, by the memory of Mies's singlemindedness.

Notes

Chapter 1

    1. Dirk Lohan interview with Ludwig Mies van der Rohe (typescript; Chicago, summer, 1968) in Mies van der Rohe Archive, Museum of Modern Art, New York.

    2. Renamed Neukölln in 1912.

    3. Mies spoke of his early years in formal conversations with a variety of friends and colleagues, most notably with Horst Eifler and Ulrich Conrads (see chap. 2, n. 24), Peter Carter (see n. 5), Peter Blake (see n. 10), George Danforth, and Georgia van der Rohe (see n. 11). Dirk Lohan's interview is longer than any of these, more thorough, and more sustained.

    4. Dirk Lohan interview.

    5. Peter Carter, *Mies van der Rohe at Work* (New York, 1974).

    6. The history of Aachen, especially during the late nineteenth and early twentieth centuries, is briefly but instructively presented, in both text and picture, in Helmut A. Crous, *Aachen: so wie es war* (Düsseldorf, 1971) and *Aachen in alten Ansichtskarten*, foreword by Werner Dümmler (Frankfurt a.M., 1977).

    7. The family records are to be found in the Aachen Stadtarchiv.

    8. Dirk Lohan interview.

    9. Personal interview with Monsignor Erich Stephany, Aachen, 1982.

    10. Peter Blake interview with Mies van der Rohe (typescript), Columbia University Oral History Project, c. 1959. Mies: "As a young boy I went to the cathedral school in my home town. It was a Latin school, but I was not very good and my father decided I should do some practical work and for this reason sent me to a kind of vocational school." This passage was edited out of the interview "A Conversation with Mies" in *Four Great Makers of Modern Architecture* (New York, 1963), pp. 93–104.

    11. Personal interview with Georgia van der Rohe, New York, April 1982.

    12. Dirk Lohan interview.

    13. Information pertaining to the early relationship of Mies with his brother was drawn chiefly from personal interviews in 1981 and 1982 with Heinrich Maillard, proprietor of the Mies-Maillard Monument Co. in Aachen, successor to the Michael Mies workshop.

    14. Mies van der Rohe personal documents, Mies Archive.

    15. Excerpt from documentary film, *Mies van der Rohe*, directed by Georgia van der Rohe, sponsored by Knoll International and Zweites Deutsches Fernsehen, Mainz, and produced by IFAGE Filmproduktion, Wiesbaden; English version, 1979, German version, 1980.

    16. Probably Wilhelm Martens (c. 1843–1910), architect, student and son-in-law of Martin Gropius; see Thieme-Becker, *Allgemeines Lexikon der bildenden Künstler*, 24 (Leipzig, 1939): 150–51.

Chapter 2

    1. Dirk Lohan interview.

    2. On Bruno Paul, see Joseph Popp, *Bruno Paul* (Munich, 1921); Stanley Appelbaum, *Simplicissimus* (New York, 1975).

3. Dirk Lohan interview. Mies: Paul "knew I had experience; other than me he had only furniture people with him."

4. Neubabelsberg, a mostly residential community, was joined with the village of Nowawes in 1938 to comprise the town of Babelsberg, which in turn was annexed a year later by Potsdam.

5. On the Riehl House, see "Architekt Ludwig Mies: Villa des Herrn Geheime Regierungsrat Prof. Dr. Riehl in Neu-Babelsberg," *Moderne Bauformen* 9 (1910): 42–48; Anton Jaumann, "Vom künstlerischen Nachwuchs," *Innen-Dekoration* 21 (July 1910): 265–72.

6. The Westend House, built in Berlin, dates from 1906, the House of Dr. B., in Klein-Machnow, from 1907.

7. In 1984 the Riehl House was being used as the administrative headquarters of the Film and Television Institute of Potsdam. Prof. T. Paul Young, of the School of Architecture of Illinois Institute of Technology, who visited the house in 1984, reported that the *Halle* had been subdivided and the veranda closed in.

8. In the Lohan interview Mies said the trip lasted six weeks. Sandra Honey, in *The Early Work of Mies van der Rohe*, the catalog for an exhibition held at the Building Centre Trust, London, October 1979, writes: "Professor Riehl sent Mies to Italy for three months before allowing design work to proceed." It seems reasonable to interpret the Italian trip as a six-week bonus rather than a three-month preparatory lesson, since it is hard to imagine that Mies arrived in Berlin in 1905, worked in Rixdorf, served in the army, spent a year with Bruno Paul plus three months in Italy and only then began designing the Riehl House, which we know was completed before the end of 1907. A large exhibition of decorative and applied art was mounted in Munich in 1908. It featured several designs by Riemerschmid. This would seem to be the show Mies remembered. Its date prompts us to presume that his Italian trip followed rather than preceded the completion of the Riehl House.

9. Most likely the Springer House, Am Grossen Wannsee, 1901, the only villa Messel built in that community.

10. Carter, *Mies van der Rohe at Work*, p. 174.

11. Dirk Lohan interview.

12. On Peter Behrens, see Stanford Anderson, "Peter Behrens and the New Architecture of Germany, 1900–1917" (Ph.D. diss., Columbia University, 1968); Fritz Hoeber, *Peter Behrens* (Munich, 1913); Alan Windsor, *Peter Behrens, Architect and Designer* (New York, 1981).

13. Cited in Windsor, *Peter Behrens*, p. 15. Windsor attributes the statement to an appeal written by Koch in the May 1897 issue of *Deutsche Kunst und Dekoration*.

14. Cited in Windsor, *Peter Behrens*, pp. 35–36.

15. Max Osborn, "Die modernen Wohnräume im Warenhaus von A. Wertheim in Berlin," *Deutsche Kunst und Dekoration* 4 (March 1903): 263, 291–93.

16. On Karl Friedrich Schinkel, see Paul Rave and Margaret Kuhn, eds., *Schinkels Lebenswerk* (14 vols.; Berlin 1939–); Karl Friedrich Schinkel, *Sammlung architektonischer Entwürfe* (reprint, Berlin and Chicago, 1981); Staatliche Museen zu Berlin, *Karl Friedrich Schinkel: 1781–1841*, exhibition catalog (Berlin, 1980); Goerd Peschken, *Das architektonische Lehrbuch* (in Rave and Kuhn, eds.); Mario Zadow, *Karl Friedrich Schinkel* (Berlin, 1980); Philip Johnson, "Schinkel and Mies," *Writings* (New York, 1979).

17. Alois Riegl, *Spätrömische Kunstindustrie* (Vienna, 1901).

18. Stanford Anderson, "Behrens' Changing Concept," *Architectural Design* 39 (February 1969): 76.

19. On the AEG, see Anderson, "Peter Behrens and the New Architecture of Germany 1900–1917"; Tilmann Buddensieg with Henning Rogge, *Industriekultur: Peter Behrens and the AEG, 1907–1914* (Cambridge, Mass., 1984).

20. On the Deutscher Werkbund, see Lucius Burckhardt, ed., *The Werkbund: History and Ideology, 1907–1933* (Woodbury, N.Y., 1980); Joan Campbell, *The German Werkbund: The Politics of Reform in the Applied Arts* (Princeton, N.J., 1978).

21. Theodor Heuss, *Hitlers Weg*, 8th rev. ed. (Stuttgart, 1932), pp. 23–24.

22. Iain Boyd Whyte, *Bruno Taut and the Architecture of Activism* (Cambridge, 1981).

23. Ibid., p. 12.

24. Mies van der Rohe in conversation with Horst Eifler and Ulrich Conrads, recorded by RIAS, Berlin, October 1964, and published on phonograph record, "Mies in Berlin," Bauwelt Archiv I (Berlin, 1966).

25. On Walter Gropius, see James Marston Fitch, *Walter Gropius* (New York, 1960); Reginald R. Isaacs, *Walter Gropius, der Mensch und sein Werk* (2 vols.; Berlin, 1983–84).

26. Dirk Lohan interview.

27. Windsor, *Peter Behrens*, p. 115.

28. Jaumann, "Vom künstlerischen Nachwuchs," p. 266.

29. Salomon van Deventer, letter to Helene Kröller-Müller, 29 August 1911, quoted in a letter of 10 August 1975 from van Deventer's widow Mary to Ludwig Glaeser, curator of the Mies van der Rohe Archive, Museum of Modern Art, New York.

30. Mies van der Rohe, letter to Adalbert Colsman, Langenberg, West Germany. Mies writes "I don't know whether I wrote you that I was with Karl-Ernst Osthaus and Heinrich Vogler on a 1910 visit to the Deutsche Gartenstadt exhibition in London."

31. Dirk Lohan interview.

32. Anderson, "Peter Behrens and the New Architecture of Germany, 1900–1917," pp. 343–44.

33. Ibid., p. 403 n.

34. Peschken, *Das architektonische Lehrbuch*, p. 35.

35. Quoted in Winfried Nerdinger, *Richard Riemerschmid, vom Jugendstil zum Werkbund, Werke und Dokumente* (Munich, 1982), p. 413.

36. On the Bismarck monument and Mies's project, see *Hundert Entwürfe aus dem Wettbewerb für das Bismarck-National-Denkmal auf der Elisenhöhe bei Bingerbrück-Bingen* (Düsseldorf, 1911); Wolfgang Frieg, "Ludwig Mies van der Rohe, Das europäische Werk (1907–1937)," (Ph.D. diss., Rheinische Friedrich-Wilhelms Universität, Bonn, 1976). See also Nerdinger, *Richard Riemerschmid*, p. 413.

37. Schloss Orianda, while never executed, was published in Schinkel, *Werke der höheren Baukunst* (Potsdam, 1848–50), and in that form would have been available to Mies at the time he was working on the Bismarck monument.

38. On the Wiegand House, see Wolfram Hoepfner and Fritz Neumeyer, *Das Haus Wiegand von Peter Behrens in Berlin-Dahlem* (Mainz, 1979).

39. Hugo Perls, *Warum ist Camilla schön?* (Munich, 1962).

40. Ibid.

41. According to Dietrich von Beulwitz, who supervised the renovation of the Perls House in 1977, it was subjected to substantial alteration in the post-World War II years. By 1950 the owner, a physicist named Bruno Lange, had had a pergola constructed which connected the Perls House to another building located to the northwest. Interior changes were also made, including

those commissioned by a society of anthroposophists who now own the house and use it as a school for retarded children. The anthroposophists, whose philosophy disdains the use of the 90-degree angle, placed diagonal "bridges" in several of the corners of the rooms on the ground floor and upstairs. Personal conversation with von Beulwitz, June 1982.

42. Mies later recalled: "When we built this house I intended to make the dining room like a fine Schinkel room. One day [Perls] just ordered [the mural] from Pechstein, the expressionist painter. He said to him 'why don't you paint these ceilings?' Pechstein . . . put his canvas around and started painting in no time. In a few days he had the whole room painted, with trees and landscapes and nudes, . . ."; from the unedited interview with Peter Blake, published in edited form in *Four Great Makers of Modern Architecture* (New York, 1963).

43. On the imperial embassy, see Tilmann Buddensieg, "Die kaiserliche deutsche Botschaft in Petersburg von Peter Behrens," *Politische Architectur in Europa*, ed. Martin Warnke (Cologne, 1984), pp. 374–97. Mies's sketch of the foyer appears on p. 393.

44. Helene Kröller-Müller, letter to H. P. Bremmer, 28 June 1910, quoted in Salomon van Deventer, *Aus Liebe zur Kunst* (Cologne, 1958), p. 51.

45. On Behrens's project for the Kröllers, see Fritz Hoeber, *Peter Behrens*.

46. At least it appears thus in the main perspective drawing. Other drawings of parts of the project do not show the connecting piece as higher, suggesting differences in the planning stages.

47. Helene Kröller-Müller, letter to Salomon van Deventer, 18 March 1911, quoted in van Deventer, *Aus Liebe zur Kunst*, p. 55.

48. Personal conversation with Tilmann Buddensieg, 1983. Anderson, in "Peter Behrens and the New Architecture of Germany, 1900–1917," p. 390 n., quotes Walter Gropius, who called Krämer "a right-hand man" in Behrens's studio.

49. Eifler-Conrads interview.

50. Ibid.

51. Even the instructional brochure on the Kröller-Müller Museum published by the museum itself (Otterlo, 1969) misidentified a photograph (p. 9) of the model of Mies's villa as that of Behrens.

52. This drawing, which Mies gave to his former Bauhaus student, the late Howard Dearstyne, is in the possession of Dearstyne's sister-in-law.

53. Meier-Graefe's letter is in the Mies Archive.

54. In a footnote to an article by Hugo Weber, "Mies van der Rohe in Chicago," *Bauen und Wohnen*, December 1950, p. 1, Mies is said to have visited the home of the critic Wilhelm von Uhde in Paris, and there to have seen cubist paintings for the first time.

55. Van Deventer, *Aus Liebe zur Kunst*, p. 70.

56. Helene Kröller-Müller, letter to A. G. Kröller, January 1913, quoted in van Deventer, *Aus Liebe zur Kunst*, p. 71.

57. *Kröller-Müller Museum* (Haarlem, 1981), p. 21.

58. Mies van der Rohe, letter to Helene Kröller-Müller, 2 April 1913, Archives of Kröller-Müller Museum, Otterlo. A question persists as to Mies's relationship with Mrs. Kröller-Müller. Was there a romantic attachment between them, or at least an attraction on his part? The suspicion is aroused, though hardly settled, by a letter written on 29 August 1911, by Salomon van Deventer to Mrs. Kröller-Müller. Greatly impressed by Mies in his first meeting with him, van Deventer tries to persuade Mrs. Kröller-Müller to trust Mies in the latter's ongoing conflict with Behrens's other assistant Jean Krämer (see note 48). Before he makes the case for Mies, however, he writes: "I

sensed from his words his great devotion to you and his wide-ranging perceptiveness; yet although the two of us in a few short hours developed a closeness that seemed like an old friendship, and while everything he said reminded me of you, I somehow felt compelled to keep him at a distance from you. This was small of me, and just because it was small, I called to the heavens for help [presumably to be objective in his judgment of Mies as an architect] and I now want to write the following." The following was van Deventer's argument in Mies's professional behalf. This passage is quoted in Mary van Deventer's letter of 10 August 1975 to Ludwig Glaeser, curator of the Mies Archive.

59. Eifler-Conrads interview.

60. On H. P. Berlage, see Manfred Bock, *Anfänge einer neuen Architektur: Berlages Beitrage zur architektonischen Kultur der Niederlande im ausgehenden 19. Jahrhundert* (The Hague and Wiesbaden, 1983); Pieter Singelenberg, *H. P. Berlage: Idea and Style—The Quest for Modern Architecture* (Utrecht, 1972); see also Hendrik Berlage, *Grundlagen und Entwicklung der Architektur* (Berlin, 1908) and *Gedanken über Stil* (Leipzig, 1905). Mies could have known these books, which were written in German. Berlage often lectured in German.

61. Berlage, *Grundlagen und Entwicklung der Architektur*, quoted by Reyner Banham, *Theory and Design in the First Machine Age* (Cambridge, Mass., 1980), p. 143.

62. Quoted by Berlage in *Grundlagen und Entwicklung der Architektur*, quoted in turn by Banham, *Theory and Design*, p. 143.

63. See Mies's letter of 31 January 1938 to Carl O. Schniewind, quoted p. 214.

64. Saint Augustine, *The City of God*.

65. Mies van der Rohe, an appreciation written in 1940 for the unpublished catalog of the Frank Lloyd Wright exhibition held at the Museum of Modern Art, New York; Mies Archive.

66. Eifler-Conrads interview.

67. Ludwig Glaeser interview with Mary Wigman, Berlin, 13 September 1972, Mies Archive.

68. Mies's associate architect on the Werner House is listed as F. Goebbels. He is probably identical with the architect whose name appears on some of the drawings of the Perls House, and he may be the same Goebbels for whom Mies worked earlier in Aachen.

69. Personal recollection of Dirk Lohan, who accompanied Mies on the visit.

70. Renate Werner, letter to Ille Sipman of the Building Centre Trust, London, spring, 1979.

71. In his Chicago office Mies kept a list of his buildings and projects, one of which was titled House on the Heerstrasse, Berlin, and dated 1913. Confirming evidence of such a work has never been found. On the other hand, he neglected to include on his list a number of buildings demonstrably by his hand, including the Werner House. That he attributed the Heerstrasse House to himself while ignoring several others lends a measure of authenticity to his claim.

72. Glaeser interview with Wigman.

73. Ada's notebooks are in the possession of her daughter Marianne Lohan of Herrsching/Ammersee, West Germany.

74. Renate Petras, "Drei Arbeiten von Mies van der Rohe in Potsdam-Babelsberg," *Deutsche Architektur* (Berlin, D.D.R., February 1974).

75. Mies's associate architect in the Urbig commission was Werner von Walthausen. The Urbig House was used as a temporary residence by Prime

Minister Winston Churchill on the occasion of the Potsdam Conference in 1945. It is now the guest house of a law school in Potsdam. Since, like the Riehl House and the Mosler House (see p. 000), it is an official government building of the German Democratic Republic, it is not easily visited and its present condition is not known (the Mosler House is now a children's clinic).

76. Personal communication from Manfred Lehmbruck, 12 January 1983.

77. Julius Posener, letter to the author, 1 December 1982, in which he attributes this account to the architect Bodo Rasch, of Stuttgart, who knew Mies in the 1920s.

78. Mies's hope that Ada would present him with a boy led to his odd habit of calling his first two daughters by masculine nicknames: "*der* Muck" and "*der* Fritz." Later, after Waltraut had arrived, he was content with the diminutive of her baptismal name: "Traudl."

Chapter 3

1. Personal conversation with Sergius Ruegenberg, Berlin, 23 June 1982. Ruegenberg relates that Mies ordered him to burn "large portions" of his files in 1924.

2. Wilhelm Lehmbruck, "Who Is Still Here?" quoted in Reinhold Heller, *The Art of Wilhelm Lehmbruck* (Washington, D.C., 1972).

3. On Bruno Taut, see Iain Boyd Whyte, *Bruno Taut and the Architecture of Activism* (Cambridge, 1982); Rosemarie Haag Bletter, "The Interpretation of the Glass Dream—Expressionist Architecture and the History of the Crystal Metaphor," *Journal of the Society of Architectural Historians* 40 (March 1981): 20–43; idem, "Global Earthworks," *Art Journal* 42 (Fall 1982): 222–25.

4. Bruno Taut, *Die Stadtkrone* (Jena, 1919), p. 69; quoted in Whyte, *Bruno Taut*, p. 78.

5. Walter Gropius, *Program of the Staatliche Bauhaus* (Weimar, 1919).

6. Quoted in Werner Haftmann, *Painting in the Twentieth Century* (New York, 1965), p. 222.

7. On *Die neue Sachlichkeit*, see John Willett, *Art and Politics in the Weimar Period* (New York, 1978); *Neue Sachlichkeit and German Realism of the Twenties*, exhibition catalog (London, 1978–79).

8. Hans Richter, letter to Raoul Hausmann, 16 February 1964, quoted in Hausmann's letter to the editor, "More on Group G," *Art Journal* 24 (Summer 1965): 350–52.

9. Theo van Doesburg, "Der Wille zum Stil, Neugestaltung von Leben, Kunst und Technik," *De Stijl* 5 (February 1922): 23–32, and (March 1922): 33–41.

10. Alexander Rodchenko, "Slogans," composed in 1921, quoted in German Karginov, *Rodchenko* (London, 1979), pp. 90–91.

11. Theo van Doesburg, writing in the Foundation Manifesto of the Constructivist International, 1922, quoted in Reyner Banham, *Theory and Design in the First Machine Age* (Cambridge, Mass., 1980), p. 187.

12. Theo van Doesburg, "First Manifesto of 'De Stijl,' 1918," *De Stijl* 2 (November 1918).

13. Mies van der Rohe, "Baukunst und Zeitwille," *Der Querschnitt* 4 (1924): 31–32.

14. Arthur Drexler, lecture at the Arts Club of Chicago, 20 September 1982, marking the opening of the exhibition, Mies van der Rohe: Interior Spaces.

15. Most of Mies's private library is kept in the Rare Book Room of the Library of the University of Illinois, Chicago. Mies's grandson Dirk Lohan and his daughter Georgia van der Rohe retain a number of titles in their private possession.

16. On Oswald Spengler, see H. S. Hughes, *Oswald Spengler: A Critical Estimate* (New York, 1952).

17. Oswald Spengler, *The Decline of the West,* abridged edition by Helmut Werner (New York, 1962), p. 31; from Edwin Franden Dakin, *Today and Destiny: Vital Excerpts from The Decline of the West by Oswald Spengler* (New York, 1940), p. 129; and Spengler, *The Decline of the West,* p. 32.

18. Mies, "Bürohaus," *G* 3 (June 1923).

19. Mies, "Die neue Zeit: Schlussworte des Referats Mies van der Rohe auf der Wiener Tagung des Deutschen Werkbundes," *Die Form* 5 (1 August 1930): 406.

20. Mies, interview by Peter Carter in "Mies," *Twentieth Century,* Spring 1964, p. 139.

21. Cited in Bruno Möhring, "Über die Vorzüge der Turmhäuser und die Voraussetzungen, unter denen sie in Berlin gebaut werden können," lecture to the Preussische Akademie des Bauwesens, 22 December 1920 (published in Berlin, 1921), p. 6.

22. Hermann Paulsen, *Preisausschreiben für ein Hochhaus Friedrichstrasse, Berlin* (Berlin, 1922), p. 9.

23. Adolf Behne, "Der Wettbewerb der Turmhaus-Gesellschaft," *Wasmuths Monatshefte für Baukunst* 7 (1922/23): 58–67.

24. Max Berg, "Hochhäuser im Stadtbild," *Wasmuths Monatshefte für Baukunst* 6 (1921/22): 101–20.

25. Ibid.

26. Mies van der Rohe, "Hochhaus Projekt für Bahnhof Friedrichstrasse in Berlin," *Frühlicht* 1 (Summer 1922): 122–24.

27. Mies's personal library contains a copy of *Die Verteidigung des Sokrates Kriton* (Leipzig, 1911). That publication date leads me to suspect Mies owned the work as early as the time of his Glass Skyscraper design.

28. One of the earliest notices, if not the very earliest, of Mies outside Germany was taken in the United States. In the September 1923 issue of the *Journal of the American Institute of Architects,* Walter Curt Behrendt, a German critic and a vigorous champion of the New Architecture in Europe, published "Skyscrapers in Germany" (pp. 365–70), in which he praised several of the Friedrichstrasse Office Building competition entries. Among these was Mies's Honeycomb, of which he said—in words that recall Mies's own in *Frühlicht*—"the peculiarity of the purpose and the properties of the materials have dictated the law according to which the form has been developed." In a reply published in the same issue (p. 370) George C. Nimmons, F.A.I.A., took a less favorable view of the plan of Mies's Glass Skyscraper: "The plan . . . is so fantastic and impractical and so impossible to divide into any kind of usable or desirable offices or apartments that it is not likely that it would ever be executed."

29. On the Novembergruppe, see Helga Kliemann, *Die Novembergruppe* (Berlin, 1967).
According to Erna Segal, widow of Arthur Segal, a member of the Novembergruppe in the early 1920s, the group was fond of a phrase coined by one of their number, "Von der Mies bis an den Rohe," which was a pun on a well-known line in the German national anthem "Deutschland über Alles": "Von der Maas bis an die Memel" (from the Maas to the Memel); Anna Wanger, undated letter to Mies, Library of Congress.

30. Ilya Ehrenburg, El Lissitzky, and László Moholy-Nagy, quoted in Willett, *Art and Politics in the Weimar Period,* p. 75.

31. On *G*, see Werner Graeff, "Concerning the So-Called G Group," *Art Journal* 23 (Summer 1964): 280–82, and Raoul Hausmann, letter to the editor, "More on Group G," *Art Journal* 24 (Summer 1965): 350–52.

32. Hans Richter, letter to Hausmann, 16 February 1964, quoted by Hausmann in "More on Group G."

33. Werner Graeff, "Concerning the So-Called *G* Group."

34. Peter Carter, *Mies van der Rohe at Work* (New York, 1972), p. 18.

35. Peter Behrens, letter in response to general inquiry offered by the *Berliner Morgenpost*, 27 November 1912, on the issue of the development of the inner city of Berlin; published in Fritz Hoeber, *Peter Behrens* (Munich, 1913), pp. 227–28.

36. Eifler-Conrads interview.

37. Peter Collins, *Changing Ideas in Modern Architecture, 1750–1950* (Montreal, 1965), pp. 42–43.

38. For an extended discussion of the Concrete Country House and the Brick Country House, see Wolf Tegethoff, *Die Villen und Landhausprojekte von Mies van der Rohe* (Essen, 1981), 1:15–51.

39. On El Lissitzky, see Alan Birnholz, "El Lissitzky" (Ph.D. diss., Yale University, 1973).

40. Mies van der Rohe, "Bauen," *G* 2 (September 1923): 1.

41. Tegethoff, *Die Villen und Landhausprojekte*, 1:21.

42. Ibid., 1:32–33.

43. Ibid., pp. 48–50.

44. Oswald Spengler, *Der Untergang des Abendlandes* (Munich, 1918), 1:331.

45. On Theo van Doesburg, see Joost Baljeu, *Theo van Doesburg* (New York, 1974); *De Stijl: 1917–1931—Visions of Utopia*, Introduction by Hans L. K. Jaffé, exhibition catalog (New York, 1982).

46. Mies van der Rohe, letter to Theo van Doesburg, 27 August 1923, Library of Congress.

47. These included models of the Glass Skyscraper and the Concrete Office Building as well as a drawing of the Concrete Country House. See correspondence between Mies and Gropius, 4–15 June 1923, Library of Congress.

48. Theo van Doesburg, "Von der neuen Aesthetik zur materiellen Verwirklichung," *De Stijl* 6 (March 1923): 10–14.

49. Mies van der Rohe, "Bürohaus," *G* 3 (June 1923).

50. On Mies's associations and writings in the 1920s, see David A. Spaeth, *Ludwig Mies van der Rohe: An Annotated Bibliography and Chronology* (New York, 1979).

51. Press release from the Zwölferring, 26 April 1924, Mies Archive.

52. Mies, letter to Friedrich Kiesler, 22 March 1924, Mies Archive.

53. Paul Henning, public lecture sponsored by Deutscher Werkbund, 19 June 1924, Mies Archive.

54. Paul Westheim, "Mies van der Rohe: Entwicklung eines Architekten," *Das Kunstblatt* 11 (February 1927): 55.

It has also been conjectured that "Haus K." was a design meant for the Kiepenheuers, a family that owned a well-known publishing house in Berlin in the 1910s and 1920s. In organizing Mies's 1947 retrospective exhibition at the Museum of Modern Art, Philip Johnson wrote Mies (23 June 1947, Mies Archive) asking him if "Haus K." was indeed the Kiepenheuer house. There is no record of any answer from Mies.

55. In 1984, Professor Fritz Neumeyer discovered drawings of the Feldmann House in the files of the Berlin Baupolizei and of the Kempner House in the Landesarchiv Berlin.

56. Mies, "Baukunst und Zeitwille," *Der Querschnitt* 4 (1924): 31–32.

57. The Dexel matter is discussed at length in Tegethoff, *Die Villen und Landhausprojekte* 1:52–55.

58. Ibid., pp. 58–59.

59. Gesellschaft der Freunde des neuen Russlands, letter to Mies van der Rohe, 12 January 1926, Library of Congress.

60. Mies, letter to Donald D. Egbert, 5 February 1951, copy owned by George E. Danforth.

According to Perls in *Warum ist Camilla schön?* he sold his house to Fuchs in a quite extraordinary transaction. Fuchs, an avid collector of Daumier, had offered the painter Max Liebermann a dozen fine Daumier prints in exchange for one of Liebermann's oils. Liebermann agreed to the deal, not once, in fact, but a number of times over, until Fuchs had traded hundreds of Daumiers for a total of fifteen Liebermann paintings. Fuchs then offered five of the Liebermanns to Perls in exchange for the house Mies had designed in 1910. Perls accepted.

To this anecdote Dirk Lohan adds a recollection of Mies himself: when Fuchs commissioned the Mies addition to the house, completed in 1928, he directed the architect to equip a room in the basement with a secret exit. In that room Fuchs kept a suitcase packed so as to make a hasty retreat in the event he might come under siege by right-wing elements. As matters developed, Fuchs was indeed required to leave Germany quickly in 1936, when the Nazis sought him out.

"The Nazis," writes Perls in *Warum ist Camilla schön?* "emptied his house. They needed several lorries to take away the 20,000 copper engravings, the 10,000 books and hundreds of paintings and sculptures and store them for the Reich of the Grand Illusion."

61. Wilhelm Pieck, speech before the German Communist party, Berlin, 17 July 1925.

62. Mies, letter to Donald D. Egbert, 5 February 1951. Literally speaking, Mies was wrong in supposing that Liebknecht and Luxemburg were "shot in front of a wall." Following their arrest in the Spartacist revolt, they were murdered en route to prison.

63. Rolf-Peter Baacke and Michael Nungesser, "Ich bin, ich war, ich werde sein," in *Wem gehört die Welt?* exhibition catalog (Berlin, 1977), pp. 280–98.

64. Hugo Perls, *Warum ist Camilla schön?*

65. This motto, taken from a poem by Ferdinand Freiligrath, "Die Revolution" (1851), was quoted by Luxemburg in her last article for the Communist periodical *Rote Fahne*. Another dedicatory inscription, "Den toten Helden der Revolution" (to the fallen heroes of the Revolution), appears with the aforementioned motto on one of Mies's early drawings for the monument. Other photographs taken as early as 1931 show no inscriptions.

66. According to Dirk Lohan, Mies recalled that at the unveiling, oil in an urn set atop the monument was ignited to produce an appropriately ceremonial fire. Instead, the combustion only gave off an enormous quantity of smoke and soot, which settled over the audience. Mies and his friends then repaired to a local tavern, where they were denied entrance by the owner, who took exception to their blackened appearance

67. Perls, *Warum ist Camilla schön?*

68. Hans Prinzhorn, letter to Mies van der Rohe, 15 June 1925, Library of Congress.

69. Walter Gropius, letter to Mies van der Rohe, 11 December 1925, Library of Congress.

70. Mies van der Rohe, letter to Walter Gropius, 14 December 1925, Library of Congress.

71. Mies van der Rohe, letter to G. W. Farenholtz, 7 December 1925, Library of Congress.

Chapter 4

1. Peter Bruckmann, statement to directors of the Deutscher Werkbund, 30 March 1925, Redslob Archive, German Federal Archive, Koblenz.

2. Mies van der Rohe, "Industrielles Bauen," *G* 3 (10 June 1924).

3. Gustav Stotz, letter to Mies van der Rohe, 24 September 1925, Mies Archive.

4. Mies van der Rohe, letter to Stotz, 26 September 1925, Mies Archive.

5. Mies van der Rohe, letter to Stotz, 11 September 1925, Mies Archive.

6. Both articles were published the same day, 5 May 1926, Bonatz's in the *Schwäbische Chronik*, Stuttgart, Schmitthenner's in the *Süddeutsche Zeitung*, Munich.

7. Richard Döcker, letter to Mies van der Rohe, 18 May 1926, Mies Archive.

8. Mies van der Rohe, letter to Döcker, 27 May 1926, Mies Archive.

9. Personal conversation with Mia Seeger, 5 July 1982, Stuttgart.

10. Mies van der Rohe, letter to Le Corbusier, 5 October 1926, Mies Archive.

11. Max Taut, letter to Richard Döcker, 9 February 1927, Mies Archive.

12. On the Weissenhofsiedlung, see Jürgen Joedicke and Christian Plath, *Die Weissenhofsiedlung, Stuttgart* (Stuttgart, 1977); Julius Posener, "Weissenhof und danach," *Baumeister* 6 (June 1981): 596–607.

13. Personal conversation with Sergius Ruegenberg, 23 June 1982.

14. Mies van der Rohe, *1. Sonderheft zur Werkbund Ausstellung, Die Wohnung, Stuttgart,* 1927.

15. Mies van der Rohe, unpublished statement, 10 March 1927, typescript, Mies Archive.

16. Lilly Reich, letter to Mies van der Rohe, 10 June 1925, Mies Archive.

17. In Christopher Wilk, *Marcel Breuer: Furniture and Interiors* (New York, 1981), the author writes: "According to Breuer, a further chapter should be added to the history of the cantilevered chair. By his account, he had been working on the idea of a cantilevered chair during 1926 and continued to construct his chair because he was unable to work with tubular steel of a proper diameter . . . Breuer calculated that he would need tubing of twenty-five millimeters in order to support the weight of a person in a chair that had only two legs." Wilk adds, "In 1927, or perhaps as late as early 1928, Breuer designed his first cantilevered side chair, which was marketed by Thonet in early 1929 as model B33."

18. See Konrad Nonn, "Zusammenfassendes über das Bauhaus," *Zentralblatt der Bauverwaltung* 47 (1927): 105; also Emil Högg, speech made to National Congress of German Architects and Engineers, in 1926, published in *Deutsche Bauzeitung* 60 (1926): 653–56, 658–64.

19. Wolf Tegethoff, *Die Villen und Landhausprojekte von Mies van der Rohe* (Essen, 1981) 1:61.

20. Mies, interviewed by H. T. Cadbury-Brown, "Ludwig Mies van der Rohe: My Address of Appreciation," *Architectural Association Journal* 75 (July 1959): 26–46.

21. Curt Gravenkamp, "Mies van der Rohe: Glashaus in Berlin (Projekt Adam, 1928)," *Das Kunstblatt*, April 1930, pp. 111–12.

22. Mies, letter to S. Adam Co., Berlin, 2 July 1928, Mies Archive.

23. Ludwig Hilberseimer, *Grossstadtarchitektur*, 2d ed. (Stuttgart, 1978).

24. Ludwig Hilberseimer, reply to Martin Wagner, "Das Formproblem eines Weltstadtplatzes," *Das neue Berlin*, February 1929, pp. 39–40.

25. For an extended discussion of the Barcelona Pavilion, see Tegethoff, *Die Villen und Landhausprojekte*, pp. 69–89.

26. Quoted by L.S.M. (Lilly von Schnitzler), "Die Weltausstellung Barcelona 1929," *Der Querschnitt* 9 (August 1929): 583.

27. Walther Genzmer, "Der deutsche Reichspavillon auf der internationalen Ausstellung Barcelona," *Die Baugilde* 11 (25 October 1929): 1654–57.

28. Although in the early stages of planning Mies's sketches indicated a reclining sculpture for the small pool, suggesting a preference for a figure by Maillol or Lehmbruck, his choice of the Kolbe piece seems voluntary rather than forced by circumstance. As Ludwig Glaeser notes, "Although Mies preferred reclining statues, he ultimately chose a standing figure for the designated place in one corner of the small pool, probably because all principal views were framed vertically"; Ludwig Glaeser, "Mies van der Rohe, the Barcelona Pavilion" (New York, 1979).

29. Frank Lloyd Wright, letter to Philip Johnson, 26 February 1932. Archives of the Department of Architecture and Design, Museum of Modern Art.

30. Ludwig Glaeser, *Ludwig Mies van der Rohe: Furniture and Furniture Drawings from the Drawing Collection and the Mies van der Rohe Archive* (New York, 1979), p. 11.

31. Grete Tugendhat, public lecture, delivered on the occasion of a retrospective exhibition of Mies's work, Brno, January 1969.

32. On the Tugendhat House, see Tegethoff, *Die Villen und Landhausprojekte*, pp. 90–98.

33. Ludwig Glaeser, *Ludwig Mies van der Rohe: Furniture and Furniture Drawings*, p. 10.

34. Reported by Julius Posener, personal conversation, 24 June 1982.

35. B. (Justus Bier), "Kann man im Haus Tugendhat wohnen?" *Die Form* 6 (15 October 1931): 392–93.

36. Grete Tugendhat, "Die Bewohner des Hauses Tugendhat äussern sich," *Die Form* 6 (15 November 1931): 437–38.

37. Fritz Tugendhat, ibid.

Mies reported his early relationship with the Tugendhats in terms less harmonious than those invoked in their own recollections. He acknowledged that Mr. Tugendhat had liked the Perls House: "He expected something similar. He came to me and talked with me. I went there and saw the situation. I designed the house. I remember that it was on Christmas Eve when he saw the design of the house. He nearly died! But his wife was interested in art; she had some of Van Gogh's pictures. She said, 'Let us think it over.' Tugendhat could have thrown her out.

"However, on New Year's Eve he came to me and told me that he had thought it over and I should go ahead with the house. We had some trouble about it at the time, but we can take that for granted. He said that he did not like this open space; it would be too disturbing; people would be there when he was in the library with his great thoughts. He was a real businessman, I think. I said, 'Oh, all right. We will try it out and, if you do not want it, we can close the rooms in. We can put wooden scaffold pieces up.' He was listening in his library and we were talking just normally. He did not hear anything. Later he said to me, 'Now I give in on everything, but not about the furniture.' I said, 'This is too bad.' I decided to send furniture to Brno from Berlin. I said to my superintendent, 'You keep the furniture and shortly before lunch call him out and say that you are at his house with furniture. He will be furious, but you must expect that.' He said, 'Take it out,' before he saw it. However, after lunch he liked it." Mies, in *Architectural Association Journal* 75 (July 1959): 26–46.

38. Bier, "Kann man im Haus Tugendhat wohnen?"

39. Grete Tugendhat, "Die Bewohner des Hauses Tugendhat äussern sich."

40. Mies, "Die neue Zeit: Schlussworte des Referats Mies van der Rohe auf der Wiener Tagung des Deutschen Werkbundes," *Die Form* 5 (1 August 1930): 406.

41. Mies, "Hochhaus Projekt für Bahnhof Friedrichstrasse in Berlin," *Frühlicht* 1 (Summer 1922): 122–24.

42. Mies, "Bürohaus," *G* 3 (June 1923).

43. Friedrich Hirz, who became Mies's assistant in 1928 at the time of the Barcelona commission, reported in a personal conversation of 28 June 1982 that Mies "read a lot of Saint Thomas Aquinas" during the time Hirz worked for him.

44. Saint Thomas Aquinas, *Summa Theologica*, translated by the fathers of the English Dominican Province, rev. by Daniel J. Sullivan (Chicago, 1952).

45. Personal conversation, Dirk Lohan, 15 March 1985.

46. Quoted in Peter Blake, *The Master Builders* (New York, 1976), p. 270.

Chapter 5

1. On the Bauhaus, see Hans Maria Wingler, *The Bauhaus: Weimar, Dessau, Berlin, Chicago* (Cambridge, Mass., 1968); Marcel Franciscono, *Walter Gropius and the Creation of the Bauhaus in Weimar* (Urbana, 1971); and Frank Whitford, *Bauhaus* (London, 1984).

2. Whitford, *Bauhaus*, p. 185.

3. Sandra Honey, "Mies at the Bauhaus," *Architectural Association Quarterly* 10, 1 (1978): 53.

4. Personal conversation with Selman Selmanagic, 28 May 1981.

5. Honey, "Mies at the Bauhaus."

6. Howard Dearstyne, "Mies at the Bauhaus in Dessau: Student Revolt and Nazi Coercion," *Inland Architect* 13 (August–September 1969): 14–17.

7. Honey, "Mies at the Bauhaus," pp. 54–55.

8. Georg Muche, "Bauhaus Epitaph," *Bauhaus and Bauhaus People*, ed. Eckhard Neumann (New York, 1970), pp. 202–4.

9. Eifler-Conrads interview.
The rivalry between Mies and Gropius relaxed as both men grew into old age, though the basic difference in their philosophies of teaching and designing was never resolved. Gropius was a devoted advocate of teamwork, both at the Bauhaus and in his American practice, while Mies remained a steadfast authoritarian. One day while visiting with Mies in the home of the Chicago realtor Robert H. McCormick, Gropius was holding forth on the advantages of collaboration in the creation of a building. "But Gropius," Mies inquired, "If you decide to have a baby, do you call in the neighbors?" Personal conversation with Ross J. Beatty, Jr., 18 June 1984.

10. Emil Nolde, letter to Mies, 10 April 1929, Mies Archive.

11. This observation is borne out by a comparison of the titles given their respective projects by the architects who participated in the Neue Wache competition. Heinrich Tessenow won first prize for "1914–18," while Peter Behrens and K. Belling called their project by alternate names: "Hindenburg" and "Ich hat' einen Kameraden." Hans Poelzig submitted "Soldiers' Tomb." Mies's title was strikingly neutral: "Raum" (space).

12. Hirz, letter to Ludwig Glaeser, 23 June 1976.

13. Conversation between Johnson, Arthur Drexler, and Ludwig Glaeser, December 1977, unedited transcript; edited transcript published in Philip Johnson, *Mies van der Rohe*, 3d ed. (New York, 1978).

14. Ibid.

15. Johnson, letter to Mrs. John D. Rockefeller, Jr., 27 March 1931, Archives, Department of Architecture and Design, Museum of Modern Art.

16. Johnson, letter to Alfred H. Barr, 11 July 1931, Archives, Department of Architecture and Design, Museum of Modern Art.

17. Johnson, letter to Barr, July 1931, Archives, Department of Architecture and Design, Museum of Modern Art.

18. Ibid.

19. Johnson, letter to Barr, 7 August 1931, Archives, Department of Architecture and Design, Museum of Modern Art.

20. Johnson, undated memo, Archives, Department of Architecture and Design, Museum of Modern Art.

21. For an extended discussion of the Berlin Building Exposition House, see Tegethoff, *Die Villen und Landhausprojekte*, pp. 110–13.

22. Johnson, "The Berlin Building Exposition of 1931," *T-Square*, January 1932; Henry-Russell Hitchcock, "Architecture Chronicle," *Hound and Horn*, October–December 1931.

23. Quoted in Russell Lynes, *Good Old Modern* (New York, 1973), p. 189.

24. Henry-Russell Hitchcock and Philip Johnson, *The International Style* (New York, 1932).

25. Hitchcock, Foreword to the 1966 edition of *The International Style*.

26. Personal conversation with Selman Selmanagic, 28 May 1981.

27. Honey, "Mies at the Bauhaus," p. 58.

28. Mies, "Die neue Zeit: Schlussworte des Referats Mies van der Rohe auf der Wiener Tagung des Deutschen Werkbundes," *Die Form* 5 (1 August 1930): 406.

29. Honey, "Mies at the Bauhaus," p. 58.

30. Wingler, *The Bauhaus: Weimar, Dessau, Berlin, Chicago*, p. 187.

31. Mies, letter to the Office of State Secret Police for the attention of Ministerialrat Diels, 20 July 1933, quoted by Wingler, *The Bauhaus*, p. 188.

32. State Secret Police, letter signed Dr. Peche, to Mies, 21 July 1933, quoted in Wingler, *The Bauhaus*, p. 189.

33. Honey, "Mies at the Bauhaus," p. 58.

34. Barbara Miller Lane, *Architecture and Politics in Germany, 1918–1945* (Cambridge, Mass., 1968), p. 204.

35. This house was built for Alois Severain, brother of Gerhard (see p. 158); letter, Albert Röck, Stuttgart, to Klaus Jürgen Sembach of Die neue Sammlung, Munich, 4 April 1970, Mies Archive.

36. For an extended discussion of the Gericke House, see Tegethoff, *Die Villen und Landhausprojekte*, pp. 114–19.

37. For an extended discussion of the court houses as a type, see Tegethoff, *Die Villen und Landhausprojekte*, pp. 124–25.

38. Some preliminary sketches of the Gericke and the Lemke houses show enclosed courts.

39. Mies, "Haus H., Magdeburg," *Die Schildgenossen* 14 (1935): 514–15.

40. Lilly Reich, letter to J. J. P. Oud, 12 February 1936, copy in Mies Archive.

41. Ludwig Glaeser, *Ludwig Mies van der Rohe, Drawings in the Collection of the Museum of Modern Art* (New York, 1969), notes on Ulrich Lange House.

42. Johnson, "Architecture in the Third Reich," *Hound and Horn* 7 (October–December 1933): 137–39.

43. Lane, *Architecture and Politics in Germany*, 172–73.

44. Ibid., p. 176.

45. It is not certain precisely when Mies joined the Reichskulturkammer, but an invitation to a Berlin Philharmonic Orchestra concert of 15 November 1933, marking the ceremonial opening of the organization and a program for that concert are in his files; Library of Congress. As late as 8 November 1938,

that concert are in his files; Library of Congress. As late as 8 November 1938, by which time he had already emigrated to the U.S., a letter (signed Eckermann) was sent to his office in Berlin by the president of the Reichskammer der bildenden Künste, a division of the Reichskulturkammer, advising him that he was expected to add to his own proof of racial purity—previously provided—some proof of that of his wife; Library of Congress. The typescript of a public notice, dated 20 January 1939 and signed Hauswald states: "On January 19, 1939 I visited the Reichskammmer Blumeshof and confirmed that Herr Mies has been absent from Germany for a year and a half, for which period he was not required to pay his dues"; Library of Congress.

46. Lane, *Architecture and Politics in Germany,* p. 176.

47. Mathies, German General Commissioner of 1935 Brussels Worlds Fair, in a draft of the commission, accompanying a letter to Mies, 11 June 1934, Mies Archive.

48. Mies, "Concerning the Preliminary Draft of an Exposition Building for the 1935 Brussels Worlds Fair," Mies Archive.

49. Walter Gropius, letter to Eugen Hönig, president of the Reichskammer der bildenden Künste, 27 March 1934, Walter Gropius Archive, Cambridge, Mass.

50. "Hitlers Kulturrede: Deutsch sein heisst klar sein," *Völkischer Beobachter,* 6 September 1934.

51. Personal conversation with Sergius Ruegenberg, 23 June 1982.

52. In a personal conversation (summer 1982), Herbert Hirche recalled for me an occasion in the mid-1930s when Mies was looking out the window of his Am Karlsbad atelier into the street below, where a group of Nazis strode by. "Sie marschieren" (they are marching), said Mies, perceptibly depressed.

53. Personal conversations with Ruegenberg, Hirz, and Hirche, summer 1982.

54. Personal conversation with Hirche, 3 July 1982.

Chapter 6

1. John A. Holabird, letter to Mies, 20 March 1936, Mies Archive.

2. Ibid.

3. Mies, letter to Holabird, 20 April 1936, Mies Archive.

4. Mies, letter to Holabird, 4 May 1936, Mies Archive.

5. Holabird, letter to Mies, 11 May 1936, Mies Archive.

6. Willard E. Hotchkiss, letter to Mies, 12 May 1936, Mies Archive.

7. Mies, letter to Hotchkiss, undated, Mies Archive.

8. Hotchkiss, letter to Mies, 2 July 1936, Mies Archive.

9. Mies, letter to Barr, 14 July 1936, Mies Archive.

10. Barr, letter to Mies, 19 July 1936, Mies Archive.

11. Joseph Hudnut, letter to Mies, 21 July 1936, Mies Archive.

12. Hudnut, letter to Mies, 3 September 1936, Mies Archive.

13. Mies, letter to Hudnut, 15 September 1936, Mies Archive.

14. Hudnut, letter to Mies 26 October 1936, Mies Archive.

15. Michael van Beuren, excerpted from two letters to Mies, 21 October and 3 November 1936, Mies Archive.

16. Hudnut, letter to Mies, 16 November 1936, Mies Archive.

17. Johnson, interview with Drexler and Glaeser.

18. Mies, letter to Hotchkiss, 2 September 1936, Mies Archive.

19. In his autobiography, *Clemens Holzmeister, Architekt in der Zeitenwende* (Salzburg, Stuttgart, Zurich, 1976), p. 101, Holzmeister writes: "As one of my last assignments at the Academy prior to the *Anschluss,* I had to find a successor to Peter Behrens. I decided on Mies van der Rohe, then in

Berlin and already internationally renowned. Mies van der Rohe answered in a long letter, consenting in tone, on March 10, 1937. . . . But there followed the blow from the Third Reich, which reduced all our capabilities at the masters' schools." Dirk Lohan suspects that Mies wrote cordially to Vienna in order to let the record show that he was prepared to remain in a pan-German environment and was not interested in emigrating to America. Personal communication from Prof. Johannes Spalt, Vienna, 25 November 1982.

20. William Priestley, letter to John Barney Rodgers, 1 September 1937, quoted in Rodgers's letter to Nina Bremer, 11 February 1976, Mies Archive.

21. Helmut Bartsch, German-born architect working at the time for Holabird and Root in Chicago, served as the chief interpreter at these lunches; Priestley, 25 January 1982.

22. Personal conversation with Priestley, 25 January 1982.

23. Edgar Tafel, *Apprentice to Genius* (New York, 1978), p. 66.

24. Personal conversation with William Wesley Peters, Spring Green, Wis., 12 October 1982.

25. Ibid.

26. Tafel, *Apprentice to Genius*, p. 69.

27. For an extended discussion of the history of the Resor House project, see Nina Bremer, "The Resor House Project," 1976, Mies Archive.

28. Rodgers suggested that the commission may have been withdrawn because "Mr. Resor worried about the war and J. Walter Thompson's European clients"; Rodgers, letter to Bremer, 11 February 1976, Mies Archive.

29. "That's when I first saw him, because he went up to Columbia, when he was in New York. Columbia was looking for a dean at that time and we all got very excited. [We] rushed to the acting dean and said what's going on. [He said] we couldn't make Mies the dean here. He can't talk English"; Daniel Brenner, in round table conversation of 8 November 1974 in offices of Skidmore, Owings, and Merrill, Chicago (with George Danforth, Joseph Fujikawa, Myron Goldsmith, and Werner Blaser), Mies Archive.

30. Mies, letter to "Mr. Schniewind," 31 January 1938, Mies Archive.

31. Rodgers, interview with Bremer, 26 January 1976, Mies Archive.

32. It appears that the Prussian Akademie der Künste itself had turned on Mies. In a letter of 8 November 1937 in the Library of Congress (Mies was at that time in New York), the president of the academy (signature illegible) wrote Mies's Berlin office, which apparently had asked earlier for some form of written acknowledgment of Mies's membership in the academy. Why this request was made is not known.

"We regret to inform you," the letter said, "that it is not possible to provide you with a certification of your membership in the academy, as your office requested over the telephone.

"We ask you to return the diploma of membership which was granted you on 11 May 1932."

33. Personal conversation with Hirche, 3 July 1982.

34. Personal conversation with Dirk Lohan, 14 April 1984.

Chapter 7

1. Frank Lloyd Wright, *An Autobiography* (London, 1943), p. 460.

2. Henry T. Heald, in *Four Great Makers of Modern Architecture* (New York, 1963), pp. 105–8.

3. Ibid.

4. Ibid.

5. This statement, which Mies occasionally varied in form ("Architecture is not a martini") became a commonplace in his conversations in the U.S.

6. The project was published in *Architectural Forum*, May 1943.

7. Personal recollection of George Danforth, in conversation, 3 October 1981.

8. Personal conversation with Katharine Kuh, July 1979.

9. Personal conversation with Lora Marx, 23 February 1981.

10. Personal conversation with Katharine Kuh, July 1979.

11. Personal conversation with Jacques Brownson, 19 March 1981.

12. In an informal conversation in Chicago, 31 June 1952, recorded by George Danforth on a tape still in his possession, Mies recalled some unfriendly words he had exchanged with Moholy-Nagy in the 1920s. "[Moholy told me] 'Gropius wouldn't mind if you retracted what you said about him.' He always phrased things so carefully! 'Listen, Moholy, I said, 'There is the door. If you don't go there, I throw you out the window.'"

13. Personal conversation with Danforth, 20 August 1984.

14. Personal conversation with Lora Marx, 23 February 1981.

15. Johnson, letter to Mies, 20 December 1946, Mies Archive.

16. Charles Eames, in *Arts and Architecture*, December 1947.

17. Wright, letter to Mies, 27 October 1947, and copy of his letter to Wright, 25 November 1947, both in Mies Archive.

Chapter 8

1. Sometime in the 1940s, according to Drexler (personal conversation, 18 March 1985), Mies gave Callery the collage of the Concert Hall he designed in 1942. It was she who replaced the seated figure by Maillol seen in earlier photographs with the cross-legged figure from the Egyptian Old Kingdom which now adorns the collage. Why she made the change—not to mention how Mies reacted to it—is not known.

2. Mies, quoted in *860–880 Lake Shore Drive*, issued by the Commission on Chicago Historical and Architectural Landmarks, undated, p. 8.

3. Peter Carter, *Mies van der Rohe at Work* (New York, 1974), p. 48.

4. Personal conversation with Lilly von Schnitzler, June 1981.

5. Charles Genther, "Habitats for American Cosmopolites," in *Four Great Makers of Modern Architecture* (New York, 1963), p. 126.

6. Mies-Reich correspondence, Library of Congress.

7. Personal conversation with Marianne Lohan, 7 May 1981.

8. Mies-Reich correspondence, Library of Congress.

9. Personal conversation with Lora Marx, 23 February 1981.

10. Personal conversation with Lora Marx, 16 September 1980.

11. Personal conversation with Marianne Lohan, 7 May 1981.

12. Personal conversation with Marian Carpenter, 25 November 1983.

13. Quoted in editor's reply to letter of Mary Z. Valatka, *Newsweek*, 29 September 1969.

14. Edith Farnsworth, Memoirs, in possession of Mr. and Mrs. Fairbank Carpenter, Lake Forest, Illinois.

15. On the Farnsworth House, see Wolf Tegethoff, *Die Villen und Landhausprojekte von Mies van der Rohe* (Essen, 1981), 1:130–31.

16. Personal conversation with Peter Palumbo, 3 October 1982.

17. Personal conversation with Alfred Caldwell, 10 August 1980.

18. Farnsworth, Memoirs.

19. Ibid.

20. Quoted in Peter Blake, *The Master Builders* (New York, 1976), pp. 248–49.

21. Anne Douglas, "Rooms Shifted at Will Inside Glass Walls," *Chicago Tribune*, from an undated clipping, Mies Archive.

22. For a technical summary of Crown Hall, see Carter, *Mies van der Rohe at Work*, 87–91.

23. Mies, quoted by Donald Hoffmann, *Kansas City Times*, 17 July 1963.

24. Mies, interview with students of the Architectural League, New York, 1951, Library of Congress.

25. For a technical summary of the Mannheim National Theater, see Carter, *Mies van der Rohe at Work*, 93.

26. Mies, "A Proposed National Theatre for the City of Mannheim," *Arts and Architecture* 70 (October 1953): 17–19.

27. Ibid.

28. For a technical summary of the Convention Hall, see Carter, *Mies van der Rohe at Work*, pp. 101–7.

29. This is the exposition hall known as McCormick Place.

30. Mies, quoted in Peter Carter, "Mies van der Rohe," *Architectural Design* 31 (March 1961): 95–121.

31. Mies, interview with students of the Architectural League.

32. Phyllis Lambert, "How a Building Gets Built," *Vassar Alumnae Magazine*, February 1959, p. 13.

33. Ibid., pp. 14–16.

34. Lambert, letter to Eve Borsook, 1 December 1954, quoted in "How a Building Gets Built," p. 17.

35. Ibid., p. 17.

36. Personal conversation with Gene Summers, 2 March 1981.

37. Personal conversation with Philip Johnson, 23 April 1981.

38. Personal conversation with Gene Summers, 2 March 1981.

39. Ibid.

40. Personal conversation with Lambert, 14 March 1985.

41. Personal conversation with Johnson, 23 April 1981.

42. Johnson, *Writings* (New York, 1979), p. 220.

43. Personal conversation with Johnson, 23 April 1981.

44. Lohan, interview with Mies, Mies Archive.

Chapter 9

1. Sandra Honey, "The Office of Mies van der Rohe in America," *UIA/International Architect* 3 (1984): 49.

2. Ibid.

3. Mies, letter to Gordon Bunshaft, 2 September 1958, Library of Congress.

4. Personal conversation with Alfred Caldwell, 10 August 1980.

5. Personal conversation with Johnson, 23 April 1981.

6. Personal conversation with Harold Joachim, 16 November 1982.

7. Personal conversation with Marian Carpenter, 25 November 1983.

8. Personal conversation with Lora Marx, 16 September 1980.

9. These and other remembered Miesianisms were written down by Lora Marx, steadily, over the years of their relationship; originals in possession of Lora Marx.

10. Samuel Marx, letter to Mies, 6 August 1956, Library of Congress.

11. Personal conversation with Lora Marx, 16 September 1980.

12. Ibid.

13. "Aus der Wüste in der Städte," *Deutsche Zeitung*, 6 June 1959.

14. Robert Venturi, *Complexity and Contradiction in Architecture* (New York and Chicago, 1966, 1977), p. 17.

15. "Mies van der Rohe," film sponsored by Knoll International and Zweites Deutsches Fernsehen, Mainz; directed by Georgia van der Rohe, produced by IFAGE-Filmproduktion, Wiesbaden; English version, 1979, German version, 1980.

16. José M. Bosch, letter to Mies, quoted in Peter Carter, "Office Build-

ing for Compania Ron Bacardi S.A., Santiago de Cuba," *Architectural Design* 28 (November 1958): 443.

17. Gene Summers, "A Letter to Son," *A+U*, January 1981, p. 182.

18. Ibid., p. 182.

19. Personal conversation with Gene Summers, 2 March 1981.

20. Ibid.

21. For a technical summary of the Berlin National Gallery, see Carter, *Mies van der Rohe at Work*, (New York, 1974), pp. 95–99.

22. Mies, quoted in "Mies van der Rohe," film directed by Georgia van der Rohe.

23. Ibid.

24. Reported by Julius Posener, in personal conversation, 24 June 1982.

25. Mies cherished his awards in America as he had in Germany. Shortly after receiving the Medal of Honor, he and Drexler dined together at the Hotel Pearson in Chicago. The head waiter, according to Drexler (personal conversation, 18 March 1985) offered his compliments to Mies, adding, "You must have won many awards by now."

"*Ja!*" responded Mies, suddenly lighting up, "Fourteen!"

26. Franz Schulze, "I Always Wanted to Know about Truth," *Chicago Daily News*, 27 April 1968.

27. Quoted by Louis Rocah in a personal conversation, 25 March 1981.

28. Personal conversation with Lora Marx, 16 September 1980. Marx recalls remonstrating with Mies: "One day I said, 'You claim to want to be a man of your time, yet you know nothing of Freud and you dislike what he stands for!'"

29. Lora Marx in conversation, 16 September 1980: "He was an avowed atheist, but he was constantly searching for a spiritual source."

30. See Rudolf Schwarz, *The Church Incarnate*, trans. Cynthia Harris (Chicago, 1958); originally published in German as *Vom Bau der Kirche* (Heidelberg, 1938).

31. Peter Palumbo, "Mies van der Rohe Mansion House Square; the Client," *UIA/International Architect* 3 (1984): 23.

32. Hans Maria Wingler, letter to Mies, 3 April 1959, Library of Congress.

33. Personal conversation with Dirk Lohan, 15 December 1984.

34. Personal conversation with Arthur Drexler, 19 February 1981.

35. Personal conversation with Lora Marx, 16 September 1980.

36. Personal conversation with Lora Marx, 17 June 1980.

37. Personal conversation with Dr. George Allen, December 1984.

38. Personal conversation with Marianne Lohan, 7 March 1981.

39. Personal conversation with Georgia van der Rohe, 3 September 1982.

40. James Johnson Sweeney, eulogy at Mies's memorial service, Crown Hall, IIT, Chicago, 25 October 1969, Mies Archive.

Bibliography

Anderson, Stanford. "Peter Behrens and the New Architecture of Germany, 1900–1917." Ph.D. diss., Columbia University, 1968.

Baljeu, Joost. *Theo van Doesburg*. New York, 1974.

Banham, Reyner. *Theory and Design in the First Machine Age*. Cambridge, Mass., 1960, 1980.

Bayer, Herbert, Walter Gropius, and Ise Gropius, eds. *Bauhaus, 1919–1928*. New York, 1938.

Beeby, Thomas. "Vitruvius Americanus: Mies' Ornament." *Inland Architect* 21 (May 1977): 12–15.

Behrendt, Walter Curt. "Skyscrapers in Germany." *Journal of the American Institute of Architects* 11 (Summer 1923): 365–70.

"Die Bewohner des Hauses Tugendhat äussern sich." *Die Form* 7 (15 November 1931): 437–39.

Bier, Justus. "Kann man im Haus Tugendhat wohnen?" *Die Form* 6 (15 October 1931): 392–94.

———. "Mies van der Rohes Reichspavillon Barcelona." *Die Form* 4 (15 August 1929): 423–30.

Blake, Peter. *The Master Builders: Le Corbusier, Mies van der Rohe, Frank Lloyd Wright*. New York, 1960.

Blaser, Werner. *Mies van der Rohe: The Art of Structure*. London, 1965.

———. *After Mies*. Chicago, 1977.

———. *Mies van der Rohe: Furniture and Interiors*. Woodbury, N.Y., 1982.

Bock, Manfred. *Anfänge einer neuen Architektur: Berlages Beiträge zur architektonischen Kultur der Niederlande im ausgehenden 19. Jahrhundert*. The Hague and Wiesbaden, 1983.

Bonta, Juan Pablo. *Architecture and Its Interpretation: A Study of Expressive Systems in Architecture*. New York, 1979.

Buddensieg, Tilmann. "Die kaiserliche Deutsche Botschaft in Petersburg von Peter Behrens." In *Politische Architektur in Europa*, ed. Martin Warnke. Cologne, 1984.

"Building Groups; I.I.T. Campus." *Arts and Architecture* 66 (Summer 1949).

Burckhardt, Lucius, ed. *The Werkbund: History and Ideology*. Woodbury, N.Y., 1977.

Cadbury-Brown, H. T. "Ludwig Mies van der Rohe: An Address of Appreciation." *Architectural Association Journal* 75 (July–August 1959): 26–46.

Campbell, Joan. *The German Werkbund: The Politics of Reform in the Applied Arts*. Princeton, N.J., 1978.

Carter, Peter. "Mies van der Rohe." *Architectural Design* 31 (March 1961): 95–121.

———. *Mies van der Rohe at Work*. New York, 1974.

Choay, Françoise. *Le Corbusier*. New York, 1960.

Crous, Helmut A. *Aachen: so wie es war*. Düsseldorf, 1971.

"Crown Hall, Illinois Institute of Technology." *Architectural Record* 120 (August 1956): 134–39.

Dearstyne, Howard. Reply (to Sibyl Moholy-Nagy. "The Diaspora," *Journal of the Society of Architectural Historians* 24 [March 1965]: 24–26) and rejoinder (by Sibyl Moholy-Nagy) *JSAH* 24 (October 1965): 254–57.

De Stijl, 1917–31: Visions of Utopia. Catalog of the exhibition at the Walker Art Center, Minneapolis. New York, 1982.

Deventer, Salomon van. *Aus Liebe zur Kunst*. Cologne, 1958.

Doesburg, Theo van. "Der Wille zum Stil. Neugestaltung von Leben, Kunst und Technik." *De Stijl* 5 (February 1922): 23–32 and (March 1922): 33–41.

Theo van Doesburg. Catalog of the exhibition at the Van Abbemuseum. Eindhoven, 1969.

Drexler, Arthur. "Seagram Building." *Architectural Record* 124 (July 1958): 139–47.

———. *Ludwig Mies van der Rohe*. New York, 1960.

Early Work of Mies van der Rohe. Catalog of the exhibition at the Building Centre Trust. London, 1979.

"Farnsworth House." *Architectural Forum* 95 (October 1951): 156–62.

Fitch, James Marston. *Walter Gropius*. New York, 1962.

Four Great Makers of Modern Architecture. New York, 1963.

Frampton, Kenneth. *Modern Architecture: A Critical History*. London, 1980.

Frieg, Wolfgang. "Ludwig Mies van der Rohe: Das europäische Werk (1907–1937)." Ph.D. diss., Bonn, 1976.

Gay, Peter. *Weimar Culture: The Outsider as Insider*. New York, 1968.

Genzmer, Walther. "Der Deutsche Reichspavillon auf der internationalen Austellung Barcelona." *Die Baugilde* 11 (1929): 1654–57.

Giedion, Sigfried. *Space, Time, and Architecture*. Cambridge, Mass., 1941, 1971.

Glaeser, Ludwig. *Ludwig Mies van der Rohe: Drawings in the Collection of the Museum of Modern Art*. New York, 1969.

———. *Ludwig Mies van der Rohe: Furniture and Furniture Drawings from the Design Collection and the Mies van der Rohe Archive*. New York, 1977.

Glaeser, Ludwig, and Yukio Futagawa. "Mies van der Rohe: Farnsworth House, Plano, Illinois, 1945–50." *Global Architecture* 27 (1974).

Gordon, Elizabeth. "The Threat to the Next America." *House Beautiful* 95 (April 1953): 126–30, 250–51.

Graeff, Werner. "Concerning the So-Called G Group." *Art Journal* 23 (Summer 1964): 280–82.

Gravenkamp, Curt. "Mies van der Rohe: Glashaus in Berlin." *Das Kunstblatt* 14 (April 1930): 111–13.

Hausmann, Raoul. "More on Group G" (letter to the editor). *Art Journal* 24 (Summer 1965): 350–52.

Heller, Reinhold. *The Art of Wilhelm Lehmbruck*. New York, 1972.

Hilberseimer, Ludwig. *Grossstadtarchitektur*. Stuttgart, 1927, 1978.

———. Eine Würdigung des Projektes Mies van der Rohe für die Umbauung des Alexanderplatzes." *Das neue Berlin* 2 (February 1929): 39–41.

———. *Mies van der Rohe*. Chicago, 1956.

Hitchcock, Henry-Russell. "Architecture Chronicle: Berlin, Paris, 1931." *Hound and Horn* 5 (October–December 1931): 94–97.

Hitchcock, Henry-Russell, and Philip Johnson. *The International Style*. New York, 1932, 1966.

Hoeber, Fritz. *Peter Behrens*. Munich, 1913.

Hoepfner, Wolfram, and Fritz Neumeyer. *Das Haus Wiegand von Peter Behrens in Berlin-Dahlem*. Mainz, 1979.

Honey, Sandra. "Mies at the Bauhaus." *Architectural Association Quarterly* 10, no. 1 (1978): 52–59.

———. "The Office of Mies van der Rohe in America." *UIA/International Architect* 3 (1984).

Jaumann, Anton. "Vom künstlerischen Nachwuchs." *Innen-Dekoration* 21 (July 1910): 265–72.

Jencks, Charles. *Modern Movements in Architecture.* New York, 1973.

Joedicke, Jürgen, and Christian Plath. *Die Weissenhofsiedlung.* Stuttgart, 1977.

Johnson, Philip. "Architecture in the Third Reich." *Hound and Horn* 7 (October–December 1933): 137–39.

———. *Mies van der Rohe.* New York, 1947, 1978.

———. *Writings.* New York, 1979.

Jordy, William. "The Aftermath of the Bauhaus in America: Gropius, Mies, and Breuer." *Perspectives in American History* 2 (1968): 485–543.

———. "The Laconic Splendor of the Metal Frame: Ludwig Mies van der Rohe's 860 Lake Shore Drive Apartments and His Seagram Building." In *American Buildings and Their Architects: The Impact of European Modernism in the Mid-Twentieth Century,* William Pearson, ed., pp. 221–77. New York, 1972.

Kröller-Müller Museum. 2d ed. Haarlem, 1981.

Lambert, Phyllis. "How a Building Gets Built." *Vassar Alumnae Magazine,* February 1959, pp. 13–18.

Lane, Barbara Miller. *Architecture and Politics in Germany, 1918–1945.* Cambridge, Mass., 1968.

Mang, Karl. *History of Modern Furniture.* New York, 1979.

"Meeting of the Titans: Frank Lloyd Wright, Carl Sandburg Talk of Life, Work, and Happiness." *The Capital Times,* 3 June 1957.

"Mies Designs Plans for the World's Largest Convention Hall." *Architectural Forum* 99 (December 1953): 43, 45.

"Mies in Berlin." Phonograph record of October 1964 interview of Mies by Horst Eifler and Ulrich Conrads, recorded by RIAS, Berlin. Bauwelt Archiv. Berlin. 1966.

"Mies van der Rohe." *Arts and Architecture* 72 (April 1955): 16–18.

Mies van der Rohe. Catalog of exhibition at the Art Institute of Chicago. Chicago, 1968.

"Mies's One-Office Office Building." *Architectural Forum* 110 (February 1959): 94–97.

Mumford, Lewis. "Skyline: The Lesson of the Master." *The New Yorker* 34 (13 September 1958): 141–48, 151–52.

"Neue Nationalgalerie Berlin." *Bauwelt* 59 (16 September 1968): 1209–26.

Neue Sachlichkeit and German Realism of the Twenties. Catalog of the exhibition at the Hayward Gallery. London, 1978.

Neumann, Eckhard, ed. *Bauhaus and Bauhaus People.* New York, 1970.

Nimmons, George C. "Skyscrapers in America." *Journal of the American Institute of Architects* 11 (September 1923): 370–72.

Pawley, Martin. *Mies van der Rohe.* New York, 1970.

Pehnt, Wolfgang. *Expressionist Architecture.* London, 1973.

Perls, Hugo. *Warum ist Camilla schön?* Munich, 1962.

Peterson, Steven K. "Idealized Space: Mies—Conception or Realized Truth?" *Inland Architect* 21 (May 1977): 4–11.

Platz, Gustav. *Die Baukunst der neuesten Zeit.* Berline, 1927.

Popp, Joseph. *Bruno Paul.* Munich, 1921.

Posener, Julius. *Berlin: auf dem Wege zu einer neuen Architektur.* Munich, 1979.

Rave, Paul, and Margarete Kuhn, eds. *Schinkels Lebenswerk.* 14 vols. Berlin, 1939–.

Rawls, Marion. "An Exhibition of Architecture by Mies van der Rohe." *Bulletin of the Art Institute of Chicago* 32 (December 1938): 104.

Richter, Hans. *Dada: Art and Anti-Art.* New York, 1965.

Rowe, Colin. "Chicago Frame: Chicago's Place in the Modern Movement." *Architectural Record* 120 (August 1956): 171–74.

Schinkel, Karl Friedrich. *Sammlung architektonischer Entwürfe.* Reprint. Berlin and Chicago, 1981.

Schulze, Franz. *Mies van der Rohe: Interior Spaces.* Chicago, 1982.

Schwarz, Rudolf. *The Church Incarnate.* Chicago, 1958. Originally published in German as *Vom Bau der Kirche.* Heidelberg, 1938.

Scully, Vincent, Jr. *Frank Lloyd Wright.* New York, 1960.

Serenyi, Peter. "Spinoza, Hegel, and Mies: The Meaning of the New National Gallery in Berlin." *Journal of the Society of Architectural Historians* 30 (October 1971): 240.

Serenyi, Peter, ed. *Le Corbusier in Perspective.* Englewood Cliffs, N.J., 1975.

"Six Students Talk with Mies." North Carolina State University College of Agriculture and Engineering School of Design *Student Publication* 2 (Spring 1952): 21–28.

Smith, Norris Kelly. *Frank Lloyd Wright: A Study in Architectural Content.* Englewood Cliffs, N.J., 1966.

Sontag, Raymond J. *A Broken World, 1919–1939.* New York, 1971.

Spaeth, David A. *Ludwig Mies van der Rohe: an Annotated Bibliography and Chronology.* New York, 1979.

————. *Mies van der Rohe.* New York, 1985.

Spengler, Oswald. *The Decline of the West.* Ed. Helmut Werner. New York, 1962.

Sweeney, James Johnson. "Le Cullinan Hall de Mies van der Rohe à Houston." *L'Oeil* 99 (March 1963): 38–43.

Swenson, Alfred, and Pao-Chi Chang. *Architectural Education at I.I.T., 1938–1978.* Chicago, 1980.

Tafel, Edgar. *Apprentice to Genius: Years with Frank Lloyd Wright.* New York, 1979.

Tegethoff, Wolf. *Die Villen und Landhausprojekte von Mies van der Rohe.* Essen, 1981.

Troy, Nancy J. *The De Stijl Environment.* Cambridge, Mass., 1983.

Venturi, Robert. *Complexity and Contradiction in Architecture.* New York and Chicago, 1966, 1977.

Westheim, Paul. "Mies van der Rohe: Entwicklung eines Architekten." *Das Kunstblatt* 11 (February 1927): 55–62.

Whitford, Frank. *Bauhaus.* London, 1984.

Whyte, Iain Boyd. *Bruno Taut and the Architecture of Activism.* Cambridge, 1982.

Wilk, Christopher. *Marcel Breuer: Furniture and Interiors.* New York, 1981.

Willett, John. *Art and Politics in the Weimar Period.* New York, 1978.

Windsor, Alan. *Peter Behrens, Architect and Designer, 1868–1940.* New York, 1981.

Wingler, Hans Maria. *The Bauhaus: Weimar, Dessau, Berlin, Chicago.* Cambridge, Mass., 1969.

Winter, John. "Misconceptions about Mies." *Architectural Review* 151 (February 1972): 95–105.

Wright, Frank Lloyd. *Ausgeführte Bauten und Entwürfe.* Berlin, 1910.

Zervos, Christian. "Mies van der Rohe." *Cahiers d'Art* 3 (1928): 35–38.

Zevi, Bruno. "Mies van der Rohe e Frank Lloyd Wright: poeti dello spazio." *Metron* 37 (July–August 1950): 6–18.

Index